The Quest for the City

"He looked for a city which hath foundations,
whose builder and maker is God."

The Epistle to the Hebrews (11:10)

The Quest for the City

The prayers of the monks through the ages of ages

These monks at Hauterive, France, mirror their brothers through past ages who for more than a thousand years have sought to find something of heaven on earth by following the Rule of St. Benedict.

Detail from the photograph
by Olivier Martel,
page 21

A.D. 740 to 1100

Pursuing the next world, they founded this one

The Christians

THEIR FIRST TWO THOUSAND YEARS

Sixth Volume

CHP

CHRISTIAN HISTORY PROJECT

THE EDITOR:

Ted Byfield has been a journalist for fifty-eight years and a western Canadian magazine publisher since 1973, the founder of *Alberta Report* and *British Columbia Report* weekly newsmagazines, and founding editor of *Alberta in the Twentieth Century*, a twelve-volume history of Alberta. A columnist for Canada's *Sun* newspapers and sometime contributor to the *National Post* and *Globe and Mail* national newspapers, he is active in evangelical journalistic outreach. He was one of the founders of St. John's School of Alberta, an Anglican school for boys where he developed a new method of teaching history.

THE EXECUTIVE EDITOR:

Paul Stanway has been a reporter, editor and columnist for more than thirty years in both Canada and the United Kingdom. Born in Manchester, England, he began his newspaper career in 1969, and has been a regular contributor to magazines and newspapers on both sides of the Atlantic. A longtime resident of Alberta, he is the former editor-in-chief of *The Edmonton Sun* and editor of *The Calgary Sun* daily newspapers. He is also a former foreign correspondent for Canada's Sun Media newspaper group, and has written extensively on Europe and the Middle East.

COVER:

This painting by Dale Shuttleworth of Alberta, Canada, depicts a community of twelfth-century monks gathered around their abbot who holds a crosier, symbolic of his office. Their undyed, whitish robes suggest the several reform orders of the late eleventh and twelfth century, most notably, the Cistercians and Carthusians, who succeeded the black-robed Cluniac Benedictines as leaders of monastic reform. For all the centuries of the Middle Ages and later, monks and nuns sought to create communities on earth that reflected the love and beauty of the eternal city of God. In the course of this quest, they left a legacy for Christian society in modern times.

CHRISTIAN HISTORY PROJECT LIMITED PARTNERSHIP

President and CEO:	Robert W. Doull
Vice President/Sales:	Kathy Therrien
Vice President/Media:	Brian Lehr
Market Development Manager:	Leanne Nash
Accounting Manager:	Tuyet Laboda
Accounting Clerks:	Kawaljit Janda, Michelle Spak
Contact Center Administrators:	Sameer Pandey, Peggy Roode
Distribution Coordinator:	Grace de Guzman
Customer Service:	Yvonne Van Ry, Jane Ikwueme, Stella Stephen, Edwin Muxlow

The Quest for the City, A.D. 740 to 1100, Pursuing the next world, they founded this one

Writers:	Paul Bunner, Michael Byfield, Ted Byfield, Virginia Byfield, Vincent Carroll, Kaye Corbett, Calvin Demmon, Matthew Francis, Louise Henein, Paul Stanway, Jared Tkachuk, Joe Woodard
Illustrators:	Richard Connor, Dale Shuttleworth, Leslie Taillefer
Volume Planner/Director of Research:	Barrett Pashak
Design Director:	Dean Pickup
Production Editor:	Rev. David Edwards
Art Researcher:	Louise Henein
Researcher:	Jared Tkachuk
Research Readers:	Greg Amerongen, Ross Amy, Judy Anderson, Margaret Armstrong, Ross W. Cleary, Caroline Fast, Matthew Francis, Rick Hiebert, Rev. John Hodgins, Rev. Gregory Kopchuk, Zenovia Kopchuk, Carol Lehr, Diane Penner, Barbara Rosof, Nicole Stanway, Liz Stolee, Aleta Voss, Frank Wiens
Proofreaders:	P. A. Colwell, Leanne Nash
General academic advisers:	Fr. Brian Hubka, priest of the Roman Catholic Diocese of Calgary, Alberta; Dr. Joseph H. Lynch, designated professor of the history of Christianity at Ohio State University; Dr. Dennis Martin, professor of historical theology, Loyola University, Chicago; Dr. Eugene Teselle, emeritus professor of Church history and theology, Vanderbilt University, Nashville, TN.
Specialist academic advisers:	Dr. Terry Carlton, professor emeritus of Slavic Linguistics, University of Alberta; Ant Greenham, instructor of religion and Islamic studies, Southeastern Baptist Theological Seminary, Wake Forest, NC; George Kurian, co-editor, World Christian Encyclopedia.

THE CHRISTIANS: Their First Two Thousand Years

(c) 2004 Christian History Project, Inc.
(c) 2004 Christian History Project Limited Partnership
Chairman, Gerald J. Maier

LIBRARY AND ARCHIVES CANADA CATALOGUING IN PUBLICATION

The Quest for the City : A.D. 740 to 1100 : pursuing the next world, they founded this one.

(The Christians : their first two thousand years ; 6)
Editors, Ted Byfield, Paul Stanway.
Includes bibliographical references and index.
ISBN 0-9689873-6-2

1. Church history—Middle Ages, 600-1500. I. Byfield, Ted
II. Stanway, Paul, 1950- III. Christian History Project IV. Series:
Christians : their first two thousand years ; 6.

BR252.Q84 2004   270.3   C2004-906445-2
PRINTED IN CANADA BY FRIESENS CORPORATION

CONTENTS

ILLUSTRATIONS

MARGIN CHARACTER SKETCHES

MAPS

The Christian History Project is deeply indebted to the work of several nineteenth century artists whose engravings first appeared in The Illustrated History of the World *(Ward Lock & Co., London and New York), and in M. (François) Guizot's* The History of France *(Estes & Lauriat, Boston). We gratefully acknowledge their contribution to this volume.*

For additional copies of this book or information on others in the series, please contact us at:

The Christian History Project
10333 178 Street
Edmonton AB, Canada, T5S 1R5
www.christianhistoryproject.com

1-800-853-5402

FOREWORD

With the publication of this sixth volume, we complete Part I and reach the halfway point in the twelve-volume series. We have now covered the first Christian millennium and moved slightly into the second, ending on the eve of the Crusades. This volume covers what will probably turn out to be the longest time span of any of them, the period from 740 to 1100—three hundred and sixty years in which four momentous developments take place.

The first is the most difficult for the modern reader to comprehend. The monk and the nun become the central figures of Christianity. The idea of giving up home, family life, all one's possessions, almost all physical comforts, and all of one's time, to the service of Jesus Christ, in common with other men or women of similar mind, will seem to many readers extreme to the point of delirium.

And yet, is it? Christians today of almost every denomination give up many of these things when they undertake foreign mission work. Others do so in undertaking work in urban ghettos. At a minimum, every Christian risks being branded a "religious kook" if he witnesses to Christ in a typical workplace. And there was a time, in the memory of many people still living, when men voluntarily gave up these same things to fight in wars from which there was every possibility they would not return. No, the depth of the commitment of the monk or nun is not entirely unknown today. Only the form of it is unusual.

But in these centuries long passed, it was not unusual. Impelled by their vision of a world to come, men and women divorced themselves from this world. Ironically, however, their effect on this one was profound and is still with us today, for they established the very foundations of our society. That is the first development covered in this volume.

The second is a great tragedy. Eastern and Western Christianity divided, to the ultimate detriment of both. Neither wanted this to happen. When it did, neither believed the rupture would be permanent. But it would become permanent, and in no small degree because of it, in Part II of the series, we will see Eastern Christians suffer almost an entire millennium of steady oppression and persecution, unrelieved and on occasion made worse by their brothers in the West.

Offsetting this reversal, however, is the third development, a truly glorious accomplishment, namely the thorough conversion of the Slavic peoples and the establishment of Christianity right across Eastern Europe. The delightful story of its crowning achievement, the coming of "the Rus" to Christ in Prince Vladimir's determination to win his Christian wife, is one of those strange love stories that happen also to be true. It concludes chapter 8.

Finally, we come to the fourth event, or series of events, of which Christians should be acutely aware. Much mention is made these days of the Crusades, which are usually portrayed as an unprovoked Christian attack on the peace-loving peoples of Islam. This is greatly at odds with the facts.

In the last volume, we showed how Islamic forces took over more than half the Christian world at the point of the sword. In the last two chapters of this one, we show how Muslims fought for the next three hundred years to finish off Christianity, conquering southern France, Sicily, Crete, the Aegean Islands and repeatedly attacking Rome itself, resulting finally in the Christian counterattack known as the Crusades. From the Christian perspective, the Crusades were morally doubtful. But they were not unprovoked. They were very provoked indeed.

Ted Byfield

An illuminated page, dating to the eleventh century,
from Augustine's The City of God. *His vision of a
heavenly city, "surpassingly glorious," inspired legions
of men and women in the Middle Ages to embrace
monastic life. The manuscript is in the Laurenziana
Library, Florence, Italy.*

CHAPTER 1

The search for sanctity that laid the foundations of the modern world

Though their minds were focused not on this life but the next, monks and nuns in their thousands began to rebuild bruised and battered Europe

If you read history, you will find that the Christians who did most for the present world were just those who thought most about the next. The apostles themselves, who set on foot the conversion of the Roman Empire, the great men who built up the Middle Ages, the English evangelicals who abolished the slave trade, all left their mark on earth, precisely because their minds were occupied with heaven. It is since Christians have largely ceased to think of the other world that they have become so ineffective in this – C. S. Lewis (Mere Christianity)

The church founded by Jesus Christ faced a desperate prospect in the early medieval era. By 750, Islam had sliced off half of Christendom, and its swords were still hacking furiously. With the ninth century came the Vikings—huge, blond, unrelentingly vicious, and arguably the best sailors ever known. They fell upon Europe's coasts and ascended far up the rivers to burn towns, pillage monasteries, murder or enslave people, and destroy whatever they couldn't steal. And from the East erupted the Magyars, successors of the Huns, and fully their equal in terror and destruction. Amid this maelstrom, every European—prince, prelate or peasant—had excellent reason to focus on staying alive.

Yet Christ's followers at that time did not focus on mere physical survival. Death being inevitable, their deeper concern was eternal salvation. In the West, Christians especially revered Augustine of Hippo, a fourth-century bishop who taught that every human heart is divided between the City of God and the City of Man. (See previous volume *Darkness Descends*.) The heavenly realm can only be served through *caritas*, acts of self-sacrificial love. In contrast, a person who acts from *cupiditas* (selfish avarice and ambition) enters an evil city, which is doomed to destruction. Through three dark centuries and for five more into the second millennium, many a good monarch and bishop served God by attempting to construct a human society that would reflect the Messiah's message of love.

At the heart of that emerging medieval civilization knelt an extraordinary figure, that of the monk or nun. He or she lived largely apart from this world, the better to concentrate on achieving holiness and ultimately an entry to the City of God. Yet these men and women had a profound impact on this world as well. In an illiterate age, they needed to read the Bible, a requirement that prompted them to reestablish scholarship in the West. Although sworn to personal poverty, monks attracted massive donations in the form of land. Thus they spearheaded a recovery of agriculture, and revived the entire Western economy. Their influence over government, charity, arts, schooling and much else was also pivotal. Without exaggeration, European and later American civilization rose on the foundation laid largely by ascetics who strove to deny this world.

Monasticism represents the highest ideals of Christianity, writes the American historian Henry Osborn Taylor (*The Medieval Mind*), and "since these often prove unattainable by men, its history is one of a continual falling away from them and return." Western monasteries, with roots dating back to the fourth century, flourished again in the eighth under the Frankish emperor Charlemagne and his son Louis the Pious. These Carolingian sovereigns strongly favored the Rule of Benedict, a monastic code originally developed by Benedict of Nursia, and in the view of many scholars, promoted by Pope Gregory the Great in the 600s. (Some, however, contend that Gregory did not actually possess Benedict's Rule, but rather a composite of several different versions of it and other rules.)

About one hundred years later, however, Benedictine monasticism, as well as much of the church, had again declined. Viking and Magyar raiders targeted the monasteries as storehouses of loot and slaves, inflicting enormous disruption. Disillusionment and sloth pervaded much of what survived. Many brothers, ignoring their vows of poverty, chastity and obedience, were living in the very cloisters with wives, concubines and children.[1] Some were highway robbers. Drunkenness was common. Church prelates functioned as merchant traders. In Rome, the men history would label as "the bad popes" outdid one another in scandal. (See sidebar, page 78.)

Even the famed house established by St. Martin of Tours during the 360s had deteriorated so abjectly by 909 that two godly men, Odo and Aldegrin, fled its slatternly premises. Yet their personal faith and calling remained strong. Odo, born to a wealthy family, had been smitten at age sixteen by migraine headaches. They grew worse until his father admitted to reneging on a vow, made when Odo was an infant, to commit the boy as an *oblate* (one offered to God) at the monastery of St. Martin. Odo therefore fulfilled the vow himself as a young man, which ended his headaches. Now thirty years old, the idealistic monk traveled the countryside with

1. The term "cloister" comes from the Latin word for a bar or a bolt. In English it is used in two ways, sometimes referring to the area within a monastery or convent that was restricted to the monks and nuns, sometimes in reference to monastic life as a whole.

Aldegrin searching for a brotherhood still dedicated to the Rule of St. Benedict. But none could be found. In despair, Odo became a hermit in the woods near Tours.

Aldegrin, the older of the pair, continued alone. One day, he entered the green valley of the Jura River (near the modern French–Swiss boundary) where the little monastery of Baume nestled against rocky gray cliffs. There his quest ended. At Baume the Benedictine Rule was still strictly kept, the monks exuding that peculiar joy in things done right that from time immemorial has marked every good regiment, every good athletic team, and every truly successful business enterprise. On hearing the news, Odo wholeheartedly enlisted at Baume. Ironically, Aldegrin failed to settle down to the frictions of communal monastic life. Now it was he who became a hermit near the monastery, although even his stringent privations never led him to complete peace. But his bones still rest in a reliquary on the high altar at Baume.

About a year after Odo's arrival, Abbot Berno of Baume received a summons from William, Duke of Aquitaine. The old duke, who was dying without an heir, told Berno that in his youth he had murdered a man, and burdened by guilt, he wanted to donate one of his estates

Tours, traditionally a place of pilgrimage to St. Martin's tomb, was the monastery from which Odo and Aldegrin set out on their quest in 909. The ruins of the fourth-century abbey are pictured in the upper photo. Below, the Abbey of Marmoutier, built in the thirteenth century, near a grotto a few miles from Tours where St. Martin used to pray.

2. The ranks of village clergy, unlike the monasteries, were open to the peasantry. "A serf could not enter the nobility, but he could enter the church. He had only to go to school and learn Latin," notes historian Henri Pirenne (*A History of the Empire from the Invasions to the Sixteenth Century*). A pig farmer named Nicholas Breakspear became Pope Adrian IV. Gregory VII, among the foremost medieval popes, was probably a peasant's son.

for a new monastery. Berno knew just the right one. But that, protested the duke, was the best hunting ground in all his domain! Would Berno please pick another? "What do you suppose will serve you best before God," Berno inquired, "the baying of hounds or the prayers of monks?" Duke William opted for the monks, and on that estate grew the most influential monastery of its era. It was called Cluny.

Its hallmarks were scholarship, discipline, missionary zeal and unstinting generosity. A network of monasteries—some already existing, others newly founded—mushroomed across Frankish lands, spreading into Britain and elsewhere. Virtually everywhere, recruiting and donations surged. Odo, who proved to be a capable successor to Abbot Berno, was himself followed by leaders who strongly influenced popes and emperors in the direction of church reform. Although alternate streams of monasticism never ceased to flow, Cluniacs would predominate in terms of shaping Western society for two centuries, until the rise of their fellow Benedictines, the Cistercians.

The Benedictine ascendancy owed much to the astonishing diversity of its monks. As historian Joan Evans notes in *Monastic Life at Cluny*, they included every kind of human being: contemplatives, men of action, penitent criminals, dedicated scholars and ambitious serfs. Historian Ludo J. R. Milis (*Angelic Monks and Earthly Men*) contends that many were highborn people who feared eternal damnation through wealth and power. Bernard of Uxelles, renowned as a great soldier, took vows at Cluny and eventually became its grand prior. Eudes Harpin, captured in war and ransomed, was prior of the monastery La Charité. Guy II, count of Macon, entered as a young married man with thirty of his knights, while their wives and daughters "took the veil" as nuns at the Cluniac convent of Marcigny. Most medieval monks and nuns hailed from the aristocracy due to social class barriers and the fact that few peasants were free to leave their farmland. Many men, and women too, joined a monastery in their gray years as the culminating act of their journey through life. A list of the monks and nuns who served the Benedictine monastery of Prémontré in its first two hundred and fifty years shows about four hundred, some ten percent, admitted as death neared.[2]

Often they bequeathed to it much of their wealth, as did Stephen, Count of Boulogne, for example, as he renounced "the transitory pomp of the world." Lord Berkeley of Bristol

Along with part of a transept, the bell tower of the Holy Water is all that remains of the original Cluny Abbey. Built in 910, the final destruction of the great edifice occurred during the French Revolution. The return of the monasteries to the strict Benedictine discipline encouraged a flood of men and women to enter monastic life: ten thousand souls in over a thousand monasteries and convents across Europe.

was buried in a monk's cowl at the Abbey of St. Augustine, leaving it a vast estate. Countess Matilda of Tuscany always kept a nun's veil handy for her final commitment to a convent. Not untypical was the testament of Robert of Alne, dated 1180:

> Know all men, present and future, that I Robert, clerk of Alne, have quit-claimed to the monastery of Winchcombe the land which I held at Medfurlong, to wit, three and a half acres, which are clearly of the Abbey demesne. Moreover, I have given to the said monks forever, to the health of mine own soul and that of Alice my wife and our ancestors, all my land at Alne between the two valleys, called Kendredsled. In return for which donation the monks have granted me twenty shillings and a monk's allowance of bread and beer such as are daily laid on the refectory table, so often as I may come to Winchcombe on their business, or mine own. Moreover, they have granted to receive me at my latter end as a monk, and then support me; and to Alice my wife they have granted her in all good deeds which are done in the convent of Winchcombe, and burial at her latter end if she desires it.

All monks are ascetics, a term drawn from the Greek *askesis*, which means "training." Just as athletic training develops physical strength, monastic asceticism develops the capacity for caritas. Monastic techniques include liturgical and individual prayer, poverty, absolute celibacy, fasting, contemplation, labor, caring for companions and more—Christian duties drawn from scripture and carefully honed by monastic leaders into life-embracing rules. Although Benedict's Rule became the most popular due to its practicality and balance, highly respected rules were also written by Basil the Great in the East, Ireland's Columban and others. Many a monastery had its own rule, tailored for local circumstances from the classics. In every case, abbots, abbesses and other monastic leaders acted like coaches, providing instruction and accountability for their spiritual athletes.

Always the goal was to emulate Jesus. The early twentieth-century British historian G. G. Coulton spent a lifetime documenting medieval monasticism. When strife and battle informed almost every man's thoughts, Coulton writes, men saw Christ himself as a warrior. In one medieval play, Jesus is depicted as bursting the imprisoning gates of hell. However, observes historian Noreen Hunt (*Cluniac Monasticism in the Central Middle Ages*), "when the monastics saw themselves as dying to the world, what they had in mind was not death in battle against the infidel, but the consummation of their pilgrimage through a real entry into the promised land." In short, the profession of a monk or nun was, in the words of the Fourth Gospel (John 3:3), to be "born again." Historian David Knowles (*Christian Monasticism*) observes that no generation ever has believed that men can become true Christians without conscious rebirth.

For many, monastic training began in childhood. Up to the thirteenth century, volunteering a son as an oblate in Christ's service was considered a meritorious act for parents, and a substantial bequest usually accompanied the youngster. At about age seven, the boy was brought before the abbot, dressed in linen shirt and monastic cloak. His commitment to the service of Christ was formally read and signed by his parents. The abbot blessed the youngster, and his cowl, and he was enrolled in the monastery school.

Oblates slept in their own dormitory, lived under a modified version of the monastic rule, and sang in the choir at the daily services. They were exempted from the more severe fasts, however, and required to attend only part of the middle-of-the-night prayer service called Matins. (If a boy began nodding, his master would give him a heavy book to hold to keep him awake.) No oblate might ever be alone with an older monk; when they met, communication was restricted to mutual bows of courtesy. No oblate might be struck with fist or palm, only punished when necessary with a stick. How rigidly such restrictions were observed is unknowable, but it probably varied. The eleventh-century monk Thietmar of Merseberg records that some of the boys there broke bounds one night and were discovered by the schoolmaster in a local tavern. Benedict would not have been amused.

At fifteen, oblates and other candidates for the novitiate were presented first before the entire assembly of the monks, called the chapter, and then before the abbot or his deputy. "What do you request?" they were asked. "God's mercy, your compassion, and we wish to share your fellowship," was the reply. The abbot then formally warned them of the difficult life they were undertaking. Did they still purpose to do so? Receiving an affirmative reply, he prayed: "May the Lord thus bring you to perfection in this undertaking, so that you may merit everlasting life." Then, before the altar in the church their beards were shaved off (if beards they had), and they were tonsured and issued the novice's cowl and habit.[3]

Their training was much concerned with scripture, including memorizing the entire book of Psalms and other biblical passages. Also mastered were the myriad rites and routines of monastic life—when to bow, genuflect, sit or stand; how to intone and chant the offices; when to allow the hands to show from beneath the habit and when not; how to use the monks' sign language during the long periods of silence. After about one year, sometimes less, the novice was formally admitted to the brotherhood, each carrying to the altar his written profession, and repeating vows of stability, transformation of life, and obedience to his monastery's rule. Prostrating themselves three times before the abbot, the novices recited the words of the psalm: "Receive me according to your word, Lord." Finally, after observing three days of dead silence wearing their new cowls, they were considered fully professed.

Prayer and care of the soul was their chief duty. The Benedictine Rule specified eight "offices" (prayer services) a day, the first at two in the morning, the last at nightfall.[4] Once daily, the Mass was celebrated, and a meeting of the chapter held where individual monks were expected to publicly confess any infractions of the rule. If a brother omitted to mention a transgression, his fellows were expected to report him. Total silence was required except for the half-hour following the chapter meeting.

Benedictine monks ate their two daily meals (dinner and supper) at long tables in a large, military-style mess hall, called the refectory. Decorated with paintings on walls and ceiling, it had three higher tables for the abbot,

3. The offering of one's child to God emulates the offering to God of Samuel by his parents (1 Sam 1:28). Initially, a boy-oblate was irrevocably a monk—he never underwent a novitiate—but later these oblates could choose to confirm their vocation at puberty. Child oblation died out entirely by the thirteenth century. Tonsuring—shaving a patch of hair from a cleric's scalp—was practiced by all medieval churches.

4. Under the Benedictine Rule, monastic offices were set, but timing varied considerably by season and institution. Here is a sample schedule:

Matins:	About 2 a.m.
Lauds:	Dawn
Prime:	One hour after Lauds
Terce:	Two hours after Prime
Sext:	Three hours after Tierce
Nones:	Three hours after Sext
Vespers:	Sunset
Compline:	Nightfall

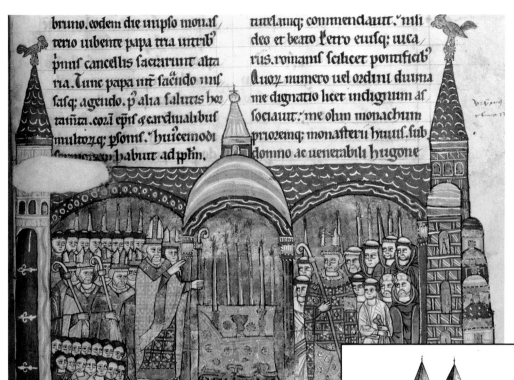

This French manuscript (left) illustrates the consecration of the Abbey of Cluny by Pope Urban II. The influential abbots of Cluny created a powerful institution, second only to Rome in Western ecclesiastical matters. Four popes, including Urban II, came from the abbey. (Below) Abbot Hugh undertook construction of the third church at Cluny, the largest abbey church in Christendom until the building of St. Peter's in Rome. The entire monastic community of Cluny covered twenty-five acres.

2. CLUNY (NO).

responsible for all Cluniac monasteries; the grand prior, in charge of monks at the motherhouse alone (at its peak nearly five hundred); and the claustral prior, director of routine administration in the motherhouse. At some point, half-width tables were developed, so the monks could all sit on one side, facing in the same direction, their attention on the reader or preacher, the hoods of their cowls preventing distraction by the man on either side. A four-monk squad, rotated daily and assisted by servants, provided the meals. The rule specified total abstinence from meat (except for the sick), which Cluny in its great days observed, though fish was allowed on Thursdays, Sundays and feast days. Dinner consisted of a dish of dried beans, plus cheese or eggs or fish when permitted, plus vegetables fried in oil (except during Lent). Every member, oblates included, got a daily half-liter of wine.

Each man was also expected to perform several hours of work daily, often the arduous task of copying manuscripts, since Benedict had stressed physical work as indispensable to spiritual development. Agricultural labor in the Cluniac period was performed by hired workers. Even so, the daily routine left many initiates exhausted. Knowles quotes one Cluniac newcomer who details a strenuous day from which the evening gives no respite: "Often before all are seated in the cloister, and before anyone has uttered a word, the bell rings for Vespers.... After Vespers, supper; after supper, the servers' meal and office of the dead; after that a reading; and so straight to Compline."

Temptations abounded, starting with the vow of poverty that must contend against the human craving for ownership. The monk must call nothing "mine" except his mother and father, and this regulation could prove tricky to maintain.

Centers of knowledge in the Middle Ages, monasteries were repositories of the great writings of civilization, sacred and secular. Important libraries were attached to many monasteries, and copies of manuscripts were created and disseminated by the highly gifted monks in the scriptoria. The beauty of the illuminations and calligraphy in these manuscripts still inspires awe today.

BIRNEY LETTICK
NATIONAL GEOGRAPHIC

Senior administrators needed allowances to travel, for example, while scholars required books and writing materials. Cardinal Hugh de St-Cher, around 1250, identifies "the greed and love of private property" as the chief cause of monastic decay. The Benedictine abbot Caesarius of Heisterbach found a halfpenny coin in a dead monk's habit. He buried him outside the abbey cemetery, throwing the coin on the body as it was lowered into the ground, with a stern: "Let your money perish with you!" The dead man was his own brother. Caesarius commented: "If he's going to be saved, the insult will do him no harm, and may profit him. And if he is to be damned, burial in the cemetery wouldn't help him. I've done this to strike terror into the rest of you. The vice of *proprietas* (ownership) separates you from the communion of the righteous."

However, some monastic reformers, Odo among them, found in sexual temptations a far graver spiritual danger. "The sins which above all others have brought man to perdition are pride and lust, especially lust," he writes. What was called "custody of the eyes" (to avoid lustful temptation) was deemed crucial by the early medieval church, but not usually to the point of condemning womankind. Veneration of the Virgin Mary, both official and popular, continued to intensify. Moreover, Cluny's convents controlled great property ably administered by their nuns. (See subchapter, page 34.) Beyond their theology, most monks were devoted to the women (often very few) whom they knew directly. Take for example the tribute of Peter the Venerable, abbot of Cluny, commending the body of his mother, a Cluniac nun, to the care of the convent at Marcigny:

> Now this humble handmaid of God lies buried under your pious eyes, and although lifeless and silent, yet addresses to you, if you give ear, earnest and frequent prayers. She is always appearing before your eyes, that you may remember her and that you may not forget yourselves. A sister, she speaks to her sisters; and dead, she addresses the living. She shows you what she is now and what you soon shall be. She recalls to you the place where you shall be buried, the sphere to which your soul shall take its flight.
>
> —From *Monastic Life at Cluny* by Joan Evans.

Laughter presented another possible pitfall. Cruel snickers and riotous guffaws were officially forbidden by Benedict, and one twelfth-century moralist provides a vision of monks being beaten in purgatory for having laughed inappropriately on earth. Yet sheer joy and a merry disposition are the universally cherished qualities of the exemplary monk, then and later. One chronicler comments that Odo's

The monk saw himself as a soldier fighting against a thick cloud of demons who thronged everywhere, mocking and tormenting, in church and cloister, workshop, field and cell.

treasured talent for making his men laugh was really a distinctive form of "spiritual gaiety" that "instilled an inner happiness in our hearts."

But the monk primarily saw himself as a serious soldier, and he sensed his enemies on every side. As Anthony and his third-century ascetics had struggled with demons in the Egyptian desert, medieval monks wrestled them in cloister, church, refectory, dormitory, workshop, field and cell.[5] "They are scattered everywhere like dust," laments Richalm, abbot of Clairvaux. "They come down upon us like rain; their multitude fills the whole world, the whole air; the whole air, I say, is but a thick mass of devils."

Hell was a huge concern. Medieval folk accepted as authoritative the teaching that at least five men would be eternally damned for every one saved, says Coulton. Even the purifying agony of purgatory, although preparatory for heaven, was seen as frighteningly arduous. A single day in purgatory would be harsher than one hundred years of combative penance against the diabolical forces in this world.

The devils were seen as highly organized, one monastic chronicler reporting that demons have their own monastic order, complete with abbots and priors,

5. The ministry of Anthony in Egypt, the pioneering leader of Christian monasticism, is described in an earlier volume, *Darkness Descends*.

scheduled routines and assigned duties. Other chroniclers claim to have overheard demons talking, often reviling the monks. "They despise us," says one account, "calling one a 'whoreson,' and another 'a filthy bald rat.'" Richalm describes a senior demon upbraiding his minions for missing Mass, where their duty was to distract and irk the officiating priest. Demons also encouraged any traits likely to irritate one's fellow monks. "All this snoring and coughing and sneezing and spitting in choir is their work," says Richalm. Some monks claim to have actually spoken with the demons. "Why don't you leave me alone?" one monk pleaded. "Not until you begin fornicating like other men," the demon is said to have replied.

But the severest test of all is the sin known as *acedia*. It translates as "listlessness," the monks recognizing it as a near-lethal paralysis of the will, which rendered every duty an unremitting bore, every prayer an intolerable burden, life itself a purposeless drudgery. Escape could become all but impossible from this depression, described by the psalmist as "the destruction that destroyeth in the noonday" (Ps. 91:6). The emphasis that monastic writers lay upon the value of helping monks who are so afflicted, and the danger of vexing them, writes Coulton, can scarcely be exaggerated.

On account of this dread disease of the soul, it is said, many a man abandoned his calling. If he later sought to return, he had to appear naked at the door, be readmitted by the whole chapter, and accept whatever penalty the abbot decreed, probably a beating. Many would not return. They saw the monastic standard as impossibly high, says Taylor, causing them to give up all moral effort entirely and descend into "all manner of sin." Augustine of Hippo concurs. "I have scarcely known any better men than those who have profited in monasteries," he writes, "but I have never known worse than those who have fallen in monasteries."

As usual, of course, the "worse" tended to command more attention. Reformers throughout the Middle Ages make their case for change by citing the conduct of monks gone bad. There was scant mention of the fidelity and holiness of the majority who did not "go bad," and whose conduct, being unremarkable, went unremarked. Records of church councils similarly tend to feature the more sordid cases.

A frighteningly graphic rendering of monks falling into temptation, this icon depicts the "ladder of divine ascent" described by the sixth-century hermit and theologian John Climacus. Good monks persevere in their struggle for religious perfection and achieve entry to heaven, the bad are dragged down to hell by devils. The icon, dating from the twelfth century, is now in St. Catherine's Monastery in Egypt's Sinai Desert.

Yet even the dour Coulton allows that the "true monk" did exist—the man "ripened by years of discipline, strict to himself, kindly to others, radiant with spiritual cheerfulness behind all his avoidance of actual laughter." Such men were "very real," he remarks.

Cluny's early abbots epitomized the strengths of true monks. The first was Berno of Baume, the little monastery that so captivated the searching Aldegrin. Berno founded Cluny itself through Duke William's bequest. From the start, it was endowed with what would prove a decisive advantage: It came directly under the pope. Unlike many monasteries, it was free of local political and ecclesiastical intervention, and just at the time when the popes were regaining control of the church. The popes therefore made the Cluniacs their agents in ridding the church of governmental control—although at times the popes themselves seemed to be agents of Cluny.

Under Berno's direction, the monastery's reputation spread far and wide, attracting so many recruits, all keen to share its rigorous life, that revenue failed for a time to cover basic necessities. When Odo took over from the dying Berno in 926, in fact, Cluny was so successful as to be bankrupt, and the brothers sometimes found themselves near starvation. Before long, however, swelling bequests caused money to match manpower.

Other monasteries began placing themselves under Cluniac direction, but some resisted vigorously. One was ancient Fleury, where rested the relics of Benedict himself.[6] At the urgent request of the Duke of the Franks, Odo arrived to set it in order, and was blocked at its gates. Fleury, he was told, was uninterested in upstart fads. Abbot Odo would not even be allowed entry unless he came on a donkey in token of humility. He cheerfully complied and Fleury's renaissance proceeded. Other monasteries produced darker reactions. At Farfa, in Lazio, Italy, two abbots were poisoned to thwart reform. A third took over the

Voices united in praise, the daily offices provide relief from the prevailing silence. Following the centuries-old Rule of Benedict, the chief work of monks, worship, includes the Mass and the daily offices and takes up much of the day. The balance of their time is devoted to work, study and individual prayer. These monks, at Hauterives, France, are of the Cistercian order.

6. The life of Benedict of Nursia is told in an earlier volume, *Darkness Descends*, but his relics have their own tale. The Lombards sacked Benedict's Italian monastery, Montecassino, in 580. A monk from Fleury (in what is now France) gathered up the bones of Benedict and his sister Scholastica, escaped a Lombard squad sent to thwart him, and brought the precious sack to his own monastery, which thereafter became a place of pilgrimage.

From bully-boys to godly mentors

The brawling monks of the East who once fatally thrashed an aged patriarch emerge from a terrible persecution as men of God with a wide respect they will never lose

When the rich young ruler asked Jesus how he could gain paradise, the Lord's uncompromising reply was: "Go your way, sell whatever you have and give to the poor, and you will have treasure in heaven; and come, take up the cross, and follow me" (Mark 10:21). It was a challenge the young man could not accept, and it has been harassing the consciences of many Christians ever since. But century after century, thousands upon thousands of believers have accepted it. Leaving families, professions, ambitions and pleasures, they embraced as monks and nuns a stern regime of rigorous prayer and ascetic discipline. However, the monastic movement in the East followed a somewhat different path than that taken in the West.

Greek-speaking monastics found that divorcing themselves from worldly pleasure was one thing, but renouncing worldly power in a society where church and state were so closely entwined was another proposition entirely. Eastern monks became fervently, often violently, involved in one doctrinal controversy after another, descending in mobs from their monasteries to disrupt church councils and occasionally inflicting physical assaults upon those whom they regarded as doctrinally errant. At one council, held at Ephesus in 449, monks joined soldiers in clubbing and kicking the patriarch of Constantinople so severely that he died a few days later. (See earlier volume, *Darkness Descends*). Such conduct has no parallel in Western monasticism.

In the East, however, it persisted into the eighth century, when the monks reacted with determined fury to the banning of icons by the emperor Leo III, bringing upon themselves a hundred years of merciless imperial

persecution. Out of that severe trial a different Eastern monasticism emerged, whose author is not disputed. The story of Theodore, who headed the Byzantine monastery at Constantinople known as Studion, is told in chapter 5. He it was who led the monks back to the ancient Rule of St. Basil the Great, father of Eastern monasticism, and who led them in suffering willingly the terrible trials of the iconoclast struggle. In so doing, they won the respect and loyalty of the Christian population, something they have never since lost.

Theodore favored a strictly disciplined communal life, on the premise that solitary challenges to Satan, especially if undertaken prematurely, could lead to self-absorption, delusion and other evils. He also stressed at Studion the importance of labor, both manual and scholarly, to balance prayer and ascetic discipline. Many other monasteries followed its example. Even so, writes Yale historian Kenneth Scott Latourette, by the end of the first millennium, the characteristics of Western and Eastern monasticism had increasingly diverged.

The monks in the East, writes historian David Knowles (*Christian Monasticism*) were regulated by decrees of church councils that later passed into common law. "This and their differing social conditions, together with the Byzantine reverence for a tradition that had never been broken, preserved Eastern monasticism as a whole from complete secularization and from the rhythm of decadence and reform experienced by the West, as it also stood in the way of the formation of new orders and the diversification of vocations."

Monasteries in raw Western lands, for example,

The Monastery of Xenophondous, built in 963, one of twenty-one monasteries on stunningly beautiful Mount Athos, Greece. The Holy Mount, completely self-governed, preserves many religious artifacts and icons of great value and is the acknowledged center of Eastern monasticism. The idyllic landscape, long a sanctuary from the turmoil of the world, belies the intensity of the spiritual battles waged in its monasteries.

reacting to the urgent material as well as spiritual needs of their people, became technological leaders in such areas as medicine and agriculture. The ancient civilizations of Asia Minor, on the other hand, were not so dependent in such matters upon monks. Then too, the new religious orders that evolved in the West made possible central supervision of whole networks of monasteries. This had no counterpart in the East, where a monastic house still typically began when disciples gathered about one saintly figure, remained a self-governing and individualistic entity under its *hegoumenos* (head), and despite the pervasive influence of Studion, often encouraged some members to live in solitary cells.

Two broad styles evolved, but were frequently combined. In "cenobitic" houses, explains British historian Rosemary Morris in *Monks and Laymen of Byzantium, 843–1118*, the entire community was seen as a "mystic body" collectively battling the forces of evil. In "lavriote" monasticism, named for the "lavra," a grouping of individual cells, members live and pray in solitude, gathering perhaps weekly for the Divine Liturgy. Practitioners of the austere lavriote regime, which harks back to St. Anthony of Egypt, usually sought solitude in the wilderness.

One location favored from early times was the rocky peninsula called Mount Athos. It juts from the coast of Macedonia, rising precipitously from the Aegean Sea and terminating in the mountain itself, a chunk of snowcapped marble over a mile high (6,670 feet). The spiny ridge, thirty miles long and 6.5 miles wide at its broadest, is deeply serrated by ravines and cliffs, and sufficiently inaccessible to satisfy even the most fastidious Byzantine hermit. Recorded history on Athos begins in 963, when monasteries on Byzantium's more vulnerable frontiers were falling victim to Muslim and other raiders, and the emperor Nicephorus Phocas sponsored the first major monastery there: the Grand Lavra.[1]

Its founder, a Bithynian monk named Athanasius, thereby earned the designation Athanasius the Athonite. Supported both by Nicephorus and his successor John Tzimisces, Athanasius managed to placate the resident solitaries, who seriously resented this organized invasion. Tzimisces issued the Grand Lavra an official charter (known as the "goat," because it is written on goatskin). Many more monasteries followed, and twenty-one are still there. At least four, including the Grand Lavra, date from Athanasius's lifetime (920–1003).

Soon known as the Holy Mountain, Athos became an enduring focus of Orthodox monasticism, as Serbia, Bulgaria, Russia and other Eastern states also established "national" monasteries there. Despite dissension among them, they learned to operate as a semiautonomous republic. They also survived pirate raids, invasion, and a centuries-long subjugation by the Muslim Turks, and although today the monks are numbered in hundreds, not thousands, their ancient pursuit of holiness continues unchanged. The peninsula itself remains pristine, practically untouched by "progress." Its monasteries, both styles, still function as repositories for (and disseminators of) scholarship, learning and art, and

Just east of Bethlehem, built into a canyon, the spectacular Mar Saba Greek Orthodox monastery has been in continuous use since the fifth century, the oldest inhabited monastery in the Holy Land. One of the few remaining from the sixty-five monasteries spread throughout the Judean desert, at its peak it was home to four thousand men.

as centers of charity and hospitality.

However, as with all Byzantine monasteries (and Western ones too, for that matter) one overriding function of these Athonite establishments has been the provision of spiritual counsel to church, state and individual Christians. St. Simeon the New Theologian (949–1022), regarded by many as the greatest of Byzantine mystical writers, was unquestionably a central influence in this. A Studion monk who became *hegoumenos* of St. Mamas Monastery, Simeon insisted that every layman—from emperor to humble soldier or farmer—needed a spiritual father. A monastery was the likeliest place to find one, he taught, though even here the seeker must take care to choose a monk sufficiently advanced in the spiritual life to possess the necessary discernment, charity and dispassion.[2]

Simeon's countrymen wholeheartedly agreed, it seems. Orthodox monastics have exerted extraordinary influence all across the East. The more the monks tried to withdraw from the world, the more the world insisted on seeking them out. "There is no doubt," writes historian Morris, "that these monastic saints were looked upon as 'living icons,' the best possible examples of the spiritual life." ■

1. A popular legend holds that the Virgin Mary made a brief visit to Athos, and so admired its spectacular beauty that she asked the Lord her Son to give it to her as a garden. However, the blessed Theotokos is the only feminine presence to find a welcome on this entire peninsula. Human females, and even female domestic animals, have been constitutionally banned from the Holy Mountain for a millennium.

2. St. Simeon taught that initial cleansing of the soul and much prayer, notes historian Morris, must go into selection of a spiritual father. "Go and find the man whom God, either mysteriously through himself, or externally through his servant, shall show you," he wrote, and century after century, Orthodox Christians have obeyed.

Two Benedictine edifices in the French countryside. Above, in the village of St. Père-sous-Vézelay, monks from the nearby monastery at Vézelay built the thirteenth-century church. An impressive example of Romanesque architecture, St. Martin-du-Canigou Monastery (below) was one of the many remarkable communities inspired by Cluny. It was founded in 1007.

abbacy by purchasing it, then successfully made the changes. While Odo yet lived, the pope placed ten monasteries under Cluniac direction, one of them St. Paul's in Rome.

"Must we not justly mourn," lamented Odo, "that Christianity, which ought to have grown stronger as it grew older, is instead bent on hastening headlong into evil?" But he remained generous-minded, admitting one distraught penitent as a novice even after discovering the man had flourished as a thief. The fellow became a model monk. On his deathbed, however, he confessed to two additional thefts. While a monk, he had taken a cloak to give to a poor man, then stolen a piece of rope to wrap around his waist as a reminder not to steal. Would God forgive him? God would indeed, said Odo, and the monk died in peace.

Before Odo himself died in 944, he had become the friend of kings and popes. Rudolf of Burgundy, king of the Franks, had conferred astonishing powers on Cluny, even authorizing it to issue its own coinage. Odo's successor, Aymar, was quite different. Shunning the company of princes, he quietly improved administration, increased land holdings, and bettered the lot of the serfs who came with every bequeathed estate. Any attack on a Cluniac serf was deemed an attack on Cluny. A knight named Richer who killed such a serf, Joan Evans recounts, was required by the Viscount of Vienne to become a serf himself. "I deliver my person and my head to the Abbey of Cluny," Richer acknowledged. "The abbot and the monks have the power to keep me in their hands, to keep me or to sell me."

After Abbot Aymar came Abbot Maiol, who declined an offer to become pope. More monasteries were constantly being added, and he strove to enhance their charitable work. When Maiol retired, exhausted and blind in 994, Cluny was entering its period of greatest growth and greatest influence. Over the next

A frail child, Odilo crept into a church and tried to stand erect by clinging to the altar cloth. Suddenly, he became strong. As a man, he healed those sick in mind and body.

one hundred and fifteen years, only two abbots reigned, both brilliantly.

The life of Odilo of Mercoeur, abbot from 994 to 1049, is surrounded by stories of the marvelous and the miraculous. As a frail toddler barely able to stand, it was said, little Odilo crept into a church, tried to pull himself erect on the altar cloth and his limbs suddenly became strong. As a man he cured the blindness of a farmer's child. Indeed he very frequently healed the sick, and restored to sanity an army deserter gone berserk. After his death, healings at his tomb were frequently reported.

In Odilo's time, a fundamental administrative change took place. Previously, each monastery had named its own abbot. Now there was to be just one abbot, at Cluny itself. Other monasteries were to be headed by men with the title "prior." Appointed by the abbot of Cluny, they would all meet there annually as a kind of grand chapter. So the movement was no longer a federation of monasteries, but a religious order. Vast building programs were launched, and hundreds of churches were staffed by Cluniac priests.[7] And still the extraordinary gifts cascaded upon it—uncultivated land, forests, fishing rights, vineyards, farms and their serfs, villages, manor houses, feudal castles. The abbot became something akin to the chief executive officer of a twenty-first-century corporation.

During the ensuing sixty-year regime of Abbot Hugh of Semur, in fact, Cluny went multinational, spreading through Italy, Christian Spain, and England. (The powerful German monasteries, however, looked for leadership elsewhere.) Estimates of the number of Cluniac monasteries vary wildly. Historian Henri Daniel-Rops (*The Church in the Dark Ages*) sets it at one thousand four hundred and fifty. In the year 1100, he writes, Cluniac monks totaled more than ten thousand. By then, only eleven monasteries seemingly called themselves abbeys, the rest having become priories.

Abbot Hugh, another confidant of popes and kings, is particularly remembered for the construction, over a twenty-year period, of Cluny's basilica, reputedly the world's largest church until the sixteenth century.[8] This tough

7. Becoming a monk did not necessarily mean becoming a priest. Most monks remained laymen. However, some were made deacons, or ordained to the priesthood, and at the pinnacle of Cluniac power, many of the bishops in western Europe were Cluniac monks. The effect was to spread Cluniac fervor and imbue much of the laity with a deeper commitment to Christ.

8. Cluny's basilica was the greatest monastic Romanesque church. It was built between 1088 and 1121, and like the Cluniac order itself, survived until the French Revolution, when it was demolished. Reconstructed in drawings, it is shown to be four hundred and fifty feet long, with fifteen small chapels in the transepts and ambulatory.

disciplinarian, says his biographer, stored food for the hungry, personally patched clothes for the needy, forgave murderers (including the man who killed his brother), and dealt patiently and adroitly with human frailty. One new monk, for instance, was the wealthy Count Guigo, accustomed to wearing fur and silk. He complained to Abbot Hugh that he could not bear the coarse monastic garb next his skin. Fine, said Hugh, go back to silk. Soon Guigo returned. The other monks thought him soft, he said, despising him as his soldiers used to despise cowards in battle. So Guigo willingly returned to the standard issue.

What did Cluny achieve? Christian historians credit the movement with spiritually awakening the whole Western church, and thereby saving tens of thousands of souls from eternal perdition. What achievement could be greater? But for secularists who would credit something more "practical," there was a great deal more. The accomplishments of Cluny's monks have, in fact, filled volumes.

To begin with, they restored the soil of western Europe to food production, and made it far more productive than ever before. Fully half of the land of Europe came into the hands of the church, writes Prosper Boissonnade in his *Life and Work in Medieval Europe*, and many a "monk" carried a pruning hook in his girdle to signify his occupation. The ecclesiastical domains pioneered agricultural science, animal breeding and husbandry, and improved forestry practices. The monks came to be recognized as highly efficient farmers and imitated by secular lords, says Paul Johnson in his *History of Christianity*.

The Renaissance painter Giovanni Antonio Bazzi painted this pious scene of a fatherly St. Benedict praying with his monks, one of a series of thirty-six frescoes from the life of Benedict in Monte Oliveto Maggiore, a Benedictine abbey in Tuscany.

"A great and increasing part of the arable land of Europe passed into the hands of highly disciplined men, committed to a doctrine of hard work. They were literate. They knew how to keep accounts. Above all, perhaps, they worked to a daily timetable and an accurate annual calendar, something quite alien to the farmers and the landowners they replaced."

The monks drained many swamps and cultivated that land. In other circumstances, they set up irrigation and water distribution systems. They created ponds and established fisheries. They constructed bridges and ran ferries across the rivers. They operated cheese factories. They also began the manufacture of linen and lace, writes the Count de Montalembert in *The Monks of the West*, wove cloth and tanned leather. Many of the great vineyards of France, Germany, Spain and Italy date from this period. The orchards of Germany began producing apples and pears in quantity.

From the ninth century onward, writes economic historian Robert Latouche in *The Birth of the Western Economy*, slavery declined in Europe. Water-powered mills and animals replaced slave labor, which the church discouraged and monks refused to use. Instead, the monasteries substituted crop sharing systems with peasant farmers, and the term *mancipia* (slaves) disappeared from title deeds. Serfdom arose due to the need for protection, but serfdom was not slavery. The serf belonged with the land and he could not be sold away from it. Very slowly throughout the Middle Ages, serfs evolved into farmers with freehold title to their land.

Where rivers could not serve, marketing crops required roads, which the monks constructed, along with hostelries to accommodate pilgrims headed for Rome or Jerusalem or the shrines of the saints. Individual monks could not own money, St. Paul describing the love of lucre as the root of all evil (1 Tim. 6:10). On the other hand, the growing towns and the monasteries themselves could not carry on without cash for buying, selling, collecting fees and so forth. Historian Lester K. Little, writing in *Religious Poverty and Profit in the Middle Ages*, points out the convenience of the bequests and gifts that initially nourished the monastic movement. "So solidly established, both materially and spiritually, was the monastic order that the transition from 'gift economy' to money economy was made without worry or reflection," Little comments.

Trade proving unavoidable, the Christian cities of Venice and Genoa became citadels of capitalism. Beyond their boundaries, the Jews labored as the first businessmen of Europe, the terms "Jew" and "merchant" becoming interchangeable. True to the monastic anti-money tradition, one preacher likened them to "filth and fecal matter," while another decried this "nation of Judases." But Jews had powerful allies as well as foes. Devout Christian monarchs, in need of trade and revenue, encouraged Jewish enterprises, even setting up some individuals in business.

But Europe's biggest enterprise was probably Cluny itself, as can be deduced at the end of the eleventh century by its building program alone. The monastic movement triggered an extraordinary period of construction, the great

Romanesque churches evolving into Gothic cathedrals that one observer called "symphonies in stone"—structures that would overwhelm the beholder right through to the twenty-first century.

Benedictine monasteries educated mainly their own monks, but their scholars laid down the medieval syllabus. In the *trivium*, the monk learned grammar, dialectic and rhetoric, followed by the *quadrivium*, covering arithmetic, geometry, astronomy and music. Meanwhile, the reading and writing of words became indispensable duties and tools of the monastic life. Bookmaking flourished. Libraries came into being. Although monks constituted barely one half of one percent of the population, says Milis, they produced between sixty-five and ninety-eight percent of all written information. In copying and preserving the classics of Greece and Rome," Johnson writes, they became "the carriers of culture."

Medieval monks regarded works of charity as even more important than learning. De Montalembert records that in the regime of Hugh, the motherhouse at Cluny annually fed and otherwise assisted seventeen thousand people. Nor were these "alms" always distributed out of "mere superfluity." The annals show that the monastery's last loaf of bread frequently went to the poor. In more festive terms, the custom of the "washing of the feet" arose in France and England. On the anniversary of the abbey's founding, the abbot would gather as many poor people as there were monks in his monastery, feast them with good food and wine, and then wash their feet—in emulation of course, of Jesus at the Last Supper (John 13:4–16).

Peasants who lived near monasteries considered themselves highly favored. Aphorisms emerged that soon became old sayings. "It is good living under the crosier," was one of these (referring to the crook-shaped staff carried by bishops and sometimes by abbots and abesses), and people spoke of "going to the charity of the monks." Thus began the tradition of care for the poor and infirm that came to characterize every Christian country, and still characterizes their descendent nations. For the monk, nevertheless, works of charity were not so much motivated by human concern as by devotion to Jesus Christ.

Traditional records indicate that Cluny's fall was almost as spectacular as its rise, even making allowances for dramatic tale-telling by reformers and rivals. Abbot Hugh's successor in 1109 was Pons (or Pontius) de Melgueil, a nobly born incompetent. The new abbot spent lavishly on the splendor of the abbey, and acquired at great cost its three most precious relics.[9] His extravagance so scandalized some of his monks, however, that they complained to Rome. Summoned by the pope, Pons resigned and undertook a pilgrimage to Jerusalem. But that was not the end of his story.

His successor at Cluny, Hugh II, died after three months in office. In 1122, the monks chose Pierre Maurice de Montboissier, known as Peter the Venerable, a Cluniac from childhood and the last of its great abbots. His regime proved turbulent, to say the least. Three years after he took office, Pons returned from Jerusalem and conspired with his many supporters.

9. A fragment of the true cross, a finger of the first martyr Stephen, and a tooth of John the Baptist. The last was kept in a jeweled reliquary hanging to the left of the high altar.

During Lent, while Abbot Peter was away visiting subsidiary priories, Pons organized a small army of renegade monks, local knights, mercenary soldiers, criminals, drifters and a mob of Cluny citizens, and led an armed attack against the motherhouse. Driving out the loyal monks, the mob looted it, pillaged its stores of grain and farm equipment, and once more proclaimed Pons abbot. He thereupon played the feudal lord, burning villages and killing anyone who opposed him.

Rome, seemingly dumfounded at first, finally ordered Pons to appear

before a synod at Lyons. When he refused, he and his supporters were excommunicated. Assailed by misgivings, the supporters deserted their leader, repented, and were forgiven. But Pons, who was imprisoned, remained defiant—no repentance for him. No one but St. Peter himself, he said, had authority to excommunicate him. He died about a year later. Peter the Venerable allowed his burial at Cluny, but over his tomb was erected the figure of the rebellious abbot, with his feet bound, his right hand amputated, and his left hand clutching a broken crosier.

Joan Evans details Peter's subsequent struggle to hold the movement together: how the younger novices rebelled against restoration of discipline; how one monk barricaded himself in a tower, threatening to stone anyone who came near

The stewardship of monks over their immense land holdings, combined with their penchant for order and discipline, enormously increased the productivity of European agriculture in the Middle Ages. These illustrations from an eleventh-century illuminated manuscript show the harvesting of olives (upper left), beekeepers at work (below), and the slaughter of a ram (upper right). New techniques and the increased use of animals introduced by the monasteries had an attendant benefit. Slavery gradually disappeared.

The curious power of saintly relics

Christians cherished them, traded in them, stole them, and believed fervently in a phenomenon that is as old as Elijah and young as a lock of Elvis Presley's hair

So it was, as they were burying a man, that suddenly they spied a band of raiders; and they put the man in the tomb of Elisha; and when the man was let down and touched the bones of Elisha, he revived and stood on his feet. (2 Kings 13:21)

Then he took the mantle of Elijah that had fallen from him, and struck the water, and said, "Where is the Lord God of Elijah?" And when he also had struck the water, it was divided this way and that way, and Elisha crossed over. (2 Kings 2:14)

Now a woman, having a flow of blood for twelve years, who had spent all her livelihood on physicians and could not be healed by any, came from behind and touched the border of his garment. And immediately her flow of blood stopped. (Luke 8:43–44)

And believers were increasingly added to the Lord, multitudes of both men and women, so that they brought the sick out into the streets and laid them on beds and couches, that at least the shadow of Peter passing by might fall on some of them. (Acts 5:15)

Now God worked unusual miracles by the hands of Paul, so that even handkerchiefs or aprons were brought from his body to the sick, and the diseases left them and the evil spirits went out of them. (Acts 19:11–12)

As the above indicates, the idea that the remains, or the apparel, or even the shadow of a person whose holiness is unquestioned, should carry with it a power over nature did not begin with medieval Christianity. It makes its appearance in both the Old and New Testaments. That it should appear prominently therefore in times of great human need, danger and suffering is hardly surprising.

Such times were the early medieval ones where Viking raids, plague, war, famine and physical injury were the common experience of many communities and of most lives. The respect paid to relics—the bones or belongings of holy men and women—soared chronically.

Thus, the new abbey, dramatically founded by England's King Henry I at Reading in 1121, became one of the wealthiest and most famous monasteries of the age, due in no small part to its impressive collection of two hundred and forty-two most remarkable relics, most of them of dubious validity. They included a shoe ostensibly belonging to Jesus Christ, his swaddling clothes, blood and water from his side, bread crumbs from the feeding of the five thousand *and* from the Last Supper, strands of the Blessed Virgin's hair, the rods of Moses and Aaron and—far from least—the complete mummified left hand of St. James, stolen from Charlemagne's imperial chapel at Aachen.

The cures and marvels attributed to Reading's miraculous array in the twelfth century attracted pilgrims by the thousands, from humble serf to noble lord. Those with means were lodged in some comfort and wined and dined in style, thus encouraging grateful donations to the abbey. Indeed, the passionate interest in holy relics, and their possession and veneration, became a central feature of economic life in Christendom, as well as a respected aspect of faith.

Saintly relics were generally believed to be a practical defense against physical suffering and the constant and malignant activities of the devil. Any promise sworn on holy relics was elevated to the status of a super-oath—with the very fires of hell waiting for those who would break such a sacred commitment. Relics were also carried into battle as an encouragement of divine support, a holy talisman of victory. Charlemagne famously campaigned with a holy spear said to be the very weapon plunged into Christ's side on Calvary. At the Battle of Hastings, William of Normandy wore around his neck a string of holy relics provided by the pope.

Relics were regarded as more valuable than gold, silver or precious gems—which were lavishly used in creating settings for these holy objects. "A huge proportion of society's liquid assets were tied up in relics and their precious settings," writes Paul Johnson in *A History of Christianity*. "Kings amassed collections as big as those of major churches, to enhance their prestige and authority. They took their best relics with them wherever they went, thus ensuring they were always within the ambit of spiritual power."

Not surprisingly, competition for ownership of saintly relics could be intense, sometimes pitting entire communities against each other. The chronicler Gregory of Tours describes what occurred at the death of St. Martin. Representatives from the towns of Tours and Poitiers (about twenty miles apart) both claimed the body, with neither side willing to back down. The standoff continued for many hours, until the exhausted men of Poitiers fell asleep. "When therefore they of Tours saw them sleeping, they laid hold of the mortal remains of this most holy body," says Gregory. "While some cast it forth from the window, others caught it outside; then the whole band floated down the River Vienne into the current of the Loire—and steered to

Tours with loud praises and abundant psalmody."

Theft of relics was commonplace, and openly acknowledged by high officials of both church and state. Some even indulged in this larcenous business themselves. Alfred, canon of Durham in northeast England, was a regular pilgrim to the monastery at Jarrow, to pray at the tomb of the Venerable Bede, for example—but only until he was successful in stealing Bede's remains and placing them beside the already potent bones of St. Cuthbert in Durham Cathedral. More squeamish kings, bishops and abbots could employ professionals to do the dirty work.

Nevertheless, the extraordinary value that Christians attached to them testified to the faith they placed in a power somehow centered in them. Many Christians still preserve, and would guard with their lives, holy relics. Just because an object is very ancient and disappears into the mists of ancient history, they would say, does not mean it couldn't be exactly what it claims to be. Until recently, it was required to have relics in the altar stone of all Roman Catholic churches. Eastern churches place them in the altar or in the *antimension*, the silk or linen cloth that confers the bishop's authority to conduct the Divine Liturgy.

"People fervently believed," writes Johnson, that "relics radiated a kind of energy, rather like a nuclear pile, and were correspondingly dangerous as well as useful. Important relics were approached with terror, and frequently revenged themselves on the profane and the skeptical. They conveyed a sense of supernatural power—constantly humming through the world—that could be switched on through access to the right liturgical and sacramental channels."

Such "fervent belief," observes the twentieth-century Christian apologist C. S. Lewis, is usually attributed to the education that people of the medieval era received, and the gullible environment in which they lived. This is said to account for their belief in miracles. But if that were so, says Lewis, it would also follow that the kind of education we receive today and the skeptical environment in which we live must account for our reluctance to believe in miracles. Medieval man expected them and was perhaps favored with them. Modern man does not expect them and is not favored with them.

In certain ways, however, modern man very definitely believes in "relics." What in the early twenty-first century might a lock of the singer Elvis Presley's hair command on the current "relics" market, one wonders. Even the clothing or habitat of a person can continue to suggest his presence—for better or for worse. Take the scene from the movie version of Neil Simons's play, *The Odd Couple*, in which Felix Unger (Jack Lemmon) has been ousted from the house by his thoroughly fed-up wife, who now phones him. "It's your wife," says his friend Oscar Maddox (Walter Matthau). "Tell her I don't want to talk to her. Tell her I've suffered, too, you know. Here, gimme the phone."

Oscar: "She doesn't want to talk to you."

Felix: "She doesn't!! Then why's she calling?"

Oscar: "She wants you to come and get your things. She's having the room repainted."

More poignantly, we hear the prophecy of the British poet Rupert Brooke on the way to the First World War Gallipoli campaign. He believes his body carries with it the presence of his country.

> If I should die, think only this of me:
> That there's some corner of a foreign field
> That is forever England.
> (from "The Soldier")

Brooke died of an insect bite before the landing and was buried on an Aegean island. ∎

A relic said to be part of the skull of St. John the Baptist (right) is contained in a gold case, studded with gems (left). The exquisite casing, originating in a Bulgarian workshop, suggests that it may have been a gift, possibly to the Byzantine court. They are now in the custody of the Topkapi Palace, Istanbul.

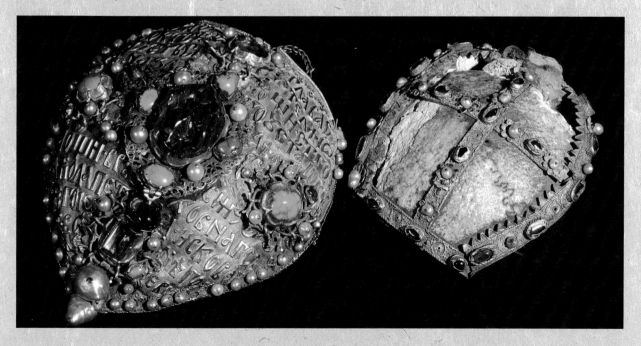

until he was issued better clothing; how another set fire to a warehouse; how one hard-line prior was poisoned by his monks, and another had to call on Rome to support him; how eighteen houses defied Peter and elected their own abbots; how the Cluny treasury, stripped by Pons, couldn't pay the bills and Peter began selling off properties until Rome forbade him to continue; and how Henry of Winchester had to donate seven thousand marks of silver to keep the monks fed.

But Peter soldiered on, his pen excoriating backsliding monks for flagrant breaking of vows. Many had taken to eating meat. "Like hawks and vultures," chided Peter, "they gather wherever they see smoke from a kitchen, wherever they smelt meat cooking." He called an assembly of all the Cluniac priors, presented to them a somewhat modified Benedictine regimen, only to discover that this too would be disregarded. Monasteries became a public scandal. Some accumulated debt, often due to grandiose building programs, and had to borrow money. Others, still prosperous, went into the loan business. One chronicler describes how his brethren quickly broke up a dice game to rush into chapel, when they heard that choristers were to be paid to sing God's praises. Another chronicler complained that monks had become so obsessed with money that "we sell Christ more shamefully than Judas did." Coulton lists ten church councils between 1000 and 1150 at which the decay of the monasteries was on the agenda, sometimes centrally.

Peter the Venerable died on Christmas Day, 1156. He was renowned as a scholar, a deft ecclesiastical diplomat, and an articulate Christian apologist against Islam and Judaism, but he had failed to restore Cluny—perhaps an impossible feat. With fitful efforts at revival, the great house held on until the French Revolution, when its bells were melted to make cannons. In November 1791, the magnificent basilica was sacked by a mob, its windows smashed, and the grave of the abbot Hugh I desecrated. The monastery's books, manuscripts, vestments and wooden statuary were all destroyed in a huge fire in the town market place. Seven years later, two local citizens bought the ruin of the abbey, and in 1811, much of what remained standing was demolished. Cluny had become a safety hazard.

But monasticism, far from vanishing with the Cluniac decline, regenerated itself once more. Between 1020 and 1120, eight new orders of monks appeared, all seeking to serve through communal life the City of God.[10] In particular, at the turn of the twelfth century (beyond the period of this volume) would come the Cistercians, whose accomplishments would rival the achievements of the black-garbed Cluniacs. Cistercian Benedictines would wear white, emphasizing their purity, and the ensuing contest between the black and white brethren absorbed the interest of medieval Europeans well into the second millennium. ∎

10. As the Cluniacs declined, new and vibrant monastic orders appeared: The Camaldulensians, founded in 1020; the Vallumbrosans, 1050; the Gramontines, 1073; the Carthusians, 1084; the Order of Fontevrault, 1094; the Antonines, 1095; the Cistercians, 1098; and the Premonstratensians, 1120. As the monastic orders developed, the color of the cowl, the hood that could be pulled over the head, came to identify the order.

Swirling fog, a clifftop setting and stately cypresses create an air of unreality about Monte Oliveto Maggiore, a Tuscan abbey dating from 1313. The great Benedictine monastery continues the traditions of the past. Its monks are involved in a school for recovery of old books, and the abbey is also noted for its series of frescoes on the life of St. Benedict.

Of noble birth and firm resolve

Far from the shy introverts popularly portrayed, the nuns were often high-born women of resolute will, fearing neither fire nor papal envoys

1. Fire was such a constant threat that William the Conqueror introduced a law requiring all domestic fires to be covered at sunset, generally with a metal cover known as a *couvre feu*, later to evolve into the English word "curfew." Owing to the lack of organized fire brigades and ready water supplies, however, this did little to prevent disastrous fires in Norman towns.

The people of the little town of Marcigny in the Grosne Valley of French Burgundy would long remember that frightening night, and history would remember it longer still. Fire, so amply fueled by timber houses, thatched roofs, straw beds and open hearths, was a terrifying, ever present peril in medieval town life. On this occasion, late in the eleventh century, it was approaching the roof of the Cluniac convent, imperiling the whole building. "Fire! Fire! Get out! Get out!" screamed the horrified townspeople as they hurried to rouse the nuns and assist their escape. At first, however, no sound at all was heard within the cloister.

But wait! From behind the locked door, a small, calm voice made itself heard. "We cannot leave the cloister," it said. "We have made the vow." Some recognized the voice of Prioress Giselda.

"Quick!" somebody shouted. "The papal legate's in town. Bring him! Have him tell these women they must get out."

He was already coming, so the story goes. Making his way through the engulfing smoke, he presented himself at the cloister door, announced his identity, and in the name of Pope Gregory VII commanded that these women now leave this building. The crowd fell silent to hear the response.

"We are under obedience to remain," said the prioress. "Only the abbot of Cluny himself can revoke the rule." There was an appalled gasp from the crowd. "But perhaps," continued the prioress, "Your Excellency might exercise your authority over the fire, and tell it to go away."

The baffled cleric threw up his hands in dismay, then clasped them in prayer, and asked that the flames be turned away. And behold, whether through a change in the wind, divine intervention, or both, the fire turned away from the convent—proving, people said, that it was easier to command fire than the iron will of the Marcigny nuns.[1]

However factual or fanciful this particular story may have been, there is no doubt whatsoever that nuns took their vows very seriously indeed. At that place and time, one must necessarily add, for in practice, the rigor of monastic life varied as widely among nuns as among monks. There

HILDEGARD ON THE GLORY OF GOD REFLECTED IN NATURE:

The loft and length of the winds and the sweet moisture of the air, and the sharp greenness of the trees and plants, which are dependent upon the strength of what is above, in which God is at work producing and sustaining them, show forth His glory. For God is glorified through the mysteries of His creatures.

were "good" eras of strict observance, and "bad" eras of neglect so chronic that papal admonitions came forth. About two hundred years later, for instance, Pope Boniface VIII found cause to officially decry the "perilous and detestable state of certain nuns, who, having slackened the reins of decency, gad about outside their monasteries." One bishop, ordered to enforce that particular decree, found himself assailed by the rebellious sisters of Markyate nunnery, near St. Alban's, England, who hurled the enclosure statute at his head as he fled their convent.

Enclosure—meaning staying put in the convent, no "gadding about"—was certainly more stringently applied to nuns than to monks, though both were bound by the Benedictine Rule to observe stability in their chosen institution, and a willing embrace of chastity, personal poverty and obedience. Hildegard of Bingen, the renowned head of Rupertsberg Abbey, considered the Benedictine model moderate, and as ideal for women as it was for men.

On the other hand, Heloise, abbess of the small Oratory of the Paraclete, near Troyes in France, pleaded for modification of the rule. "No one would lay on an ass a burden suitable for an elephant," she wrote to her mentor and former lover, Peter Abelard, the brilliant and controversial scholar who for a time was abbot of St. Gildas monastery in Brittany. Abelard disagreed. The great problem, he maintained, was to curb "gossip," and the only known remedy for it was perpetual silence—"at prayer, in the cloister, the dormitory, refectory, and

during all eating and cooking, and from Compline onwards"—in other words, most of the day. The nuns, like the monks, developed an elaborate system of hand signals to observe the letter, if not the spirit, of the Rule.[2]

But the medieval nun was not the timid, compliant female of popular notion. She was often of noble birth, independent and spirited, commonly a widow, or a wife encouraged to enter religious life for some reason of family expediency. Such women frequently possessed excellent leadership qualities. Then too, nunneries were convenient places to dispose of unattached female relatives; they probably attracted their share of brokenhearted lovers, women fleeing marriage, and lonely widows looking for security in their old age. Young girls, some of them infants, some handicapped, some illegitimate, were brought to the convent and remained there for life. And while medieval poetry likes to lament the tragedy of the reluctant nun, many women embraced the life fervently, the willing and devout brides of Jesus Christ.

Nunneries had small populations, twenty to one hundred women. Marcigny, for example, was never to exceed ninety-nine, while the Virgin Mary was the

2. One of the great romances of the Middle Ages was the ill-starred love affair between Peter Abelard, an enormously gifted but enormously contentious theologian and teacher, and Heloise, niece of Canon Fulburt of Notre Dame. The couple fled together, but Fulburt had them pursued and Abelard castrated. Heloise agreed to take vows at the Oratory of the Paraclete (which Abelard had founded). Abelard pursued his controversial career elsewhere for another two decades, but at length was reconciled with church authorities and died in peace at Cluny.

HILDEGARD ON THE CONVERSION OF THE SOUL:

In the same way as creatures have strengths so also does the soul. For the beginning of just desires blows in the soul like a wind and the taste of goodwill plays over it like the air and the completion of finished deeds flourishes in it like the greenness of the world to advance it.

HILDEGARD ON LEADERSHIP:

Beware lest you climb higher than your abilities will allow, but in all your doings embrace the most sweet mother of virtues, that is, Discretion, and be guided by her in all things and you will not fail. For the shepherd who wields the rod of correction without discretion is not pleasing to God and will not be loved by his flock but rather hated.

3. The community of nuns at Fécamp, anticipating the onslaught of the Normans, cut off their lips and noses as a defense against rape. The Normans did return, but this ghastly measure provided no protection; they were summarily butchered.

presumed hundredth, with a place set for her at table and a seat reserved for her in chapel. Most were established by wealthy patrons or modest local landowners who pooled their funds, with the papacy and church playing a surprisingly negligible financial role. Humorously, the names of some of these humbler patrons are not particularly indicative of piety: Jerorius Fat Lips, Ogerius Sword-Rattler and Raginald Who Folds Up Peasants. These benefactors enjoyed some privileges: Prayers would be said on their behalf by the nuns, a home and care provided for their aging widows, and they could be buried in the convent cemetery.

By the eleventh century, English and continental nunneries had largely recovered from the hideous Viking and Magyar invasions of the ninth and tenth.[3] More than four hundred new communities for women were established in France and England. Some dual monasteries (side-by-side communities for men and women) still existed in the eleventh century, and not infrequently were headed by an abbess. Dual monasteries offered certain advantages; the men could provide liturgical services and perform heavy chores while the women provided domestic assistance, sewing clothing and baking bread.

Convents could be extremely wealthy or devastatingly poor. Highborn women entering nunneries brought sizable entry gifts (dowries) of land, mills, houses, or vineyards. Hildegard's monastery was clearly a wealthy community, owning twenty houses, several vineyards, land and servants in various locations, as well as extensive property around Bingen. The financial solvency of any religious house depended on property acquired, other gifts and the "dowries" that accompanied wealthier entrants. Poor communities could be truly destitute—their buildings derelict, with unrepaired roofs, at constant risk of fire or collapse, and the nuns relying on friends for their basic needs. Desperate measures were sometimes called for, pawning liturgical silver, renting out land, the nuns themselves begging.

Monastic hospitality could be also ruinous. Given that any stranger in need must be viewed as Christ himself (Matt. 25:31–46), the king, noble families or a bishop could require monasteries or convents, in exchange for one lump sum, to provide lodging and board to certain persons for the rest of their lives, a practice known as *corody*. Since some of these pensioners proved unexpectedly long-lived, eating far more food than envisioned, and seriously overcrowding the available accommodation, corody could be problematic. In one instance, a man acquired one corody, then moved into the convent with his wife, three children and a maid.

Not all nuns lived in community; renewed interest in the eremitic life found some living as recluses in huts, caves and rooms attached to churches.

Christina of Markyate typifies this life. When very young, she made a vow of virginity, which was put severely to the test by her forced betrothal to a nobleman. Disguised as a man, she fled and spent many years in hiding, living first with an anchoress, then with a hermit. (Much later, Christina was able to return to Markyate, where she became prioress.) Women living as recluses or anchorites were more likely to observe extreme ascetic practices. In the late thirteenth century, Mechthild of Magdeburg, who practiced flagellation as well as extended fasting and vigils, declared: "These were the weapons of my soul with which I conquered my body so successfully that for twenty years there was never a time when I was not tired, sick and weak."

The cloister, however, was also the point of convergence for medieval women with scholarly or artistic aspirations. The abbess Heloise vividly expressed the difficulty of living a scholarly life anywhere other than a convent: "What harmony can there be between pupils and nursemaids, desks and cradles, books of tablets and distaffs, pen or stylus and spindles?" she wrote to Abelard. "Who can concentrate on thoughts of Scripture or philosophy and be able to endure babies crying, nurses soothing them with lullabies, and all the noisy coming and going of men and women about the house?"

Another nun of talent was the tenth-century abbess and writer Hroswitha of Gandersheim, raised in the convent from her youth, who wrote Latin poetry and was the first known European post-classical dramatist.[4] Elisabeth of Schönau and

Mechthild of Magdeburg are remembered for their mystical writings. But Hildegard is the most notable example of a woman whose myriad gifts in writing, theology, music, art, science and medicine were able to find full expression in the monastic milieu.

Scholarship and learning were not prerequisites for an abbess, however. It was much more important that she demonstrate an exemplary life, and possess the holiness and wisdom to guide the women committed to her charge—and who, if the rule was followed, elected her to this lifelong office. She must also, of course, be

4. The well-educated nun, Hroswitha, strove to make her plays appealing by copying the comedic style of the classical dramatist Terence, while maintaining a higher moral plane. But this did present a problem. "I have often hesitated with a blush on my cheeks through modesty," she wrote, "because the nature of the work obliged me to concentrate my attention on and apply my mind to the wicked passion of illicit love and to the tempting talk of the amorous, against which we at other times close our ears." Her dramas were revived in the nineteenth century by a marionette troupe, and presented in New York and London.

Hroswitha of Gandersheim is depicted reading to her nuns. A tenth-century abbess, Hroswitha entered the convent as a youth and found the scholarly and ascetic environment conducive to developing her considerable literary gifts as a poet and dramatist.

capable of managing a large establishment, of ensuring the material well-being of all its residents, lands and buildings, and of dealing shrewdly and competently with the outside world. Thus an abbess was generally a mature woman, of noble birth, born in wedlock, preferably previously married, and well practiced in the rule.

The position carried high prerogatives as well as heavy responsibilities. Well-connected abbesses were able to use their influence to enrich the holdings of their houses. A rare few actually presided over courts of their own, struck their own coins, and influenced church councils and national assemblies. On a personal level, senior churchmen, monarchs and even popes sought the advice on occasion of abbesses noted for their spiritual and prophetic wisdom.

The abbess of a large nunnery relied on many assistants. The treasuress received and disbursed funds; the chantress was responsible for books, music and singing instruction; the infirmarian cared for the sick. The wardrober managed the shearing of sheep, the provision of linens and sewing tools, and the making of clothing ("shapynge, sewynge, makyng, repayryng and kepyng them from wormes" in the words of one rule). The cellaress controlled all cultivation and harvesting of food, including animals and bees, the hiring and firing of servants, the purchase of supplies and the sale of crops, hides and wool. The portress (doorkeeper) not only received guests, but also washed the feet of poor women if required. The sacristan tended to church furnishings, and hired candle-makers. Laundry, cooking and the brewing of ale was often done by the nuns themselves, though wealthier houses could afford servants to perform such household tasks. Laborers were hired for the farm work.

The daily offices, as in the men's monasteries, were central to the nuns' life and work. When not in chapel or doing chores, they prayed, read, studied, and did needlework and weaving, including the sewing of vestments. A typical day allowed for eight hours of sleep, four hours of prayer, four hours of study and eight hours of work, the Benedictine combination of routine and variety. Simplicity governed their needs. Their meals were prepared from locally available produce (nothing exotic) and they slept in dormitories. The nun's habit consisted of an undergarment and a robe, a cloak for cold weather, shoes and stockings and a white band around a shorn head covered by the black veil. The veils of consecrated virgins were to be marked with a white cross "as a deterrent to any of the faithful against burning with desire for them," as instructed by Abelard in a letter to Heloise.

Cloistered nuns, of course, were nonetheless subject to the frailties of human nature. Overindulgence in food or drink may have been common, along with gossip. Other infractions concerned the wearing of secular clothing, visiting with outsiders or keeping pets. More serious

consequences still could follow from sexual temptation. Too often, observed Aelred of Rievaulx, the sisters might "think it enough to confine the body behind walls while the mind roams at random." And in some cases the body followed, so that some nuns bore children from illicit liaisons with clergy or eloped with itinerant craftsmen or passing minstrels. "Nothing is less under our control than the heart," wrote Heloise in one tormented letter to Abelard.

By virtue of their vocation, however, most nuns went about their quiet lives of work and prayer anonymously; only a few names are remembered for individual accomplishments in scholarship or artistic endeavor. But the compassionate care dispensed at every convent in the name of Christ, to travelers, abandoned children, and to the sick, elderly or troubled, were the precursors of the hospitals, almshouses and hospices that would become the fundamental social network of modern life. ∎

HILDEGARD ON MUSIC IN WORSHIP:

The body is the garment of the soul and it is the soul which gives life to the voice. That's why the body must raise its voice in harmony with the soul for the praise of God. God should be praised with crashing cymbals and with all the other musical instruments that clever and industrious people have produced. For all the arts serving human desires and needs are derived from the breath that God sent into the human body. And that is why it is fitting that God be praised in all.

The Sybil of the Rhine

Hildegard of Bingen, a nun of brilliant mind and powerful convictions, has been called 'a Renaissance figure before the Renaissance'

Dubbed by one *New York Times* article "a Renaissance figure before the Renaissance," the twelfth-century nun Hildegard of Bingen had a renaissance of her own more than nine hundred years after she died. A recording of her music made in 1982 prompted wide interest in her genius, and in 1998, there was an exuberant celebration of the nine hundredth anniversary of her birth. Previously known only to medievalists and musicologists, she was thereafter appropriated by New Agers, lesbians, pantheists, environmentalists, avant-garde composers, holistic healers and feminists, all seeing in her work some validation of their respective causes.

Not a few of these new admirers would surely have astonished Hildegard. A commited and orthodox Christian, she was the tenth child of a noble German family. At the age of eight, she was offered as a tithe to God, a not uncommon act of piety, and became a companion to a recluse named Jutta. She took monastic vows at fourteen, succeeded Jutta as abbess of the small community of nuns attached to the male Benedictine house at Diessenberg, and at fifty-two founded a new women's monastery near Bingen, on the banks of the Rhine, not far from the city of Mainz. A daughter house was established fifteen years later, and Hildegard served both as abbess.

Contemporary fascination with this devout monastic (the "Hildecraze," as one wag called it) is doubtless due to the misperception that she willfully broke barriers of gender, culture and position. But Hildegard was no militant medieval feminist; her actions and writings resonated from deep faith, firmly grounded in tradition, and her own conviction that she acted "as the mouthpiece of God." Her gift of writing also found expression in plays, poetry and works of natural science and medicine. She was the only known female composer of her era, possibly the most prolific identifiable composer of the Middle Ages.

About one gift, she was very secretive. Prophetic visions burdened her at age three, when she first witnessed "a dazzling heavenly light." Although she never doubted that these came from God, the consequences of revealing her gift, and thereby opening herself to censure and ridicule, filled her with dread. A divine command to write about it, in her early forties, left her no choice. Validation eventually came from papal envoys who investigated her visions, and endorsed them as indeed unique and genuine.

They come down as prophetic, cosmic and apocalyptic, but what they

"Humanity stands in the midst of the structure of the world." Often compared to those of William Blake, Hildegard's mystical paintings translated her visions into something tangible and iconographic. This painting, titled Universal Man, *is from her* Liber divinorum operum. *Hildegard herself is in the bottom left corner, receiving the vision.*

actually mean is far from self-evident. Uniquely, Hildegard experienced them while wide awake with her ordinary sight uncompromised (that is, not in a trance or dreamlike state), which enabled her to reproduce in iconography their vivid colors and images. Visionary episodes were invariably accompanied by debilitating illness, pain and heaviness—symptoms that some modern commentators attribute to severe migraines. But for Hildegard, the "living light" provided a release: "And when I look upon it all sadness and pain vanishes from my memory, so that I am again as a simple maid and not as an old woman."[1]

Her fervent devotion finds further expression in her music. Often her elaborate, haunting chants, a departure from the traditional Gregorian, are still able to inspire awe nearly a millennium later. Their continuing appeal is attested by the fact that over a million copies have been sold. In *Scivias*, Hildegard explains the power of music in worship: "The words symbolize the body, and the jubilant music indicates the spirit; and the celestial harmony shows the divinity, and the words the humanity of the Son of God."

In a time of political and religious turmoil, Hildegard's convictions and brilliant mind drew many to her, prompting one writer to refer to her as "abbess of the world." Nearly four hundred of her letters have survived. They range from compassionate to caustic, offering spiritual advice and encouragement to monastics and laymen alike, while upbraiding popes, bishops and kings for sloth, injustice and abuse of power. Like many medieval abbesses, she traveled to other communities "to reveal there the words which God ordered me."

The fame of the visionary "Sybil of the Rhine," as she came to be called, grew rapidly, attracting many more women to the monastery. Thus in 1148, Hildegard determined to leave crowded Diessenberg and found her own convent. When foiled, she took to her bed, paralyzed, blind and in torturous pain, until the authorities granted permission—which miraculously cured her infirmities. Rupertsberg, established on the ruins of an old monastery at the junction of the Rhine and the Nahe rivers near Bingen, like most self-sufficient monasteries, boasted farm buildings, a mill, stables, gardens, workshops, church, cemetery and infirmary.

No mere showpiece for her extraordinary gifts, Hildegard's community reputedly excelled in "lively devotion," obedience and useful activity. She herself is described by early sources as humble, fair and generous—but also autocratic and tempestuous. Characteristically, she made few concessions to advancing age. In her sixties and seventies, she continued to give talks in monastic houses throughout Germany, and very near the end of her life engaged in a battle of wills with the archbishop of Mainz over the burial of a man who had supposedly been excommunicated.

Hildegard's stylistically unique paintings are colorful, detailed and almost mathematically organized, striking modern viewers with their graphic originality. Art historians suggest that elements of her painting—the brilliant colors, shimmering light, flames and dots—indicate the work of a migraine sufferer. This painting, The Four Seasons, *is from the manuscript* De Operatione Dei.

Although she is considered by many to be both a saint and a "Doctor of the Church,"[2] official canonization has eluded Hildegard. But within fifty years of her death, proceedings for canonization were initiated; she has been beatified, one step short of canonization. Her writings have been publicly circulated, studied and published since her lifetime. At the very least, her devotees endorse the summation of Christopher Page, director of the first recording of her chants: "A remarkable woman in an age of remarkable men." ∎

1. The texts of Hildegard's visions, along with some of her illustrations, are published under the titles *Scivias* (an abridgement of *Scito vias Domini* or "Know the Ways of the Lord") and *De Operatione Dei* ("Book of Divine Works"). *Scivias* so impressed Pope Eugene III that he read passages aloud to assembled clergy at the Synod of Trier. Both are available in modern editions.

2. Only three women have been officially recognized by Rome as "Doctor of the Church," that is as "an eminent doctrinal writer." They are St. Teresa of Avila, St. Catherine of Siena and St. Thérèse of Lisieux.

A regal Charlemagne by German artist
Albrecht Dürer, held by the Germanisches
Nationalmuseum, in Nuremberg, Germany.

CHAPTER 2

In a bold act of faith Charlemagne envisions a Christ-ruled empire

All his life he studied Augustine's *City of God*, but his Christian empire had to tame the Saxons who respected only the sword, and perished by it

At prayer in his chapel at Aachen, the man known to history as Charles the Great, or Charlemagne, was not an impressive sight. The conqueror of much of western Europe ordinarily wore tunics and leggings of mainly linen and wool, rather than the dazzling silk robes affected by Byzantine royalty in the East. Court etiquette and architecture were similarly unpretentious in western Europe's first northern-based empire. The sole adornment of the Frankish sovereign's marble throne, for example, was a wooden plank embedded in its seat, symbolic of his dynasty's tribal origin in the Germanic forests. On that austere chair, however, thirty emperors would be crowned. None so much as dared to alter its simplicity, so imperishable was the legacy of the man from whose realm would spring both Germany and France, each of them hailing Charlemagne as founding father.

By eighth-century standards, the emperor was a big man. Antiquarians, passionately pursuing precision, would open his tomb a millennium later and measure the skeleton at six feet, three and a half inches.[1] He was large in other ways as well, large in battle, large in lust. He rarely met his match as a general, while his unbridled sexual enthusiasm would complicate royal genealogies for centuries to come. His fifty-three military campaigns permanently reshaped

1. A study released in 2004 by Prof. Richard Steckel of Ohio State University showed that early medieval people were approximately the same height as those of the twenty-first century. Towards the late Middle Ages, however, human beings shrank, becoming smaller still until the eighteenth century, when the size began to increase again. He attributed the phenomenon to changes in climate and the growth of cities in the later Middle Ages, which spread communicable diseases.

Europe, creating an empire that reached from Rome to the North Sea, and from the Spanish Pyrenees to the Hungarian plain.

Of even greater influence in the long term, however, was this man's respect for scholarship. Intellectual effort became the signature of his reign—an exceptional, even astonishing, trait in a Germanic warrior. Often he awoke in the night, so it was said, to practice writing on the tablets he kept under his pillow. But to him, scholarship must be focused. The duty of a Christian king was to shape the kind of kingdom, the kind of laws Jesus Christ was calling for, however difficult that may be to achieve. He therefore studied Augustine's *City of God* much of his long life, absorbing the fifth-century theologian's enunciations on what a Christian society should believe and how it should act. But whether he read it himself, or had it read to him, remains debatable.[2]

Charlemagne's role in history proved pivotal. During his lifetime, the ancient classical world expired and the medieval age emerged, a new culture whose roots would be Christian, not pagan. Moreover, military power within Europe would shift northward, never to return south. Charlemagne's men-at-arms would form

Charlemagne was exceptional among rulers in his zeal to learn. Chroniclers said that the king would often awake at night to practice writing on tablets kept under his pillow.

the earliest archetype for the chivalrous knight, arguably the most influential model of manhood ever created, and certainly the most romantic. And the Christ-centered society launched by this emperor would ultimately give birth to rationalism, the dominant philosophy of the post-Christian era we live in today.[3]

Northern Europe at the time appeared a most unlikely place for a cultural blossoming. In the ancient world, while urban communities rose to glory from China to Mexico, the Germanic and Celtic tribes had gloried in their forests, composing superb sagas to illuminate their lives, but they were barely literate. Their agricultural technology amounted to little more than scratching at the soil with sticks and herding. The Germans in particular proved as immune to urban life as the desert-bred nomads of Arabia. Neither Germans nor Arabs ever really yielded to Rome, militarily or culturally, and it was their ragged brigades who eventually seized most of the empire.

Rome was not wrecked in a day. Working with the few records that survived the city's fall in the fifth century, the Belgian historian Henri Pirenne (1862–1935) pieced together what became of its economy (his sweeping, still-controversial thesis is outlined in *Mohammed and Charlemagne*). Pirenne postulated that business continued around the Mediterranean, keeping cities alive for another two hundred years. The invading German barbarians were not against trade; most of the revenues for their new semi-civilized dynasties came from taxing it. However, the effect of the Arab invasion in the seventh and eighth centuries was apparently much more severe. They almost totally extinguished the

2. Controversy continues about whether Charlemagne could read and write. A reasonable guess would be that the great emperor was indeed literate, but often preferred to listen. As to writing, he may have had difficulty mastering the new form of script developed by his own industrious scholars.

3. Charlemagne's empire would become, among other things, France and Germany, which would be the seedbed for Jacobinism (the extremist ideology of the French Revolution), as well as Marxism and Nazism. All three ideologies, each profoundly hostile to Christianity, generated dictatorship and mass murder.

Mediterranean trade (see chapter 9), and constant Muslim raids along the northern coastline forced entire Christian populations to flee inland. Meanwhile new waves of invaders from the east isolated western Europe from Byzantium. Charlemagne and the Franks had no option but to forge their own northern society, and his most effective tool was the Christian church.

He was born to power ten years after his grandfather, Charles Martel, stopped the Muslim invasion of the future France at the Battle of Tours in 732, and founded what became known as the Carolingian dynasty. (Carol, Carl and Charles are different English versions of the same name.) He was a devout man and doubtless pondered Christ's injunction, "Love thine enemies" (Matt. 5:44). But for Charlemagne, loving did not imply that injustice or aggression should be tolerated by a good ruler. For example, his grandfather had whipped the Franks' Muslim enemies at Tours, enabling his successors to drive the Arab armies back across the Pyrenees into Spain.

There were other Christian questions to consider. His mother had not wed his father, Pepin the Short, until Charlemagne was about seven. So was he illegitimate? And did it matter? His grandfather Martel was similarly illegitimate—hardly surprising, given that the mating habits of Frankish monarchs until the ninth century were scarcely distinguishable from Islamic polygamy. No one at the time seemed scandalized, Christian or not. What mattered to the nobility was Pepin's success in consolidating power for his son's later triumphs.

Something else did vex the Franks, one and all. It was the matter of who should be king. Martel, Pepin and their forebears for generations had been called "Mayors of the Palace," prime ministers to the line of Merovingian monarchs. For years, the Merovingian kings had reigned while the mayors ruled. But when one mayor did try to claim the crown, he wound up jailed, tortured and executed. Pepin sought to put an end to this charade by appealing to the Church at Rome where the quasi-mystical authority of the once-mighty Roman Empire had devolved upon its Christian bishop, the pope, successor to Peter himself. Would Pope Zacharias therefore decide who was king of the Franks? Pepin had requested in or around 750.

The pontiff had good reason to cooperate. The papacy by then ruled its own lands in central Italy, and Zacharias desperately needed

Charlemagne's austere throne, fashioned from white marble, was used by thirty Holy Roman Emperors, until the sixteenth century. Following his coronation in Aachen Cathedral, Germany, Charlemagne would have sat here to receive the homage of his court.

military help against the Germanic Lombards who were trying to seize them.[4] So
Pope Zacharias wrote a judgment commanding the Franks to crown and obey
Pepin and his heirs. The ruling was accepted, and the last Merovingian king was
tonsured as a monk, thereby rendering him ineligible to reign. Archbishop
Boniface, the pioneering Apostle to the Germans (see page 64), crowned Pepin
and anointed him with holy oil, following the ancient Hebrew coronation
custom, never before performed in Europe.

The next pope, Stephen II, crossed the Alps in winter (a hazardous journey)
to plead in person for armed help in Italy, and Pepin sent his handsome young
son as escort to this august visitor. For Prince Charles, that day—January 6,
754—must have been memorable. This tired old man with his splendid clothing
and alien tongue held the keys to paradise itself. Near the royal villa, Pepin
himself appeared. Dismounting, he prostrated himself before the pope, then
walked beside the prelate's horse like a groom.

Later that day, however, the pope equaled if not surpassed his host in
humility. He came to the royal chapel dressed in sackcloth, his head heavily
sprinkled with ashes. Falling at the feet of the Frankish ruler, the old man
tearfully bewailed the depredations of that veritable spawn of hell, the
Lombards. With his own hands, Stephen later re-crowned Pepin and his wife
Bertrada, as well as Charles and his younger brother Carloman. He also invested
the three men as patricians of Rome, thereby elevating them to the nobility of

4. Medieval pontiffs believed that
only through effective control of a
broad area around Rome could
they ensure the independence of
the church, a belief that would
thoroughly enmesh them in
worldly politics for years to come.

that "eternal" city. Although Pepin promised in exchange to subdue the Lombards, he knew that to mount an invasion of Italy, he would have to convince his own nobles that the papal case was just.

In a further curious development, Pepin's brother appeared. Also named Carloman, he had earlier abdicated the throne of Austrasia to become a monk, but now unexpectedly left his Italian monastery to urge his brother to stay out of Italy.[5] In the ensuing debate, Pope Stephen prevailed. During 755, Pepin and Charlemagne led an army against Pavia, capital of the Lombard king Aistulf, which soon surrendered. On Aistulf's promise to leave the papal territory alone, Pepin withdrew. The Lombards thereupon resumed the attack, ostensibly butchering nuns and desecrating churches. The pope denounced Aistulf as *impius, crudelissimus, malignus, atrocissimus* and more. When Pepin refused further intervention in Italy, Stephen took to threatening his family. The king, he wrote, would forfeit heaven

Pepin handed the pope the clanking keys of 23 Italian cities. Now the papacy need not be under Constantinople's thumb. Would it, though, be subject to a Western emperor?

should he fail to protect Rome, and so would his sons Charles and Carloman (five years old at the time). So the Frankish army returned to Italy, and this time the outcome was more decisive. Aistulf fell from his horse while hunting and died.

To the victorious Franks there now came a top-ranking delegation from Byzantium whose suave emissaries besought Pepin to return to the Byzantine Empire the city of Ravenna and the other Byzantine holdings in Italy lost to the Lombards. Pepin politely demurred and instead handed the clanking ceremonial keys of twenty-three Italian cities to the pope. It was a decisive act. Never again need the papacy be subject in any sense to Constantinople. But now another question presented itself. Would the pope be subject to a Western emperor instead? Certainly Charlemagne and his imperial successors would come to that point of view, but future popes would vigorously disagree. Pepin did not press the issue, but neither did he eliminate the Lombard kingdom.

The next pope, Paul I, proved more adept at wooing the Frankish royal house. After Pepin's queen, Bertrada, gave birth to a daughter, Gisela, Paul had the baby's baptismal garment placed in the burial chapel of Saint Petronilla whom tradition, if not history, remembers as a daughter of Saint Peter, and had himself proclaimed godfather. Thereafter, Charlemagne considered himself brother not only to Gisela, but to Petronilla, and kings of France called themselves brothers to the fisherman's daughter, adopting her resting place as their royal chapel in Rome.

Pepin died in 768. In accord with the generous if politically perilous custom of the Franks, the kingdom was divided between Charlemagne and Carloman, the younger prince receiving the biggest territories, including Paris. Given the simmering sibling jealousies, civil war appeared imminent. In addition, a rebellion broke out in Muslim-imperiled Aquitaine, a region in southern France

5. Frankish territory at one stage consisted of two kingdoms: Austrasia comprised parts of what are now France, Germany, Belgium and Holland, while Neustria covered most of northwestern France. Charles Martel, after uniting the Franks, left Neustria to Pepin and Austrasia to his younger son, Carloman. In 747, however, Carloman retired to become a monk, reuniting the Franks under Pepin.

divided between the two brothers. Carloman refused to help quell the uprising. However, fortune favored Charlemagne, now in his later twenties. (Whether through the grace of God or blind luck, it always would.) First, he suppressed the Aquitaine revolt unaided. Second, Carloman died of natural causes at age twenty. His death united the kingdom.

The Franks had no fixed capital then. Charlemagne used Roman villas at convenient points as royal palaces, ruling his rural people as a physical presence, and making decisions while his court toured his realm. With the king were his family and the *comitatus*, a traditional committee of seasoned men, some

Armor gleamed and banners waved in a brightly-colored cavalcade as the warriors, priests and women of Charlemagne's court followed the king in a stately tour of his realm.

military, some civilian. The latter, who had to be literate, almost invariably came from the church. The modern words "clerk," "cleric" and "clergyman" all derive from the same Latin term, *clericus*.

On the move, Charlemagne and his simple government must have made a sobering sight. The court included young warriors, eager to earn praise and reward from their king. Banners floating, the cavalcade of grave priests and beautiful women would always be thoroughly protected by mounted men in armor. In the lead rode Charlemagne and his sons. His wife and daughters, possibly with a glint of gold or jewels on their cloaks and garbed beneath in the reds and greens beloved of the Franks, followed at the rear with a specially-selected bodyguard.

That bodyguard consisted of heavily armed cavalry, and therein lay an irony. Alone among the Germanic peoples, the Franks in particular had eschewed horses. Martel's decisive victory at Tours, where the Frankish infantry had stood "like a wall of ice," was an infantry triumph over the light Muslim cavalry. But it was Martel himself who initiated the change to horses. Indeed, the church had condemned him after the battle for distributing its properties to his armed followers. But he needed the revenues to finance a new and mounted Frankish army, because a military innovation, as significant as the machinegun eleven centuries later, had changed warfare. This was the stirrup, which enabled a mounted warrior, his feet firmly planted in these U-shaped devices, to drive a lance through an adversary at full gallop without being swept off his horse. Heavy body armor added weight to his thrust, while protecting him against an infantryman's spear. Stirrups had been advanced before. So why was it the footslogging Franks who first adopted them? That, writes the historian Russell Chamberlin in *Charlemagne: Emperor of the Western World*, "is impossible to say."

Charlemagne carefully fostered the change. By the end of his reign, any man who owned four *mansi* of land was expected to muster as a fully equipped cavalryman. (One *mansus* was the amount of land needed to support a household; the actual acreage varied with the property.) Those with insufficient land came as foot soldiers or supported those who had enough. Any landholder who failed to register as either fighter or contributor stood to lose half his land. Every soldier had to bring food, weapons and tools. Alert officials vigilantly tracked compliance.[6] But the system opened a gulf between the landed and the landless, the noble and the peasant, the one utterly distinct from the other, but for one factor, the Christian conviction that each person has a soul beloved of God and possesses the same potential for full citizenship in heaven.

Charlemagne strove, at least initially, to palliate this social rupture. He allowed poorer peasants to band together, equipping just one of their number as a mounted fighter. But this proved impractical, and practicality must rule. For Charlemagne had enemies on every side—the Lombards to the south who again rose defiant, and the Saxons to the north, belligerent, relentless, dishonest, and still sacrificing human beings to their gods. Beyond Saxony lived the Vikings, seaborne marauders launching their two-hundred-year pillage and slaughter of northern Christianity. Among the Germans, the dukedom of Bavaria had been inherited by Tassilo, Charlemagne's fifteen-year-old nephew, who had deserted his uncle during the Aquitaine campaign, a treason of the first magnitude. To the east, the swift cavalry of the Hun-like Avars, roaming unchecked from Constantinople to the Baltic, might at any instant unleash new horrors on his frontier. Most ominous of all, Islam lay beyond the Pyrenees and Mediterranean, convinced of its divine mission to destroy and supplant Christianity. Its rising civilization in Spain far outclassed the Franks in commerce and learning. In such trying times, what mattered was what worked.

The Franks had at least one further strength. Their economy, chiefly agricultural, was rising. Harvests improved through the early medieval era through the development of the new iron-edged plough, better draught animals and sowing patterns. But these farms must be protected against the nearest threat, the Saxons. Their incessant raids must be stopped. Charlemagne declared war in 772, the first of eighteen campaigns he would conduct against the Saxons over thirty-two years.

The Saxons had no urban life. When their small fields were exhausted, they would abandon them for others. Their scattered bands were governed by chiefs who convened to make national decisions through a primitive parliament. Their warriors combined courage and cunning. Rather than directly confronting organized armies, they melted into the forests in the old German way, then emerged unexpectedly in massive ambushes of Frankish troops.

Charlemagne began confidently. His army marched through Saxony almost unopposed, and seized the fortified point where stood the *Irminsul*, a sacred tree or wooden pillar precious to the Saxons. He hewed it down, and served notice

Giving a huge competitive edge to Frankish cavalry, the stirrup enabled mounted soldiers to attack at speed without being swept off the horse, and to stand in the stirrup to deliver a killing blow to enemy infantry. These iron stirrups date from the eighth century.

6. In *The Barbarians: Warriors and Wars of the Dark Ages*, author Tim Newark notes that the Franks valued a shirt of chain mail alone as worth six oxen. Because no peasant could afford a full set of armor and weapons, a knightly class developed, supported by the peasantry as infantrymen.

After eighteen battles in thirty-two years, Charlemagne was determined to pacify the unruly pagan Saxons, forcing baptism on them. Earlier he had chopped down their sacred tree, the Irminsul. *From Guizot's* History of France.

J. ROBERT

that conquered pagans must become Christians. The alternative—a continuation of incessant warfare, human sacrifice and ritual cannibalism—was not acceptable. Having made their show of force, the invaders returned home.

None too soon, for he now found his kingdom in a war set off by a botched attempt to make a lasting treaty with the bellicose Lombards. His mother, who, though pious, held the Germanic Lombards in higher regard than the smooth-spoken Latins of Rome, had negotiated a marriage between her son and Desiderata, daughter of the new Lombard king Desiderius. Charlemagne agreed, though it meant putting aside Himiltrude, a respectable Frankish woman, long his unwedded spouse and mother of a hunchbacked eldest son named Pepin. So

Himiltrude disappeared from court, Charlemagne married Desiderata, and Rome fervidly denounced the whole idea of a Frankish–Lombard alliance. Then fate, or perhaps God, intervened. The Lombard girl turned out to have a physical deformity, probably could not bear children, and perhaps could not please the insatiable Charlemagne in bed. So Charlemagne's bride was sent home, her father exploded in wrath, and his army once again marched against the papal lands.

Charlemagne, not eager to fight, offered Desiderius fourteen thousand *solidi* to return to the papacy those cities he had captured, but the Lombards insisted on war. The Franks forced their way through a well-fortified Alpine pass and again besieged Pavia. Then occurred an event that shaped Charlemagne's view of the world and the course of subsequent European history. During the siege, he made a pilgrimage to Rome.

It was Easter, 774. As a medieval Christian, Charlemagne was not visiting Rome, nor the pope, but Peter himself, the apostle, whose presence was believed to pervade the city. Rome was not a beautiful place in the eighth century, but a big

The king climbed the stairs, sinking to his knees to kiss each step. At the top, a waiting Pope Adrian took his hand and led him to the tomb enshrined as the resting place of St. Peter.

one, bigger than Charlemagne had ever seen. He slept outside the walls, humbly asking the nobly born Adrian I, now pope for two years, for permission to worship as a plain pilgrim. Entering the city, he would have beheld the huge and ancient basilica of Saint Peter, its mismatched chunks of marble scavenged from pagan temples rising majestically. He ascended the wide flight of stairs up to the basilica, sinking to his knees to kiss each step. Adrian, waiting at the top before a massive door plated with gold, took the king by the hand, and led him to the tomb enshrined as the resting place of the apostle himself. The two leaders would remain friends through the twenty-three years of Adrian's rule (among the five longest papacies on record).[7] On hearing of Adrian's death years later, Charlemagne wept.

Notker the Stammerer, a monk of Saint Gall and a chronicler of Charlemagne's reign, describes his return to his troops after the pilgrimage: "…There came from the west a black cloud which turned the bright day to horrid gloom. Then could be seen the iron Charles, helmeted with an iron helmet, his hands clad in iron gauntlets, his iron breast and shoulders protected with an iron breastplate; an iron spear was raised high in his left hand…. All who followed after him imitated him as closely as possible. The fields and open places were filled with iron…. A people harder than iron paid universal honor to the hardness of iron…. The resolution of young and old fell before the iron." Pavia soon fell, too. Desiderius was tonsured as a monk, and after two centuries of independence, Lombardy's crown passed to a Frank.[8]

Soon after, the king married Hildegarde. Of aristocratic Frankish lineage, and only about fourteen years old at her wedding, she bore him three sons and four

7. According to Roman Catholic records, Adrian was the fifth longest serving pope at twenty-three years and ten months (772–795). The longest was the apostle Peter himself at approximately thirty-five years (32–67), followed by Pius IX at thirty-one (1847–1878), John Paul II at twenty-six years when this volume was published (1978–), and Leo XIII, who served for a quarter of a century (1878–1903).

8. When Charlemagne invaded Italy and defeated Duke Desiderius at Pavia, the two nephews of the Lombard chief are thought to have been permanently consigned to monasteries. But perhaps not. A medieval poem numbers one of them among Charlemagne's courtly knights, called paladins.

daughters before dying in her mid-twenties. During that time, however, Hildegarde also wove a deeply loving domestic life around her husband. Both she and his mother exercised over him "a strong influence for good," observes the *Catholic Encyclopedia*. And although reputedly given to affairs with beauties of all classes, he responded warmly to the affection of his family.

But his public life was neither warm nor affectionate. In every year of his reign, he would be at war, leading campaigns himself or through his sons as they matured. While he was engaged with Lombardy, there came a dangerous development among the Saxons. Coalesced around a single leader, Wittekind,

There was worse to come. Basque Christians, siding with the Muslims, descended like a cloud of wasps in the valley called Roncesvalles. The flower of his army perished.

they resumed their raids into Frankish territory. Charlemagne's troops, now equipped with amphibious carts whose hide coverings could be converted into pontoons, made the perilous crossing of the Rhine, and captured the two main Saxon forts. Wittekind fled to Denmark. So complete seemed the Saxon subjugation that when Charles held the Frankish annual assembly within Saxony itself in 777, Saxon delegates obediently showed up. Baptisms ensued in the thousands—total immersion in a convenient river for all but the aristocrats, who were accorded the privilege of a tub. How much these illiterate, largely uninstructed candidates understood about the sacrament is doubtful, but they certainly grasped that their old gods were being abjured.

This apparent triumph would soon prove murderously incomplete, like another deceptively good development at that assembly. A Umayyad Muslim leader, escaping the bloody Abbasid revolution at Damascus, had fled westward and invaded Muslim Spain. The exotic figure of the Abbasid ruler at Barcelona on the Mediterranean appeared before the assembly seeking a Frankish ally in holding the Umayyad intruder off. Charlemagne eagerly seized the chance to organize Christendom's first major counterattack on Islam, and warriors by the tens of thousands answered his call. The Christians moved easily through the Pyrenees. Some cities, including Barcelona itself, surrendered. But the Muslim garrison at Saragossa held out, and Charlemagne ordered a withdrawal from Spain.

There was worse to come. On August 15, 778, Basque Christians, siding with the Muslims against the Franks, ambushed Charlemagne's forces moving unwarily through the valley called Roncesvalles in the Pyrenees. They allowed the main army to pass, then hurled huge boulders down on the rearguard, scattering their ranks and disabling hundreds. Heat-exhausted and uncertain of their bearings, the heavily armored Frankish cavalry could not contend with the fleet-footed mountaineers, who descended like a cloud of wasps. "The Gascons [Basques] slew their opponents to the last man," laments one mournful account. "Then they seized upon the baggage, and under cover of night, they fled with the utmost rapidity."

The fiasco at Roncesvalles mutated into the most influential saga of all chivalry, the eleventh-century *Song of Roland*. This paean, written anonymously, exemplifies later medieval attitudes to Charlemagne and the chivalrous code of warfare, which in the popular imagination harkened back to his knights, or paladins. In this fictional version, the Basque mountaineers at Roncesvalles become well-equipped Muslims whose treacherous king accepts baptism, surrenders Spain, accepts Charlemagne as his feudal lord, then hatches a conspiracy with a Frankish traitor. The impetuous Roland, greatest of Charlemagne's knights, refuses to summon aid by blowing his great horn, and with the twelve finest knights in the Christian host makes a hopeless stand against overwhelming odds. Translator Glynn Burgess, in his 1990 version published by Penguin, New York, portrays Roland, with most of his men dead, finally sounding a mighty blast on his "olifant" (a horn fashioned from an elephant tusk). Charlemagne hears it too late, and Roland is cut down. But dimly aware of the Muslim warrior grabbing his gold-inlaid weapons, he with a final effort smashes the man's skull with his horn:

> So Roland felt his sword was taken forth,
> Opened his eyes, and this word to him spoke
> "Thou'rt never one of ours, full well I know."
> Took the olifant, that he would not let go,
> Struck him on th' helm, that jeweled was with gold,
> And broke its steel, his skull and all his bones,
> Out of his head both the two eyes he drove;
> Dead at his feet he has the pagan thrown.

Dying himself, Roland does not neglect his personal honor:

> Turning his head towards the pagan race,
> Now this he did, in truth, that Charles might say
> (As he desired) and all the Franks his race;—
> 'Ah, gentle count; conquering he was slain!'

The Cathedral Treasury in Aachen is one of the most important collections of ecclesiastical treasures in Europe. The shrine of Charlemagne holds relics of Jesus and the Virgin Mary collected by Charlemagne. The relics have been displayed every seven years since the fourteenth century for the benefit of pilgrims.

Yet honor is far from being uppermost on the dying man's mind. Devout to his last heartbeat, this archetypical knight counts his own virtues as besmirched by guilt. He must rely solely on salvation through the risen Christ:

> And with one hand upon his breast he beats:
> "Mea Culpa! God, by Thy Virtues clean
> Me from my sins, the mortal and the mean,
> Which from the hour that I was born have been
> Until this day, when life is ended here!"
> Holds out his glove towards God, as he speaks
> Angels descend from heaven on that scene.

By 782, at Charlemagne's annual assembly deep within Saxony, near the present site of Hamburg, thousands of Saxons paid their respects. Even a delegation of Avars showed up, doubtless taking the measure of this Germanic ruler, yet nevertheless talking peace. But soon afterward came the unwelcome news that Wittekind was back, scorning the pusillanimous submission of the other chieftains. The Saxon peasantry, including some women fighters, had risen en masse at his call. The coarsely garbed Saxon infantry, rank upon rank across a hillside, had made a final stand against the mounted and armored Franks. But the confident Frankish commanders, seeking individual glory, had abandoned their attack plan, charged prematurely up the slope into a thicket of Saxon spears and axes—and were thereupon cut to pieces.

Over the Rhine with the full weight of his army came Charlemagne, uncharacteristically enraged. The Saxon farmers, as usual, evaporated into their forests, Wittekind with them. Charlemagne surveyed what they had been up to. In village after village, he found the mangled corpses of priests and nuns amid the charred ruins of churches. Enough, he decided, was enough. No more phony baptisms and false promises. He ordered the Saxon nobles to identify and arrest the individual rebels within their domains. They obeyed.

According to medieval chroniclers, forty-five hundred men were ordered beheaded. But what shook both his contemporaries and posterity was neither the numbers nor the severity, for it was age in which death was always familiar, in which contagious disease and famine routinely killed thousands, child mortality claimed one in four, and mothers risked death with every birth-giving. It was Charlemagne's view of the deed. He showed no regret whatever, quite the reverse. He imposed Christian practices upon these former pagans. It must be baptism, tithing, Lenten fasting and every other rule, or it must be death. A guilty party could only escape execution if a priest determined that he had sincerely repented of his crime.[9]

Within two years, Wittekind surrendered and accepted baptism, Charlemagne himself standing as godfather. Over time, he softened his original code, and his son Louis would have the gospel story recast into an Old Saxon tale. Portrayed in the finest vernacular verse, Jesus becomes the Chieftain of mankind, born in the hill-fort Nazareth. Sheep and shepherds, lowly beings in Saxony, are transformed into the far nobler figures of horses and horse-guards.

9. This slaughter begs comparison with Mohammad's killing of eight hundred Jewish males at Medina (see previous volume, *The Sword of Islam*), but the two are not precisely parallel. Charlemagne punished individuals who had themselves conducted slaughters. Medina's Jews had slain no one. Neither comes close in extent, of course, to the vast secular exterminations of the twentieth century.

J. ETTLIN

Roland at the gorge of Roncesvalles summons help from Charlemagne by blowing on his "olifant" horn; too late, alas, to save his men. Roland himself, succumbing to his wounds, grieves for his fallen comrades, and with his last strength hews down an enemy who tries to grab his sword. From Guizot's History of France.

Christ fasts for forty days deep in the forest, and later reveals the secret runes of the Lord's Prayer. Swayed by threats and seduction, wooed by hundreds of humble priests and monks, the Saxons eventually thrived as a pious people.

His wife, Hildegarde, and mother, Bertrada, both died in 783, in a summer of great heat and pestilence. The grieving Charlemagne, accustomed to relying on their prudence and devotion, apparently gave overly free rein to his fourth spouse, whom he married within months: Fastrada, daughter of a Frankish noble. The early chronicles depict her as a high-handed meddler. In this "new period of his life," the *Catholic Encyclopedia* wryly observes, "signs begin to appear of his less amiable traits." He never permitted any of his daughters or his sister Gisela to wed, a policy so unusual as to prompt scandalized speculation, but possibly Charlemagne simply wished to limit the number of his legitimate descendants to reduce future political friction. In any case, no evidence of misconduct ever came

Also from Guizot's History of France, *this engraving depicts Wittekind finally submitting to Charlemagne in 785, and accepting the Christian faith. Charlemagne himself stood as godfather for the Saxon warlord.*

to light. Gisela, although consigned to a nunnery, continued to enjoy dances and other court functions. Only later in life did her genuinely devout nature prompt her to adopt a strict regimen of prayer and contemplation. One royal daughter apparently took a lover, a poet named Angilbert, and bore him two children out of wedlock. Charlemagne, far from objecting, made Angilbert an abbot in charge of constructing Europe's largest monastery.

Meanwhile, he increasingly intertwined clerical and lay functions. Key churchmen staffed his government. He divided Frankish territory into about three hundred counties, each headed by an officer called a count, whose church counterparts were bishops. A cleric could find himself organizing supplies for war, or named one of the *Missi Dominici* ("Envoys of the Lord") to review local administrations. "We have been sent here by our lord, the emperor Charles," declared one, "for your eternal salvation, and we charge you to live virtuously according to the law of God, and justly according to the law of the world. We would have you know first of all that you must believe in one God, the Father, the Son and the Holy Ghost." He added ominously: "Nothing is hidden from God. Life is short and the moment of death is unknown. Be ye therefore always ready."

In the 780s, the envoys figured centrally in one of Charlemagne's most ambitious initiatives—the education of the clergy, many of whom did not even understand the Latin of their liturgies, and beyond them the laity. Priests and monasteries were ordered to establish schools where men might send their most talented sons, free of charge, to be instructed in the ways of God and literacy. Some bishops and abbots did establish schools, and the concept of educating the best minds regardless of class origin would remain an enduring medieval aspiration.

Foremost among the scholars who launched what became known as the Carolingian Renaissance was Alcuin, an English monk and a foreigner in Frankish eyes, who had supervised the reconstruction of the great cathedral at York after a fire. As a young librarian for York, he had traveled Europe seeking rare manuscripts for the monks to copy, and at age forty-six in 781, was retained by Charlemagne to oversee the palace school where promising youths were trained to administer the growing empire. The monk of Saint Gall, writing in the late ninth century, said that even the king considered himself a disciple of Alcuin in a scholarly sense.[10]

With other English scholars, Alcuin worked to establish a clear and standard Latin, vital to future study in the West, separating it from the corrupted Frankish Latin that was already becoming French. As well, he promoted a beautiful but practical script, known as "Carolingian Miniscule," to replace the ugly, largely illegible scrawl then in use. It was destined to form the basis of printed type. And the illumination of manuscripts would evolve into an art form.

Charlemagne's court included a galaxy of other scholars, like Theodolf, a bishop of Gothic descent whose influence rivaled Alcuin's; the scholarly Arno who became first archbishop of his native Salzburg; Einhard, a diminutive but inexhaustible Frank, who was both Charlemagne's biographer and a practicing architect; and Paul the Deacon, a Lombard fluent in Greek, who indentured himself to Charlemagne if the king would pardon his rebellious brother. The king did, and composed a farewell poem to Paul when he eventually allowed this much loved companion to return to Lombardy. No longer would he hear Paul's celebrated debates with the academic Peter of Pisa. These and other Carolingians would compose enough poetry to fill four massive volumes.

A gentle egalitarianism attended Charlemagne's home life. At banquets, the ruler himself enjoyed serving his guests, some of whom, along with the king himself, were assigned nicknames to bridge the social gulfs. Charlemagne retained regal status as "David." One daughter became "Dove," while Einhard was "Bezaleel," after the biblical artist who decorated the Tabernacle in the wilderness. But on the diplomatic front a

10. On occasion, Alcuin and Charlemagne by a royal messenger would exchange riddles, an intellectual amusement much beloved of the English. Here is one sample: "I lately saw a man standing, and a dead man walking, even one who never was. What was it?" Answer: "A reflection in water."

The learned Alcuin, foremost scholar of his age, was urged by Charlemagne to remain in his court, where he became an adviser to the king and an influential writer and educator. He is credited with establishing a significant library at Aachen, and helping to develop the Carolingian miniscule script.

In addition to his military prowess, Charlemagne's contributions to culture were significant. His palace school, the source of the Carolingian renaissance, moved with the king's court. As well as a traditional school, it was also a venue for discussion and the source of many copied manuscripts of ancient literature. From Guizot's History of France.

H. DUTHEIL

very different concept was taking shape. In 799, Alcuin, by then the abbot of Saint Martin's at Tours, proposed that Charlemagne be made emperor in the West. In a letter to one pope, doubtless inspired by his priestly courtiers, Charlemagne referred to himself as "Lord and Father, King and Priest, the Leader and Guide of all Christians." He would protect the church across his vast realm while the successor of Peter prayed for it, a chaplain's role.

But what preoccupied the king was neither the papacy nor his international status. It was the perpetual problem of sedition—like the revolt in 786 of Tassilo, duke of Bavaria, and the Lombard duke of Benevento, both backed by the Byzantines. The royal espionage service, alert as always, discovered the plot, and Charlemagne's lightning response brought the Lombard duke swiftly to heel. The Byzantines too backed off, and three Frankish armies sliced into Bavaria. Tassilo, in a public ceremony, formally submitted himself to Charlemagne, one of the first formal acts of feudal homage in Europe. But Tassilo's loyalty proved short-lived. He soon rebelled again, this time in alliance with the pagan Avars. Tassilo was subdued, arrested, convicted in open court and condemned to death. But Charlemagne, citing the love of God, sent him to a monastery instead, and Bavaria was thereafter ruled directly by the king.

The time had now come, he decided, to deal with the Avars, horsemen from the Asian steppes who had used their curved swords to slash their way into Europe. Breaking the Avars meant breaking their fabled, never-conquered Fortress of the Nine Rings, which they had built on the Hungarian plain. Each ring consisted of massive ramparts of heavy timbers and earth, skirted by an impenetrable hedge of thorn. Stashed in the center lay the loot and tribute they had accumulated in two hundred years of raid and pillage. It included the eighty thousand gold solidi per year they had extorted from Byzantium for over a century, the largest hoard of bullion that Europe would know until the Spanish conquest of Mexico and Peru in the sixteenth century.

The Franks paused for three full days of prayer before they crossed the Danube into Avar territory, Charlemagne leading his army in person for what would prove the last time. At first all went well, with the enemy forced back to the Rings. Then plague decimated the Frankish cavalry, and a rebellion had to be suppressed at home.[11] When the campaign resumed, the Avar resistance grew. Charlemagne poured men and material into the attack, constructing new landing craft to cross rivers, even starting a canal to link the Rhine and Danube. (Heavy rain and inadequate equipment foiled the project, but even the attempt was prophetic; it demonstrated that northern Europeans had already begun to entertain monumental visions.)

It took five years for the Franks to smash their way through the innermost ring, but the booty exceeded all expectations. Fifteen large wagons, each pulled by four oxen, hauled it to Aachen, the fabulous cavalcade crossing the Rhine on a new five-hundred-foot bridge,

11. The rebellion this time centered on Charlemagne's eldest son, the illegitimate Pepin. The unfortunate hunchback, passed over by his father to the point that even his name had been transferred to a legitimate son, had been beguiled by stronger personalities into outright treason. Upon the king's return, this episode ended with Pepin banished to an exceptionally strict monastery.

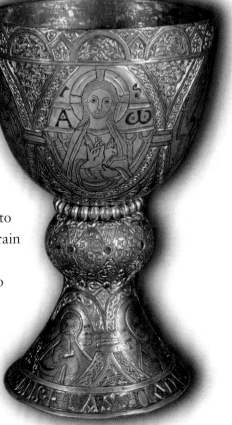

The Carolingian renaissance in arts and crafts produced masterpieces such as this one, the Tassilo Chalice, of gilded copper with inset medallions of Christ and the four Evangelists. The influence of Irish design is evident in this piece, still in the Kremsmünster Abbey in Austria, where it was a gift from Duke Tassilo of Bavaria and his wife Liutberga, in 770.

The cathedral of Charlemagne in the German town of Aachen (left), along with the rest of the city, was heavily damaged in the Second World War. The tower (above) was all that was left intact. The cathedral has since been rebuilt, and is a UNESCO World Heritage Site.

constructed near Mainz. It was distributed without stint to the men who had shared the risks of battle, to the pope and to key monasteries laying the foundations of the new Western civilization.[12] The defeated Avars, previously the terror of half a continent, accepted baptism (how willingly they did so is unknown), then slowly disappeared into the surrounding population. But their place was soon taken over by their cousins from the steppes, the Bulgars and later the Magyars, whose bloody raids reached as far west as Tours in central France. Over time, the Magyars (eventually known as Hungarians) would themselves become a Christian bulwark.

The city of Aachen, a former Roman spa, (near the future Belgian border, forty miles southwest of Cologne), was becoming the favorite royal residence, appreciated for its hot sulfur springs and its central location in the Frankish heartland. Here Charlemagne established his seat of government, complete with a hillside palace, some of which was still functioning in the twenty-first century as a municipal building, qualifying it as Europe's oldest structure in continuous use. A nearby chapel also survives intact, despite

12. Gold had become so scarce in the agricultural West that Charlemagne converted the entire coinage to silver. Emulating the Roman emperor Constantine's currency, the *livre*, or pound, was divided into twenty *sous* (shillings), each in turn divided into twelve *penigs* (pennies). These "sterling" coinage denominations would be retained by the British until February 15, 1971.

intensive bombardments by both sides in the Second World War.

To Charlemagne's court in 799 came another refugee pope. Leo III had succeeded Pope Adrian and begun cleaning up corruption in the papal administration. Two of Adrian's nephews had attacked him, intent on tearing out his eyes and tongue. Though wounded, Leo fled to Frankish territory, escorted by one of Charlemagne's trusted Lombard generals. Spokesmen for his adversaries also arrived, accusing Leo of many crimes. To investigate, Charlemagne traveled to Rome and satisfied himself of Pope Leo's innocence. Thus it came about that on Christmas Day, 800, Charlemagne donned classic Roman garb, and kneeling before Leo at St. Peter's, was crowned emperor and augustus. Whether he wished to receive the honor, or was surprised by the pope, at least in some aspect the coronation has been much disputed, and the grand title was notably vague in terms of jurisdiction. Still, the act infuriated the Byzantines, whose emperors considered themselves successors to the Roman caesars, and Christendom's supreme authority. They denounced the act, but they did not fight. The pope, for his part, was altogether satisfied. As he saw it, he had conferred upon the papacy the authority to consecrate the emperor.

In the meantime, peace and stability worked their usual magic. French historian Prosper Boissonnade (*Life and Work in Medieval Europe*) estimates that the population of the future France rose to eight million under Charlemagne. The number of villages in the Frankish heartland trebled, while people of Italy, writes Paul the Deacon, "multiplied like ears of corn." Charlemagne required not only that every male over the age of twelve must swear loyalty to his sovereign, but must also promise to aid the poor and obey the other precepts of Jesus Christ. With age, the emperor recognized and angrily protested against corruption among his own officials, and he sometimes despaired entirely of human wickedness. All too clearly, he knew that the City of God is not of this world. But as a Christian ruler, he had to continue striving to govern with love, working both justice and charity, on his own journey to that heavenly city.

Charlemagne did not see his

The ninth-century Codex Aureus Gospel, in a jewel-studded binding depicting Christ and the four Evangelists: within the book are illuminated pages, beautiful examples of the mastery of Carolingian craft. The Gospel is now in the Bayerische Staatsbibliothek, in Munich.

The elephant Abu al-Abbas, along with other curiosities of the Middle East, was a gift from the Abbasid caliph Haroun al-Rashid. It is known that Charlemagne built a house for the beloved pet, and brought it along on many campaigns. Abu al-Abbas died on a campaign against the Danes.

ANDRE DURENCEAU
NATIONAL GEOGRAPHIC

empire as permanent. On his death, he wanted to divide it among his three legitimate sons, in the old German way, exhorting them to rule in amity. However, his sons Pepin and Charles—both tough, competent men—died before their father, and so did the hunchbacked Pepin. Only Louis, pious and studious but not a commanding figure, remained. Charlemagne crowned him his heir in the chapel at Aachen in 813—notably ignoring any putative claim of church authorities for a hand in the process—but he did not abdicate. Still strong at seventy-one, he regularly indulged his passion for hunting. Yet the end was near. First the tall figure, with iron-gray hair falling to his shoulders, was felled by a fever accompanied by a sharp pain in his side. Ignoring his doctors, the emperor insisted upon fasting, which likely weakened him further. Einhard recorded that Charlemagne "received holy communion, and then he died, at nine o'clock in the morning on 28 January." The year was 814.

The Carolingian empire, a sprawling bramble of peoples, which lacked both revenue and effective central institutions, did not long survive him, but its influence endured, forging the pattern for medieval society. On that foundation, westerners would erect modern science and technology, capitalism and democracy. Small wonder, then, that later generations would fuse Charles to the Latin word *magnus* to become Charlemagne. From that time on, only he among European monarchs would have the word "great" embedded directly within his name. ∎

Charlemagne on his deathbed, at the age of seventy-two, after having reigned for forty-two years. An active man, he had been hunting until shortly before his death. This fifteenth-century manuscript, Le Miroir Historial, *is now in the Musée Condé, France.*

The foremost apostle to Germany

The irrepressible Boniface converted over 100,000 German tribesmen
before his head was split open by an angry Frisian's sword

Near the little settlement of Dokkum, pagan warriors angrily watched their fellow Frisians gathering at the riverside camp of the accursed archbishop. Boniface, an Anglo-Saxon, had already helped draw more than one hundred thousand German tribesmen to Jesus Christ. Although the veteran missionary was now at least seventy-five years old, he had led this band of fifty or so clergy deep into the swampy flatlands beside the North Sea, far from any helpful army commander or friendly chieftain. That day—June 5, 755—he planned to baptize the latest newcomers to his flock. But shortly after dawn, the hostile pagans suddenly charged toward the still quiet tents of the Christians.

First to confront the assailants was Hildebrand, the archbishop's personal attendant. He was immediately hacked to death. Hahmund, Hildebrand's brother, stepped into their path, and died just as quickly. The Christians and their converts rallied, swinging the few weapons they had among them—until Boniface, who had been praying in his tent, emerged with lifted hand to forbid any attempt at defense. "Let us not give evil for evil!" he cried. The entire party was then slaughtered, a Frisian sword cleaving Boniface's head. So died the foremost Christian apostle to the German tribes.

Boniface, baptized as Winfrid, had been a natural leader since childhood in southern England. His Saxon parents were of good family, farming on the frontier between the Saxon kingdom of Wessex and the Britons of the southwest peninsula. Their raw and often violent district had few churches, and monks would preach instead beside stone crosses erected at central locations. Listening to these regular visitors convinced Winfrid that he wished to join them, a notion flatly rejected by his parents, although they were Christian. After recovering from a deadly bout with the plague, however, his stalwart father relented and gave up his promising son to God.

The boy was sent to a small monastery at nearby Exeter, governed by Abbot Wolfhard, a practical if not especially learned soul, who soon realized that his young charge was both intelligent and mature beyond his years. At age fourteen, the already popular Winfrid became a full member of the religious community, a vow that normally would have bound him to Exeter for life. Instead, Wolfhard dispatched his talented protégé to a more scholarly and sophisticated monastery at Nursling near Winchester, capital of Wessex. At Nursling, Winfrid soaked up the pious learning appropriate to a monk, while learning to write fine Latin, and it seems that practically everyone loved him and trusted his sturdy common sense.

The king even sent him to represent Wessex in important church discussions with the archbishop of Canterbury, and fellow monks assumed that their talented and holy brother would in due course become abbot at Nursling.

Since boyhood, however, Winfrid had yearned to spread the gospel to pagan tribes across the narrow seas that separate southern England from Belgium and Holland. He now unexpectedly reported an inner call from God to evangelize the Frisians in what would become northern Holland, and his abbot agreed, albeit reluctantly. When the mission was cut short due to Frisian hostility, however, Winfrid decided to secure from Rome a mandate and support for his work. This long journey in 718 presented its own perils, especially from the unfriendly Lombards of northern Italy, but letters of introduction from ecclesiastical authorities in Wessex ensured that bishops and abbots would provide food and shelter along the way.

Many of his hosts, Winfrid realized, fell drastically short of the mark as Christian leaders, especially among the Merovingian Franks. As he later wrote to the pope: "For the greater part, the sees of bishops in our cities here have been handed to grasping laymen or adulterous clergy...." Winfrid was shocked to discover bishops and priests who performed the sacraments even though they "sleep with four or five mistresses, yet neither blush nor fear to read the gospel at mass...." In Rome, Pope Gregory II quickly fell under the spell of this earnest, attractive monk, conversing with him for days about his distant homeland.

The visitor in turn felt confirmed in his already profound commitment to institutional discipline, ensured by strong papal leadership and authority over the whole church.

In May 719, Gregory commissioned Winfrid to evangelize the German tribes, renaming him Boniface. His roving assignment took him far into the lonely forests and wild hill country of Germania, domain of the Thuringians, Alamanni and allied tribes. Most of them were still outright pagans, while others had slipped back into paganism after earlier evangelization by pioneering Irish monks. Even the Christians among them

Boniface is martyred in the top right of this image, while on the left his labors in Germany come to fruition as German pagans are baptized. From the sacramentary of the church of St. Salvatoris, Fulda, Germany.

Boniface chops down the sacred tree of the Bortharians, in an illustration by Heinrich Maria von Hess from the St. Bonifatius Basilica, Munich. To the surprise of the heathen, Boniface remained unscathed after committing this act. So impressed were they that they immediately converted to the Christian faith.

reportedly wore magic amulets, ate meat sacrificed to heathen gods (after making the sign of the cross over it, however), and sold slaves for human sacrifice. In Thuringia, an outbreak of "free love" was being led by Christian renegades. Preparing himself to deal with this turbulent flock, Boniface apprenticed for two years as assistant to Archbishop Willibrord (another English Saxon) in Frisia. He then journeyed up the Rhine Valley, where he attracted thousands of converts and backsliders into the embrace of the church.

Back in Rome in 722, he conferred with the pope before launching his main offensive, and Gregory II decided to make him a bishop—but one with no geographically defined see. It was an unusual appointment, in which he would report directly to the Vatican. Bishop Boniface took as his first

challenge the Bortharian tribe, who worshiped around an ancient tree at Geismar, the Thunder Oak, sacred to the god Woden. To their unmitigated horror, Boniface took an ax to it, and the astonished tribesmen watched wide-eyed as the oak crashed to earth. Even so, this lunatic Christian, as his onlookers saw him, remained inexplicably unharmed. Rather than kill Boniface on the spot, they accepted this remarkable phenomenon as proof of the truth of his message, and many accepted Jesus as savior. They even used timber from the felled oak to construct a small church.

Other churches sprang up as Boniface continued his work. He also found himself frequently writing to Rome concerning pastoral problems, posing questions that provide wonderful insight into the difficulties he faced.

Should he conduct the lighting of the Easter candle even though his ex-pagan converts confused the ceremony with the practice of lighting a great fire in spring to honor the rising sun? (Yes, replied the pope.) Is a baptism valid if conducted by a priest who had participated in pagan rites, or if it was performed in a native language or in bad Latin? (Baptisms were valid so long as the intent was clear, the pragmatic pope ruled.) Being short of priests, could he ordain men at age twenty-five rather than thirty? (Yes, indeed.) Would the pope permit a man of noble rank to marry a widow who happened to simulta-neously be his cousin, his aunt by marriage and a nun who had abandoned her vows? (Certainly not.) Could Rome relax its prohibition against marriage between even fourth cousins, a severe restriction for a people who lived in small villages? (One pope agreed, a later one did not.) Could lepers be given Holy Communion? (Yes, but separately.)

Oh, and one more question: Would the pope forgive a bishop for the late arrival of a report? He had been busy replacing thirty churches burned by Saxon raiders, said Boniface.

Boniface would never see England again, yet he kept in constant touch via correspondence with an astonishing number of people. The English were proud of him. For example, King Aelfwald of East Anglia wrote that his name was remembered during the seven daily rounds of prayer at every monastery in his realm. Boniface on occasion expressed anxiety for the good name of his country, in 747 admonishing Cuthbert, archbishop of Canterbury, to "stop your married women, and your nuns, from going so often to and from Rome. Many of them meet their ruin; few remain unharmed. There are very few cities of the Lombards in Italy, of the Franks in France, in which some courtesan or prostitute of English race is not found."

When pressed for funds, he sometimes asked a friend to send him a cloak or other simple items. Unbidden, kings and abbots dispatched silver cups, spices and other gifts, but what Boniface wanted most were books. The future of German monasteries and schools depended on assembling collections of those costly, handwritten works of scholarship.

East Anglia's monks sent up their prayers seven times every day for Boniface's safety.

The charismatic prelate, drawing many aristocratic youths to the religious life, closely ordered their lives. For instance, he ruled that Sturm, a young nobleman, should work for his fellow monks in the kitchen while others performed more prestigious offices. The humbly obedient Sturm later became the first abbot of Fulda, the most important monastery Boniface founded. But the abbot was a reasonable man. "Let each of you, according to his strength and character, try to preserve his chastity," he advised his monks, which implies that unchastity was far from unknown among them, religious enthusiasm and commitment notwithstanding.

Almost ten years after he became a bishop, Boniface received from Rome an archbishop's pallium. He still ruled no specific territory, but with years of hard work, he had created three bishoprics within his broad jurisdiction. (Finding enough brother bishops to consecrate their leaders had been a final difficulty, since Boniface would not work with any Frankish ecclesiastic whom he regarded as corrupt.) The new pope, Gregory III, approved of all his methods and innovations, despite doubts that the small, isolated settlements of Germania could soon build an imposing cathedral or provide the civic prestige considered appropriate for a bishopric in Italy and Gaul.

Boniface, who had added Frankish to his languages, staunchly supported Charles Martel in his resistance to Muslim incursions from Spain, though the two were not personally friendly. He grew close to Martel's son, Carloman, after he inherited his father's eastern territories. Carloman and Boniface, both pious men, organized the first German synod in 743, a pivotal conference that among other things forbade the clergy to indulge in fornication, go to war, or hunt, and adopted the moderate yet firm Benedictine Rule for monasteries. Carloman returned church lands and revenues that had been seized by his subjects, thus helping to finance expanding Christian endeavors in Germania.

This secular connection was crucial to preserving Nicene orthodoxy in a time of considerable religious confusion. The most popular heretic in the region was a telepathic miracle-worker named Adalbert, who claimed that his powers had been given him by an angel. Calling himself "the saint of saints," Adalbert sold his own nail clippings and hair as relics, and reportedly lived in luxury. Three genuine bishops had actually consecrated Adalbert to the episcopacy (critics charged that they were bribed, which was altogether possible), and he proceeded to build churches. One Clement was another supposedly legitimate bishop. He had a wife and two children, denied the teaching authority of the church fathers, and proclaimed the Jewish custom that a man should marry his deceased brother's widow. Boniface and Rome, backed by synods, repeatedly condemned Clement and Adalbert, prompting the Franks eventually to imprison them. Their ultimate fates are unknown.

Boniface had his prejudices, of course. He long remained at odds with Pirmin, an abbot in the neighboring lands of the Alamanni tribe, who was supported by one of their chieftains. But Pirmin's monastery at Reichenau, on Lake Constance, became one of the great centers of medieval scholarship, and over time Boniface grew to respect his adversary's commitment to the Benedictine Rule. Toward the end of their lives, these two giants of the

A heretic 'saint' sells his own nail clippings to the gullible public as religious relics.

early German church warmed to each other.

In the meantime an entire corps of distinguished priests and bishops matured under Boniface's tutelage. Lullus, also of Wessex, a fine scholar who struggled lifelong against ill health, nevertheless became archbishop of Mainz (amid great controversy), and finally founded a monastery at Hersfeld. Leoba, a much younger cousin of Boniface, had to be disciplined when she was a spirited young novice, for stomping on the grave of an older nun whom she had disliked. On maturity, Leoba founded a nunnery near the Mainz River, and was a close friend of Hildegard, Charlemagne's influential wife. Many of her nuns became abbesses of their own convents.

Lebuin, another Anglo-Saxon, was renowned for boldly entering a Saxon assembly and calling the pagans to Christ. The Saxons, much impressed, made no attacks on Lebuin's missions so long as he lived. Gregory of Utrecht, who joined Boniface in early youth, became an abbot and founded a famous school of learning, while humbly refusing episcopal consecration as too high an honor.

Through men and women of this caliber, Christianity gradually took root in central and northern Europe. Yet no one matched the public renown accorded to the Apostle of the Germans. When King Carloman retired to a monastery, and the two Frankish kingdoms were united under his brother Pepin, Boniface conducted the coronation ceremony, anointing

Pepin as king. It was a telling precedent for Western Christendom. Kings and bishops, working in partnership, would come to define the values of medieval civilization. As for the aging Boniface, he returned to his missionary work, and less than five years later, was martyred by the Frisians—the very people among whom he had begun that work more than four decades earlier. ■

The resting place of Boniface, in the St. Salvator and Bonifatius Church, in Fulda, Germany. Fulda grew up around the site of an abbey founded by Boniface and Sturm, one of his disciples, from which Christianity spread throughout Germany.

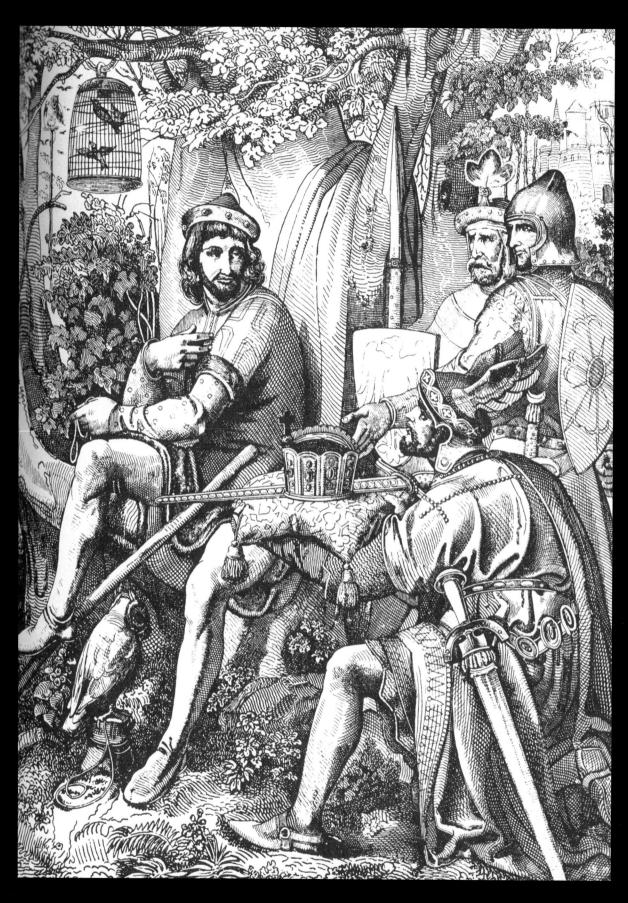

*Henry the Fowler, Duke of Saxony, has his hunting party
interrupted by an envoy from the dying Conrad, King of the East
Franks, urging Henry to take his throne. First king of the German
Ottonian dynasty, Henry did not go to Rome to be crowned, so was
never styled "emperor."*

CHAPTER 3

Rising imperial power creates a deadly clash of emperor vs. pope

When penitent Henry IV stood barefoot in the snow for three days to seek Pope Gregory VII's absolution, the showdown seemed at hand, but it was far from it

Charlemagne's empire disintegrated after his death. "It is difficult to exaggerate the horror and confusion of the dark age that followed its collapse," writes British historian Charles Dawson in *The Making of Europe*. Through the ninth century, seven kings ruled in their great predecessor's western territories, eight over the vanished empire's eastern lands. In reality, however, regional warlords freely battled each other while Viking and Magyar pagans wreaked havoc. Then, in the year 918, came an astonishing event. Conrad I, king of the East Franks, made a crucial decision as he lay dying. For seven years, he had fought the Saxons to the north. Calling his brother to his deathbed, the Frankish monarch made a startling suggestion: his crown should go to Henry, Duke of Saxony. A union between Christian adversaries would best enable their peoples to survive and prosper.

And so it was done. An ancient legend relates that the Frankish envoy found this inveterate foe of his people hunting with his falcons deep in the Harz Mountains. "God save you, Henry of Saxony," said the messenger, kneeling before the formidable duke. "I come to announce the death of King Conrad and to tell you that the nobles [at his suggestion] have elected you to succeed him as king of the Germans." In *Famous Men of the Middle Ages*, American authors John Haaren and A. B. Poland describe Henry's reaction. "For a moment the duke was speechless with amazement. Then he exclaimed: 'Elected me king? I cannot believe it.

I am a Saxon, and King Conrad was a Frank and a bitter enemy to me.'" The tough warlord then reportedly begged heaven's help in leading the new folk.

Although this tale may be romanticized in detail, Henry I did found the Germanic kingdom that would later develop into the Holy Roman Empire (a title based on territories held in Italy by Germanic rulers). That new imperium, along with the emerging kingdoms of France and Britain, would preserve European Christendom while the papacy at Rome endured the darkest, most chaotic years in its entire history. (See sidebar, page 78.) As the papacy recovered, however, Germanic emperors would vie with popes, at times brutally, for control of the church within their own lands.

Henry I, known as the Fowler, was descended from Wittekind, the pagan leader who had so fiercely resisted Charlemagne. Christianity long sat lightly on the Saxons. For two generations after their enforced conversion, many warriors fought sporadically to restore their pagan rites. Even so, says Henry's monk-biographer in *The Three Books of the Deeds of the Saxons*, the king succeeded in uniting his subjects as "one people in the Christian faith, even as we see them today."

Unity was sorely needed. The forty or so Germanic tribes of antiquity had evolved into a handful of dukedoms, whose hereditary leaders began to select kings from within their own ranks. Royalty and nobility alike struggled

Kings, nobles and marauders fought each other, while armed bands pillaged the peasants in the horror and chaos that followed the dramatic falling apart of Charlemagne's empire.

incessantly with neighbors for land, their armed bands pillaging helpless farmers. Simultaneously, the peasantry suffered from pagan marauding of indescribable savagery. From this lethal turmoil slowly evolved a new military hierarchy. It is commonly called feudalism, though the term itself was not coined until the eighteenth century, long after medieval civilization had disappeared, and many twentieth-century historians argued that the system was so varied and unsystematic that there was really no system at all.

Whatever its merits, feudal theory discerns an overarching pattern throughout much of Medieval Europe. Besides kings who ruled kingdoms and dukes who ruled dukedoms, there were counts who ruled counties. In frontier lands threatened by barbarian invaders, the counties became known as "marks." In England they were called "marches"—the "Welsh Marches" to the west, the "Scottish marches" to the north. In Europe a mark was ruled by a "graf," and out of the term "mark-graf" came the title "margrave," or "marquis."

The key feudal values were land and personal loyalty. Lords allotted fiefs of territory among the lower aristocracy. At the local level, farmers enjoyed the use of their fields in exchange for providing food and other benefits to the increasingly heavily armed knights. Some peasants remained legally free sharecroppers, others became rent-paying serfs tied to their farms, but everyone

1. Byzantium stood in striking contrast to the West during this epoch. Manufacturing and trade, the basis of a monetary economy, generated tax revenue to pay professional soldiers and administrators.

except outright slaves had some property rights.[1] The warrior vows of fidelity to a liege lord, undertaken with impressive solemnity, were considered sacred, the basis of the community's survival when enemies appeared.

But courage was not just for warriors. A constant battle also raged within every individual, noble or commoner. Each Christian was seen as conducting his own life-and-death struggle between good and evil, between committed loyalty to Jesus Christ, or the path of self and Satan. Just as the peasantry looked to knights for protection in worldly conflicts, the embattled Christian turned to specialists in heavenly warfare, the priests and monks, whose weapons consisted of the holy sacraments and exceptionally disciplined prayer. The consequences of temporal conflict with marauders were temporary; the consequences of the spiritual conflict were eternal. So two medieval hierarchies, secular and sacred, would mature roughly in parallel, the knight in his manor beside the priest in his parish, the duke or count beside the bishop, the emperor at the secular pinnacle, the pope at the spiritual, with all professing submission to Jesus Christ.

The primary scriptural basis for this division between secular and spiritual—in medieval parlance, the two swords—was, Christ's injunction to "render unto Caesar the things which are Caesar's, and unto God the things that are God's" (Matt. 22:21). As long as the religious and worldly authorities cooperated, the

Henry I reunited the Christian kingdoms of Saxony and east Francia, using this restored power to fortify the country and train an excellent army. His work paid off; he defeated the Magyars for good at Riade in 933. In this illustration, he receives the accolades of his people after the victory.

Otto I had this crown fashioned from gold, cloisonné panels and precious stones, for his coronation in 962, in Pavia, Italy. The cross was added in the early eleventh century. The painter Albrecht Dürer (1471-1528) "borrowed" the crown for his imagined portrait of Charlemagne (see page 42) who, of course, reigned two centuries before the crown was made. The crown is now housed in the treasury at the Kunsthistorisches Museum, Vienna.

principle was workable. But strife within Christendom remained painfully common. Churchmen blamed it on individual sinfulness, especially the greedy and egotistical feuds of secular lords. Yet the papacy itself suffered glaringly from its own sinful misbehaviors.

The unlearned Henry the Fowler, by vigorous campaigning and dynastic marriage-making, added Swabia, Bavaria and Lorraine to his Saxon–Frankish kingdom. He bought nine years of peace with the Magyars by returning a captive Magyar prince and by paying an annual tribute, using the nine years to add cavalry units to his army. When he cut off the tribute, his cavalry defeated the predictable Magyar attack. Henry I died in 936, and his work of expansion and unification was mightily reinforced by his twenty-year-old son, known to history as Otto the Great. Like Charlemagne, he would be crowned as the Holy Roman Emperor.[2]

Otto I's view of his responsibilities considerably exceeded that of his father. "He was fully penetrated with the sense of his divine mission," writes the British historian Thomas Frederick Tout in *The Empire and the Papacy*, and was "filled with the high ideals of kingcraft." Thus he had himself crowned and anointed in Charlemagne's chapel at Aachen. But his religion was deeper than kingcraft. In the whirlwind of familial wars, one of them against his brother who plotted his murder, a crucial battle turned against him. He flung himself on his knees, begging God to protect his followers. A nearly miraculous victory followed, and Otto's faith became deeply personal.

He added to his realm Slavic Bohemia, which would one day become the Czech Republic, and in 955 he so thoroughly thrashed the Magyars at the Lechfeld in Bavaria that they never invaded German lands again. As his territories grew, he lavished lands upon the church, in part so bishops would have the resources to carry out their religious duties. But the prince-bishops who ruled these powerful sees exercised civil as well as ecclesiastical authority. Otto found them far more controllable than feudal lords, less likely to rise in rebellion, while their celibacy made it legally impossible for them to form competing dynasties. Like Charlemagne, he also brought to his court the best theological and legal minds of his time.

Since the prince-bishops reported to the king, not to Rome, Otto had created what amounted to a state-controlled church, independent of the papacy, a reality that he made explicit in the

Otto II, although short-lived, left some legacy of his reign with these striking artifacts. The golden relief of the Last Supper is an antependium, a hanging for the front of an altar or pulpit, still at the Palatine Chapel in Aachen. The Cross of Lothar (below) is fashioned from gilded copper and precious gems with an inset cameo of Caesar Augustus. It is now in the Louvre, Paris.

ordination and investiture ceremony. When a bishop took office, the king played the dominant role, handing the candidate a signet ring that bestowed the authority to legally undertake secular duties, and the crosier, the ornate staff based on the shepherd's crook that recognized the bishop's spiritual pastorate over his people. The "glebe" also came from the king, a lump of earth that conveyed authority over church-owned land.

While few reformers disputed that the bishops were properly vassals of the secular ruler in right of their fiefs, Otto's actions raised the question of where spiritual authority lay. Within the Roman Empire, bishops had been selected by the people of their sees, with prominent families playing the most notable part in the process. In medieval times, those prominent families had become royal and ducal, so they assumed the right to invest the bishop with the spiritual symbols of ring and staff. The pope's involvement in investing ecclesiastical authorities was represented solely by the pallium, a white woolen stole worn over the neck by archbishops (formally called metropolitan bishops because they exercise supervision over fellow bishops). This garment had to come from Rome.

But a bishopric offered power and a luxurious life. Soon some sees were being auctioned to the highest bidder in the practice known as "simony,"[3] and a return on the investment was expected. Cluniac reformers and many other devout Christians came to deplore the practice, and doubtless looked to Rome to reform it. Kings naturally defended this important source of income and political influence. In any case, the papacy was in no condition to reform anything for decades to come. In fact, the pope of the day, John XII, was appealing to Otto I for help. It was when Otto responded, and knelt before the pope to receive the

3. The crime of simony is named for Simon Magus. The scriptural reference (Acts 8:18–21) reads: "When Simon saw that the Spirit was given at the laying on of the apostles' hands, he offered them money and said, 'Give me also this ability so that everyone on whom I lay my hands may receive the Holy Spirit.' Peter answered: 'May your money perish with you, because you thought you could buy the gift of God with money! You have no part or share in this ministry, because your heart is not right before God.'"

imperial crown on February 22, 962, that the Holy Roman Empire was restored.

Crowned with his father was Otto II as co-regent king of Germany and Italy, who six years later became co-regent emperor. Four years after that, he married the Byzantine princess Theophano. His father died a year later. A warrior worthy of his parentage, Otto II suppressed revolts in Bavaria, Lorraine and Bohemia, fended off the West Franks by marching almost to the walls of Paris, claimed suzerainty over Poland, then invaded southern Italy to oust the Muslims and acquire from them the former Byzantine lands that were supposed to come as his wife's dowry. That endeavor failed. The Christian army was ambushed and scattered in a Calabrian valley. In an epic escape, Otto made it to the coast, swam to a passing vessel, then jumped ship and swam to shore before the vessel entered a Muslim port. While planning another offensive, Otto II died of an overdose of medicine given to him to combat a fever. He was twenty-eight. His son, Otto III, was three years old.

Conferred on bishops and abbots at their investitures, the crosier is a symbol of their authority. A bishop's crosier has a curved top, somewhat resembling a shepherd's crook, appropriate to his role as "shepherd of his flock." An archbishop's crosier is topped by a cross, rather than a crook. This example is Irish.

Of the three Ottos, the third was the most unusual. His Byzantine mother, an intelligent and politically effective regent, raised him in an atmosphere of exceptional religious idealism, and imbued in him the conviction that he was born to be the theocratic monarch of a sacred empire. The child-sovereign was eleven when his mother died, and historian Tout notes that he was thereafter educated entirely by bishops under the rising influence of the Cluniac movement. (See chapter 1.) Thus, from time to time throughout his short life, he would shed his royal finery, abandon his gold dinner plates, and dress in a rough cloak to visit secluded holy men and shrines.

At sixteen, Otto III crossed the Alps, responding to yet another papal cry for help when Pope John XV sought protection against the Roman mobs in general, and against antipope Boniface VII in particular, who had just starved to death his predecessor. John died before his rescuers arrived, so Otto appointed as his successor, the first German pope: Bruno, aged twenty-four, his own cousin and also a Cluniac sympathizer. Bruno became Pope Gregory V, and began the urgently needed papal reform. However, he died just three years later, and the squalor continued at Rome.

Upon his death, Otto turned to a remarkable monk, Gerbert of Aurillac, a gifted mathematician, born to poverty in Spain, who had crossed the Pyrenees as a young man and found service with the Capet family. The Capetians, who were the counts of Paris, made him archbishop of Reims. In 987, prodded by Gerbert, Hugh Capet persuaded the French nobility to name him king of the West Franks. Hugh's descendants, filtering down through two dynasties, the Valois and the Bourbons, would rule France until the revolution in 1789. However, once safely enthroned, the ungrateful Hugh had Gerbert fired as archbishop, so he sought work with Otto III, and was warmly received—so warmly that on the death of Gregory V,

Otto saw Gerbert made Pope Sylvester II.

The king's own aspirations were mushrooming alarmingly. Still influenced by his dead mother, he introduced Byzantine titles, eunuchs and elaborately rigid ceremonial to his court. His German nobles had to twist their rough tongues around the alien intricacies of Greek. Rome must become the capital of a new Western empire, Otto decreed, where seven clerics (a mystical number) would consecrate the emperor and elect each new pope. From this sacred and eternal city, operating in intimate partnership, emperor and pope would reform the world.

None of this particularly enthused the German nobility. Then Otto and Pope Sylvester made a move that distinctly disenchanted them. He created native archbishoprics for Hungary, land of the Magyars, and for Poland. From the Christian viewpoint, this made sense. It deeply embedded Latin Christianity in two important emerging nations. But it infuriated the Germans, especially their ecclesiastics. For generations, iron-fisted Teutonic nobles had been expanding eastward, consolidating their victories by appointing German bishops over the Magyar and Slav Christians. Now their young sovereign was not only aping the preposterous manners of the effete Greeks, but also undermining the political strength of his own people along their eastern border. Most of the German church thereupon rebelled against Sylvester, refusing to attend his councils.

So much royal territory had been given to the prince-bishops and to the monasteries that Otto's family held relatively little land of its own. In need of funding, the royal youngster returned to Germany, hoping to reestablish harmony. Strange stories came with him. He sought guidance, said one account, by entering the crypt under Charlemagne's chapel at Aachen, and gazing in contemplation upon the imperial cadaver still seated on a throne with scepter in hand. The Germans remained disenchanted. So crossing the Alps for the last time, Otto tried settling again in Rome, only to find he wasn't wanted there either. The city's ever-fickle mob had little love for Germans and they set about driving him out.

His dreams collapsing, he appealed again for help from Germany, meanwhile visiting Romuald, a miracle-working hermit who dwelt in the swamps near Ravenna, with whom he was said to have shared in self-mortifications and scourging. But no help came. Returning to Rome, he was beset by a sharp fever, probably smallpox, and died in 1002 at twenty-two, leaving no children. Within a year, Pope Sylvester II followed his emperor to the grave.[4]

Another cousin of Otto's succeeded him as Henry II, put down the customary rebellion of the nobility, suppressed revolts in both Bohemia and Poland, intervened in Italy where the wrangles and bedlam around the papacy continued, supported the German bishops against the dominant power of the Cluniac movement, and died childless in 1024 after reigning as emperor for ten years. (He and his wife, Cunigunde of Luxembourg, were said to have taken a vow of

A stern Pope Sylvester II is captured by an anonymous painter. Born in poverty as Gerbert Aurillac, he used his gifts and his wits to attract the attention of Emperor Otto III, rising to the highest episcopal office, the first French pope.

4. William of Malmesbury, a twelfth-century monk, credulously recorded the widespread fable that Pope Sylvester II was a magician who sealed a pact with Satan. Medieval chroniclers were often reasonably well informed about events close to home, but wildly credulous about distant places. William himself wrote many reliable accounts about his own land in his *History of the Kings of England.*

A dark hour for the Papacy

The bizarre 'Synod of the Corpse' ushered in the era of 'the bad popes,' marked by mob violence, poisonings, strangling, graft and sexual depravity

While the German monarchy under Otto the Great reinforced the church and supported its finest scholars, the papacy at Rome descended into one of its darkest eras. Awash in mob violence, poisonings, stranglings, graft and sexual excess, the 900s became the century of "the bad popes." It began in January 897, with a bizarre council in Rome known as the *Synoda Horrenda* (or in English as "the Synod of the Corpse"). It continued through the next twenty-seven popes until the German Bruno of Carinthia, reigning as Gregory V, began a gradual restoration of the Throne of Peter a hundred years later.

Amid the chronic anarchy of the Italian Peninsula itself, Roman factions competed viciously for the papal post, which represented an unparalleled opportunity to enrich themselves. Few holds were barred. Thus for the Synoda Horrenda, Pope Stephen VII exhumed the nine-month-old corpse of his predecessor, Formosus (891–896), who had been championed by a rival faction. The magnificently robed cadaver, propped upon the throne, was tried for allegedly accepting the papal office while still bishop of another diocese.

Pope Stephen yelled accusations. The cleric appointed to defend Formosus prudently remained as silent as his client. The corpse was convicted. The three fingers of benediction were chopped from its right hand, and the corpse was hurled into the Tiber. (Some kindly fishermen retrieved and reburied it.) But Formosus's supporters strangled Pope Stephen that autumn, and in half a dozen years, five more popes rapidly followed each other—four of them dying amidst the lethal squabbling.

The next in line, Sergius III, backed by the Roman senator Theophylact of Tusculum, lasted from 904 to 911. Theophylact's powerful clan controlled the region at the mouth of the Tiber, and his beautiful wife, Theodora, and their daughter, Marozia, would take papal scandal down to new levels of degradation. Marozia began by becoming, while still in her early teens, Pope Sergius's lover.

The most complete account of the Theophylacts comes from Liutprand, Lombard bishop of Cremona and protégé of Otto the Great. Lushly detailed and aggressively biased, his work nonetheless impressed Baronius, the sixteenth-century cardinal who compiled the first major history of the papacy. Liutprand portrays Theodora as dominating the Tusculan faction after Sergius died, deftly managing the next three popes. Two expired quietly after short incumbencies. The third was her current lover, the young bishop of Ravenna, who ruled from 914 to 928 as Pope John X.

Marozia, not yet twenty, had meanwhile married one Alberic, a capable soldier. He and Pope John X, whatever their other qualities, proved their military mettle in a campaign that decisively crushed Muslim forces advancing against Rome. However, Liutprand next depicts John X as trying to appease Marozia by naming her a senatrix and patrician, while conferring the kingship of Italy upon Hugh of Provence to ensure his support. (There is no further mention of Theodora.)

But the lovely Marozia, now paired with King Hugh's half brother, Guy of Tuscany, was far ahead of Pope John. Guy's soldiers seized him, and he died in a Castel Sant' Angelo dungeon—probably, writes E. R. Chamberlin in *The Bad Popes*, of starvation or suffocation. Guy of Tuscany also conveniently died in 929, putting within Marozia's orbit both papacy and kingship. She hastened to install upon Peter's throne, as Pope John XI, her son by Sergius III. Then Hugh of Provence, serenely untroubled by the murder of John X (and perhaps Guy as well), hurried to her side, and they were wed by her son the pope.

Papacy and monarchy now seemed united as the dynastic property of one criminal family—yet things did not go quite as Marozia planned. Hugh the bridegroom quarrelled with her other son, another Alberic, who raised a Roman mob against him. Hugh fled, and Alberic confined his beautiful forty-year-old mother in Sant' Angelo. No more is heard of her after that, but Alberic became prince of Rome, governed relatively well for two decades, and in 954 was peacefully succeeded as prince by his son, Octavian, then seventeen.

A year later, Octavian became Pope John XII, with the Theophylact clan now at the peak of its power. As the eighteenth-century British historian and vehemently anti-Catholic Edward Gibbon would acerbically comment: "The bastard son, grandson, and great grandson of Marozia—a rare genealogy—had all been seated on the Chair of Saint Peter."[1] Unsurprisingly, however, Octavian proved to be an unsatisfactory prince and a worse pope—best known for the kind of activity that caused Cardinal Baronius to call the Theophylact regime a "pornocracy."

Briskly described by one *Catholic Encyclopedia* as "a coarse, immoral man," Pope John XII loved hunting, gambling and women, not necessarily in that order. He is said to have invoked pagan gods, filled the Lateran Palace with loose women, and presented the golden cups and crosses of St. Peter to his paramours. His Roman subjects loathed him, and his one military venture was a sad failure. Thus when the Lombard duke Berengar of Ivrea marched southward in 960, John made a fateful move. He asked Otto the Great for help, and that devout monarch quickly responded, for reasons both spiritual and political.

German forces were soon respectfully camped outside the walls of Rome, and Otto and Pope John XII made a momentous deal. Otto promised to deal with Duke Berengar and otherwise defend the papacy; John readily promised to mend his worldly ways. Then, as the German monarch knelt humbly in St. Peter's, the profligate pope crowned him ruler of the Holy Roman Empire. No sooner had Otto's forces marched against Berengar, however, than the pope resumed his plotting, shopping the imperial crown to Berengar, and making overtures to the Magyars, to Byzantium, even to the Muslims.

When these machinations came to light, the emperor assembled a synod of some hundred bishops to review Pope John's record. Witnesses testified that he had caused the death of one cardinal by castrating him, blinded the man assigned as his spiritual mentor, and copulated with his own niece (among other things). From a refuge at Tivoli, twenty miles away, John threatened to excommunicate the entire synod, but it elected a new pope nonetheless. Liutprand wrote that John XII was later beaten to death by a cuckolded husband, but credited Satan himself with the blow that actually killed him.

Despite intermittent efforts at reform, peace and stability remained elusive at Rome. In 996, three decades and seven popes later, Pope John XV was also forced to seek help against feuding factions, this time from the pious young emperor Otto III. He died before Otto's troops reached Rome, and so the twenty-two-year-old emperor put his cousin Bruno, twenty-four, upon the papal throne as Gregory V—the first German pope. Both enthusiasts for the Cluniac reform movement, the two young men began a gradual restoration of the papacy.

But this process was to prove very gradual indeed, not least because the Roman factions continued acutely troublesome far into the eleventh century. In 1045, in fact, the whole city was a battlefield, with three warring camps fighting for supremacy, each with a papal candidate already installed. One was Pope Benedict IX, grandson of Count Gregory of Tusculum, and reputedly a notable teenaged libertine. This enterprising youth allegedly sold his august title to his godfather, a wealthy archpriest, who became Pope Gregory VI, and to another contender as

well, who claimed office as Pope Sylvester III.

This time, it was the Roman populace itself, sated with anarchy, that called in Emperor Henry III. He briskly settled matters, for the time being, and paid close attention to the election of the next four popes. The wonder is, of course, that the papal office lived on—and even throve—despite all the abuse inflicted on it by human greed, pride, and debauchery. As Cardinal Baronius remarked of the infamous John XII, to survive such a miscreant, the papacy as an institution must indeed enjoy divine protection.

Historians note another very cogent point. The great danger to the individual is sin, but the greatest danger to the church as a whole is heresy, which can divide the entire Christian body, sometimes for centuries, pitting very devout Christians against one another. Not a single one of the "bad popes" was ever accused of heresy. Their minds were occupied with other things. ∎

1. Protestant Christians (and not a few Catholics) used to believe a persistent legend, which asserted that a British woman named Joan, in the ninth century, had managed to disguise herself as a monk, and had became pope. Gibbon, who helped scotch the Pope Joan story, suggested that it might well have been inspired by popular awe at the authentic power wielded by the Theophylact women.

The aptly named Synoda Horrenda *witnessed the grisly spectacle of the exhumed corpse of Pope Formosus put on trial by his successor, Stephen VII. The defendant, predictably silent, was pronounced guilty. Three fingers were cut from his right hand, and his body hurled into the Tiber. The macabre scene is reproduced here by Jean-Paul Laurens; the painting is now in the Museé des Beaux-Arts, Nantes, France.*

chastity. The church canonized them both.)

The German monarchy now passed to descendants of Otto I through the female line.[5] Conrad II, elected king by his fellow magnates, added the kingdom of Burgundy to the empire, but his most significant contribution to the German kingdom came through his marriage to Gisela of Swabia, a widowed duchess and his distant cousin. She was a strong-minded and intensely Christian woman, and when the marriage produced a son named Henry, his parents supplied him with a more thorough formal education than any previous German monarch. Like the three Ottos, the young Henry grew

Henry IV, about to be deposed by Pope Gregory VII, humbly requests intervention on his behalf from Countess Matilda and Abbot Hugh of Cluny. Their pleas resulted in Henry's absolution. This illustration is from an illuminated manuscript of the eleventh century.

up believing his kingship to be a sacred obligation, dedicating himself to establishing greater peace for the common people. With the death of his father in 1039 he became king of Germany, and seven years later was crowned Emperor Henry III. Although this sovereign determinedly backed the cause of church reform, the great showdown between the empire and the papacy began to unfold during his reign.

Henry was not universally popular. His reforming efforts against married prelates and simony antagonized some German bishops upon whose influence royal authority depended, and his high taxes annoyed practically everyone. Yet Henry's determined support provided immense prestige for the Cluniac reforms, and he validated his theology in his personal life, preaching to a synod in southern Germany, for instance, clad in the drab garb of a penitent. So when his empress, Agnes of Poitou, and Abbot Hugh of Cluny urged Henry to intervene in the endless imbroglio at Rome, he complied. Three popes were currently trying to reign at once, an intolerable scandal. Respecting the canonical principle that no king may judge the bishop of Rome, Henry summoned a synod. It directed Pope Sylvester III to a monastery, accepted the resignation of Pope Gregory VI for simony, and expelled Pope Benedict IX to his native Tusculum.[6] Henry then orchestrated the nomination of the next four popes, achieving the zenith of imperial power

5. Becoming emperor required first becoming king of the Germans. German kings had been elected since deep in the tribal past by the tribal chieftains. By the ninth century, the electors had become the dukes of the Franks, Saxons, Bavarians, Swabians and Thuringians. Up until the sixteenth century, the elected king would travel to Rome to be crowned emperor by the pope.

6. Peter Damian, a hermit whose incessant letter-writing made him the most influential publicist of his period in Italy, recorded a popular tale that Pope Benedict IX, one of three simultaneous claimants to the papacy in the mid-eleventh century, suffered a particularly awful fate after his expulsion from office. He reportedly was seen in the form of a half-human, half-ursine monster, condemned to wander the earth until the Final Judgment. More plausibly, there is some evidence that Benedict eventually repented and became a devout monk.

over the papacy. One of these, however, gave evidence that the long era of papal degradation was about to come to an end.

This was Leo IX, a strong-minded German who initiated his ministry with an unprecedented tour of his scattered flock, traveling north and west to Germany and France, then down to southern Italy, his garments varying from monkish homespun to majestic robes as occasion demanded. He drew to Rome a competent team of young reformers who worked swift and sweeping changes in the papal administration. Safer roads meant that papal envoys (usually called legates) could move more freely abroad, enabling the papacy to routinely intervene in such matters as church property squabbles, previously settled by regional bishops. Education of the clergy advanced. Married priests came under increasingly intense condemnation. All this was backed by Henry, but it strengthened the papacy as a rival to his own imperial authority within the church. Moreover, Leo first warred, and then allied with the rising Norman presence in southern Italy, furnishing the papacy with a military power that could oppose that of the empire. Leo died a broken man (see chapter 9), but his alliance with the Normans would change the balance of political power within the empire.

Germany itself was teetering toward disorder when Henry III died in 1056 at age thirty-eight. Henry IV was not quite six when his father died and his mother Agnes assumed the regency. Also an enthusiast for church reform, she failed to quell unruly nobles and zealous bishops who seized on the royal minority as their chance to reduce imperial authority. In a particularly catastrophic error, Agnes allowed strategically important German lands to slip from royal control into the hands of potentially unfriendly dukes. And while secular lords warred endlessly over their various interests, the church was developing greater internal order, sharpening the religious sword while the secular blade grew blunt.

Soon, a challenge was being boldly articulated. Why should emperors and kings—habitually violent, often uneducated, and rarely even faithful to their wives, let alone celibate—have the right to appoint bishops, whose sacred role was central to the well-being of the church? Hadn't the venerable church fathers explained that the primary interest of worldly rulers was worldly, not heavenly?[7] Didn't the Bible clearly state that the leadership of the church, and responsibility for its welfare, lay with the apostle Peter, whose successor was the pope in Rome?

These contentions led to action. Popes Stephen IX and Nicholas II assumed office with no reference to the emperor. Then in 1059, Nicholas II convened a synod at the

7. Historian Allan J. MacDonald, in his biography of Gregory VII, cites a glaring, but not unusual case illustrating the routine secular abuse of church offices: "Guifred of Cerdagne, a boy of ten years old, received the archbishopric of Narbonne in 1016, after the payment of one hundred thousand solidi had been made by his relations. He held the see until 1079, and easily recouped himself and his relations for the purchase price from the revenues of the see."

Leo IX instituted sweeping reforms, strengthening the medieval papacy. He acquired the nickname "Pilgrim Pope" as a result of his travels throughout Europe. The salutation of this document: "Leo episcopus servus servorum Dei" identifies it as one of his papal pronouncements.

Lateran Palace that revolutionized the papal election process. Future popes must henceforth be elected solely by the cardinals,[8] with strong preference for a Roman candidate. The role of royalty in papal selection was reduced to a vague right to be consulted—after the fact. The Nicholas formula, with modest modifications, became permanent and survives to this day.[9] The same synod, attended by one hundred thirteen bishops, specifically forbade investiture of any church officials by secular rulers.

That last provision was incendiary. The German monarchy, dependent for its very survival on its prince-bishops and abbots, could scarcely accept any prohibition against investiture by laymen. In retaliation, the empress Agnes sought to oust Nicholas by backing the election of a rival pontiff, but her plan failed for lack of military support. Who, after all, wanted to take on the Normans? The Germans regarded the upstarts' principalities in Italy as illegitimate and dangerous, but what could they do about them?

Meanwhile, Henry IV, the monarch who would have to contend with this amazingly revived papacy, was growing up. Archbishop Anno of Cologne became

8. The office of cardinal was created in the eighth century to help alleviate the increasingly demanding workload of the papacy. The cardinals at Rome ranked as Roman princes immediately after the pope, and became his chief counselors. A cardinal's insignia has traditionally been a red hat (changed to a biretta in 1969), which was worn only once, and then placed on his tomb at death.

9. Scripture itself affords no exact formula for choosing a bishop, and the method of selecting the pope had varied over the centuries. A tradition that St. Peter had named his own successor was never officially accepted. In earliest times, the clergy of Rome chose their bishop, probably with the people playing some part. Later on, Roman emperors exercised a frequently decisive influence, as did German emperors and Roman nobles later still. But Pope Nicholas II in 1059 put the matter into the hands of the cardinals.

The intense eyes of Hildebrand are evidenced in this sketch made from a woodcut by Otto Knille and preserved in the Bettman Archive. Hildebrand became Pope Gregory VII, regarded as the most aggressive champion of papal power in the Middle Ages. His fierce conflict with the equally persistent Holy Roman Emperor Henry IV violently sundered the empire and papacy during the late eleventh century.

regent for the boy-king. Although Anno would be sainted soon after his death, he did not impress his contemporaries as spectacularly devout. Medieval chroniclers relate how he had gained the regency. A former soldier, he invited the twelve-year-old Henry to tour his superbly equipped barge, then seized him and pressured Agnes to retire. The prince, outstandingly athletic, reportedly jumped into the Rhine to escape. Caught and dragged back, he never did warm to the stern archbishop. Still, Anno fought for the king's rights. He agreed to recognize the new pope Alexander II only in exchange for a promise that his royal charge would be crowned emperor.

As Henry IV grew older and more rebellious, he was transferred to the care of Adalbert, archbishop of Bremen, who courted the favor of his royal ward by letting him run wild. The opportunistic Henry took control of his kingdom at age sixteen, girded himself with his knight's sword, and set out after his old intimidator Anno, intent on running him through, so it was said, but his mother and Adalbert restrained him.

Meanwhile at Rome, two other figures were rising to prominence in the administration of Pope Alexander II. One was a brilliant and outspoken monk named Hildebrand, who embraced a view of the papacy as unassailable. The authority of the pope, he said, was universal, overriding emperors, kings, dukes, everyone in Christendom. The steadfast ally of both Pope Alexander and Hildebrand was Matilda, countess of Tuscany. Again and again, against Romans, Normans and Germans, she would risk her strategically located province to provide vital defense for the emerging papal power. An immensely wealthy heiress, left fatherless and brotherless at age six, she had learned to fight with sword and ax, and personally led an army of knights whose battle cry was "For Saint Peter and Matilda." Upon her death, the countess's will added these fertile lands to the papal states that spread through central Italy.

Like Matilda, Hildebrand was also a Tuscan, born on a marshy stretch of the Italian coast, seventy-five miles north of Rome. According to the unverifiable traditions that are still so common in this era, he was the son of a village carpenter, but John Gratian, then an influential abbot in Rome, enabled the youngster to join the papal Schola Cantorum (school for choristers).[10] The boy had a feeble voice and was short and ungainly, but his eyes glittered with intelligence and determination. Gratian bought the papacy and became Gregory VI, and was one of the three deposed in the cleanup directed by Henry III. Young Hildebrand loyally followed his uncle into exile.

When John Gratian died, Hildebrand is thought to have visited Cluny, served in Rome as archdeacon, been a legate to France at age thirty, and returned to Rome to supervise, among other things, the hiring of mercenary troops. Here the record becomes more sturdy. When Alexander II died in 1073, clerics and laity alike all but compelled Hildebrand to accept the chair of St. Peter. Honoring Gregory the Great and his own uncle, he took the name Gregory VII. He would become the most aggressive pope of the Middle Ages.

He well may have expected an immediate confrontation with young Henry IV over the archbishopric of Milan, one of the last western jurisdictions to

10. John Gratian's father, known as Benedict the Christian, was a banker and a Jewish convert, who married one of Gregory's aunts. Benedict helped finance Gratian's purchase of the papacy, according to Cambridge historian A. J. MacDonald. Benedict's son Leo, also a banker and a leader of the emerging Italian commercial class, would play a key role in the career of his cousin Gregory, providing cash to pay troops during the costly fight against the German monarchy.

resist papal oversight of its internal affairs. Both Henry and Gregory assumed they had the right to appoint its bishop.[11] For whatever reason, the new pope, characteristically taking the initiative, wrote several times to the twenty-three-year-old monarch, initially in kindly terms. But the position assumed by this pontiff would become uncompromising indeed. The pope, in his view, exercised supreme spiritual power over the church, limited solely by his own conscience before God. Therefore, the temporal power invested in secular officials like Henry must give way before the papacy's spiritual authority in the event of dispute. This power must apply not only to the empire, but to all Europe.[12] Papal rulings were implicitly buttressed by the threat of excommunication in the event of noncompliance.

Gregory cannot be justly accused of singling out Henry IV. The king of France, for instance, also faced a serious threat of excommunication. Nor did

Gregory's sweeping claims horrified the rulers of Europe. He said the pope had the right to depose emperors and was beyond the judgment of mere mortals.

Gregory ignore previously Christian countries now under Muslim control. Before his dispute with Henry IV reached complete rupture, he would try to mount the first crusade against the Muslims. Henry, the warrior-king of Germany, must have raised an eyebrow when he learned that this projected campaign, which was to involve fully fifty thousand troops, would be led by the unwarrior-like pope in person, accompanied by the empress Agnes and Countess Matilda. The pope's plans, however, would fail to spark sufficient enthusiasm to be carried out.

Henry, facing another massive Saxon revolt, responded to the pope's extraordinary claims in diplomatically submissive terms that would doubtless have bolstered Gregory's confidence. However, compliance with the papal orders nowhere occurred. They were simply ignored. So in 1075, Gregory mounted a carefully prepared legal campaign, issuing a decree prohibiting lay investiture of bishops. He followed this with the *Dictatus Papae*. Among the twenty-seven claims of this memorandum (which may have been a speculative musing intended for internal consideration only) were the following: That the Roman church was founded by God alone. That only the Roman church is rightly called universal. That the Roman church has never erred, and never will. That the pope may be judged by no human being. And more controversially, that the pope's name alone is to be cited in the diptychs (liturgical prayers for the church and its people). That only the pope may use imperial insignia [i.e., not the German emperor]. That all monarchs must kiss the foot of the pope, rendering such homage to no one else. That the pope has the right to depose emperors. That the pope may release the subjects of an unjust ruler from oaths of fealty to that ruler.

That very year, however, King Henry had finally amassed sufficient support among his nobles to crush the Saxons. He deliberately invested two German

11. In dispute between the Archdiocese of Milan and the papacy was clerical marriage, a religious controversy intensified by Milan's political rivalry with Rome. The ongoing question of priestly marriage and celibacy will be addressed in the next volume.

12. To support his claim to papal political power, Gregory advanced the so-called "Donation of Constantine." In this document, the emperor Constantine the Great confers on the papacy "our palaces, the city of Rome and all the provinces, places and cities of Italy and the regions of the West." In legal terms this transformed the pope into the secular ruler of all western lands. This document was respected as authentic for seven centuries, until the Italian scholar Lorenzo Valla conclusively proved it a forgery.

bishops, hoping that the German and Lombard churches would stand behind the concept of anointed royal investiture. On January 24, 1076, he convened twenty-six bishops in the council of Worms (Worms is a city on the Rhine, thirty miles southwest of Frankfurt). Led by a cardinal, they agreed to depose the pope for exceeding his authority. The letter Henry dispatched to Rome was addressed to "Hildebrand, no longer pope, but a false monk," and climaxed with: "I, Henry, king by the grace of God, with all my bishops say to thee: 'Descend! Descend, thou ever accursed!'"

Like a medieval comic strip, these panels illustrate the tempestuous relationship between Pope Gregory VII and Henry IV. In the top panel, Henry is pictured with the antipope, Clement III, while Robert Guiscard rescues Pope Gregory form the Castel Sant' Angelo. The bottom frame illustrates Gregory's death.

In the course of this confrontation, one Roman noble, an ally of Henry's, seized the pope and carried him off to a fortified stronghold in the city. Gregory, suffering a deep but not fatal gash in the chest, was quickly rescued by loyal supporters. Throughout his ordeal, he displayed by all accounts a calm valor. He treated even his kidnapper kindly, and was equally gentle with the royal envoy who had to read out loud—to the synod in Rome—King Henry's violent deposition order: "Ye [the people of Rome] are bidden to receive another pope from the king … for this man is no pope but a ravening wolf." When angry Romans drew swords, Gregory personally shielded the messenger.

For King Henry himself, however, there was no papal forbearance. On February 22, 1076, Gregory declared before the assembled dignitaries of Rome: "I forbid anyone to serve him as king." Thus, for the first time ever, a pope excommunicated—and in effect deposed—a reigning monarch. It was amazingly effective. Henry's cause collapsed with shocking speed. His own mother, living as a penitent in Italy, sided with the pope, writing that her son "trusts in the words of fools." The king's stoutest supporter among the German aristocracy, Godfrey the Younger of Lorraine, was murdered. By Easter, the German bishops began deserting him in droves, each striving to make his peace with the pope. The Saxons rose again. The German dukes, their feudal obligations to Henry of null effect, invited the pope to preside over an assembly at Augsburg, scheduled for February 1077, to choose a new king.

Gregory agreed, and with some difficulty, traversed the frozen Apennines as far as Mantua, a Lombard center east of Milan. At this crucial point, however, King Henry decided that he must surrender. The desperate sovereign crossed the Alps during an exceptionally bitter winter, his men frequently crawling down the icy slopes on hands and knees. Gregory, learning that his foe was in Italy, retreated to the countess Matilda's mountain fortress at Canossa. (Matilda, incidentally, was a

Henry IV, barefoot and penitent at the gates of Matilda's fortress at Canossa. Left to shiver outside in a bitterly cold winter, he was admitted to the castle on the fourth day, once Pope Gregory agreed to pardon him.

second cousin of Henry's.) The king's allies, still numerous in Lombardy, urged him to attack, but he refused. Instead, he appeared before the walls of Canossa clad only in the woolen garb of a penitent, barefoot in the snow.

This put Gregory in a quandary, as Henry well knew. If the pope absolved the king, the rebel German aristocrats would feel heavily betrayed. On the other hand, how can any priest refuse absolution to a repentant sinner? And if he did refuse it, how would that look to the church and the world? Henry shivered outside Canossa for three days (although some Catholic historians insist that his physical suffering has been romantically exaggerated). Inside the castle, Matilda so strenuously urged mercy for her cousin that Gregory grew irritated with her. Abbot Hugh of Cluny, Henry's godfather, also petitioned for his forgiveness. On the fourth day, after Henry agreed to face a German assembly on all accusations brought by his nobles, Gregory relented. The castle gates opened. The king, it is said, wept with relief.

In principle, Canossa represented a papal victory. The most powerful ruler in Western Christendom had yielded to Rome. But Henry was free to rally his forces, and thereafter never did express the slightest remorse for defying the pope. With the Roman anathema lifted, German nobles and bishops flocked back to his banner. The pope could offer them neither troops nor money, and with the help of the increasingly influential merchants of the fast-growing towns along the Rhine, Henry reestablished his control of his territories. In full counterattack, he then appointed an antipope from Ravenna, who took the name Clement III. Gregory prophesied that his enemy would die within a year—but Henry failed to oblige. In the spring of 1082, he arrived with an army in the vicinity of Rome. He besieged the city three times, inflicting little damage and behaving with the utmost respect for the people. He finally took Rome in 1084, forcing Gregory to find refuge in Castel Sant' Angelo. With the support of many cardinals, Henry formally deposed Gregory VII and enthroned Clement III, who in turn crowned his German patron as emperor.

Responding to Gregory's appeals, the Norman Robert Guiscard marched on Rome with thirty thousand infantry and six thousand cavalry, drawn from southern Italy and Sicily, and including many Muslims. Henry retreated, while his Roman allies tried to hold out. Guiscard conducted vicious street battles and burned perhaps one-third of the city. Lines of women, including nuns, were marched with hands bound into the tents of the Norman soldiers and their Muslim allies. Slavery became the ultimate fate of thousands. Gregory, who must have been shattered by the abominable behavior of his uncontrollable ally, nonetheless accompanied Guiscard when he withdrew from the devastated city. To remain would have been suicidal. Despairing but defiant, the pope died the following spring in Salerno, uttering the famous words "I have loved righteousness and hated iniquity, therefore I die in exile." But he neither lived nor died in vain. In many men's minds, the church stood independent, possibly even supreme. Never again would the bishop of Rome be considered the mere chaplain to a theocratic emperor.

Henry, beset by the usual succession conflicts, fared only marginally better. When his rebellious eldest son, Conrad, cornered him in northern Italy, he escaped and had his second son crowned co-monarch as Henry V. But this ungrateful whelp, conspiring with rebellious nobles, imprisoned his father and forced him to abdicate. Henry, elusive as ever, escaped again, and waged vigorous war against his treacherous heir until 1106, when death suddenly took him at the age of fifty-five.

The controversy surrounding the investiture of bishops would flare up sporadically well into the twelfth century, and occasionally even later. A compromise was first worked out in England and France, followed by Germany. Typically, the clerics of a cathedral chapter would elect a candidate for their bishopric. If the pope agreed, then his delegate (normally an archbishop) would invest the nominee with ring and staff. The new bishop would then vow loyalty to his king or emperor in right of his feudally held lands. But the underlying issue of supremacy between church and state remained unresolved, a conflict that would intensify with the emergence of powerfully integrated nations, above all France. Thus, the two swords, spiritual and secular, would continue to clash. ∎

Pope Gregory sought refuge in the Castel Sant'Angelo, a second-century fortress by the Tiber River, where he was subsequently freed by Norman general Robert Guiscard. Connected to the Vatican by a secret passage, the imposing fortress, now a popular museum, has been used as a prison and a papal refuge.

A Viking longship rides a North Atlantic storm.
At the end of the eighth century, these sleek,
durable vessels, packed with Norse privateers,
burst out of Scandinavia to bring terror and ruin
to the Christian world and beyond.

HERVEY GARRETT SMITH

CHAPTER 4

Horror from the sea, the Vikings butcher and loot Christendom

Huge, brave and arguably the greatest sailors ever, they all but destroy the church in the North until apostles, braver than they, bring them to Christ

Two huge stones, carved twelve hundred years ago with bold Scandinavian runes, stand in the quiet lake country southwest of Stockholm. One memorial celebrates a warrior named Gudver, who "went westward to England … and manfully attacked the Saxon towns." The second stone recounts how Torsten, another local man, "fell fighting in the East, in Russia, the chief of the army, the best of his countrymen." At the end of the eighth century, thousands of men such as these, armed with battle-ax and broadsword, and helmed with iron, burst suddenly out of the remote North to lay waste Christendom. From the Irish isles to the walls of Byzantium, the mere appearance of these far-wandering warriors evoked a near-paralyzing terror for more than two centuries. They were the Vikings.[1]

The peoples of what are now Sweden, Norway and Denmark spoke a common dialect, Old Norse. They worshiped an assortment of gods—Woden, Thor, Freya and others—who rode from heaven to earth along a rainbow bridge. Generous but capricious, the gods unrelentingly pitted their courage and cunning against the evil genius Loki, terrible ice giants and other demonic figures. The Viking equivalent of saints were the berserkers, a species of warrior who lost all sense of self-preservation and pain in the frenzied bloodlust of battle.

1. In Old Norse, the word vik referred to a bay or inlet, and to go viking may originally have meant sailing Scandinavia's rugged coastline. The word could also link to the Old Norse word for battle, vig. Viking became a catchall label for the seafaring raiders of Norway, Denmark and Sweden.

Besides bravery, this harsh folk cherished practical jokes, sometimes decidedly gruesome. The Jomsburg Saga tells how Earl Haakon, himself a Viking, tied a bunch of his captured foes (also Vikings) along a log, seated side by side. At the earl's order, the captives were beheaded one by one, none flinching from the fatal blow. Any cowardice would mean forfeiting the sacred spark that bound the clans of gods and men alike. Only valiant warriors could be received into the celestial Valhalla, where they would feast forever with their ancestors.

In due course, the executioner reached Sigurd Buisson, a prisoner who had an exceptionally fine head of hair. "I fear not death," cried out Sigurd, "but let no slave touch my hair, nor blood defile it." Deciding to grant that wish, a man-at-arms stepped forward and held Sigurd's long locks up and away from his neck.

The hazardous voyages of Viking ships across some of the world's most dangerous saltwater only served to strengthen the valor of men who had been born and brought up to fight.

But when the executioner swung, the victim jerked downward, pulling the other man's wrist into the path of the ax. That ruse, although it cost their companion his hand, so amused the captors that they spared the lives of Sigurd and the remaining Jomsburg Vikings.

The Scandinavians trickled into recorded history initially as barely-noticed traders and occasional auxiliaries with Roman armies. All Vikings, linguistic cousins of their German neighbors, practiced polygamy, human sacrifice and slavery. Even so, this class of independent freeholders was large and libertarian. Kings traditionally ruled more by influence than coercion over populations of farmers and craftsmen. Viking smiths in particular were widely admired, transforming iron from native ore deposits into sharp weapons and tools. Equally skillful shipwrights applied those blades to the plentiful northern timber, creating ships that would become the bane of ninth- and tenth-century Europe.

The earliest Viking vessel discovered intact dates to about A.D. 300. Although the ships grew larger over the next five centuries, all carried just one square sail. Each had a pointed prow and stern, with steering provided by an oar at the stern (always on the right, hence the nautical term starboard, or "steerboard"). All of these "sailing canoes" were clinker built, the overlapping planks of oak providing the strength needed to endure the storms of the north Atlantic. Although the superbly graceful craft featured the high dragon's head at the bow and rose again at the stern, their steeply curved sides amidships rode just three-and-a-half feet above the waterline, allowing the crew to row. Also, the ships lacked a deep keel, so a seventy-foot longship carrying a couple of hundred fighters could be rowed upriver against the current in waters as shallow as two or three feet.[2]

Historian Michael Hasloch Kirkby, author of *The Vikings*, refers to the dragonships as "oceangoing landing craft." Like the horses that carried the Central Asian hordes across their far-horizoned steppes, like the Arabs racing

2. A royal longship could reach one hundred sixty feet in length, carrying two hundred fifty men, but most were perhaps half that long. One model, known as the Knörr, was a rarely-rowed sailing design, better suited for crossing the Atlantic and hauling cargo, with broader beams and higher freeboards.

across their sandy wastes on camels, the Viking longships provided a mobility that their Christian enemies could not match. Furthermore, their vessels' bellies could carry plenty of passengers and cargo, including horses, enabling warriors to move quickly on land as well as water. And the ferocious storms encountered on passages across some of the world's most frightening saltwater only strengthened the valor of men born and bred to fight.

"Seafaring was in their blood," writes British historian and philologist Eleanor Duckett (*Alfred the Great*). Even so, precisely what prompted the eruption of these violent rovers at the end of the eighth century is still debated. Local raiding had been practiced since time immemorial, and overpopulation was a recurring problem in a marginal subarctic agricultural region. Whatever their motive, when the Scandinavian pirates first landed on

Viking raiders sack a monastery at Clonmacnoise, Ireland, in the early years of the ninth century. The pagan early Vikings viewed the abbeys and churches of Christendom as nothing more than poorly defended storehouses of portable wealth.

foreign shores they met little resistance from their fear-paralyzed victims.

On June 8, 793, a Viking flotilla drew up on the broad beach at Lindisfarne, a small island off northeast England. Its monastery, founded by the saintly Aidan more than a century and a half earlier, had become the most revered site in Britain. (See previous volume, *Darkness Descends*, chapter 9.) The pagans seized the weapons stored in wooden chests fixed to the decks, and loosed the black and yellow shields tied along the gunwales of their ships. Roaring their war cries, they charged. Simeon of Durham described the attackers as "running hither and thither like ravening wolves ... they lay waste to everything in sight—trampling holy relics and defiling them underfoot.... Some of the monks they killed outright, others they overpowered and carried away with them. Many they taunted and abused and flung out naked. Some they drowned in the sea."[3]

In 795 came the turn of another iconic island, Iona, home to a monastery established by Columcille. Iona recovered briefly after the first assault by the northerners but they returned in 806, slaughtering sixty-eight monks. Similar orgies of butchery were inflicted all along the coast of western Scotland. These

A chronicler describes the attackers as laying everything waste, savagely abusing the monks and drowning them in the sea. They trampled holy relics and foully defiled them.

early pirates were likely Norwegians. At this stage, their ships were small (perhaps no more than fifteen or twenty crew members) and the raids limited to a few vessels. But the success of the first forays spurred others to go a-viking for profit and fame. Raids spread to Ireland. The *Annals of Ulster* record how hardly a year passed without the "devastation of the Kingdom by pagan raiders." Everything became a target, from the wealthy monastery at Bangor to a solitary hermit on the ocean-girt barren rock of Skellig Michil.

For Celtic Christianity, the Vikings were a decisive disaster. "Somewhere between 795 and the middle of the ninth century, the Irish missionary church completed its work by carrying Christianity to Iceland," says British historian C. F. Keary (*The Vikings in Western Christendom*). "Almost immediately there began the process of undoing its work at the hands of the Vikings, who were not only murdering all the communities of monks whom they found scattered over the north seas and the Scottish coasts and islands, but had already struck at the very root or fountainhead of the 'movement' in Ireland itself." Their strategy was crude but efficient. Raids of appalling violence would yield not only large quantities of plunder but also hefty payments from people willing to buy off the invaders. Bribed or not, however, the Vikings would keep returning until a district had been stripped clean.

Raids by Danish Vikings along the Frankish coast remained modest in scale during the initial devastation of Britain. Meanwhile, the Franks tried to introduce Christianity in Denmark. In 826, the Danish prince Harald Klak traveled with much pomp to be baptized in the cathedral at Mainz, and an

3. The first recorded Viking raid upon England happened about the year 790, when three Norwegian ships, assumed to be merchants, landed near Portland. They were met by a customs official for Wessex, but paying taxes was not an idea congenial to the Northmen. They slaughtered the inspector and his men on the spot.

energetic young Saxon monk named Ansgar returned home with him to establish a mission in southern Denmark. Ansgar, full of youthful enthusiasm, would become the first major figure in Scandinavian Christianity.[4]

But Ansgar soon realized that Harald's baptism had more to do with politics than religion. A rival had recently deposed him, and he needed powerful allies. The Danish mission stalled. Then, in 829, the Swedish king Björn asked the Frankish court to send priests for the growing number of his people "who had a leaning towards Christianity." In compliance, Ansgar and two companions sailed to the Swedish trading center of Birka. The trip turned dreadful when pirates seized the books and other gifts that the emperor Louis the Pious (son of Charlemagne) was sending to the Swedish king. Even so, Ansgar's biographer and disciple, Rimbert, says Björn willingly granted permission to preach the gospel of Christ in his realm.

Trade from the East and plunder from the West fueled unprecedented prosperity in Scandinavia. Its first urban settlements began to sprout, including Birka. Björn appointed a prefect to regulate the growing port, and that official,

4. Ansgar (or Anskar), known as "the Apostle to the North," was a Saxon born in Picardy in 801. Tonsured at age thirteen, he became a noted teacher by his twenties. *The Oxford Dictionary of the Christian Church* notes that Ansgar did help mitigate the horrors of the slave trade in Scandinavia, and his constant calm in the face of potential martyrdom was worthy of any Viking.

Alfred the Great's England

Iona

Lindisfarne

BERNICIA

STRATHCLYDE

North Sea

NORTHUMBRIA

Bangor

CUMBRIA

Stamford Bridge

York

DEIRA

River Humber

MERCIA

EAST ANGLIA

WALES

ESSEX

London

Thames R.

KENT •Canterbury

Ethandun

N

WEST WALES

WESSEX

SUSSEX

Hastings

Winchester

English Channel

✕ Battles

✝ Monastic Sites

Hergeir, accepted Christ. But the king refused to convert to the new religion and virtually all of his people, difficult to even reach in their isolated farms, proved equally resistant. Ansgar persisted. Appointed the first archbishop of the North, he had the satisfaction of seeing Rimbert, now a bishop, build two churches in Denmark. In 851, Sweden's first church rose at Birka.

As sometimes happened elsewhere, slaves provided the finest initial seedbed for Christianity in both countries. Their value was low, about the same as the domestic animals whose legal status they shared, their numbers were distressingly high. The trade mushroomed, particularly after 845, when Christian kingdoms in the West under church prodding outlawed slave transport across their lands. The Vikings' route through the Slavic lands to the east became the preferred alternative for shipping them via Constantinople to the Muslim world. There the demand, especially for women, seemed insatiable. The number of Slavs, Celts and Saxons sold into bondage, although unknown, must have reached hundreds of thousands.[5]

More than any other European people, the Vikings enjoyed imaginative nicknames, with scarcely a king or leader lacking his colorful moniker.[6] Typical was Ragnar Lodbrok ("Hairy-Breeches"), who led a Danish assault on Northumbria, a

5. Human beings were probably the Vikings' biggest trade item. A single ninth-century raid on Armagh, Ireland, netted fully a thousand slaves. Most slaves were shipped via eastern routes to Muslim lands, but not all. A Scandinavian burial dated circa 879 contained a Viking chieftain and several hundred slaves—men, women and children—sent along to provide for his every comfort.

6. Viking nicknames were often picturesque and unflattering—Cod-Biter, Bluetooth, Belly-Shaker, Flatnose, Unwashed, Seal-Head, Barelegs, Boneless and so forth. Another odd Scandinavian habit for the period was the weekly bath, normally done on Saturday.

kingdom in northeastern England. Its ruler, Aelle, captured the barbarian chief and had him thrown into a pit of venomous snakes. Hairy-Breeches, who had four sons still at home, glared up at his Saxon tormentors and snarled, "The little pigs would grunt now if they knew how it fares with the old boar."

Winston Churchill describes the legendary reaction of those sons in his *History of the English-Speaking Peoples*. The eldest gripped his spear shaft so hard that he left the print of his fingers on it. Another clenched a chess piece so tightly that blood spurted from under his nails. A third, paring his nails, cut through to the bone. The youngest turned red, blue and pale by turns. Their revenge on northern England is also on record. In 851, the Danes seized the cathedral city of York (which the Romans had called Eboracum and the Vikings renamed Jorvik or Jarvik) in Northumbria. Ragnar's vengeful sons slit open King Aelle from throat to crotch and ripped out his "still-palpitating" lungs. There was worse to come. Following the pattern already established in Ireland, the raiders began staying year-round in the north of England, and dividing up its soil between their warriors.

The year before, the Danes had already hit the south. The *Anglo-Saxon Chronicle* reports that three hundred and fifty ships intruded into the estuary of the river Thames. Thousands of Danes sacked the cathedral city of Canterbury,

Ansgar, known as the Apostle to the Vikings, preaches the gospel to a group of Northmen on the shores of the Baltic, in a painting by Gustaf Olaf Cederstrom (1845–1933). His message was embraced by many of the Vikings' slaves, but Ansgar made little headway among the Northmen themselves.

then attacked London. In 864, the Saxons of Kent paid a massive bribe in silver, but their region was put to the sword anyway. The campaign of terror now turned on East Anglia. Its king, Edmund, went down to a valiant defeat. The Danes asked the royal prisoner to share sovereignty with a Danish chief, but Edmund refused to associate himself with a pagan monarchy. So the Vikings used him for target practice, then lopped off his head. St. Edmund the Martyr remains a symbol of English resistance to this day. Mercia fell next, leaving only Wessex unconquered. The Saxon ascendancy in England, about four centuries old, appeared on the brink of an immediate and bloody conclusion. But the indomitable spirit of one man still stood in the way.

Alfred of Wessex was born in 849, youngest son of King Ethelwulf. With three older brothers, he seemed to have little likelihood of ruling. His father sent him at age four with an entourage of reliable warriors on the long road to Rome. Seeking papal benediction had become a trend among western Europe's royal houses after Pope Adrian blessed Charlemagne's two sons, Louis and Pepin. With Vikings swarming across Britain, the royal family of Wessex had need of divine favor.

Only when Mass was finished did Alfred rally his Saxon troops to repulse the Danish hordes as they charged down the hill. The battle was intense but Alfred emerged victorious.

In fact, the Vikings also menaced the young prince's pilgrimage through Frankish lands, sweeping "like a savage hurricane" upon the two great monasteries of St. Martin at Tours and slaughtering 126 monks. But Alfred's trip proved so satisfactory that two years later King Ethelwulf himself went to Rome, taking Alfred along. They stayed almost a year, also visiting the court of Charles the Bald, king of the West Franks. What impression these travels made upon the six-year-old child can only be surmised, but they exposed him to the religious, cultural and administrative centers of Western Christendom. Perhaps the experience helps account for his later piety, love of learning and administrative skill.

Across northern and eastern England, Viking destruction "left nothing standing but roofless walls," records Simeon of Durham, writing a century later. The once-great kingdoms of Northumbria, Deira and East Anglia would never reemerge. Alfred's youth would leave him memories of ever-larger Danish raids upon Wessex, causing the death of two of his brothers. King Ethelwulf died in 865. The third brother became King Ethelred I, and Alfred at sixteen was expected to stand at his side in defense of their patrimony. In December 870 the Vikings crossed the river Thames in force. The two armies faced each other in Berkshire, near the gigantic image of a white horse cut in prehistoric times into the chalk hillside (it can still be seen today). Legend has it that the king insisted on finishing the Mass in his tent as the battle began, leaving his brother Alfred to rally the English as the Danish horde rushed down the slope. Had the Danes won that attack, historian Keary contends, "the course of history would have been rolled back; Christianity would have been driven out."

But the Saxons held the field after a day of intense combat, then spent several months pursuing the Vikings. However, Viking reinforcements kept arriving from the mainland in discouraging numbers. In March, the English lost a key battle. Ethelred died soon after, and at twenty-two, Alfred found himself king. Over the next year, he doggedly fought nine major engagements and many smaller ones. Finally, the Danes accepted a heavy payment to withdraw, sacking London as they retreated. But in 877, they attacked Wessex again under a fearsome leader, Guthrum, and this time the English forces simply evaporated. "Now the whole opposition to their [i.e., Viking] movements seems to have collapsed," Keary observes. "Alfred himself was not wanting, but his subjects, wearied with their long vigil, their marchings and their countermarchings, seemed to have given up hope, to have begun to think of submitting to the inevitable, as the Northumbrians and East Anglians and Mercians had submitted."

Alfred, accompanied only by his *housecarls*—the professional army of the royal household—took refuge in a fort hidden amid the almost impenetrable marshlands of Somerset. He skulked in this reedy waste for months, staying in touch via covert messengers with important comrades across his fully overrun realm, and working out with them a plan to revive the resistance. One by one, they secretly committed themselves and their men to the cause. Meanwhile, according to an immensely popular English tale, which could easily be true, Alfred sat one day by the fireside in a woodsman's cottage, pondering strategy. The peasant's wife, unaware of who her raggedly garbed guest was, asked him to mind a pan of baking biscuits. He agreed to do so, but then got lost in thought until the smell of burning alerted his hostess. "Alack, man," cried she, "why have you not turned over the bread when you see it is burning—especially as you so like eating it hot!" Alfred, far from taking offense, humbly apologized for his carelessness.

That spring, he emerged from the swamp at the head of a guerrilla army, assembled so it seemed out of nowhere. "To their beloved leader, with hearts rejoicing, came all the inhabitants of Somerset, Wiltshire and Hampshire," exults *The Anglo-Saxon Chronicle*. Near the ancient fort of Bratton Castle, at Ethandun, now Edington in Wiltshire, Alfred's men crested a windswept summit and beheld the enemy. A mass of heavily armed Vikings was advancing toward them, the pagans confident that a final victory over the English was at hand. In wedge formation, the grim men of Wessex stormed through the Danes, and sent them flying for shelter to their fortified camp a few miles away. This time, the hitherto all-but-irresistible invaders had been thoroughly thrashed.

Alfred the Great, the only English king ever to bear that title, now showed his

The Alfred Jewel, discovered in the seventeenth century in the marshes of Somerset, where legend says the embattled king took respite from the Viking wars. The jewel's provenance is not in doubt. Inscribed in gold filigree are the Saxon words 'Aelfred Mec Heht Gewyrcan'—which translates as 'Alfred Had Me Made.' It is designed to be worn as a brooch.

Know ye the barbarian, then and now

Chesterton's epic poem of Alfred's defeat of the Danes warns that barbarism will be back

G. K. Chesterton's stirring, book-length, narrative poem, The Ballad of the White Horse, *describes King Alfred's seemingly hopeless, but ultimately triumphant, struggle against King Guthrum's Viking Danes. The full poem consists of 544 verses, twenty-five excerpted here. As the excerpts show, the ballad is also a timeless allegory, filled with thrilling battles and visions of the ongoing war between Christianity and the forces of nihilistic destruction.*

King Alfred strives in vain against the conquering Danes

A sea-folk blinder than the sea
Broke all about his land,
But Alfred up against them bare
And gripped the ground and grasped the air,
Staggered, and strove to stand.

For earthquake swallowing earthquake
Uprent the Wessex tree;
The whirlpool of the pagan sway
Had swirled his sires as sticks away
When a flood smites the sea.

Our towns were shaken of tall kings
With scarlet beards like blood:
The world turned empty where they trod,
They took the kindly cross of God
And cut it up for wood.

He bent them back with spear and spade,
With desperate dyke and wall,
With foemen leaning on his shield
And roaring on him when he reeled;
And no help came at all.

There was not English armor left,
Nor any English thing,
When Alfred came to Athelney
To be an English king.

The despairing king, in prayer, is rewarded with a vision of the Virgin Mary

"Mother of God" the wanderer said
"I am but a common king,
Nor will I ask what saints may ask,
To see a secret thing.

"But for this earth most pitiful.
This little land I know,
If that which is forever is,
Or if our hearts shall break with bliss
Seeing the stranger go?"

The Virgin responds with a hard message, reminding him what it means to be a Christian

"The men of the East may spell the stars
And times and triumphs mark,
But the men signed of the cross of Christ
Go gaily in the dark.

"The men of the East may search the scrolls
For sure fates and fame,
But the men who drink the blood of God
Go singing to their shame.

"For you and all the kind of Christ
Are ignorant and brave,
And you have wars you hardly win
And souls you hardly save.

"I tell you naught for your comfort,
Yea, naught for your desire,
Save that the sky grows darker yet
And the sea rises higher.

"Night shall be thrice night over you,
And heaven an iron cope.
Do you have joy without a cause,
Yea, faith without a hope?"

Alfred, inspired by the vision, rallies his reluctant liegemen once more

"Out of the mouth of the Mother of God,
More than the doors of doom,
I call the muster of Wessex men
From grassy hamlet or ditch or den,
To break and be broken, God knows when,
But I have seen for whom!"

The resurgence of battered Wessex catches the powerful Danish king Guthrum unaware

The live wood came at Guthrum,
On foot and claw and wing,
The nests were noisy overhead,
For Alfred and the star of red;
All life went forth, and the forest fled
Before the face of the king.

Then bursting all and blasting
Came Christendom like death,
Kicked of such catapults of will,
The staves shiver, the barrels spill,
The wagons waver and crash and kill
The wagoners beneath.

Alfred sees that the battle has turned in his favor, that the Danes are faltering

The high tide, King Alfred cried,
The high tide—and the turn!*
As a tide turns on the tall gray seas,
See how they waver in the trees
How stray their spears, how quake
   their knees
How wild their watchfires burn!

Alfred sentences his fallen enemy—to baptism

When the pagan people of the sea
Fled to their palisades,
Nailed there with javelins to cling
And wonder smote the pirate king,
And brought him to his christening
And the end of all his raids.

Chesterton foresees the barbarism that was yet to come

They shall not come in warships,
They shall not waste with brands,
But books be all their eating,
And ink be on their hands.

Yea, this shall be the sign of them,
The sign of the dying fire;
And man made like a half-wit,
That knows not of his sire.

What though they come with
   scroll and pen,
And grave as a shaven clerk,
By this sign you shall know them
That they ruin and make dark;

By all men bond to nothing
Being slaves without a lord,
By one blind idiot world obeyed
Too blind to be abhorred.

By thought a crawling ruin,
By life a leaping mire,
By a broken heart in the breast
   of the world
And the end of the world's desire.

By God and man dishonored
By death and life made vain
Know ye, the old barbarian,
The barbarian come again.

* The second line of this verse was the headline on the *London Times* editorial marking the British victory in the Battle of El Alamein, which with the Russian victory at Stalingrad three months later, was the turning point of the Second World War.

This majestic statue of King Alfred the Great by Hamo Thorneycroft was unveiled in the city of Winchester, England, in 1901 on the millennial commemoration of the king's death. (He actually died in 899, but the Winchester populace persistently observes the later date.) The resolute fortitude conveyed by the figure is altogether consistent with the historical record.

DEDICATION

Christian journalist, essayist and poet G. K. Chesterton

Chesterton dedicated "The Ballad of the White Horse" to his beloved wife, Frances, who helped to lead him to Jesus Christ. He writes:

Lady, by one light only
We look from Alfred's eyes.
We know he saw athwart the wreck
The sign that hangs about your neck,
Where one more than Melchizedek
Is dead and never dies.

Therefore I bring these rhymes to you,
Who brought the cross to me,
Since on you flaming without flaw
I saw the sign that Guthrum saw
When he let break his ships of awe,
And laid peace on the sea.

Viking raiders attack a manor in the Seine Valley of north-central France. The attacks prompted Charles the Bald, king of the West Franks, to begin a program of massive fortification of towns, monasteries and even bridges, the walls and towers of which would become emblematic of the Middle Ages.

quality. Even if he could annihilate his present foes in their weakened state, more Scandinavian pirates would continue to arrive. But at the moment, he was in a position of power—perhaps only fleetingly, but enough for a chance at a lasting settlement. The treaty that Alfred concluded with Guthrum—a copy still exists— acknowledged a permanent Danish presence in England for those who wished "to plough the land and make a living for themselves." They would be governed by Danish law. In return, Alfred demanded, the mighty Guthrum must accept baptism and agree to rule as a Christian king, treating equally and fairly both his Viking and English subjects. To all this, Guthrum agreed.

And so, writes Churchill, King Alfred "received Guthrum with thirty prominent buccaneers in his camp. He stood godfather to Guthrum; he raised him from the font; he entertained him for twelve days; he presented him and his warriors with

costly gifts; he called him his son." The price of the treaty was high. The Danes acquired most of central and eastern England, but there was no realistic alternative. While Guthrum issued coinage under his Christian name Aethelstan, Alfred gained a fourteen-year respite to heal his people.

Continental Europe enjoyed no such reprieve. Viking fleets plundered at the mouths of the Rhine and Loire. Always they sought out monasteries, where treasure troves had been conveniently collected and an effective defense was mounted only rarely. Their pagan depredations could scarcely have been better designed to damage the fledgling civilization emerging in the West. And the Frankish church, thoroughly demoralized by being singled out for excruciating torment and the starvation conditions imposed on its human flocks, failed to rally the sheep against the predators.

The raiders probed further southward along the Atlantic coast and into the Mediterranean, where they encountered Islamic Spain, a land far richer than any Christian realm of the West. But Muslim armies consisted of experienced regular soldiers; their swift war galleys were manned by hard-bitten veterans. Despite rich winnings from some cities, the Vikings' own losses prompted them to permanently avoid the Iberian Peninsula. In Germany, by contrast, the largest Viking fleet yet seen—some six hundred ships—sailed into the river Elbe and attacked Hamburg. In a day and a half of murder and rape, the frontier town's new church and monastery were looted, its other buildings burned.

Yet another northern fleet made its way into the Seine, its crews smashing into Paris. There they began their usual pitiless routine—until, according to both Viking and Frankish histories, a strange and almost impenetrable fog enveloped the city. The unnerved brigands returned to their ships, many getting lost in the process, so the Parisians were able to kill quite a few. But that success proved as ephemeral as the fog. Across France, the Vikings ravaged at will for years to come.[7] "All men

7. Viking operational bases were usually easily defended island lairs: Thanet and Sheppey in southeast England, Walcheren off the coast of Flanders, and Noirmoutier near the mouth of the Loire. Their largest base of all, Oissel in a loop of the Seine, was the first Norse settlement in what would become Normandy.

A nineteenth-century depiction of the Vikings before the walls of Paris, from Guizot's History of France. *This last great assault on the city, in November 885, proved to be a watershed in the Franks' defense of their realm—and the beginning of the end for the rapacious Northmen.*

give themselves to flight," reads a chronicle of the time. "No one cries out, 'Stand and fight for your fatherland, for your church, for your countrymen.' What they ought to defend with arms they shamefully redeem by payments. The commonweal of Christendom is betrayed by its guardians."

Charles the Bald, ruler of the West Franks and Charlemagne's grandson, urged every man who could maintain a horse to do so. He authorized the fortification of towns, monasteries and strategic bridges, which became standard medieval procedure. The king offered Weland, chieftain of a large Viking force on the Somme, three thousand pounds of silver to attack other Vikings in the Seine Valley. Weland took the money, failed to honor the deal, and the next year demanded a double payment. With this in hand, he finally did move against the Seine Vikings—until they offered him another six thousand pounds of silver to leave them alone.

The Frankish nobility meanwhile, consistently protected their own interests rather than uniting for the common good. Feudal lords disbanded peasant militias that had formed in desperate attempts at self-defense, the aristocrats sometimes using brutal measures to assure their own continued dominance. News of easy pickings in Francia reached England, attracting men who preferred war to farming in the domain ruled peaceably by Guthrum. In 879, these freebooters began looting the lands that are now Belgium and Holland, later joining forces with comrades who had been similarly occupied in Saxony. Together they easily pillaged the entire lower Rhine Valley. Cologne's churches were reduced to ash. Aachen, Charlemagne's old capital, fell in 881, the Vikings stabling their horses in churches built by the emperor.

On one notable occasion, Charles the Fat, grandson of Charles the Bald, assembled a sizeable army and surrounded a contingent of those same Vikings in an old royal villa. Instead of attacking, however, the Frankish king cravenly offered payment to move on. As negotiations proceeded, the Vikings threw open the gates of the villa and began a gigantic sale of their plunder. Crowds poured in: curious gawkers, merchants, clerics hoping to redeem holy relics and treasures from half the Rhineland abbeys and churches. Then in the midst of the sale, the Vikings withdrew their token of safe conduct (a shield hung outside the wall), clanged shut the gates, and fell upon the captive crowd, putting many to the sword.

By this time, all organized attempts to convert the Viking homelands to Christianity had foundered. The mission at Birka was abandoned, and its priest moved to the Danish port of Hedeby, but that church lasted little longer. Ansgar's death in 865, followed by the faithful Rimbert three years later, ended virtually all Christian contact with Scandinavia. As a result, Christians could no longer be ransomed from the northern slave market (Rimbert himself had been one of Ansgar's earliest purchases).

In November 885, another record-setting Viking fleet—by report, seven hundred longships plus many smaller barks—sailed up the Seine. Again the goal was Paris. But Count Odo, the regional lord, led a truly gallant defense despite rivers of blood and a serious outbreak of plague. Amid the clouds of arrows, the city's spirited bishop fell wounded but survived. On the strength of this victory rested the initial prestige of the name Capet, a dynasty that would rule France for longer than any other. (See page 76.) The Vikings never again threatened Paris.

In 891, another great contingent of Northmen was slaughtered by King Arnulf of the East Franks near Louvain in present-day Belgium. Their raids, often destructive, would continue until the middle of the tenth century, but the worst was over for the continent. Some of the invaders joined their compatriots already settled in Ireland and England, and these families soon converted to Christianity. But others renewed the assault against Alfred in Wessex.

Now, however, the great king was prepared. A particular problem had been the English militia, called the *fyrd*. Its ranks of farmers had traditionally sworn to fight for forty days at a time. During planting and harvesting seasons, however, they returned home to produce food. In response, the Viking armies of full-time pirates often avoided battle until the fyrd had depleted. But once Alfred ruled all of the English outside the Danish territories, he split his increased manpower into two levies, one draft always on active duty while the other worked at home.[8]

Fortresses with permanent garrisons dotted the land, often beside strategic bridges, offering refuge for people, livestock and portable wealth. At the king's command, Wessex also constructed sixty-oar warships, larger and stronger than almost all Viking longships. This navy, England's first, restricted the enemy's previous freedom of the sea. After four fruitless years of fighting, this renewed Viking offensive burned itself out in 896.

Alfred had won. Throughout the long struggle with the Northmen, the devout Christian never lost his wish to win souls of all stripes. In fact, he viewed Viking piracy as a divine punishment for his own people's sins. A scholar himself, the king personally translated *Pastoral Care*, the manual composed by Pope Gregory I that became a textbook for medieval bishops. In his preface, Alfred wrote: "We were Christians in name only, and very few possessed Christian virtues."

Like Charlemagne, Alfred established a code of laws, drawing on principles

8. Alfred's forces now included West Saxons, Angles, Mercians, Welsh and Frisians. *The Anglo-Saxon Chronicle* refers to Alfred's army simply as "the Christians." Across western Europe, the prayer "Libera nos a furore Normanorum" (From the fury of the Northmen, deliver us) became common, a testimony to terror. The prayer's use survived in some places until the modern era.

from the Book of Exodus and earlier Saxon laws. Although the king avoided unnecessary changes to custom, he restricted the blood feud and dictated harsh penalties for breaches of oath. He also rescued education. "Learning had declined so thoroughly in England," the king wrote, "that there were very few men on this side of the River Humber who could understand their divine services, or even translate a letter from Latin into English, and I suppose that there were not many beyond the Humber either. There were so few of them that I cannot recollect a single one south of the Thames when I succeeded to the kingdom." To right the situation, Alfred offered patronage to scholars from Wales and the continent, learned Latin himself, and opened schools.

By the time this archetypical medieval monarch died in 899, while no Saxon or Dane would have imagined himself to be living in an earthly replica of Augustine's City of God, former foes could nevertheless conceive of living together in a community. From that mutual respect emerged a single kingdom, England. Over the next several decades Alfred's descendants extended his realm to include all of the Danelaw, and reclaimed the ancient Christian centers of the north.[9]

This reconstructed Viking village (lower photo) is at Hedeby, north Germany, near the border with Denmark. Originally a Danish Viking trading base, Hedeby became the original foothold for Christianity among the Northmen. A twelfth century "stave church" at Borgund, Norway, (inset below), is one of the thirty remaining from about a thousand that existed in medieval Norway. A series of vertical posts (staves) provides the framework, rather like shipbuilding. Viking craftsmanship is evident in the all-wood construction (no nails used), in elaborate carvings and in typically Viking dragonheads on the exterior.

Across the English Channel, Danish Vikings established their own fiefdoms on the fertile lands of the lower Seine. Their leader was Rollo, a man said to be so large that no horse could support him, so he customarily walked. In 911 a new king of the Franks, Charles the Simple, recognized Rollo's control of the region now known as Normandy. In exchange for his dukedom, Rollo accepted baptism, acknowledged Charles as overlord and married Charles's daughter Gisele. His heathen comrades quickly intermarried with Christian Franks. This new branch of the Viking stem would itself soon become a force to reckon with as far afield as Asia Minor.

At about the same time, an Arab by the name of Ahmad ibn Fadlan traveled up the Volga River in the Khanate of Khazaria. There he met the Rus. "Never before have I seen

men of such magnificent bearing," ibn Fadlan wrote. "They are all as tall as palm trees, with reddish-blond hair, and their skin is fair." Those Rus were, in fact, Vikings, most of them Swedish. In the eighth century, they had explored south from the Baltic coast, portaging their boats over the Valdai Hills, the source of rivers flowing into the Baltic, the Black Sea and the Caspian Sea.[10]

Thus the Northmen gained an overland access to Constantinople, to the Muslim empire and to the fabled Silk Road to China. The physical barriers, starvation and other hardships encountered along the rivers were as punishing as the storms of the North Sea and Atlantic. During the 830s, the first group of Rus reached Constantinople via the Dnieper, exhausted and reduced by many deaths. Emperor Theophilus permitted them to return by the Mediterranean, and the *Annals of St. Bertin* recorded their arrival at the Frankish court.

The Rus built trading centers at Novgorod and Smolensk. By 882, their chieftain Rurik had organized a kingdom controlled from Kiev, capital of modern Ukraine. His descendants would rule Russia until the sixteenth century. Under Rurik, the Rus brought furs, slaves, weapons, honey and wax to the south. Silver, glass, spices and Chinese silk made the return trip to Scandinavia.

A tenth-century Arab traveling up the Volga described the Rus as tall as palm trees, with reddish-blond hair and fair skin. He had come face to face with Vikings from Sweden.

In 950, the Byzantine emperor Constantine Porphyrogenitus recorded: "In winter, life is hard for the Rus. In the beginning of November, their chiefs and all the Rus at the same time leave Kiev and make the rounds of the lands of the Slavs and other tribes subject to their taxation. They settle there for the winter, but return to Kiev in April when the ice melts on the Dnieper. There they buy boats from the Slavs, which the latter have hewn in the forest during the winter."

The emperor also described the gathering of the Rus merchant fleet downstream from Kiev, at a fortified camp. Every June, a convoy would descend the fast-flowing Dnieper, negotiating the river's infamous rapids. The arrival in Constantinople of these heavily armed, backwoods freebooters was clearly not without its problems. A treaty signed in 945 stipulated that the Rus "must enter the city with an imperial inspector, by a gate which will be shown to them, unarmed, by groups of no more than fifty, and do their trading."

That caution was warranted. Viking fleets from Kiev attacked Constantinople around 860, 907 and 941. The Byzantines repelled the Rus with Greek fire (a fearsome secret weapon described in the previous volume *Sword of Islam*, chapter 10). The Vikings also assailed the Muslims, raiding Azerbaijan in 912 and 943. Muslim valor and dysentery defeated those offensives. In general, the eastern Vikings found more profit through trade treaties than war, but their relationship with Byzantium remained edgy until the extraordinary prince Vladimir reigned in Kiev. (His story is told at the end of chapter 8 of this volume.)

9. Alfred was followed by rulers who united England and brought much of Scotland and Wales under Saxon control. Equally outstanding churchmen (most notably Dunstan, archbishop of Canterbury, and Oswald, archbishop of York) helped create a prosperous kingdom, its peace marred only by several Viking attempts to reestablish control of York and the northeast.

10. The word Rus is believed to be a Slavic form of the Finnish name for the Swedes, ruotsi ("river folk" or "rowing folk"). Over the course of time the Byzantines, Muslims, and even the Franks used this name to describe the Slavic peoples who came to be ruled by the Rus, the Russians.

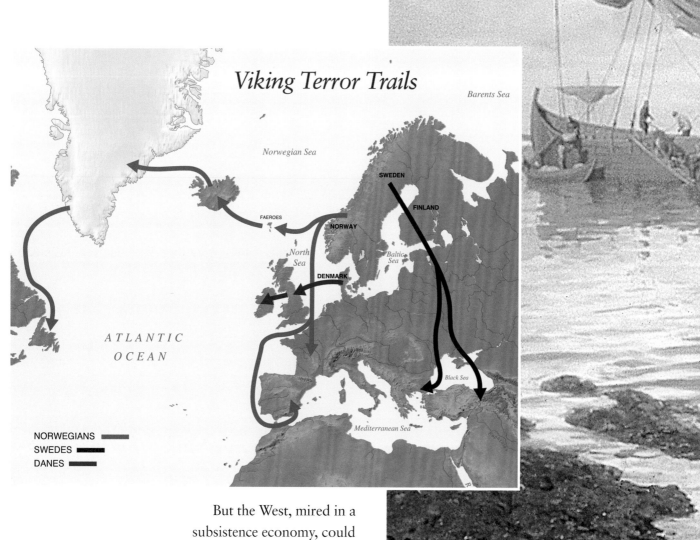

Viking Terror Trails

Barents Sea

Norwegian Sea

SWEDEN

FINLAND

FAEROES

NORWAY

North Sea

Baltic Sea

DENMARK

ATLANTIC OCEAN

Black Sea

Mediterranean Sea

NORWEGIANS

SWEDES

DANES

11. The progress of the Norman invaders can be deduced from the Bayeux Tapestry, a visual record of their conquest in 1066. The ships, armor and weapons of Duke William's army are all still clearly in the Viking style.

But the West, mired in a subsistence economy, could not buy off Viking aggression by permitting access to rich markets. Again the Danes assaulted England—but this time with unexpected gains to Christianity. After its king, Ethelred II the Unready (more properly translated, say some scholars, as "Ethelred the Ill-Advised"), died in 1016, the country ended turmoil by accepting Canute (or Knut), a Danish prince, who later inherited the crown of his native land as well. This steel-willed warrior, who had mutilated hostages and committed political murder, fell under the influence of Archbishop Wulfstan of York. Therefore, Canute rebuilt the English churches and monasteries, and constructed new ones. He performed the pilgrimage to Rome, and under his protection, English missionaries flooded into Sweden and Denmark.

In Norway, King Olaf Haraldsson proclaimed his territory officially Christian. By the time he died in 1030, his Vikings charged into battle bellowing, "Forward Christ's men, Cross men!" rather than the names of the Norse gods. Olaf became the patron saint of Norway, which fought its way to independent nationhood. Canute, who had tried to add Norway to his conquests, died in 1035. His northern empire broke up within seven years, England reverting to its old Saxon royal line.

In 1066, the relentless northmen tried again. England's Harold II shattered a Norwegian army in the north, then fell himself at Hastings in combat against Duke William of Normandy (see subchapter page 111). There Saxon royal rule over Britain ended, finally and forever. In a remarkably short time, the Normans

Viking settlers coming ashore with their families, belongings and livestock. By the end of the first millennium, the Norse had established permanent settlements from the lower Seine Valley in France (Normandy), through eastern England, Ireland, and across the North Atlantic on the Orkney, Shetland and Faeroe Islands, as far as distant Iceland and Greenland.

had evolved from illiterate barbarism into the most tightly knit feudal realm of all Christendom. William, a close ally of the papacy, soon fastened a tightly woven net of military and ecclesiastical authority over his new kingdom.[11]

Paganism was now in retreat across the northern lands. Swedish kings became Christian after Ansgar's early mission was revived at the beginning of the eleventh century, with much help from English monks and nuns. Thousands accepted baptism, churches sprouted and bishoprics formed, although so many Swedes resisted that their Christian rulers continued to officiate at pagan state ceremonies. The chronicler Adam of Bremen noted that mob violence in Sweden's heartland made it a heathen bastion in 1075, but in the face of that popular fury, King Inge abolished the pagan royal ceremony five years later. Rebels killed the bishop and forced Inge to flee southward to territory where Christian Swedes predominated. The king rallied his forces, broke the revolt and pulled down the great Viking temple at Uppsala, for centuries the heart of Swedish worship. Inge built a church on the site.

Generations would pass, however, before the old gods were completely eradicated in rural Scandinavia. An exasperated twelfth-century monk named Elnoth complained that Vikings too often linked Christianity to prosperity: "But if the wind changes for the worse … if storm or fire causes suffering, then they

The Christian Viking explorer

The convert Leif Ericsson traced the coast of North America to the fabled Vinland
after his troublesome father Eric planted a Viking colony on Greenland

In the second half of the ninth century, Viking adventurers from the fjords of Scandinavia began sailing westward into the vast and for the most part unexplored North Atlantic Ocean. Their search would take them to Iceland, to Greenland, and eventually to the eastern shore of North America itself, about five centuries before Columbus. Among all the achievements of the Northmen, these legendary voyages, the great "sagas" of Viking exploration, have most strongly impressed themselves upon the modern imagination.

However, the Vikings were not the first to take up the challenge of the North Atlantic. Irish monks, their names for the most part long lost, who set out in tiny boats to seek solitude and God beyond the western horizon, were before them. According to the Irish chronicler Dicuil, writing in 825, they reached the Faeroe Islands, midway between Scotland and Iceland, in the early eighth century. Several decades later other monks discovered a larger island far to the northwest of the British Isles, which Dicuil called Thule. Clearly, this was Iceland.[1]

The Irish monks had the Faeroes and Iceland to themselves only until the arrival of Viking raiders. After that, any who did not flee were either killed or enslaved. "On these islands, hermits who have sailed from our Scotia [Ireland] have lived for roughly a hundred years," Dicuil writes. "But, even as they have been uninhabited since the world's beginning, so now, because of Norse pirates, they are again empty."

But not for long. Iceland's climate was considerably milder than it is today. Despite its position just south of the Arctic Circle, it had rich pasturage for animals and crops, particularly grains, besides abundant fish. The Vikings began colonizing the islands of the North Atlantic around 870, and before the end of the century, there were even a few Christian families in the Icelandic settlements. The origins of their faith are not known, but it too may have come from Ireland. Not until the late tenth century did the first missionaries begin to arrive from Norway—and for once the issue of conversion was settled, not by royal example alone, but by vote at an assembly of freemen, known as the *Althing*.[2]

In about the millennial year, tension between pagan Icelanders and the growing Christian population seemed likely to lead to civil war, and the chieftain who presided over the assembly, Thorgeir, was asked to arbitrate. He proposed a compromise. Iceland should become officially Christian, Thorgeir suggested, but sacrifices to the old gods would still be permitted in private. This eminently practical solution

was adopted by a substantial majority. Such a compromise could not long endure in an offcially Christian society, however, and it did not. Within five years, all pagan practices were abolished.

As for the Greenland saga, it began with Erik the Red, a native of southwestern Norway, and an inveterate troublemaker. Thrown out of Norway for manslaughter, Erik was later twice banished from Iceland for similar crimes. On the second occasion, he sailed west in search of land that had been sighted some fifty years earlier by other Vikings, and he discovered an island larger than Iceland. It was even more rugged, but in the milder climate of the time, it too boasted grassy coastal hills and abundant fish and game. Erik optimistically named it Greenland, spent three years exploring it, and sailed back to Iceland to recruit settlers. The first colony, of some four hundred and fifty people, was established in 986.

One of the ships in Erik's fleet, blown off course, may have made the first Viking sighting of North America. Fifteen years later, Erik's son, Leif, a Christian convert recently returned from Norway with the first party of missionaries to Greenland, acted on this information. The Norse sagas detail Leif's voyage along the North American coastline, naming various regions as he sailed south—from Flatstone Land (Baffin Island) to Wood Land (Labrador), and eventually to the fabled Vinland (Wineland), where grapes and grain reportedly grew wild on a hospitable shore.[3]

Just how far south Leif, and those who followed, actually ventured remains a subject of debate, but excavations in the 1960s unearthed a Viking settlement of eight buildings at L'Anse-aux-Meadows on the northern tip of Newfoundland, confirming that the Northmen made it at least that far. They also made several subsequent attempts to establish a foothold in this new world, but hostile natives finally convinced them that their numbers were too few, and support and supplies too far away.

So the Norse abandoned their continental settlements, but not before Gudrid, the Christian wife of an expedition leader, gave birth to Snorri, the first recorded North American of European ancestry. Gudrid is believed to have returned safely from North America, incidentally, and there is even a story that in 1024, she visited Rome and was received by Pope Benedict VIII. Perhaps she regaled the pontiff with tales of Vinland.

Except for a few oblique references to Greenlanders visiting Wood Land in search of timber for their ships, there is just one more mention of Norse in North America. Eric Gnupsson, Bishop of

Greenland, reportedly sailed west a century later, in 1121, to revisit Vinland and preach the gospel. After that, both the bishop and North America disappear from Norse records.

However, Viking settlements in Greenland prospered for another two hundred years before beginning a long, steady decline to extinction. At its height, in the fourteenth century, Greenland's Norse population likely numbered around three thousand, but colder weather, ice-clogged seas, famine, and attacks by Inuit invaders of the Thule culture, advancing as relentlessly as the ice, apparently sealed the colony's fate.

In 1540, crewmen on a passing Icelandic merchant ship thought they glimpsed people on Greenland, but venturing ashore, they found only one emaciated corpse. In 1605, a Danish expedition was dispatched to discover the fate of the colonists, and could find hardly any trace of them. The last Greenland Vikings had died in lonely obscurity, had been carried off by the Inuit, or—as some believe—had disappeared into the vastness of North America. ∎

1. Viking settlers in western Greenland were told by the Inuit there that a group of strangers had long ago established themselves on the "opposite coast"—presumably meaning North America. They wore pale robes, the Inuit said, and walked in procession while singing in a peculiar fashion. There is also a very real possibility that the legendary voyage to North America of St. Brendan of Clonfert, in the sixth century, was not just legend (see earlier volume, *Darkness Descends*).

2. Popular assemblies were a feature of life among all the Germanic peoples of Europe, but particularly among the Vikings. Their assemblies ranged from farmers' gatherings to regional and national meetings, and those still in existence in Iceland, the Faeroes and the Isle of Man (in the Irish Sea) are among the world's oldest democratic institutions. In addition to destruction and bloodshed, the Vikings also spread the seeds of democracy.

3. The chronicler Adam of Bremen suggested in 1075 that grapes grew in Leif's Vinland, citing Svein Estridsson, king of the Danes, as the source of his information, but modern historians note that *vin* in Old Norse signified meadow or prairie. Since the Norse sagas were first written down some two centuries after the event, and more than a century after Latin-educated Adam, they may have repeated a mistaken assumption.

Gathered at the Althing parliament in the year 1000, Icelanders debate whether to abandon the ancient Norse gods in favor of the cross of Christ. Iceland would become the only country to embrace Christianity as the result of a democratic vote of its people.

TOM LOVELL NATIONAL GEOGRAPHIC

Tom
LOVELL

The Vikings' image has recently undergone a significant overhaul, with the murderous pirates now often transformed into fun-loving party animals. This Norwegian soccer fan (left), attending the women's soccer final between Norway and the United States at the 2000 Olympics in Sydney, Australia, wears a plastic helmet to emphasize her proud heritage. The Up Helly Aa Festival at Lerwick, in the Shetland Islands, has a much longer history, but these jolly make-believe Vikings (right) appear to be enjoying themselves. Even serious historians now emphasize the positive aspects of the spread of Viking culture, but it should not be forgotten that the Norse spread death and destruction across much of Europe, and posed a dire threat to developing Christendom.

turn on the faith they pretended to respect ... and take it out on the Christians." In Elnoth's own day, however, King Erik of Sweden organized a crusade aimed at conversion of the pagan Finns. But the Finns stubbornly clung to their own heritage that lay, not with the Vikings, but with Siberian peoples to the East. Not for another century and a half would Finland really accept Christian tutelage.[12]

A people less likely than the Scandinavians to accept the Prince of Peace would be difficult to imagine. Early Christians repeatedly noticed that Vikings, from kings to thralls, had genuine difficulty in appreciating either sympathy or remorse as virtuous. Historian Keary, in *The Vikings of Western Christendom*, cites the example of a leader who stopped his men from tossing captive children up in the air and playfully catching them on their spears. His men, who found his tenderheartedness eccentric, gave him the nickname "Börn" (meaning child).

Why did men of these inclinations yield to a religion that preaches love of God and care for fellow humans as a central principle? In part, Viking kings came to recognize that the medieval church hierarchy could be a useful, even crucial ally in organizing their free-spirited folk. But the immense upwelling of dedication to Christ across the Germanic peoples could hardly have been forced by royal decree. Fueling that surge was the figure of Jesus, presented as the god-man whose courage dwarfs the bravest warrior, the divine brother whose self-sacrifice surpasses the deepest motherly devotion, the Savior who will lead his church to final victory over all evil. As it happens, the English word hell descends from the Norse term Hel, the dead land ruled by the malignant trickster Loki. Scandinavia had had enough of Loki. They had found the truest Viking of them all. ∎

12. Unlike the Swedes, Norwegians and Danes, the Finns are not Scandinavians, but a Finno-Ugric people who speak a non-Germanic language. Their paganism centered on shamans, with strong elements of magic and spell-casting. Heathen practices survived into the late nineteenth century. Photographs of the last Finnish shamans in their bark and feather costumes look remarkably like North American aboriginal shamans of the same era.

The birth of the Norman French

A descendant of the Vikings, Duke William seized control of England, but he died regretting his 'rivers of blood' and his burial was macabre

The battle-hardened barons of Normandy must have had a few doubts in 1035 when their duke, Robert the Devil, presented them with his son and heir. How could their stormy duchy be governed by an eight-year-old boy, frail and sickly, the bastard son of a lowly tanner's daughter?[1] A century earlier, Viking freebooters had settled in the coastal province, and their descendants, though by now half-Frankish, Christian and French-speaking, had lost none of their ancestral ferocity. And Duke Robert insisted that William must rule. "He is little," Robert told his assembled chieftains, "but he will grow, and—if God please—he will mend." And so he did. William the Conqueror would seize and rule England, too, becoming in his era the most famed champion of Christendom's most effective fighting breed, the Normans.

Robert the Devil, after securing recognition for his son, made a pilgrimage to Jerusalem, but died along the way. His overlord, Henry I of France, brought William up in his own court. The prince devoured logic, geography, arithmetic and the classical languages, becoming brilliant at chess and gambling. He was also lucky, surviving many assassination attempts in his youth. In 1047, for example, a killer plunged a knife into a friend sleeping beside the young duke, but William himself remained unharmed.

Well-muscled, he also proved adept with the heavy weapons of the time. Legend claims that no other man could draw the great bow he carried into battle. He was equally strong of purpose.

1. Robert is said to have greatly loved William's mother Herleve, a gracious woman by all accounts. With his approval, Herleve married his friend Herluin of Conteville, thus achieving respectability. But William was touchy about his ignoble birth. When his men attacked Alencon, its citizens hung out animal skins, shouting, "Hides for the tanner!" When the duke took the town, he had its leaders skinned.

Scenes from the Bayeux Tapestry, now housed in a modern museum in Bayeux, France. This page (left), Harold at his coronation. One of the men on the left offers the crown, to the right is the archbishop of Canterbury and a group of admiring Saxons. (Right), The appearance of Halley's comet, an inauspicious omen, and a vignette of Harold and his advisor with their heads together, ghostly ships beneath them a portend of what's to come. (Following pages), The chaos of the Battle of Hastings, the bottom margin suggesting the toll of horses and troops. A group of Anglo-Saxons on a hill make a bold defense; two of their injured tumble down.

When he took control of his duchy, his immediate demand for complete obedience and administrative order triggered a baronial rebellion, but to his aid again came King Henry, in personal command of thousands of troops.

Across the English Channel (which the French prefer to call "La Manche," meaning "the Sleeve"), the lineage of Alfred the Great was about to fail. Edward the Confessor, pious and childless, had spent much time with William in their younger days, hunting and talking for hours on end. William claimed, without proof, that his close friend had promised him the English succession. The other major royal contender was Harold Godwinson, Earl of Wessex. By a twist of fate, Harold in his own youth had been shipwrecked on the Norman coast, and become the unwilling guest of its duke. To obtain his release, the prisoner may or may not have promised support for William's claim to the English throne.

When Edward died on January 5, 1066, Harold was immediately crowned at Westminster Abbey (which had itself been consecrated just eight days earlier). He was supposedly Edward's choice, and in any case, the powerful house of Wessex controlled four great fiefdoms. But hot-tempered William summoned his barons to a council of war and petitioned the pope for approval of his own claim. Pope Alexander II, over the reported opposition of some of the cardinals, blessed an invasion and consecrated a banner to be carried by the Norman army. (Blatant politics, say Alexander's critics; the Normans in Italy were allies of the papacy. Not so, say Alexander's defenders. The pope sought the ouster of the current archbishop of Canterbury, a notorious trader in church offices.)

By now, William had transformed Normandy into a realm of remarkable efficiency. Viking fashion, he organized his English campaign as a business enterprise, the prospect of loot and lands drawing volunteers from as far away as Italy and Denmark. Norman shipbuilders produced up to three thousand watercraft, led by Viking-style warships with dragon prows. The fleet sailed on September 27, 1066, with twenty-five thousand men on

board, prompting the English to flock into churches and pray for deliverance.

But Harold II simultaneously faced another threat, direct from the Viking homelands. His disgruntled brother Tostig, Earl of Northumberland, had decided to support a royal claim from the Norwegian king, Harald Hardrada ("Hard Ruler"). This former commander of the Byzantine Varangian Guard (see sidebar page 146) landed with an army of nine thousand in northeastern England. Harold, vowing to cede to Hardrada no more than "seven feet of good English earth" (i.e., for his burial), met them in battle at Stamford Bridge, near York, on September 25. Hardrada was killed; only twenty-seven ships from the Viking fleet of three hundred survived to return home.

Just three days later, the Norman fleet appeared off England's south coast. William ordered his troops to plunder and burn, remarking, "Harold will not stand by to see the England of the Saxons lighted by Norman firebrands." The Saxon monarch and his housecarls, his personal troops, slogged southward, gathering the southern militia as they marched. On October 14, the English assembled on Senlac Ridge, near the town of Hastings. The well-armored, orderly Normans advanced across marshes and meadows to the attack.

The invaders fared poorly at first, even fearing at one point that William himself had fallen. But then they feigned a retreat, prompting the less disciplined Saxon militia to break ranks and pursue them. The Norman duke rallied his troops for a counterattack, his mounted knights making bloody work of the Saxon infantry in more open country. Volleys of arrows decimated the English ranks, and Harold II reportedly died instantly when a shaft pierced his eye. His kinsmen and housecarls fought a heroic last stand, but as the day faded, the Battle of Hastings was lost.

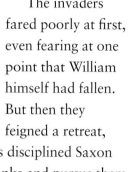

Harold died instantly when a Norman shaft plunged into his eye.

With its leader dead, England surrendered, and on Christmas Day at Westminster Abbey, the archbishop of York placed his country's crown on the head of the Norman duke. "I have conquered," declared William I. For the next two centuries, England's rulers would speak French.[2] The king kept ninety-five hundred manors (estates) for himself, and parceled out many others among his supporters. Powerful forts, including the Tower of London, sprang up to guard strategic locations, and Saxon resistance was stifled by unremitting butchery. The thoroughness of Norman administration was exemplified by the Domesday Book, a detailed census of population, land and goods, which facilitated taxes on the conquered population. Another tribute to Norman organization is the fact that England has never again suffered foreign conquest.

The church in England, still reeling from the Viking depredation, was rife with "pluralism, simony, lax observance of the canons, contented ignorance, worldliness in every aspect," writes British historian Sir Charles Oman (*History of England Before the Norman Conquest*). The Normans brought with them the reform spirit of Cluny and the great Frankish monasteries. Lanfranc, an Italian-born monk, theologian and former abbot in Normandy, became archbishop of Canterbury, and by 1070 only two Saxon bishops remained in office. Separate secular and religious courts were established, and Archbishop Lanfranc ran the government as William's regent when the king was absent (even bloodily squashing a Saxon revolt). Pope Gregory VII wrote approvingly that William, "though in certain respects not as religious as we would wish, still shows himself more acceptable than other kings.... He neither

2. By the time the Saxons and Normans merged into one people, French had contributed upwards of ten thousand words to the English language. These often reflect the Norman–Saxon class structure—with words like "beef" and "pork" from French, "cow" and "pig" from Anglo-Saxon. Naturally, such words as "government," "court" and "monarch" derived from French; along with, of course, "bureaucracy."

destroys nor sells the churches of God, and he binds priests by oath to dismiss their wives."

Yet the victor was not entirely blessed. The new French king, Philip, is said to have scoffed that William had grown so fat he looked pregnant. When war ensued, William fell in 1087, during an assault on the town of Mantes. The chronicler Ordericus Vitalis records the king's dying words: "I tremble, my friends, when I reflect on the grievous sins which burden my conscience, and now, about to be summoned before the awful tribunal of God, I know not what I ought to do. I was bred to arms from my childhood, and am stained from the rivers of blood I have shed…. It is out of my power to count all the injuries which I have caused."

He plainly knew that he would not be fondly remembered. In their rush to safeguard their own interests, his sons left his body unburied. Servants stripped the corpse and dumped it naked on the floor. A dispute over payment for his burial ground delayed the burial, and an arm fell off the decomposing body as it was lowered into the grave. Some five hundred years later, a party of Calvinists destroyed his tomb. A substantial new monument was built, and what could be found of William's remains—a single thighbone—was reinterred. Even this monument was destroyed in the French Revolution. The remains of England's last conqueror now rests beneath a simple stone slab in a church at Caen. ∎

TOM LOVELL, NATIONAL GEOGRAPHIC

Norman knights charge up Senlac Hill near Hastings on October 14, 1066. The Normans had adopted the use of heavy cavalry as the heart of their army, while the Saxon English still relied upon their traditional shield wall. Using a tactic well known to their Viking forebears, the Normans feigned retreat—and when the Saxons opened their shield wall to rush in pursuit, the outcome could not be in doubt. England's Saxon era was brought to a bloody conclusion, and a French-speaking Norse people became the new aristocracy of the island kingdom.

The Virgin Hodegetria (Indicator of the Way). Mary points to Jesus as the way to salvation, from the Icon Gallery, Ohrid, Macedonia.

CHAPTER 5

The veneration of icons sets Eastern Christians at war for 117 years

Icons preside at horse races and become godparents until a hero-emperor calls it idolatry, orders a purge, and thousands are slain and jailed defending them

mperor Leo III, "the Isaurian," was a magnificent soldier, accustomed to command. It was he who had so decisively defeated the enormous Muslim assault on Constantinople in 717, saving all Christendom from Islam. (See previous volume, *The Sword of Islam*, chapter 10.) It was he who then reformed Byzantium's tax code, military command structure, and rural, maritime and civil laws. And it was he, who like many soldiers, conscious of the narrow gap between life and death, would attribute his triumphs to Divine Providence, and give every evidence that he meant it.

Yet, when Leo contemplated the state of the church within his own empire, everything within him rebelled at what he saw. While the rural population slowly shrank, the monasteries were bloated and running wild. Hairy, wild-eyed monks, exempt from imperial service, would jump their cloister walls and stir mobs of women into pious frenzies. The monasteries, exempt from imperial taxes, were growing ever richer, charging ignorant peasants and craftsmen to kiss and caress their most revered icons.

To Leo, icons were mere paintings of Christian faces and depictions of Christian events, harmless in themselves, but being taken to the point of idolatry. Iconolatry, it might be called. As a child in the Isaurian Mountains near the

St. Luke, acknowledged as the first iconographer, creating the icon of the Virgin and Child. Tradition holds that Mary appeared to Luke and gave her blessing to the work. Abesalom Vujicic created this icon in the seventeenth century.

Syrian border, Leo had been exposed to Muslim and Jewish taunts that Christians were idolaters, worshiping "graven images."

Were these charges valid? Everywhere Leo looked, there were icons: icons of the Lord, icons of his mother, icons of countless saints; icons draping churches, in shops and homes, sewn to clothes or painted on drinking cups, furniture and trinkets; icons kissed and caressed, wreathed in garlands and candles, and lathered in incense smoke. People made icons godparents at their children's baptisms, scraped the pigment into cups as tonics for illnesses, and sang hymns to them. Icons presided at horse races. An icon of Christ dominated the Bronze Gate of Leo's own Sacred Palace. Icons were placed in the path of fires to prevent them spreading. Icons were paraded instead of spears, to defend the walls of a city. In the Divine Liturgy, the consecrated elements must touch an icon.

Thus in the ninth year of his rule, 726, Leo the Isaurian resolved to stop it. In so doing, he set off a 117-year crisis that would pit Christians against Christians, Asians against Greeks, the Eastern Church against the Western, and soldiers against women and monks. Tens of thousands of churchmen would be deposed, exiled or killed. It would see a revered empress blind her emperor son. Two emperors would be assassinated, one executed, two forcibly made monks, one killed by attacking barbarians who made a drinking cup of his skull. When it was all over, midway through the ninth century, icons would be formally reinstated, amidst great public rejoicing, an event annually celebrated by Orthodox Christians ever since. The whole affair would create "the most serious crisis that has ever attacked Eastern Christianity," says historian Henri Daniel-Rops (*The Church in the Dark Ages*), and from that day to this, the cause and fury of the conflict would remain largely incomprehensible to Western Christians.

This incomprehensibility, however, did not mean that the icon controversy was in any sense trivial or frivolous. When Leo III set the battle lines between "iconoclasts," who condemned the use of images in worship, and "iconophiles," who defended them, he raised a core doctrinal issue of Christianity: Can God be depicted in human terms? "Do not the Ten Commandments condemn the worship of graven images?" demanded the iconoclasts. "Yet even the Jews portrayed their religious history with images," replied the iconophiles. "And was not the whole point of God's becoming human to reveal himself in terms we could understand?" To which the iconoclasts replied: "Any attempt to portray Divine reality must of necessity be impossible and therefore blasphemous." And the iconophiles responded: "Words themselves are created by man and are used to portray God. Are they also blasphemous? Is the whole Bible therefore blasphemous?"

Christian art was hardly new, of course. In the catacombs, it appeared in symbols—Jesus Christ as a fish or lamb, the Holy Spirit as a dove—all codes to foil the authorities. This reticence began diminishing, however, after Constantine decreed public toleration of Christianity. Narrative pictures of the Holy Family, apostles and martyrs became common, even fashionable, by the late fourth century, although depictions of Christ alone were rare. One bishop, circa 400, who criticized the fad of embroidering gospel stories on clothing, was more troubled by the ostentation than the pious sentiments. Still, there was that seemingly uncompromising commandment: "Thou shalt not make unto thee any graven image, or any likeness of any thing that is in heaven above, or that is in the earth beneath, or that is in the water under the earth; thou shalt not bow down thyself to them or serve them" (Exodus 20:4–5).

Most Jewish and Christian theologians concluded that the commandment, in the full biblical context, prohibits only those images that are manufactured as the focal point of worship in themselves (i.e., blatant idolatry). God had approved, after all, the golden cherubim on the Ark of the Covenant, and the graven bullocks in Solomon's Temple. While not essential to salvation, images can play a constructive role in religious life, just as music or poetry. But both faiths were deeply concerned that any image-making not offend the second half of the commandment—that is, slide into

Clinging to terraces in a gorge in the Isaurian Mountains, the majestic remains of the fifth century Alahan Monastery have now been silent for fourteen hundred years. At one time on this site, there were two basilicas, living quarters, a cave church, a baptistery, and a necropolis. Monasteries frequently became refuges for iconophiles under Leo III.

idolatry. Fear that Christians might appear to be worshiping idols, for example, had caused a Spanish synod in 305 to ban any painting in a church.

The great Christological controversies of the fourth and fifth centuries, debating Christ's divine and human natures, sharpened the issue. Since Jesus of Nazareth was God Incarnate, his human form—and image—must constitute a legitimate vision of God. Furthermore, a great many people were illiterate. They depended on images because they could not read. So in 599, when the bishop of Marseilles tore the images from his churches, Pope Gregory I admonished him: "Pictures are the books of the illiterate. They should be permitted, though not worshiped." A council of 692 decreed that Christ ought always to be depicted in human form, not as a lamb, "so all may understand, by means of it, the depth of the humiliation of the Word of God."

In time, images of saints were venerated as well, and the most revered of all, in both East and West, were images of the mother of Jesus, known in the West as the Blessed Virgin Mary, and in the East as the Theotokos, the Bearer of God. Always, in both East and West, official church teaching was that the spiritual focus must be on the person represented, not the physical

The representation of Christ in icons reopened discussion of his nature. The Council of Trullo in 692 decreed that Christ must be depicted in his humanity, a reminder of his Incarnation. This icon of the "Holy Face" is located in the Tretyakov Gallery, Moscow.

artifact. Kissing a holy image, or bowing or genuflecting before it, signified only respect for the personage depicted, as one might reverence him or her in natural life. And only Jesus Christ himself may be actually worshiped—not his image, however beautiful or beloved.

As the centuries passed, a notable difference would develop between the art of Eastern and Western Christendom. Western artists, led by men like Raphael and Michelangelo, developed the naturalistic, representative style that became the glory of European art, and produced thousands of revered paintings and sculptures. In the East, meanwhile, three-dimensional representation was not allowed, so Eastern churches could contain no statues. God the Father, never having taken corporeal form, may not be depicted at all (though some Orthodox churches in North America have disregarded the rule). The Holy Spirit is usually shown as fire or a dove, both scriptural images. Jesus Christ and the Theotokos predominate, along with legions of equally stern saints, and angels of martial appearance. These austere, sometimes forbidding, severely stylized faces that gaze from church walls and ceilings baffle westerners. None looks precisely human—nor are they meant to—for Eastern icons have a purpose beyond instruction and beyond sentiment.

The iconic image, as the revered fathers of the church consistently explained, is a window through which may be perceived the reality of eternity and the presence of God. It is in representing the divine that it becomes sacred, not the paint and wood. Thus the making of an icon (which is called "writing" it, not "painting") is to be done by the "iconographer" with prayer, fasting and minimal stylistic change. "When depicted in an icon," wrote St. John Maximovitch of San Francisco[1], "the Savior must be [portrayed] so that we sense that he is a man, a real man, yet at the same time something more exalted than a man, that we not simply approach him as we approach a visitor or an acquaintance."

Whether in the East or West, however, such subtle distinctions are easily blurred, be it with the miracle-working icon of Jesus Christ at Edessa, the images

Images seemed real persons. In pious legends, they speak, move about like supernatural beings, still tempests, put evil spirits to flight and ward off diseases.

of the Virgin of Guadalupe, or even a much-venerated family Bible. In eighth-century Byzantium, this human inclination had evolved into a feverish piety that burst all bounds. Theologians then as later, writes historian Charles Diehl in *The Cambridge Medieval History*, "were accustomed to explain that the saint was mystically present in his image, and that respect paid to the image penetrated to the original, which it represented." But now, it seemed, "the populace no longer drew this distinction. To them, the images seemed real persons, and Byzantine history is full of pious legends in which images speak, act and move about like divine and supernatural beings … they stilled tempests, put evil spirits to flight, and warded off diseases."

The tendency, however, was not universal, and it became repulsive to those Christians having to contend with Islam. One of these was Leo III. The Muslim caliph himself, trying to persuade him that Islam was the true faith, had accused Christians of idolatry. The caliph did not convert Leo, of course, but he did succeed in convincing him that "image worship" was the main obstacle in converting Muslims and Jews to Christ.[2]

Now, within his empire, he saw the icon craze arousing the erratic enthusiasms of monks and women, feminizing the church and alienating the army. Most of his soldiers came from Armenia and Asia Minor, and sometimes seemed to respect their image-hating Muslim foes more than they did many Christian priests, at least in the matter of images. Unrest in the army was not something Leo could afford. As for the clergy, Patriarch Germanus of Constantinople was a confirmed iconophile, but many bishops, especially in Asia, were not. Then in 726, there came an incident that persuaded Leo to act. A volcano devastated the Aegean island of Thera, darkening the skies for days, writes the ninth-century chronicler, the monk Theophanes, and following that an earthquake shook Constantinople itself. Two such disturbances in close succession struck Leo as heavenly portents.

He began his reform by ordering the removal of icons that were receiving

1. St. John of Shanghai and San Francisco, born Michael Maximovitch in Kharkov, Russia, 1896, was an extreme Orthodox ascetic, and a man of action. For forty years, he reputedly slept just two hours nightly on the floor, ate one meal a day (except in Lent, when he often fasted completely) and went barefoot in the coldest weather. As bishop of Shanghai, he shepherded a large expatriate Russian flock through the Japanese occupation, and before the Chinese Communists took over, he arranged its entire evacuation to Australia and America. His body, found to be incorrupt when it was moved in 1994, is enshrined at the Cathedral of the Theotokos in San Francisco.

2. Among the most uncompromising of image-haters were the Manichaean dualist sects of Asia Minor, such as the Paulicians, who believed physical matter to be hopelessly infected with evil, and thus forbade images entirely. Particularly strong in Armenia, they too may have influenced Emperor Leo III. ("Paulician" in fact became a general iconophile slur against all iconoclasts.)

what he regarded as excessive public devotion, among them the greatly revered *Christos Antiphonetes* ("Christ the Responder"), which dominated the Bronze Gate of his own palace. This came like a declaration of war. While the soldier trying to remove it was still aloft, a crowd of frantic women gathered, yanked his ladder out from under him, and murdered the man. Although more guards were sent out, rioting spread. People were killed or mutilated, and many were jailed. The violence that would detonate again and again for more than a hundred years had begun.

Declaring himself the "high priest of the empire," Leo wrote to Rome, ordering Pope Gregory II to remove religious art from his churches, and to convene a synod that would forbid all image worship. Gregory replied that the emperor "ought not to concern himself with matters of faith, nor change the ancient doctrines of the church." He later expressed a pious hope that some demon might sufficiently torture Leo on this matter as to save his soul. Iconophile Greece and Christians in the Byzantine lands of Italy sided with the pope. The much-respected monk (and future saint) John of Damascus, residing in Muslim territory beyond reach of the emperor, plunged into the controversy. Calling iconoclasm "an abnormal fear of matter," he bombarded Constantinople with pro-icon pamphlets. The iconophile patriarch Germanus, who *was* within Leo's reach, was promptly deposed and replaced by Anastasius, a more cooperative ecclesiastic. By now, extreme iconoclasts were condemning as well the practice of praying to the saints to intercede with God. They believed that Christians must focus on Jesus Christ alone as the sole avenue to salvation.

Rome regarded Leo's ousting of Patriarch Germanus as a clear assault on the authority of the church. Pope Gregory convened a synod, as requested, but far from banning images, with Gregory's support, it proceeded to excommunicate all iconoclasts. Meanwhile, the rebellious Byzantine-held city of Ravenna in Italy opened its gates to the pope's allies, the barbaric Lombards. In southern Italy, the Calabrians lynched the imperial exarch, the emperor's representative, and the Duke of Naples. Pope Gregory refused to remit any further taxes to Byzantium, and had himself declared Duke of Rome. From now on, the pope would often act as its secular lord, supported by the rising power of the Franks. Although over the next year the emperor regained control of southern Italy, Rome itself remained beyond him. He had to content himself with confiscating the papal possessions in Sicily, Calabria and Illyricum.

All this notwithstanding, Leo's official anti-icon measures remained relatively mild. He continued to suppress their public use, and replaced Christ's portrait on coins with his own. He closed iconophile church schools. (One was torched, some claimed, with a

Being a safe distance from Constantinople, John of Damascus's residency in the caliphate gave him greater freedom to speak, which he zealously utilized to oppose the emperor, Leo the Isaurian, on his iconoclast position. This portrayal of John of Damascus is Russian, of the Novgorod School.

dozen clerics inside). Above all, he patiently packed the church hierarchy with iconoclast bishops. Nevertheless, at his death in 740, the iconoclast war was well under way. It would divide into two phases. The first, conducted over a seventy-six-year period, pitted Leo and his immediate successors against the monks and iconophiles. The victor was the empress Irene, who had declared herself to be both empress and emperor. The second phase raged in the ensuing forty-one years of political chaos that Irene left behind her, during which seven emperors ruled. One died in battle, two were assassinated, and two were deposed as incompetent. Only two died in bed. It was finally won for the iconophiles by the empress Theodora.

With the accession of Leo's twenty-two-year-old son, there came radical change. Like his father, Constantine V would become an able general and administrator, campaigning successfully against Muslims, Slavs, and Bulgars, improving Constantinople's water supply, and forcibly resettling the city after a terrible plague. Unlike his father, he was widely hated and widely jeered. At

Pope Gregory told Leo to stop meddling in matters of faith, and he expressed the pious hope that a demon would torture him enough about this to save his soul.

baptism, the infant Constantine had supposedly defecated in the font, an ominous sign that won him the nickname *Copronymus* (literally, dung-named, or dung-christened). Obsessed with horses and riding, he was also mocked as *Cabillinus* (Stable Boy). And though he married a Khazar princess, writes Edward James Martin in *A History of the Iconoclastic Controversy*, "he cannot be completely acquitted of the accusation of sodomy." He derived from his religious education a belief in a single and transcendent God, not unlike Islam's,[3] and became a convinced iconoclast, particularly contemptuous of any veneration of the Virgin. "Mary gave birth to Christ as my mother gave birth to me," he bluntly told the patriarch, and on another occasion mused: "Of what value is a wooden box that once held gold?"

Constantine began his reign with a fight. His brother-in-law seized control of Constantinople, promising to restore the holy images. Constantine besieged the city, starved it into submission, and blinded the usurper. He had the aged patriarch Anastasius, who had weakly supported the takeover, flogged and paraded naked in the amphitheater, seated backwards on an ass—then contemptuously left him in office. Soon he had largely succeeded in clearing Byzantium of religious imagery. Most icons surviving from his reign or earlier come from Muslim territory.

When Anastasius died in 753, Constantine called a church council at Hiera, near the capital, attended by 338 iconoclast bishops, none representing Alexandria, Antioch, Jerusalem or Rome. The council observed that any image of Jesus Christ would necessarily portray him as either divine or human.

3. Whether or not Leo III and his son Constantine V were attracted by the simplicity of Muslim doctrine, writes Alice Gardner (*Theodore of Studios*), they had seen in battle how "a religion without asceticism, without external symbols, without saint-worship or religious orders, possessed a power ... [that] enabled ordinary men to forego private inclinations and face imminent death."

The mysterious practice of iconography

These ancient images are not said to be painted but 'written,' after fasting and prayer, and viewing them is intended to enable the Holy Spirit to act upon the soul of the viewer

Icons are two-dimensional images depicting Jesus, Mary and the saints. They are said to be "written," not drawn or painted, and the images do not reflect merely human personality. Rather, say Eastern Christians, the Holy Spirit expresses divine truth through the artist, whose labor is a form of prayer. That's why icons must adhere to certain formalities of color, design, pattern and gesture. The images are not strictly realistic but representational, even abstract. Similarly, a Christian who views an icon should do so as a form of prayer, enabling the Holy Spirit to act upon his soul through the figure. It is in this spiritual purpose, not in the paint and wood, that the sanctity of icons lies. They are regarded as "windows to heaven." Iconography spread from Constantinople to Russia, Greece and the Balkans, with some variations in regional style. Two monks, one in his workshop in a Finnish monastery (1) and a second in Cyprus (2), remind us that monasteries are the natural habitat for iconographers, who prepare for their task by prayer, fasting and study. Many monks help to maintain their monasteries through the sale of their work. A visual reminder of prayer and of the closeness of Christ and his saints in the lives of the faithful, these icons are for sale in a sidewalk stall in Crete (3). A Cypriot monk (4) displays the icon he has painted of St. Nectarius. The name of the person depicted is always identified, as in the top right corner of this icon. Museum displays, such as this one in Athens (5), infuse an appreciation for iconography in the curious and the devout from all over the world. ∎

Therefore, since neither one would represent his full nature, any attempt to depict him must by definition be misleading. Prayer to the Virgin and other saints for intercession should be allowed, it was decreed at Hiera, but any veneration of images was idolatry. It would now be considered heresy, and deserving of death. But the iconoclastic victory proved illusory. Acts of defiance kept recurring—like that of the lone monk who crept into the palace to denounce Constantine as an apostate to his face, earning himself death by flogging.

In Greece, being predominantly an Orthodox nation, hand painted icons are for sale everywhere, as in this Athens' street market. Icons adorn the walls of churches and homes of Orthodox faithful; many people have small icons in their cars and offices as well, a constant reminder of the presence of Christ.

Furious, the emperor began an all-out war against the monastic celibates, who together with women were the most stubborn iconophiles. In 764, he forced the patriarch to take a wife. His army made free with clubs and torches against what he termed "idolaters worthy only to be forgotten." One abbot, seen reverencing an icon, was torn limb from limb. Monks in chains were herded into amphitheaters, spat upon, and forced to parade hand-in-hand with giggling harlots. Monks' nostrils were slit, their tongues cut out. They were tied into sacks and tossed into the sea.

Iconophiles by tens of thousands fled westward beyond Byzantine jurisdiction, while in Constantinople, the emperor cracked down harder. He instituted an iconoclast oath, backed by blindings and executions, to thoroughly purge his army and administration. He installed as patriarch an almost illiterate

Slavic eunuch. Prayers to saints were prohibited outright, and even common exclamations like "Mother of God!" In Thrace, hundreds of monks and nuns were ordered to marry or be blinded; most submitted, but not all. On Cyprus, monks' beards were soaked in wax and set aflame, so that their last struggling breaths seared their lungs. At Ephesus, thirty-eight elderly contemplatives were buried alive under a public latrine. Theophanes claims that the emperor congratulated the prefect responsible for that barbarity as "a man after my own heart."

Such savagery turned the public against the emperor, and cast doubt on his thinking. "It revolted the common sense of the day to think that Christ was inaccessible to the prayers of his mother," writes historian Martin. Despite the peril, many women remained faithful to their well-loved traditions. Constantine's own daughter, Anthusa, hid icons within the palace. Jailers' wives brought icons to shackled monks. Some women turned viciously on the army, once catching a soldier alone and tearing him limb from limb. But as an administrator, ruler and general, Constantine could not be faulted. When he died in 775, after reigning thirty-four years, he left his empire with a well-filled treasury and mastery over external foes on every front.

His son Leo IV, called Leo the Khazar because of his mother's ancestry, inherited his father's religious outlook, but not his ferocity, and was moreover frail in constitution. Though the iconoclast laws remained on the books, the persecution slackened. Leo even restored the Eastern practice of limiting the office of bishop to celibate monks, but it was his wife who would prove the supremely effective defender of the icons. Her name was Irene.

She was an Athenian, fifteen at her marriage, almond-eyed, olive-skinned, hauntingly beautiful, and possessed of a razor-sharp mind. The imperial pair produced a son, and soon after their coronation, Irene persuaded her husband to crown the boy co-emperor. Later on, however, when Leo found icons in Irene's apartments, he coldly banned her from the imperial bed. Moreover, as his health began to fail, Leo's iconoclast patriarch played on his conscience, so that suddenly imperial offices were being searched, many icons discovered, and officials by the dozen beaten and dragged through the streets to prison.

But the violence came to an abrupt end. Leo died in 780, and Irene became regent for Constantine VI, then ten years old.[4] She immediately halted the persecution. Iconophiles ecstatically hailed her as the "lionhearted, God-fearing woman" who had valiantly championed their cause. Monks streamed from the prisons, and the *Christos Antiphonetes* was returned to its place above the Bronze Gate. But the army—still iconoclast—did not share in the rejoicing. These things, grumbled the senior officers, were being done by a woman—and not only by a woman, but by an idolater. Their first coup attempt came within six weeks, but Irene's agents discovered it. The conspirators were flogged and banished, and a military revolt in Sicily was crushed.

She looked westward for help, betrothing her son to Charlemagne's oldest daughter, and writing in conciliatory tones to Rome to propose an ecumenical council on the icon issue. Pope Adrian I cautiously agreed to send legates, and

4. The monk-chronicler and militant iconophile Theophanes claimed that Leo IV so coveted jewels that he appropriated to himself a spectacular crown on display behind the altar of Hagia Sophia. Through wearing it, he broke out in boils and this caused his death. That the iconoclasts refuted the claim is altogether likely, but none of their writings survived the controversy.

Theodore of Studion, defender of icons and the first patron saint of Venice, is seen atop this column by every tourist who visits St. Mark's Square in the heart of the city. The column, a symbol of early Venice's strong alliance to the Byzantine Empire, was raised in 1172 after reportedly being stolen from Constantinople.

two deacons slipped quietly out of Egypt through the Muslim blockade to speak for the patriarchs of Jerusalem, Antioch and Alexandria. But the council, meeting in Constantinople, got off to a bad start. Soldiers of the imperial guard burst into the hall at the opening session, bellowing, "Death to monks and idolaters!" As the swords began to flash, however, a number of iconoclast bishops who were in attendance, mistakenly concluding that this show of military threat would secure their victory without actual bloodshed, jostled the warriors from the hall with glad cries of, "We have conquered! We have conquered!" The iconophile majority then prudently suspended proceedings.

Irene had appointed eunuchs to key administrative posts in her government, headed by the cunning Stauracius as her chief executive. He now dealt with the imperial guard, dispatching this elite regiment on a supposed Asian campaign. Once it was well away from the city, he dismissed all its members, and recruited half-trained Slavs to replace them in the capital.

What was to become Christianity's Seventh Ecumenical Council reconvened safely at nearby Nicea in 787. Here the iconoclast bishops crumbled completely, recanting their prior opinions and begging to retain their offices.[5] Despite the bitterness of many monks, who had not forgotten their agonies, Irene's politically astute patriarch (her former chancellor, Tarasius) insisted on reconciliation. There must be no counter-persecution. However, the council unanimously condemned iconoclasm, rejecting it as akin to Manichaeanism, Judaism and Islam. Holy images of Christ and saints were approved for display anywhere they might spiritually profit God's people. God could be worshiped through an icon of Jesus Christ. Saints, too, could be venerated through their icons.

At this point, however, Irene revealed the other side of her character, a naked political ambition—with her own son as her rival. She had kept Constantine VI, now seventeen, unloved and unschooled. Soon she canceled his betrothal to Charlemagne's daughter, substituting a pretty Armenian girl, a clear signal that

5. The monk-historian Theophanes reportedly attended the Seventh Ecumenical Council at Nicea in 787, "in a coat of hair, with his shepherd's staff in his hand." His attendance had to be compelled by his superiors, because, it was said, Theophanes so hated meetings.

nothing must threaten his mother's dominance. His despair curdling into resentment, he plotted the arrest of Stauracius. When Irene found out, she tortured and banished his confederates, publicly slapped Constantine, then had him thrashed and confined to his chambers. "God does not want your son to reign," Stauracius assured her. So she decreed that her name must precede Constantine's on all imperial documents, and required every soldier to swear: "So long as you live, we will never accept your son as emperor."

Now she had gone too far. The Armenian troops mutinied, declaring Constantine their emperor, and the entire army followed, compelling her to release her son. So the roles reversed. Irene was confined to her private palace, Stauracius was flogged and banished, and in a brief glory, Constantine VI received the raucous homage of his army. But as a general, he failed conspicuously. With the army weakened by the conflict, he lost ground quickly to both the Muslims and Bulgars. Within a year he allowed Irene, followed by Stauracius, to return to court, where with subtle slanders they turned this weak young man against the Armenian general who had helped put him in power. The blinding of this officer cost him the army's support. New conspiracies erupted with increasing violence. Disaffection spread.

A Byzantine era icon of the angel Gabriel at the Annunciation. Egg tempera paint, used for brilliance and luminosity, is applied to a prepared wooden surface; paint and varnish can add up to thirty layers, allowing the icon to last for centuries. Gold leaf or gold or silver casings may enhance the finished icon.

Lured on by his mother, Constantine now divorced his Armenian wife in order to marry a lovely young woman named Theodote, a member of a particularly devout and orthodox family. Patriarch Tarasius, aghast at this unlawful divorce, refused to perform the wedding. When the emperor threatened to adopt iconoclast policies, Tarasius permitted a lesser ecclesiastic to marry the couple, but the divorce and second marriage cost Constantine the support of the more zealous religious, including members of the empress's own family.

It was this extraordinary family of Constantine's new wife Theodote, however, that now entered the story, epitomizing the steadfast, self-sacrificial heroism that would cause the ultimate iconophile triumph. The family had a curious history. Early in the eighth century, a plague had orphaned a sister and brother at Constantinople, Theostica and Plato. In destitution, they educated themselves, learning to read, studying the Christian faith and putting it into practice. Despite her poverty, Theostica found a loving husband high in the ranks of the civil service. Her brother Plato also reached the senior echelons of the imperial administration. But the brother abandoned this comfortable life, became a monk in the desert, then with his sister, her husband and their four children formed a Christian community in the wilderness. One of the four children was destined to play a decisive role in the iconoclast controversy.

He is known as Theodore of Studion, and by the reign of Constantine VI, he and his uncle Plato had become the two most respected monks in all Byzantium. They defiantly disapproved of both the emperor's divorce and his illegitimate marriage to their young cousin Theodote. Declaring that kings are not above God's laws, they refused to even meet with Constantine when he waited upon them in a monastery vestibule. The emperor responded by having both men beaten and jailed. On August 15, 797, guards loyal to Irene seized Constantine VI. Upon his mother's orders, his eyes were gouged out in the Purple Chamber, his birthplace twenty-seven years earlier. Some sources say the deposed monarch survived another two decades, a husk of a man haunting the back halls.[6] His second wife, Theodote, was immured in a convent, as his first wife had been.

As for Irene, she now proclaimed herself not merely empress, but emperor. She believed in the value of charm. She charmed the people by parading in shimmering purple through the capital, scattering coins. She charmed the monks by recalling Theodore and Plato and expelling the priest who had officiated at Constantine's second wedding. And she charmed everybody by recklessly remitting taxes for five years. Everybody, that is, but the army. To charm it, she would have had to deliver victory on the battlefield, something she singularly failed to do. So the soldiers remained restive, and as her health began to fail, the palace eunuchs (chief among them Stauracius, whose incessant conniving was finally thwarted by his death) hatched plots within plots to seize power.

Then as she approached the age of fifty, there occurred the unexpected. Frankish envoys arrived with a proposal of marriage from Charlemagne himself, uniting the two imperial crowns. She accepted eagerly. The Byzantine aristocracy was appalled. To them, Charlemagne was little more than the tribal chief of a barbarian dynasty in the hinterland. Was this German aboriginal, they fumed, to rule all Christendom? Were they to be vassals to a savage? The end came swiftly. Even as the marriage contract was being drawn up, Irene was arrested on October 31, 802. Her chancellor, an aristocrat named Nicephorus, had himself crowned Emperor Nicephorus I the General Logothete, by the pliant patriarch Tarasius. "Pious Irene, lover of God," as she was still praised by the monks, was exiled to an Aegean island, where she was required to spin wool until she died eight months later. Thus ended the dynasty of Leo the Isaurian and phase one of the iconoclast struggle.

The new emperor Nicephorus I began by tackling the financial problems left by Irene, raising taxes and making himself very unpopular in the process. Meanwhile, the power struggle between palace and church intensified. Determined to demonstrate his ascendancy, Nicephorus demanded reinstatement of the hapless priest who had performed the second marriage of Constantine VI. Theodore of Studion stood firmly opposed, and thereby earned himself another month in jail.[7] Then Nicephorus became bolder. He convened a synod, which dutifully declared that Constantine's second marriage was legitimate, that emperors were above church laws, and that all dissenters with this view must be excommunicated.

It was open war with the monks, and here something had been occurring of which Nicephorus was unaware. A new and powerful spirit of self-sacrifice had ignited within the monastic movement, and a stream of eager Christians were

6. Some records claim that Constantine VI died from the blinding. Others indicate that Irene's successor had the victim brought to the Sacred Palace well over a decade later, to pump him for information about where his mother had hidden her treasure, and that he told all.

7. Theodore of Studion has been criticized for staying silent on Irene's blinding of her son Constantine, while storming about the "scandal" of his second marriage. But Irene never demanded ecclesiastical approval for the blinding. Following the reasoning of St. Paul in Romans 14:20–21, "scandal" in theological terms is not defined simply as sin, but as any action, even an innocent one, or a failure to act, that is likely to induce another person to do something that is morally wrong.

A tree by persecution pruned

*The value Eastern Christians ascribe to icons is not easily explained,
say their theologians, because the phenomenon must be experienced,
rather than understood. Perhaps John Betjeman, poet laureate of
Britain from 1972 until his death in 1984, came closest in his
enchanting description of a Greek Orthodox church.*

The domed interior swallows up the day.
Here, where to light a candle is to pray,
The candle flame shows up the almond eyes
Of local saints, who view with no surprise
Their martyrdoms depicted upon walls
On which the filtered daylight faintly falls.
The flame shows up the cracked paint—sea-green blue
And red and gold, with grained wood showing through—
Of much-kissed ikons, dating from, perhaps,
The fourteenth century....

Thus vigorously does the old tree grow,
By persecution pruned, watered with blood,
Its living roots deep in pre-Christian mud,
It needs no bureaucratical protection.
It is its own perpetual resurrection.

The Triumph of Orthodoxy is the subject of this icon, a celebration of the church's victory over the iconoclasts. The Theotokos (Mary) is flanked by the chief players in the struggle to restore the use of icons: a regal Theodora and the young emperor Michael III on the left, and Patriarch Methodius of Constantinople and three monks on the right. Bishops, monks and a nun display icons below.

dedicating themselves to the celibate life. The spark for this revival was Theodore. In the iconophile peace of Irene's five-year reign, he had returned from exile and revived Constantinople's Monastery of Studion, which had been emptied by the persecutions of Constantine Copronymus. Its discipline was now based upon prayer, manual labor and study, all with strict accountability. Fully seven hundred monks belonged to the famous monastery. It became the center and model of Eastern monasticism, says *The Oxford Dictionary of the Christian Church*, including the monasteries of Mount Athos.

So the Studites declared their rejection of Nicephorus's council, Theodore further angering his sovereign by appealing to the bishop of Rome as the "first of pastors." He and his aging uncle Plato were again imprisoned, and the Studite monks either jailed or scattered. The army, according to Theophanes, was encouraged "to use bishops and clerics like slaves."

But the emperor's foreign enemies were not so easily subdued. The Muslims took Cyprus and Crete, and in 811, Nicephorus died in a campaign against the Bulgar khan Krum, who commemorated his victory by casting a silver-lined memorial cup, made of the skull of the late emperor. In the pandemonium that followed, two emperors, Nicephorus's son and his son-in-law, were enthroned and deposed for incompetence within two years. Krum meanwhile pressed Constantinople hard, offering peace only on condition that the masses of Thracian refugees in the capital be turned over to him to become slaves. Byzantine authorities would have complied, but one voice dissuaded them. It was Theodore's. He quoted St. John's Gospel: "Whoever comes to me, I will by no means cast out" (6:37). The generals acceded. They believed the Bible.

It was the army in Asia that produced the next emperor, Leo V, known as the Armenian. Swarthy, curly-bearded and energetic, he led rapidly reorganized troops to victories against the Bulgars. Krum's death in 814 ended that war. But the war over the icons blazed up anew. Leo was an iconoclast, and promptly restored the laws against images. In protest, on Palm Sunday, 815, Theodore led a thousand Studites in procession, bearing icons and singing, "We venerate your sacred images, blessed saints." Leo responded with a judiciously selected synod that declared icons "mere idols." Soldiers stoned the *Christos Antiphonetes* over the Bronze Gate, and Leo removed it "for safekeeping."

Back to prison went Theodore, where he wrote hundreds of letters, some in cipher, exhorting the faithful to stand firm. (Patrician ladies reportedly helped smuggle them out.) Leo repeatedly ordered him lashed, but only one warden is said to have actually carried out the order. Other monks were tortured or executed, however, and many—counseled by Theodore to avoid martyrdom whenever possible—went into exile. Meanwhile, Leo V freely reinstated iconoclast priests and abbots. His network of informers weeded out iconophiles, bringing men and women alike under the lash. Then in 820, the rule of Leo V ended in a suitably horrific climax.

Leo uncovered a plot by a fellow general called Michael the Stammerer. The appropriate penalty, he decided, was to skewer the offender on a spit, together with a monkey, and roast the two of them in the palace furnace. But it was nearly Christmas, scarcely an appropriate time for executions, however novel, said his

The emperor grabbed a cross from the altar and started swinging. 'Time for killing, not sacraments,' snarled an assailant, and Leo was murdered in the cathedral's holiest part.

wife, who persuaded him to postpone the gruesome event over the holiday. The delay proved fatal. Through his priestly confessor, Michael told his fellow conspirators that they'd better rescue him or he'd see that they joined him. Thus on Christmas morning, while the emperor Leo was at the Divine Liturgy, several men vested as priests appeared with drawn swords. The iconoclast monarch ran to the altar, grabbed its large gold cross and started swinging it in self-defense. "Time for killing, not sacraments," snarled one assailant, and Leo V was thereupon hacked to pieces in the holiest part of the cathedral. Michael the Stammerer, brought from prison with feet still fettered, was proclaimed Emperor Michael II.

Michael II came from Amoria in Asia Minor, where he had been raised amid the eclectic doctrines of a fringe Jewish sect.[8] His sole religious concern seems to have been with public conformity. He first declared an amnesty, and the monks joyfully proclaimed him "a new David," but then he unilaterally appointed a new patriarch. When the pope protested, the emperor had the man who brought the papal message, a monk named Methodius, flogged and jailed. Theodore of Studion asked that public icons be restored, and Michael refused; they would be tolerated only in private. He formally requested the Frankish emperor, Charlemagne's son Louis, to destroy all religious images in Rome—which Louis (known as "the Pious") could not do, and in any event, presumably would not.

The Eastern empire began to roil into almost hallucinogenic anarchy. One of Emperor Michael's supporters, Thomas the Slav, claimed to be Irene's son, Constantine VI, defender of the holy images, with his sight miraculously restored, and was crowned patriarch of Antioch. This caused a massive peasant revolt in Asia Minor. Rebel forces besieged Constantinople for a full year, until the Bulgars attacked again, dealing a deathblow to the insurgency. Michael II then cornered the last hold-outs, and impaled and dismembered Thomas.

8. The idiosyncratic interpretations of the Bible favored by Emperor Michael II must have caused his ecclesiastical advisers much head shaking. Among other things, he reportedly believed Christ's betrayer Judas to have been saved, on the assumption that "Judas" meant "Jew." And he refused to believe in Satan, because the devil was not mentioned in the Mosaic books.

The final act of the icon controversy now began to unfold, and women again would play the key roles. The wife of Michael II, mother of his son Theophilus, had died during the Bulgar siege. Seeking legitimacy, Michael II now insisted upon marrying Euphrosyne, daughter of Constantine VI and the last blood descendant of Leo the Isaurian. The emperor saw no detriment in the fact that this woman was a nun, and despite vehement protest from Theodore and the Studites, the marriage took place. It was Theodore's last protest. He did not live to see the icon controversy settled. In 826, at sixty-seven, he died in exile on the Black Sea coast, surrounded by brethren chanting from Psalm 119: "Princes sit and speak against me, but your servant meditates upon your statutes."

Michael II died peacefully three years later, and was succeeded by his son Theophilus, sixteen.[9] The boy had been thoroughly versed in iconoclast theology, but it was Euphrosyne who made the move that would prove decisive. She herself probably had little or no personal choice in either making or breaking her vows as a nun. In any case, she was a devout Christian and also a believer in the veneration of icons. It was she who set up and supervised the bridal contest to find a wife for her stepson.[10] All the candidates were of course beautiful, but one was far more stunning than the rest, and the young emperor unerringly chose her. As Euphrosyne well knew, she was an ardent iconophile. Her name was Theodora.

9. All the other plotters behind Michael II came to a sudden and violent end in the reign of his son Theophilus. At a public assembly in the Hippodrome, Theophilus held aloft the gold altar cross with which Leo V had tried to defend himself, and posed a question. What punishment, he demanded, should befall those who smite God's appointed monarch in God's house? "Death!" roared the crowd—so Theophilus executed his father's allies.

10. One of the key functions of the beauty contests held from time to time to choose a bride for an emperor, writes historian Judith Herrin in *Women in Purple*, "was to keep the provincial families vying ... Even the poorer members of the provincial aristocracy, every mother and a good many fathers, must have hoped that their daughter's beauty would result in fame and fortune for the entire family."

Her influence was certainly not immediate. Emperor Theophilus made the fervid and articulate iconoclast John the Grammarian patriarch, and began another violent persecution. He had the hands of an icon-maker named Lazarus grilled on hot metal plates. He summoned prominent iconophiles, and alternately debated with them in his palace or had them chained in his dungeons. To win these debates was dangerous. When two Palestinian monks caught him misquoting Isaiah, he had the misquoted lines tattooed on their faces. He had Methodius, the papal messenger who had been flogged and jailed, brought from his prison cell to argue the iconophile case. The manufacture of Christ's image demeaned Christ's dignity, declared the emperor. If so, countered the courageous monk, the emperor's dignity would be enhanced by banning his own image, too. This earned Methodius six hundred lashes, applied slowly.

Nevertheless, in his thirteen-year reign, Theophilus became an effective administrator and an impressive patron of the arts.[11] Although he remained a determined iconoclast; he was surrounded by devoted iconophile women—his stepmother Euphrosyne, his mother-in-law, his wife Theodora—plus his five daughters. When he died in 842 (from dysentery), Empress Theodora became regent for their son Michael, then two.[12] With iconoclasm seemingly fading in the army, Theodora shunted John the Grammarian into retirement and the courageous Methodius became patriarch. Then she summoned what the chronicles call "a divine and holy synod," and had to plead with it not to condemn her beloved husband. On his deathbed, she swore, the repentant emperor had venerated a holy image. The assembled ecclesiastics swallowed their

11. The emperor Theophilus filled his palace with marble pavilions inset with golden mosaics. A tree of gold shaded the imperial throne. Golden lions and griffins, jewel-encrusted, guarded it. When foreign ambassadors entered the throne room, the golden birds in the tree fluttered and sang. The griffins sat up on their pedestals. The lions rose, lashed the air with their tails, and uttered metallic roars. It left such visitors awestruck.

12. Theodora's eunuch-dominated domestic administration seems to have been competently managed, and she skilfuly directed foreign policy except in one instance, a serious one. She ordered a persecution of Byzantium's onetime allies, the iconoclast Paulicians, on the Syrian border. After many of them died in Armenia, the Paulicians went over en masse to the Muslims, and became a constant thorn in the empire's eastern border.

To this day, the restoration of icons is celebrated in the Orthodox Church on the first Sunday in Lent. Churches have colorful processions with icons and banners, such as this one depicted in a nineteenth-century painting by Ilya Repin, Religious Procession in the Province of Kursk.

doubts, and refrained from anathematizing the late emperor Theophilus.

So on the first Sunday in Lent in the year 843, a date celebrated ever since by the Holy Orthodox Church as the Sunday of Orthodoxy, the empress Theodora, her imperial son Michael and the scarred patriarch Methodius led a solemn procession of holy icons into Hagia Sophia. With his damaged hands, the iconographer Lazarus restored the *Christos Antiphonetes* to its place above the Bronze Gate of the palace, where it would remain for another six hundred years.

Patriarch Methodius then rid the church of hundreds of iconoclast bishops and abbots in a purge so thorough (although relatively bloodless) as to settle the issue once and for all in Eastern Christendom. Back from his Black Sea exile came the revered bones of Theodore of Studion, to lie in honor beside his valiant relative, Plato. Back, too, were brought the bones of the more questionable Irene, for interment in the imperial crypt. Her sins seemingly were black, but her defense of the holy images would earn her canonization. The emperor Michael III, last of the line, would be assassinated. (See following sub-chapter.)

Was this preservation of icons worth one hundred and seventeen years of bloodshed and appalling cruelty? And what of the iconoclasts? They too fought from Christian conviction. Eastern theologians firmly agree that the battle was worth fighting and the outcome satisfactory. The icon question touched on the central Christian claim, they say, that God actually and literally "became flesh." St. Paul wrote that Jesus Christ was "the image of the Father" (II Cor. 4:4), undoubtedly basing this claim on the Lord's own words: "He who has seen me has seen the Father" (John 14:9). Thus it follows that human art can portray, however inadequately, this image of God, and, as lovers know, to venerate the image is to reverence the beloved.

Moreover, thanks to Theodore of Studion and his many allies, the monastic movement emerged from the violence as the disciplined core of the Eastern church, a role its monks continue to maintain. The church became "not only stronger, but purer for the conflict," concludes historian Diehl.

Nevertheless, say its critics, iconoclasm was both imposed and repudiated on imperial authority. Thus the whole controversy was an exercise in "caesaro-papism," the subservience to state authority of which the Eastern church is chronically accused. Against this charge, its defenders merely point to the hundreds of thousands of Christian martyrs under emperors, caliphs, khans, sultans, czars and commissars over the centuries. Their blood, they say, refutes the criticism. ■

As well as standing alone, icons may also adorn liturgical vestments, banners and church vessels. Enameled icons of Christ and the saints embellish this Byzantine chalice, from the treasures of St. Mark's, Venice.

The clay heart of a golden era

While intrigue, betrayal, dalliance and murder grip the imperial household Byzantium soars to cultural heights unequalled in the contemporary world

The emperor Michael was drunk—nothing notable about that. He swilled himself into a stupor that September evening in the year 867, at a great feast laid for him in the sumptuously decorated banqueting hall of the Palace of St. Mamas in Constantinople. During this revel, few noticed one lanky, heavily muscled, sinister figure steal quietly from the hall. He made his way to the emperor's chambers, and deftly crowbarred the heavy bolts on the doors so that they could not be locked. Then he inconspicuously returned. Michael was drowsy now and nodding, babbling that it was time for bed. All rose as the emperor stumbled from the hall.

Soon the conspirator left too, and joined eight colleagues to complete the evening's work, notably the assassination of Michael III, emperor of Byzantium, also known as "Michael the Drunkard." For security, Byzantine emperors never slept alone, and tonight Michael's longtime drinking companion Basiliscianus was on duty. Basiliscianus had noticed the damaged bolts, and was lying uneasily awake when the door opened to admit the nine assassins, headed by the dark man. Basiliscianus leaped for his sword, but one conspirator ran him through. Another approached the snoring emperor and struck off both his hands. Blood spurted over the royal bedsheets. A third man, with one plunging stab, ended the life of Michael the Drunkard.

All now looked to the tall, dark leader, their designated candidate for the imperial throne: Basil I, called the Macedonian. Thus with a bloody murder began the Macedonian dynasty, and with it the "Golden Age" of Byzantium's twelve-century history. Basil had planned carefully. Within a week, the Senate, the nobles, the army, and the people (represented by the mob in the Hippodrome) unanimously acclaimed him as autocrat over what in the succeeding two centuries would become the world's most magnificent and mighty empire, unequalled even by the much larger Muslim empire on its eastern flank.

Basil's domain was a preeminently Christian one, where rich and poor alike accepted with profound belief the person of Jesus Christ, his teachings, the doctrines derived from them, and orthodox ecclesiastical authority. Churches by the thousand were packed on Sundays and great feast days. Every district had its monastery, tens of thousands of monks and nuns devoting their lives to Christ's work. From the magnificent churches of the capital— Hagia Sophia (Holy Wisdom), Holy Apostles, Saints Sergius and Bacchus— precious icons were carried in colorful, chanting processions for all to venerate, with the emperor himself, as

The marriage of Eudocia, favorite concubine of the emperor Michael III to the future Basil I, performed at Michael's request to legitimize Eudocia's status. While priests and attendants prepare Eudocia at left, Basil receives instructions from the seated Michael. The image is from the only illustrated Byzantine chronicle in existence, written by John Scylitzes, and enhanced with 564 miniature paintings.

1. Emperors and empresses of the Macedonian dynasty were: Basil I (867–886), Leo VI the Wise (886–912), Alexander III (912–913), Constantine VII (913–959), Romanus I "Lecapenus" (919–944), Romanus II (959–963), Nicephorus II Phocas (963–969), John I Tzimisces (969–976), Basil II (976–1025), Constantine VIII (1025–1028), Romanus III (1028–1034), Michael IV (1034–1041), Michael V (1041–1042), Zoë (1028–1050), Constantine IX (1042–1054), Theodora (1054–1056), Michael VI (1056–1057).

patron and protector of the church on earth, often at their head.

Yes, the empire was undeniably Christian, but all Byzantine dynasties, and the Macedonian in particular, exhibited shocking degrees of unchristian behavior in the personal lives of many rulers. Of the fourteen emperors in the Macedonian line,[1] one was bludgeoned to death, one was kidnapped and forced into a monastery by his two sons, one died in what is believed to have been a faked accident, one ruled with his concubine beside him on state occasions, one was a demented epileptic, and two were fatally poisoned.

To expedite dynastic shifts, regicide had always been a favored method. Since Constantine moved the capital from "Old Rome" to the city that bears his name (see earlier volume, *By This Sign*, chapter 6), there had been six imperial dynasties. The transition varied little. A strong contestant would wrest power from the last surviving emperor of the previous dynasty. His heirs (or their spouses) would rule for several generations, until a powerful

contestant—usually a soldier with strong military support—would assassinate or banish the sitting emperor and establish his own dynasty.

Royal credentials were not essential. Basil, for example, had reached the capital ten years earlier as a young refugee—penniless, street-smart and lucky. His biographers, whether from fact or for flattery, provided him with an Armenian pedigree connecting him to the kings of ancient Parthia. As a youth, Basil was enslaved by invading Bulgars, but escaped to Constantinople, where he worked as a groom for an influential family. His patroness, the Lady Danielis, attracted (both spiritually and carnally) by his quick mind, physical beauty and raw muscular strength, lavished money upon him, providing him with a household and a staff of thirty slaves.

Fortune continued to smile upon him. A brawny Bulgarian wrestler challenged all comers at a royal exhibition, handily defeating them one by one. Then Basil, who had no love for Bulgars, came forward, hurled the man to the ground and stood on his neck. The crowd went wild, none more so than the man in the imperial box, Michael III, and Basil became his favorite—an unofficial but prestigious office, though chronically short-lived and often fatal.

For one thing, the emperor expected special favors. Would Basil be kind enough, for instance, to marry the emperor's concubine, the Lady Eudocia, thus legitimizing her status? Basil was already married to Maria, a Macedonian, and they had a son, Constantine. This was awkward, but the emperor must be accommodated. So Basil divorced Maria and married Eudocia, who nevertheless continued as the emperor's mistress. She was pregnant when he was assassinated, and no one appears to have doubted that the child was Michael's.

Basil was well aware of the perils of his preferred position, but he knew, too, that Michael was widely detested. When drunk he would order executions, then when sober would denounce and brutalize the men who had carried them out. He would don patriarchal robes and play the buffoon, serving a parodied communion of vinegar and mustard to his besotted companions, and obscenely jeering the most cherished icons—this in pious Constantinople. Furthermore, in one short reign he bankrupted the treasury.

With his death, deemed by most a service to the state, began the Macedonian era. Its first nine emperors, up to and including Basil II, would among them accomplish unprecedented foreign victories, reform the justice system, set limits on the empire's ravenous aristocracy and increase economic prosperity. Their patronage of art, learning and culture generally, reflected in the splendid liturgies of the church, would entrench Orthodox practice in the Eastern world for the next millennium. Macedonian emperors, however sanguinary their conduct, saw themselves as agents of the mighty Christ Pantocrator (Christ the All-Powerful), establishing his kingdom upon the earth.

Basil I embarked with characteristic vigor upon his most pressing task, the

The Scylitzes Chronicle *enlivens the events described in its history through illustrations such as this one. Here Byzantine foot soldiers, shown on the left with the long shields, desert their general, under attack from Muslim forces, with the round shields.*

bankrupt treasury, personally examining bureaucratic accounts, calling in government debts, vigorously prosecuting embezzlers and miscreants. More controversially, he revamped the tax system to press harder on the landed aristocracy of Asia Minor and the wealthy church elite, while easing the burden on small freeholders, tradespeople and peasant farmers. Wider right to purchase property was conferred on the poor and military class. His successors would sustain these initiatives toward the poor for more than a century.

Meanwhile, Basil overhauled the legal system, updating codes promulgated by Justinian three hundred years earlier and publishing a new handbook for lawyers. He vetted judicial appointments, personally took part in trials of serious cases, and acted as a court of last resort. Some hundred churches, built during his reign, testify to his faith. Not so his handling of the major tragedy of his life—the early death of his son by Maria, Constantine, upon whom he had pinned his hope for a brilliant succession. After this he became morose, harsh and vindictive, and ultimately perished in a hunting accident, which most historians agree was probably murder.

Basil had one enemy in particular, his son Leo. Or was he Michael's son? While Constantine lived, Basil treated Leo with wary contempt, first tonsuring him as a monk, then forcing him to marry a woman in whom he had no interest, and once imprisoning

him for implication in an insurrection plot. But the early death of the boy Constantine made Leo heir apparent. Thus when Basil died, Leo practically proclaimed himself the son of Michael the Drunkard, and reinterred Michael in full splendor at the Church of the Holy Apostles while providing minimal honor for the late Basil.

The chief problems of Leo VI were marital. Theophano, the wife forced upon him by Basil, died six years after he became emperor.[2] Leo then married his longtime mistress, but she too soon died. So did his next wife, a young Phrygian girl. Since not one had produced a male heir, Leo resolved on a fourth marriage (his new mistress being pregnant with a potential heir), something strictly forbidden by the church. The pope at Rome finally ratified it, the patriarch of Constantinople resigned over it, and the public wrangle went on until Leo's own death. This fourth wife, Zoë by name, did bear a son, the future Constantine VII.

Though Leo had repudiated Basil I as a usurper, his public policies upheld everything Basil began. He codified Basil's legal reforms. He published a manual for the imperial bureaucracy, covering everything from palace ritual to tax administration. He established rules for the craft guilds on apprenticeship terms, working hours, wages and prices. All such skilled crafts as weaving, dye making, and manufacture in wood, gold and ivory, licensed by the emperor, were prime revenue sources.

> The emperor Leo VI was dubbed 'wise,' but he bungled plans for the royal succession.

2. Theophano, first wife of Emperor Leo VI, was later canonized. Leo divorced her three years after their marriage, when he was arrested in a plot to usurp his father's throne. Retiring to a monastery, she became known for unstinting benefactions to the poor, care for widows and orphans, and spiritual advice for the bereaved. Leo offered to build a church dedicated to her, but Theophano forbade it.

3. The concentrated contempt of historian Edward Gibbon descends upon Leo the Wise: "His life was spent in the pomp of the palace, in the society of his wives and concubines; and even the clemency which he bestowed, and the peace which he strove to preserve, must be imputed to the softness and indolence of his character.... His mind was tinged with the most puerile superstition.... His oracles are founded on the arts of astrology and divination." However, Professor Albert Vogt in the *Cambridge Medieval History* vigorously disagrees, calling Gibbon "grossly unfair," and declaring that Leo "completes and crowns" the work of Basil.

Because of his education and cultural interests, Leo VI became known as Leo the Wise, much to the disgust of the acerbic and classic historian, Edward Gibbon (*Decline and Fall of the Roman Empire*).[3] His plan for the succession, however, was very unwise. When he died in 912, his son by Zoë became Constantine VII, at age seven. Not until he was thirty-nine would he get hold of the reins of government, which meanwhile were grasped by a succession of regents, usually recognized as emperors. Leo's (probable) younger half brother, the dissolute Alexander, served as regent for a year and died—too soon, it later appeared, for him to carry out his intention to castrate the boy emperor so his own family could claim the succession. But on his deathbed, Alexander established a council of regency.

This set off a contest for the crown, soon won by a soldier-adventurer, Romanus I Lecapenus, who legitimated his claim by marrying his daughter Helena to fourteen-year-old Constantine. But Romanus had himself proclaimed emperor, his wife empress, and his three sons the equivalent of princes. He was, in short, an ambitious upstart like Basil. Also like Basil, he proved an able administrator, and in his twenty-five-year reign made effective treaties with the warlike eastern European tribes, helping to tie them to the Greek church rather than the Latin.

Romanus won little popular support, however, and for reasons never explained his two younger sons rebelled against him. (The eldest had died.) They immured him in a

Constantine VII, son of Leo VI by his fourth wife, Zoë, is finally crowned emperor after a succession of regents. A depiction such as this of Christ placing the crown on the emperor's head is intended to validate the emperor's power and divine authority. This wood carving from the tenth century is now in the Pushkin Museum, Moscow.

Basil II, "the Bulgar Slayer," is shown crowned and in military dress standing triumphant over prostrate Bulgarians. This image, from the frontispiece of a psalter dating from around the year 1000, is now located in the Biblioteca Marciana, Venice.

with a sarcastic smile, and after a just reproach of their folly and ingratitude, presented his imperial colleagues with an equal share of his water and vegetables." Such was the monastic diet.

But Constantine, although adored by the people, allowed his government to slide into corruption. Absorbed by his art and his books, he let Helena run the empire for the next fifteen years, assisted by an incompetent prime minister quaintly known as "Basil the Bird." Two conspiracies led by the Lecapenus family were suppressed with ferocious cruelty. Constantine did greatly advance learning, however, giving the arts new impetus, and appointing men of high reputation as writers, philosophers, historians and scientists to senior teaching positions. Byzantines appreciated this, for a great many of them could read, a skill confined in the West to monks, clergy and the wealthy.

Constantine and Helena failed in another crucial respect. Their son, destined to become Romanus II, grew up handsome, indolent, dissolute and wicked, and chiefly distinguished himself by marrying a woman generally regarded as the most ghastly female ever to reign as Byzantine empress. This was Theophano—not to be confused with the repudiated, though saintly, first wife of Leo VI. There was nothing saintly about this Theophano. Daughter of a pub-keeper, she was a beautiful and

monastery on the island of Proti in the Sea of Marmara, intending to assassinate Constantine VII and become joint emperors. Instead they were confronted by an angry mob that favored a very unexpected candidate— Constantine, no less. Their sister Helena, loyal to her husband, had betrayed them. So Constantine VII, long since reduced to poverty and making a living as an artist, finally came into his inheritance at age thirty-nine. The two conspirators were banished to Proti with their father, where Gibbon portrays their arrival: "Old Romanus met them on the beach conniving Hippodrome prostitute, skilled in the use of poison, who became a society courtesan. Malicious gossip was rarely lacking in Byzantine society, and it was said that she persuaded Romanus to poison his father, Constantine VII. Four years later, her detractors said, she herself poisoned Romanus. But this undoubtedly powerful lady (whose name means "manifestation of God") did bear two sons and two daughters. One son became Basil II, second greatest of the Macedonian emperors. One daughter, Anna, became Grand Duchess of Kiev, participant in one of the great romantic marriages of medieval times and founder with her husband of Christian Russia. (See Chapter 8.)

Ironically, however, the outstanding accomplishment of the Macedonian era occurred in the reign of the debauched Romanus II. This was the rise of the master military strategist Nicephorus Phocas, who regained Crete from the Muslims and whose armies reconquered much of Syria and reached the very gates of Jerusalem (as described in this volume's last chapter). This hero-soldier was a complex individual, rigidly disciplined and passionately Christian, who after the deaths of his wife and son vowed to become a monk at Mount Athos. Then he met the newly widowed Theophano, and everything changed. As regent for her sons, Basil and Constantine, both under six, she wanted a powerful backer. Nicephorus, the pledged monk, struck her as ideal.

Abandoning all monastic aspirations, Nicephorus had his army proclaim him emperor, marched into the capital, and was crowned by the patriarch. News that he intended to marry Theophano, however, lost him much popular support.[4] The monks, formerly his friends, condemned this marriage. So did the patriarch, who excommunicated him for a year, and relented only after Nicephorus assembled a council of sympathetic bishops and coerced its approval. As emperor, he then avenged himself on the monks by forcing them to sell their city properties, using the proceeds to finance his victorious war against the Muslims in Syria. Meanwhile, the burden of wartime taxes on the populace furthered his unpopularity, but the crucial factor was Theophano's infatuation with another man, Nicephorus's cousin, fellow general and longtime friend, John Tzimisces. This proved fatal to Nicephorus, and his assassination was particularly brutal.[5]

Tzimisces, as famed as Nicephorus for his courage and success against the Muslims, vowed to serve solely as regent for young Basil, now eleven. The patriarch refused to recognize him at all, however, until he banished Theophano to a convent, turned in his fellow assassins, and returned the monastic properties. He did all three. Theophano did not take exile well. She cursed and clawed her erstwhile lover. She beat poor Basil (who bore it stoically) and declared him the bastard offspring of one of her illicit liaisons.

> Nicephorus coerced a council of bishops into giving approval to his marriage plans.

4. The historian Albert Vogt (*Cambridge Medieval History*) explains the fall from popularity of the war hero Nicephorus Phocas: "There was something distinctly scandalous in the spectacle of this man of fifty marrying a woman in her twenties. This austere general, ascetic almost to a fault, who had vowed to end his days as a celibate in a monastery, now suddenly uniting himself to Theophano, one of the most ill-famed and vicious of women, was utterly repulsive in the eyes of the religious world."

5. Admitted to the heavily guarded palace by Theophano's ladies-in-waiting, the conspirators found Nicephorus asleep on a tiger skin. They kicked him awake, slashed his face wide open with a sword, then dragged him before Tzimisces, who heaped insults on him, knocked him down, held him with his foot while he pulled his beard out, then smashed his skull with a sword. They buried him secretly next day in the Church of the Holy Apostles. Thus perished at the hands of his countrymen one of the greatest military heroes in the annals of Byzantium.

ΚΩΝCΤΑΝΤΙΝ ΕΝΧΩΣΤΩ ΘΩ ΑΥΤΟΚΡΑΤΟΡΠΙCΤΟC ΒΑCΙΛΕΥCΡΩΜΑΙΩΝ Ο ΜΟΝΟΜ

ΙC ΧC

+ΖΩΗ ΗΕΥCΕ ΒΕCΤΑΤΗ ΑΥΓΟΥCΤΑ

Dressed in imperial ceremonial garments, the empress Zoë and Emperor Constantine IX (Monomachos) present offerings, a purse of gold coins and a scroll detailing donations to the church, to an enthroned and blessing Christ. The face of the emperor has been changed from the original, suggesting alterations in the portrait for each of Zoë's three husbands.

But she too was carted off to Proti, and Tzimisces ruled Byzantium for seven years. He died, it was generally agreed, of natural causes.

Theophano's son then became Basil II at age twenty-seven, in a chaos of civil war between two of his generals, each intent on assassinating him. With the help of a Viking contingent from Kiev, he emerged from this triumphant, having promised his sister Anna to the Viking leader, Vladimir of Kiev, in exchange. This was a central factor in the conversion of the Russians to Greek Christianity, undoubtedly the most lasting success of Basil's reign.

But it was Basil's military triumphs that won him most renown at home. Tenth- and eleventh-century Byzantium had three fearsome enemies: the Muslims, whom he kept in check; the Viking-led Rus, with whom he signed a lasting treaty; and the fearsome Bulgarians, whom he taught a terrible and permanent lesson. (See chapter 8.) To the people, this made him Basil *Bulgaroctonos* ("the Bulgar Slayer"), yet they never loved him. Indeed, many detested him. He was reportedly a cold, austere man, vowed to celibacy, neither drinking wine nor eating meat, wearing a monastic habit under his robes and armor. The heavy taxes he imposed, combined with his contempt for literature, art, and culture generally, also ensured that his death in 1025 was little mourned.

In its final thirty-two years, the Macedonian dynasty produced eight more emperors, none distinguished. Indeed, their history reads like an increasingly bad soap opera. The childless Basil was succeeded by an elderly brother who reigned three years as Constantine VIII. When he died, a respected senator was forced on pain of execution to marry Zoë, one of his three daughters. This unfortunate man reigned for six years as Romanus III, until Zoë poisoned him in order to marry a paramour, who became Michael IV. But her new husband turned out to be a demented epileptic who wandered through cemeteries lamenting his sins, while his eunuch brother John robbed the treasury. When Michael died, John coerced Zoë into adopting his nephew.

This nephew became Michael V, moaning that he didn't want the job and cursing as they placed the crown on his head. As emperor he promptly dispatched his benefactress Zoë to a monastery, a deed so offensive to the mob that they stormed the palace, blinded Michael, exiled him instead, and installed Zoë on the throne along with her sister Theodora, a nun. But the sisters quarreled, Theodora returned to her convent, and Zoë, now sixty, married her third husband, who insisted that his mistress also live with them. Zoë consented, and thereafter the new emperor, Constantine IX, routinely appeared in public flanked by his wife and his concubine.

Constantine outlived them both, but died without an heir. The aged nun Theodora was thereupon recalled from her convent, served as empress for eighteen months, and on her deathbed named a retired soldier as successor. This was Michael VI. Senile, and nearly blind, he lasted less than a year, until Isaac Comnenus briskly defeated him and brought to power the Comnenian dynasty. Before long, Michael VI died, peacefully it seems, the last of the Macedonians. ∎

> *Sex and intrigue make the final years of the dynasty sound like a bad soap opera.*

Mighty men of the North

Formidable Viking warriors from Kiev, the Varangians served as trusted and elite bodyguards for generations of Byzantine emperors

The emperor Basil II was in trouble. His Byzantine army had just crawled back to Constantinople, after a thorough trouncing by the Bulgars, when a rebellion broke out. Worse followed. Phocas, the disgruntled former general sent to quash the revolt, entered instead into negotiations with the rebels and agreed to lead them. Declaring himself emperor, with the support of nearly all the officers in the imperial army, Phocas prepared to march on Constantinople.

There remained one last, desperate chance, and Basil took it. He sent an envoy to Kiev to forge a treaty with the barbarian Vladimir, ruler of the Kievan Rus. The result was an offer from Vladimir of six thousand lusty Viking mercenaries. That would do it. In the year 989, Basil led the imperial troops still loyal to him, reinforced by these Northmen, to a resounding victory. That this force of Vikings had been instrumental in defending Byzantium was a notable first; it would not be the last.

The Scandinavian barbarians who began appearing in northeastern Europe late in the eighth century were known to the Byzantines as Varangians.[1] Formidable warriors and capable merchants, they came to dominate the land between the Dnieper and Volga rivers, along with the Slavic tribes they found there. This particular contingent was made up of relatively recent imports, needed by Vladimir to secure his ascendancy over his brothers. Nestor, a chronicler of early Russian history, notes that Vladimir warned Basil not to keep them all in Constantinople, "for then they will only give you trouble, as they have given me, but divide them up into many places, and do not let one man come back here again."

Basil had no desire to send them back. He soon realized, writes historian Sigfus Blondal in *The Varangians of Byzantium*, "what a treasure he had gained in these mighty men of the North." From the victory against Phocas onwards "no hand was raised against Basil inside the empire, nor could any hostile foreign power withstand him to the uttermost." Wherever he went, a picked contingent of Northmen went with him. Basil's Varangian Guard, as they were known, became the heart of the imperial army, spearheading some of its greatest victories.

Moreover, these warriors, who were too hot for the formidable Vladimir to handle, swiftly transformed themselves into an elite and trusted bodyguard for Basil. Why not for Vladimir? The explanation is likely found in the magnetism of Byzantine culture, and at least equally significant, the promise of wealth and prestige. Military historian Tim Newark in *The Barbarians* describes a company of Varangian mercenaries returning home to Sweden from service in Constantinople:

> Their leader wore a tunic and trousers of silk, over which hung a cloak of scarlet. His sword hilt was ornamented with gold thread wound round the grip. On his head, he wore a gilded helmet and he carried a scarlet shield. Wherever they stopped, native Nordic women could not keep their eyes off the brilliant warriors.

However, the Varangians were never completely cured of their natural unruliness. During a Syrian campaign in 999 they set fire to the fortified Monastery of St. Catherine, then comprehensively plundered it, stripping even the lead and copper from the roof. Blondal also cites an incident in Armenia the following year, when a Greek soldier allegedly stole some hay from a Varangian. In the ensuing skirmish the Varangian was killed, "whereupon the whole Viking force, some six thousand men, mobilized for a fight ... armed with spears and shields." The outcome is not recorded.

The Varangian Guard was used in campaigns against the Bulgars, Khazars, Georgians and Normans. In Georgia, it was they who carried out Basil's merciless order to kill every man, woman and child within twelve districts. The job took them three months, Blondal writes, and they were particularly brutal about it. On the other hand, they were not without honor. When they wintered in Thrace in 1034, one soldier tried to rape a local woman, and in defending herself she killed him. His comrades "gathered together and honored the woman by giving her all the possessions of the man who had attempted to rape her, and they threw his body away without burial."

Although never again used quite so effectively as under Basil II, the Guard remained for two hundred years a vital component of the imperial army. One notable who served in its ranks was Harald Hardrada, later King Harald of Norway (killed at Stamford Bridge in 1066 while attempting an invasion of England, see page 113).

Long after Harald Hardrada returned to Norway, covered in wealth and honor, the Guard got some unexpected recruits in another seemingly hopeless situation. Constantinople was under siege by the Turks and expected to fall at any time, when one day the harbor filled with some three hundred and fifty ships. Hordes of warriors charged ashore, the Muslim attackers quickly faded away, and Emperor Alexius Comnenus welcomed the rescuers.

The rescuers, it turned out, were Saxons. Driven from England by the Normans who invaded that island in 1066, they had made the long journey into and through the Mediterranean. "The English were much distressed by their loss of liberty," the chronicler Ordericus Vitalis explains, "...A number of them, with the fresh bloom of youth upon them, went to distant lands." The grateful emperor offered them whatever they wanted, and they wanted two things: land, and membership in the famed Varangian Guard. From then on, the Guard was no longer composed solely of Vikings.

Its ultimate demise coincided with two developments. One was the launching of the Crusades. In the mid-twelfth century, many Varangians joined the European crusaders. The other was the decline of Constantinople. The Guard was entirely attached to the person and the city of the emperor. That its splendor should dim along with his was entirely predictable and appropriate. When Constantinople was sacked by the Franks in 1204, says Blondal, only "the ghost of the regiment" remained. ∎

1. The historian Sigfus Blondal defines the word Varangian as "a companion, a man who has entered into a contractual fellowship of merchants and soldiers, and gives security, accepts responsibility towards his companions, as they accept responsibility for him."

Taken into Constantinople's army as mercenaries, the Norse Varangians proved to be fearless and loyal. A gift to the emperor Basil from Vladimir, Prince of the Kievan Rus, they were transformed into the elite Varangian Guard, the imperial bodyguards. The excellent pay attracted mercenaries from all over Europe, who often returned home wealthy at the end of their service.

DURENCEAU

In 869 the Byzantine emperor Basil I and Pope Adrian II were mutually intent upon reconciliation. The result, depicted above by the seventeenth-century artist, Cesare Nebbia, was a synod held in Hagia Sophia, the cathedral in Constantinople, one of the last two councils where both East and West were represented. Attended by 102 bishops, four patriarchs, and two papal representatives, it confirmed the pope's condemnation of Patriarch Photius of Constantinople (already deposed and banished by Basil), but also required every Eastern bishop to pledge obedience to decisions of the Roman see. Ten years later, however, Photius would be back. (The painting is now held in the Vatican Museums.)

CHAPTER 6

The worst blow falls as feuds over authority split East from West

Clashes between pope and patriarch make starkly clear the gulf between Eastern and Western Christendom, though the disputants themselves were appalled by it

In the year 1000, when the Christians entered their second millennium, their prospects were something less than promising. Islam's assault three to four centuries before had overrun more than half of their churches and people. Muslim armies still pressed upon them from the west in Spain, from the south across the Mediterranean, and from the East in Persia and Syria. The hideous Viking raids from the north that had destroyed hundreds of churches and monasteries had largely stopped, but most of the Scandinavians were still pagan and still threatening. Finally, from the great steppes to the east, the fearsome Turks were moving towards Islam spiritually, and toward the Christian lands militarily.

To be sure, not all was grim. Christendom's demoralizing string of retreats and defeats had been somewhat offset by stirrings of revival: the founding in the West of the Cluny monastery with its contagious spirit of reform; a renewed confidence in the East as the Byzantine Empire held the Muslim legions at bay; and the recent baptism of Grand Prince Vladimir that portended the conversion of Russia. But as the historian Kenneth Scott Latourette observes, Christianity at the end of its first millennium was still "far less prominent on the total human scene than it had been in A.D. 500"—so much so, in fact, that someone then reviewing

Christianity's setbacks and the combined strength of its enemies might well have imagined it shrinking into insignificance during the next few hundred years.

The last thing Christians needed in the year 1000 was another catastrophe to weaken their ranks, and yet one was quickly approaching, and would climax before the century had passed.

This disaster would be internal: a decisive showdown between East and West. The Byzantine Empire, though now stripped of Muslim-held Syria, Palestine, Egypt and North Africa, still controlled most of Asia Minor, Greece and eastern Europe south of the Danube, and still called itself "Roman." Its emperor at Constantinople and most of his subjects spoke Greek, and viewed the people of the West as barbarians, and their Latin language as barbarous. To them, the bishop of Rome, increasingly referred to as the "pope," was merely "the Patriarch of the West." True, he was the senior of the five patriarchs in Christendom—the others being those of Constantinople, Alexandria, Jerusalem and Antioch—but being senior, they contended, did not empower him to approve the appointments of the other four, or intervene in their internal affairs. In addition, they said, he was still a "subject" of the emperor at Constantinople.

The placidness of this illustration belies the astonishing precedent of the action taking place. In hopes of establishing a united Christendom, Pope Leo III crowns Charlemagne, thereby reviving the Western empire and securing protection for Rome from its heathen enemies. The Western church benefited from the munificent wealth bestowed on it by Charlemagne, much of which was used to assist the poor.

To the Latin West, most of these contentions were absurd. Had not Jesus Christ himself, to preserve unity, named Peter to lead the apostles as they led the Church? Had Christ not given Peter, they asked, the steward's "keys to the royal household" and thus the authority to "open and close," that is, to govern (as in Matt 16:18–19 and Isa. 22:20–22)? Had not Peter become bishop of Rome and therefore did not all his successors in that office inherit this authority to govern? And did not this authority apply to the whole Church?

Moreover, said the West, the bishop of Rome was no longer a subject to the Byzantine Empire, but subject to God as coruler with the emperor of the true Roman Empire, now restored to the West and established by Charlemagne, who had been crowned by the pope himself in the year 800. Finally, the West saw the Constantinople patriarchate as a latecomer, an upstart, not even heard of until the fourth century. Surely, the patriarchs of Antioch, Alexandria and Jerusalem, though now under Muslim control, held far more venerable and respected offices.

By the second millennium after Christ, an East-West schism had been brewing for five centuries. Six times it had boiled over, and Rome and Constantinople had severed relations with each other. Twice popes had been kidnapped and held hostage by Byzantine emperors. With the Muslim calamity, however, the whole structure of the church had changed, particularly in the East, where three of its four patriarchs must now somehow safeguard their imperiled flocks under Muslim governments that prohibited the preaching of the gospel to Muslims on penalty of death. Under such anxious conditions, church leaders had become more sensitive than ever to practices that diverged from what they considered the settled traditions of the church.

This growing vigilance was apparent as early as 692, at the Trullan Council (literally, "under the Dome" in the imperial palace in Constantinople), whose canons highlighted a number of differences between the Eastern and Western churches. The emperor Justinian II convened the gathering to settle unresolved matters from the Fifth and Sixth Ecumenical Councils, but also because it was a

The council called to settle vital issues turned into a fiasco. The pope bridled at its declaration that Constantinople should have equal privileges with the see of Rome.

moment fraught with urgency for the church. With so many of the faithful newly subject to a psychological state of siege within the Muslim orbit, it was important to tie up loose ends regarding what was permitted and what was not. Solidarity and unity were the orders of the day.

Alas for unity, the council turned out to be an Eastern affair, with not one of 215 bishops in attendance hailing from the West. Even the representative of the pope, Basil of Gortyn in Crete (which for the moment remained within papal control), did not appreciate how badly several of the canons would go down in Rome. Given the growing sense of papal prerogative, however, it is no wonder Pope Sergius I would bridle at a declaration that "the see of Constantinople shall have equal privileges with the see of Old Rome, and shall be highly regarded in ecclesiastical matters as that is, and shall be second after it." That last phrase may have softened the blow somewhat, but the statement remained no more palatable to Sergius than a similar declaration, more than two hundred years before at Chalcedon, had been to Pope Leo I.

Several other canons at the Trullan (or Quinisext) Council also showcased the East-West divide. One insisted that clergy below the rank of bishop could continue to "live with a lawful wife," but could not marry after they were ordained, while bishops could not be married at all; another banned the depiction of Christ as a lamb; a third denounced the custom of fasting on Saturdays. All three insulted entrenched Western practices, and the defense of lesser clergy who remain married is especially notable as the first evidence of East-West tension over celibacy.

The council also approved a canon that foretold a most bitter dispute in the future involving the type of bread used in the Eucharist. "Let no one in the priestly order nor any layman eat the unleavened bread of the Jews," Canon XI declared in part. Although the thrust of the entire canon clearly aimed at barring close association between Christians and Jews, its frontal assault on unleavened bread no doubt raised eyebrows in the West. The Latin Church believed Jesus could not have used leavened bread in the Last Supper, given the account in the synoptic Gospels, which indicate it occurred on the Jewish day of Passover, the first day of a week in which only unleavened bread could be consumed; the Eastern fathers, on the other hand, drew quite a different conclusion, based upon their reading of the Gospel of John, which suggests

Troops mutinied when the emperor ordered the pope arrested. Only the personal intervention of the pope himself saved the arresting officer, found cowering under the pope's bed.

Jesus was crucified on the day of Preparation, or in other words before the Passover meal. This was not a new disagreement, but for most of early church history, it simply had not mattered. "The Roman and Byzantine rites had long coexisted in the ancient world without conflict," observes historian Mahlon H. Smith (*And Taking Bread: Cerularius and the Azyme Controversy*). But the two spheres of Christendom were drifting apart, and soon those who saw advantage, or religious duty, in demanding that the other side reform its ways would seize upon these differences.

When Pope Sergius withheld his approval to the canons of Trullo, the emperor decided to bring the recalcitrant pontiff to heel and ordered his arrest. But this was easier said than done. No sooner had the captain of the imperial guard arrived in Rome to inform the pope that he was being summoned to Constantinople than the Italian-born troops who were supposed to enforce the decree mutinied in the pope's defense. Only Sergius's personal intervention saved the emperor's emissary—who at one point was reduced to cowering under the pope's bed.

Relations between East and West would soon improve again, but the fragile amity of the early eighth century quickly plunged into even more radical estrangement when Emperor Leo III began destroying religious icons in 726, and Rome refused to follow suit (see chapter 5). Suffice it to say this would be the last century in which a pope visited Constantinople; the last century in which a pope paid imperial taxes; the last in which he would date his proclamations according to the reign of the emperor in Constantinople; and the last in which any pope would be Greek.

In many ways, ironically, the relentless Muslim advance conspired to accelerate the separation of East and West. Muslim assaults tied down

Byzantium at key moments when the papacy might have looked to it for military help, thus prodding the pope, who faced Arab scares of his own, to scan the horizon for an ally with a more reliable mailed fist. And as East and West alike sought to compensate for the loss of regions once under their influence, they sent forth missionaries who competed on the same spiritual frontiers.

Even so, the single consistent thread in the on-again, off-again relationship between the Eastern and Western churches was the tension over papal claims to ecclesiastical primacy and Constantinople's insistence on all-but-equivalent prestige and autonomy. No episode illustrates this central fact more clearly than the "Photian schism" of the late ninth century, the single most significant confrontation in the long run-up to the decisive break between East and West that occurred two centuries later.

When the empress Theodora restored image veneration in 843, many of the iconoclasts she suppressed had no intention of accepting the new order.[1] They represented a continuing threat in the eyes of their triumphant enemies, particularly those of the zealous Studite monks. These anti-iconoclasts demanded a patriarch of impeccable credentials, a resolute and uncompromising leader, and they got their wish with the elevation of the saintly Ignatius to the post in 847.

The younger son of the late emperor Michael I, Ignatius had been castrated, tonsured a monk and imprisoned on Princes Islands when his father was deposed in 813. By the time he became patriarch, Ignatius was renowned for his ascetic rigor and stubborn fearlessness—a reputation that subsequent events were to vindicate in full. But although Ignatius was a sincere and holy man, his virtues did not include an instinct for diplomacy. His background was nearly bereft of secular learning or experience in the wider world, and it showed in his prickly dealings with those who did not fully share his priorities. Indeed, Ignatius's blunt, abrupt style sparked a confrontation at his own consecration as patriarch with a bishop from Sicily, Gregory Asbestas, who was in Constantinople to deal with a charge that he had violated church rules. When Ignatius insisted the Sicilian vacate St. Sophia's because of his uncertain status, the bishop exploded. He denounced the patriarch as a wolf, smashed his own candle against the floor and stalked out of the church leading a procession of allied clerics.

And this was only the beginning of the clash. Ignatius called a synod that condemned Asbestas and his followers, but the move inspired the Sicilian to

A twelfth-century illustration from Augustine's City of God *in the archives of Hradcany Castle, Prague, Czech Republic. The idealized holy city, Jerusalem, described in the book of Revelation, is depicted with Christ, his angels and his saints, surrounded by the city walls.*

1. The lingering strength of iconoclasm after its repudiation was such that authorities were careful not to provoke its partisans with a rapid restoration of images. Indeed, an icon of the Virgin installed at Hagia Sophia in 867—nearly a quarter century after the suppression of iconoclasm—was one of the first in that citadel of Orthodoxy.

escalate the confrontation. He appealed to Rome, complaining not only of his own treatment, but also of the irregular way Ignatius had been designated patriarch by Theodora and her advisers, who had failed to convene the usual synod. Pope Leo IV was not reluctant to get involved, and wrote to the patriarch asking that copies of papers on the Gregory Asbestas case be sent to Rome for Leo's inspection. Ignatius evaded this trap with a flat refusal, and then gave the same answer when Leo's successor, Benedict III, repeated the request.

The stubborn Ignatius was willing to assert his autonomy not only against the faraway pope. He also refused to kowtow to a figure of far more potential menace to himself, Theodora's brother Bardas, who served as regent for her son, the emperor Michael III. Persuaded by rumors that Bardas enjoyed an incestuous relationship with his daughter-in-law, Ignatius resolved as his holy duty to stop the perversion. On the feast of the Epiphany in 858, the patriarch made his move: He withheld communion from Bardas in full view of other congregants, a humiliation that provoked the caesar into a controlled but vengeful fury. It was now only a matter of time before Ignatius's downfall, but it would not occur until the patriarch once again had proved his valor.

At Bardas's prodding, the adolescent emperor was persuaded to seize sole control of the government by the device of banishing his mother to a monastery. To solemnize the deed, the emperor ordered Ignatius to perform the ceremony of the tonsure on Theodora and her daughters, a shameful duty for a man who owed his position to the empress. But to his lasting credit, Ignatius chose personal loyalty to Theodora over his own welfare, and rejected the emperor's demand on the ground that the empress's abdication was coerced. Now Bardas had Ignatius where he wanted him. It would not require much more evidence to convince the emperor that the stiff-necked patriarch was a liability, and Bardas was capable of manufacturing the sort of tale to which any ruler must pay attention: He linked Ignatius to a traitor. The patriarch was arrested, resigned his position, and was banished to the island Terebinthus.

The great Hagia Eirene (Divine Peace or St. Irene) is one of the largest churches in Constantinople. This building dates from the time of Justinian, and unlike its sister church the Hagia Sophia, has never been converted to a mosque, but has served as both an arsenal and a museum in recent times. Centuries of earthquakes, fire, iconoclasts and neglect have rendered the walls almost bare of decoration.

At this point, we encounter one of the most intriguing yet elusive individuals in the medieval church. Photius is a pivotal historical figure who nonetheless comes down to us in such contrasting portraits, depending on the allegiance of the source, that a mist of contradiction swirls around him still. Was he an unprincipled aggressor in his confrontation with the pope, or a defender of New Rome's prerogatives forced reluctantly into his role? Were his attacks on Western practices, especially the use of the Filioque clause in the creed, heartfelt? Or were they a mere pretext for driving a wedge between the Greek and Latin Churches?

For a thousand years, Western theologians and scholars hewed to the most unflattering answers, thus ruling out the slightest sympathy for Photius and his position. Yet even his most savage critics have always agreed to this extent with his enthusiasts: Photius was one of the most brilliant men of his age, and easily the most learned. The son of an old, aristocratic family—Greek, but with an admixture of Armenian on his mother's side—his knowledge and understanding of classical literature not only dazzled his peers and his students at the university of Constantinople, they impressed much later scholars as well, who credited him with preserving a wealth of classical culture that otherwise would surely have been lost.

Photius's interests were not confined to the secular classics. A deeply religious man, he had mastered the subtleties of theological literature, too—his facility being such that at one point before he was patriarch, he published a heresy as a prank to test whether the intellectually less nimble Ignatius, then patriarch, would detect it.

The regent Bardas may have been a ruthless man, but this vice was in part redeemed by an admiration for subtle judgment and erudition, and he could hardly fail to appreciate the talents of Photius. He and the emperor were naturally pleased, therefore, when the synod that met to nominate a successor to Ignatius chose Photius as a compromise candidate who could attract the support of all but five bishops. There was just one problem with this selection: Photius was a layman. He would have to proceed through the entire ecclesiastical sequence— lector, subdeacon, deacon, priest, bishop—before he could become patriarch. But no matter. The task was accomplished in a sprint that began on December 20, 858, and concluded on Christmas Day, with none other than Gregory Asbestas, the sworn enemy of Ignatius, among those presiding at the consecration.

Unlike Ignatius, Photius understood the uses of a conciliatory compliment or a gracious expression of concern, and he genuinely tried to win over those such as the Studite monks and a handful of influential bishops who would not be reconciled to his predecessor's abdication. It was to no avail. The Abbot of Studion would not take communion with Photius. The dissident bishops, meanwhile, met in the church of *Hagia Eirene*, declared Ignatius patriarch and excommunicated Photius, a bold but hopeless gesture given the balance of power. Soon those bishops too were deposed, a crackdown accompanied by a general persecution against the now routed allies of Ignatius.

The pope at the time was an aristocrat, Nicholas I, who in his own way was as remarkable as Photius. Not for nothing was Nicholas the last pontiff to earn the title "the Great." In his nine years as bishop of Rome (858–867), he set about to heighten the authority, prestige, and independence of the Roman see, which he insisted must rank as the final court of appeal in church affairs. No bishop, he maintained, could be appointed or deposed without the pope's approval, and because the pope functions as the apostle Peter's deputy, his authority takes precedence over the decisions of any synod, too.

So the pope seized his opportunities as they arose, bringing the independent-minded archbishops of Ravenna and Reims to heel, for example, through the excommunication of the first and a threat of the same to the second. (Despite their long-standing Byzantine connection, both Ravenna and Reims fell under the Roman patriarchate.) When a synod of servile Frankish bishops agreed to let King Lothar of Lorraine divorce his wife, Theutberga, in order to marry his mistress, the pope stiffened again. He ordered the king to return to his wife, excommunicated two archbishops who sided with Lothar (and who returned fire by denouncing Nicholas for "making himself emperor of the whole world"), and refused to back down even when Lothar's brother

Historians have long sparred over how the emperor managed to win over those papal legates. Did he bribe them, threaten them, or convince them?

marched on Rome and forced the pope to seek asylum in the shrine of St. Peter's. It was the king, in the end, who would capitulate.

"The Lorraine divorce case showed Nicholas at his courageous best," contends historian Eamon Duffy (*Saints and Sinners: A History of the Popes*), "defying emperors, archbishops and regional councils in defense not only of papal prerogatives but of a friendless woman. The same determination marked his relations with the emperor and churches of the East, but here the consequence was to be a tragic split between the churches of East and West."

In their letters to Nicholas informing him that Ignatius had been deposed as patriarch, both Emperor Michael and Photius carefully avoided asking for the pope's approval. But the pope hardly required an invitation to assert his oversight in such important business. He responded to the emperor that his legates, who would be delivering the reply in person to Michael, would "make a careful inquiry into [Ignatius's] deposition and his censure, with a view to discovering whether the canons have been observed or not; then, when the matter has been reported to us, we shall direct by our apostolic authority what is to be done, so that your church, daily shaken by these anxieties, may henceforth remain inviolate and unhurt." Nicholas's letter to Photius was shorter and somewhat curt: It objected to the elevation of a layman to bishop, but added that the pope would await the judgment of his legates on the new patriarch's character.[2]

Some historians describe Nicholas's intervention as little more than a cynical exercise intended to wrest Illyricum in the East, plus the Italian district of Calabria

2. Although unusual, the elevation of a layman to bishop was by no means unprecedented, in East or West. The most notable example in the West, which partisans of Photius never permitted the Latin Church to forget, was the elevation of Ambrose to bishop of Milan in 374. Ambrose was the Roman governor at the time of his election.

and the island Sicily in the West, from the jurisdiction of the patriarch of Constantinople, since the pope raised that possibility with the emperor. Yet if Nicholas was prepared to strike a deal, it is just as apparent that he actually wanted both the disputed territory and the last word on whether Ignatius had been justifiably deposed. In the event, discussion on the topic of the Balkans never seriously got under way. What did occur in Constantinople in the spring of 861 was far more remarkable: a retrial of Ignatius for the benefit of the pope's legates, Rodoald and Zachary. This was a major concession to the Roman see, even if the emperor was at pains to insist the retrial was merely a courtesy to the pope. The rehearing was also a political risk, since it was sure to reignite pro-Ignatius passions and demonstrations, which had to be put down with ugly force. At the council, meanwhile, the papal legates at first sought merely to gather information to take back to Rome, but Michael reared up against this limited agenda. He insisted the pope's representatives render a decision on Ignatius on the spot, and his wish was eventually granted—although historians have sparred ever since over how he managed to win the legates over. Did he bribe Rodoald and Zachary? Threaten them? Or were they moved simply by the logic of the situation? After all, they found Photius to be suave and respectful, while Ignatius seemed oblivious to his opportunity and adopted a truculent attitude that rejected their authority to consider his case at all. Moreover, they must have come to realize that Ignatius was more isolated in Byzantium than the pope had been led to believe.

Whatever their reasons, Rodoald and Zachary capitulated to Michael's demands, exceeded their orders, and in a serious abuse of power, passed sentence on Ignatius—condemning him—before anxiously heading back to report to Nicholas.

The pope was anything but pleased. His legates had failed to restore Illyricum to the papal orbit and had preempted his rightful decision to rule on the retrial of Ignatius. The latter affront became increasingly hard to bear after the arrival in Rome of an eloquent defender of Ignatius, the abbot Theognostos, who had fled Constantinople in disguise just steps ahead of the emperor's agents. Theognostos regaled Nicholas with lurid stories of the Ignatians' abuse at the hands of Michael, and no doubt reminded the pope of the equally sensational origins of Ignatius's downfall: His refusal to grant communion to Bardas over allegations of grave sin. Nicholas had proved before that he was not afraid to buck unfavorable odds in the name of principle, and it wasn't long before he had resolved to repudiate his legates and rally

A beautifully preserved pendant, less than three inches in height, is hinged at each end, revealing a small cavity to hold a relic, possibly a fragment from the true cross. The reliquary depicts the Virgin Mary in prayer flanked by Basil the Great on the left and Gregory Thaumaturgus on the right. The enameling process silhouettes the figures against a background of bare metal, then highlights details with rich colors. Found at the Great Palace of Constantinople, it is now held by the British Museum.

The Harbaville Triptych, opened, reveals Christ being entreated by the Virgin Mary and John the Baptist on behalf of mankind, surrounded by apostles, martyrs and soldier-saints. This tenth-century ivory masterpiece still has traces of gold leaf, hinting at even greater elegance in its original condition. Now in the Louvre, Paris, the exquisite piece signaled the resurgence of interest in ornamental sculpture of the Byzantine era.

to the cause of Ignatius, whether the crusty ex-patriarch liked it or not. Thus it was that in 863, Nicholas took the fateful step of calling a council in Rome that restored Ignatius to power and excommunicated Photius, unless he resigned his see at once.

Official Constantinople was shocked at the news from this Lateran council, but stewed in silence for nearly two years, until at last the emperor—no doubt in concert with Bardas—could stand it no longer. He dispatched to Rome what the historian Owen Chadwick calls "one of the rudest letters of Byzantine history," denouncing the pope for cultural backwardness and ignorance of Greek, and threatening to march on Rome if the pope didn't abandon his allegiance to Ignatius. Nicholas softened a bit at this thunderbolt, but his official reaction was as symbolic as was the emperor's threat of a military campaign. Come to Rome, Nicholas urged Michael and Photius, and we will examine the matter again, together.

Photius of course had no intention of prostrating himself in such fashion, and in any event, had a scheme afoot involving overtures to Western bishops who chafed under Nicholas's aggressive leadership. In effect, the patriarch was betting on a putsch within the Latin Church. But Photius's patience was not boundless, and he watched with increasing irritation as Western missionaries made inroads among the Bulgars, whom he felt by proximity and imperial right ought to cleave to Constantinople (and eventually would; see chapter 8). Since Photius by this time had given up all hope that Nicholas would ever come round to his side, the patriarch decided to force the issue and see if the pope could survive the resulting furor. He summoned a synod, which met in the fall of 867, to consider the pope's responsibility in permitting a number of heresies to take root in the West and be exported to Bulgaria. Photius enumerated these outrages in a letter sent to the other three Eastern patriarchs before the council got under way. They included the West's exemption of milk and cheese from the Lenten fast; its ban on married clergy; fasting on Saturdays; and the insistence that bishops alone apply the chrism of confirmation.[3] But the greatest offense by far, according to Photius, was the teaching by Frankish missionaries that the Filioque clause belonged in the creed. The Filioque clause, which describes the Holy Spirit proceeding not only from God the Father but also

3. Confirmation became separated from baptism in the West, because as infant baptism became common, priests (and deacons) had to become the main ministers of baptism. The bishop could not possibly get around quickly to each house where a child was born. Either the priest had to administer an accompanying initiation rite to baptism, or if it was to remain tied to the bishop, it would have to be temporally separated from baptism until the bishop could come. That was the Western solution, and eventually confirmation became treated as another initiation sacrament. In the Orthodox tradition, a new member is admitted to full communion as an infant at baptism, when the chrism, or "holy oil," is placed on the infant's forehead, eyelids, lips, breast, hands and feet by the priest. An adult convert to Orthodoxy is similarly "chrismated" by the priest.

from the Son, "merits a thousand anathemas," Photius solemnly proclaimed.

With the emperor Michael presiding, the synod of 867 condemned the pope in what later would be seen as the major watershed leading ultimately to the final break between the Eastern and Western churches.

Western church historians have often been tempted to view Photius's indignation at the Filioque as a cynical means of elevating a power struggle into a doctrinal clash and thus give it more substance, but subsequent events left little doubt regarding his sincerity. As far as the patriarch was concerned, the Filioque amounted to rank heresy. Never mind that it did not belong in the creed; in his view, it did not belong in Christian theology. Did not Scripture itself say that the Holy Spirit proceeded from the Father (John 15:26)? From the Greek Church's perspective, moreover, Photius seemed to have a monopoly on the arguments. The Filioque did not appear in the creed as it emerged at the Second Ecumenical Council in Constantinople in 381, where the phrases referring to the Holy Spirit were added to the Nicene version.[4] Nor had any of the early Greek fathers accepted the dual procession, although several popes and fathers of the church in the West clearly had. The Latin model of the Trinity had in fact been decisively shaped by the writings of Augustine, but such was the intellectual isolation of East from West that his works were still unknown to Eastern clerics, except by reputation. Incredibly, given Augustine's immense prestige in the West, no one had yet bothered to translate his works into Greek.

The first insertion of the Filioque into the creed occurred in Spain, as a way to emphasize the divinity of Christ against the Arian heresy. From there the practice seems to have migrated by way of Ireland and England to the Carolingian Empire, where the Franks became the Filioque's untiring, uncompromising promoters. Realizing that Rome still resisted the Filioque as an addition to the creed, the Franks had dispatched a delegation to Rome in 810 to urge its adoption. But Pope Leo III felt so strongly that it did not belong in the liturgy—although he absolutely agreed with its doctrinal truth—that he told them such a design was "illicit" and later had two silver shields engraved with the Nicene-Constantinopolitan Creed installed on either side of the Confession of St. Peter. However, the Franks ignored the pope's admonitions and the Filioque continued to gain ground in the West throughout the ninth century.[5]

Pope Nicholas died in the same year he was condemned by Michael and Photius. But soon, fortune turned against them as well. Michael's great favorite, the capable but ruthless Basil the Macedonian, demonstrated his gratitude first by murdering Bardas with his own hands, and then conniving to have the emperor killed, too. (See subchapter, page 137.) At this point, Photius could not have been hopeful about his own chances—Basil disliked him and had allied himself with the Ignatians—and soon his premonition would prove correct. Photius was banished to a monastery as Ignatius was tapped once more to lead the Eastern church.

It was Rome's hour again, too. The emperor Basil was intent on reconciliation with Rome, and Pope Adrian II was more than happy to oblige—but on

4. The Nicene Creed of the First Ecumenical Council of 325 affirmed that Christians believe "in the Holy Spirit," but did not elaborate further. Only at the Second Ecumenical Council of 381 was the phrase lengthened to include, "and in the Holy Spirit, the Lord and the Giver of Life, who proceeds from the Father, who together with the Father and the Son is worshiped and glorified." In the English rendition, the Filioque adds to the phrase "proceeds from the Father" the words "…and the Son." Western proponents of the Filioque argued that if the Nicene Creed could be added to once, as in 381, it could be added to again.

5. Pope Leo III was also at the center of the first significant East-West clash over the Filioque, which occurred when two Latin monks residing in Jerusalem introduced the clause in the creed after hearing its use during a visit to the Carolingian court. The monks were astonished at the bitter reaction of the Greek monks in Jerusalem, who charged them with heresy. This prompted the Latin monks to write the pope in 807 asking for guidance. In his response to the monks, which he sent to "all churches of the East," the pope strongly affirmed that the Filioque was the inviolate doctrine of the church.

his own triumphant terms. Adrian shared his predecessor's expansive vision of the papacy, and was also determined to be the instrument of Nicholas's vindication. After presiding over a synod in Rome that reaffirmed the condemnation of Photius, Adrian sent representatives to Constantinople to lead a council there on the same issues. Here again, however, conflicting goals between East and West led to friction. Basil wanted Rome's support for deposing Photius and elevating Ignatius. He did not want to prostrate the Eastern Church before papal authority—which was, as it happens, exactly what Adrian's legates insisted upon. Not only was Photius condemned anew and his ordinations rejected at the Synod of 869, but also every Eastern bishop in attendance was required to sign a document pledging obedience to the decisions of the Roman see in order to restore relations. Such was the resentment at this last demand that these signed statements at one point were stolen from the legates' quarters and "recovered" only after tremendous furor. The skullduggery may not have ended there, either. The legates were delayed

Basil did not want to prostrate the Eastern Church before papal authority—which was, as it happens, exactly what the pope's legates insisted on.

on their way home and then waylaid by Slav pirates who seemed to exhibit a curiously intense interest in the papal archives. In any event, the papers were seized and lost to posterity, with the only surviving account of the synod being a Latin translation carried independently to Rome by an alternative route.

As unlikely as Ignatius's ecclesiastical resurrection had been, it was followed by one even more extraordinary: that of Photius himself. Byzantine politics being what they were, the emperor found he needed the moderate wing of the clergy in his corner, too—or at least not chafing in resistance to his every move. And so within a few years, Photius found himself being eased back into respectability, even to the point of being able to offer comfort to Ignatius on his deathbed in 877. "When he fell ill and asked to see us," Photius later wrote, "we visited him, not once or twice, but frequently, doing everything we could to relieve his suffering."[6]

By this time, no one in Constantinople was surprised to see Photius regain the patriarch's throne, but his appointment did of course present a most delicate problem: What about Rome? How would it react to news that the arch-schismatic had clambered back into Basil's good graces? Fortunately for Basil and Photius, Pope Adrian's successor, John VIII, had more important things on his mind than nursing grudges. The Arabs were on the attack again in southern Italy, and the Franks were tied down elsewhere and unable to come to Rome's aid. John was willing to smooth over clashes of the past in return for assistance from the emperor's fleet and a proper apology from Photius for his conduct a decade earlier. So once again, a pope's legates headed east with instructions that could not possibly be followed to the letter, given attitudes in the imperial capital. Photius had no intention of apologizing; in his mind

6. A group of Byzantine sources known as the Anti-Photian Collection deny any such reconciliation took place between Photius and Ignatius, and indeed charge Photius with continual scheming for power from the moment he returned from his banishment. But the emperor Leo, no friend of Photius, referred to the reconciliation in his funeral oration in honor of his father, so there is little doubt today that it took place.

he had nothing to apologize for, and had suffered much too much humiliation already. Instead, he orchestrated a synod in late 879–880, with the legates in attendance, from which he emerged not only with recognition of himself as ecumenical patriarch (although East and West differed as to what precisely this phrase meant) but even with an agreement that nothing be added to the Nicene Creed "provided that the devil starts no new heresy."

The triumph of Photius was now complete, and he was able to savor it for a few more years before another shudder in Byzantine politics put his position in peril again. Basil's death in 886 catapulted to the throne an illegitimate son, Leo VI, who despised Photius, and the young emperor lost no time in charging his former tutor with various intrigues. Photius was stripped of his title and sequestered in a monastery, where he died a few years later.

For all the Eastern accolades and Western imprecations that would rain down upon Photius's memory in the centuries to follow, it remains a remarkable fact that Rome and Constantinople were in communion during all but a few months of his career. So what then accounts for his reputation through the ages as chief author of the Great Schism that was still to come? As the historian J. B. Bury explains, Photius "formulated the points of difference between the two churches that were to furnish the pretext for the schism; he first brought into the foreground, as an essential point of doctrine, the mystery of the procession of the Holy Ghost." Photius was not in fact the first Eastern churchman to object to the Western attachment to the Filioque, but he attacked it with a gusto and sophistication that were to remain unmatched for all time. Easterners increasingly recognized in Photius a model of fearless independence from what they considered Rome's bullying pretensions, while westerners came to view him as the crowning example of how unprincipled ambition hitched to imperial power would shatter the unity of the church.

Even so, since Photius and Ignatius both died completely reconciled to Rome,

The emperor Leo VI humbly prostrates himself before a blessing Christ, begging forgiveness of his sins. The ninth century mosaic at the Hagia Sophia is in a tympanum, a niche above the lintel of the "emperor's door," one of the nine doors leading from the narthex into the church proper.

Successive emperors Basil I (the Macedonian) and his illegitimate son, Leo VI (the Wise), are depicted receiving gifts from Daniel. The illustration gives no indication of the enmity that existed between father and son.

optimists were confident the East-West controversy would die with them. But of course it did not, since its central issue—what are the powers of the patriarch of the West over the church of the East?—was no closer to settlement. For more than 150 years, the question lay smoldering, while Rome endured the era of what even some Catholic historians call "the bad popes" (see sidebar page 78). None seemed capable of ruling in the West, let alone the East. Meanwhile at Constantinople, Basil's descendants, despite court feuding that made the word "Byzantine" synonymous with "treachery," provided the Eastern empire with its golden era, raising it to economic, military and cultural heights it would not surpass in its entire eleven-century history. Certainly none of the "bad popes" was ready to challenge it.

Indeed, the Roman see reverted to such indifference regarding its rights that by 1024, Pope John XIX was prepared to embrace a declaration suggested by an Eastern embassy that read, in part, "the church in Constantinople should be styled universal in its sphere"—a concession of nearly full autonomy. But then something occurred that warned of a sea change to come in the Western church's attitude: Disciples of the Cluniac reform movement raised such a din of protest over this perceived affront to papal authority that John had little choice but to repudiate the deal.

This time, church reformers had flexed their muscles as outsiders. The full force of their campaign for the renewal of Christian life and an end to such practices as simony and clerical marriage would only be felt, however, when they gained control of the papacy itself. This was not far off, either. Beginning in 1046, the German emperor Henry III began appointing a series of such reformers to the papacy, the greatest of whom by far was the third, Pope Leo IX (1049–1054), a relative of his and a distinguished churchman.

Like Nicholas nearly two centuries before, Leo set the tone of his papacy at once. He surrounded himself with talented advisers—the first Roman Curia with a truly international flavor—and embarked upon a whirlwind schedule of travel throughout Italy, Germany, and France that included numerous synods at which he would condemn such corruptions as simony and the practice of laymen appointing bishops. Leo's travels helped him appreciate the growing threat of the

Normans, too—freebooters who would smash the Muslims in Sicily but whose incursions into southern Italy threatened both Byzantine lands and the pope's own patrimony. Leo could hardly face them alone, however. When sufficient help from Henry failed to materialize, the pope parleyed with General Argyos, a Lombard in Byzantine pay who favored a partnership. Not that the resulting deal did Leo much good. When the pope dashed south in 1053 to protect his interests, he ended up sending his own makeshift army into battle against a combat-hardened Norman force. The pope's troops were an untested if fervent multitude of volunteers leavened with a few hundred fearsome Germans, and despite stout resistance from the latter, the Norman surge turned into a blood-soaked rout, with the pope escaping just ahead of the slaughter.

In the history of medieval warfare, Pope Leo's quixotic venture might rate a footnote at best, but its implications for church unity turned out to be profound. Leo had already irritated the Eastern patriarch, a formidable churchman named Michael Cerularius, by holding councils condemning the creeping acceptance of Byzantine-rite ceremonies in Latin parishes in the south, and by appointing an archbishop to Sicily, once part of the patriarch's domain. Leo's hobnobbing with

In Cerularius, Pope Leo now encountered a rival every bit as remarkable as himself. Indeed he would prove more adept than the pope at achieving his personal ambitions.

General Argyos had gone down hard with the patriarch, too, who had clashed with the general over his preference for unleavened bread. Moreover, the patriarch was understandably concerned the emperor might reward the pope for any assistance he could muster in holding the Normans in check. Leo's foray south compounded these unintentional affronts by reconfirming the pope's unquenchable interest in an arena in which the patriarch deeply feared Latin hegemony.

In Cerularius, Leo now encountered a rival every bit as remarkable as himself, and every bit as attentive to his own interests. Indeed, for a brief spell, the patriarch would prove even more successful than the pope at achieving his ambitious goals. No Byzantine patriarch, before or after, would ever accumulate the power that Cerularius eventually wielded. Critics would cite this as a testament to his personal ambition and pride, noting for example his stated belief that his position was "not one whit inferior to that of the purple or the diadem," as well as his penchant for wearing boots of royal crimson. Admirers, on the other hand, would insist Cerularius sought nothing more than the sort of ecclesiastical autonomy that eventually prevailed in the West, and which had been pursued ever since Ambrose. If we are left guessing regarding the patriarch's true motives in the imminent drama of the schism, it is in part because he authored no body of writing comparable to that of Photius. Yet Cerularius's personal qualities, including high intelligence, decisiveness and a penchant for intrigue, are not remotely in doubt.

Cerularius first bolts into historical view as a patrician conspirator in an unlucky plot to topple the emperor Michael IV in 1040; it seems probable Cerularius hoped to occupy the imperial throne himself. But the fiasco propelled him into a different career: He was banished to a monastery, where he took up the religious life with characteristic seriousness and lofty aspiration. Such were his talent and force of personality that he was impossible to overlook when a new emperor, Constantine IX Monomachos (1042–1054), sought learned advisers, and by early 1043, when the patriarchate became vacant, Cerularius was poised to be elected to that office.[7]

However irritated Cerularius might have become with Rome, the opening broadside from the East was unleashed not by the patriarch but by a Bulgarian archbishop, Leo of Ohrid, who fired off a testy letter in 1053 to the Greek bishop of Trani, Italy, warning him against Latin rituals and disciplines, most notably the use of unleavened bread. The letter was copied and passed around, as it was meant to be, and soon wound up in the hands of the pope. Did Cerularius put his friend Leo of Ohrid up to this stunt? Possibly. Even if he did not, he certainly agreed with the letter's contents, although he most likely failed

Though banished for plotting to overthrow the emperor, Cerularius's talent and his forceful personality led to his election as patriarch of the Eastern church.

to realize the degree to which they would incite Western resentment.

Cerularius likewise lent support to a far more truculent anti-Western treatise composed by the Studite monk Nicetas Stethatos, who interspersed discussion of various intolerable practices—the use of unleavened bread, the Saturday fast, priestly celibacy—with naked insult. Finally, the patriarch seems to have ordered the closing of Latin-rite churches in Constantinople, although the evidence for this is not quite so clear-cut as has sometimes been portrayed.

In any event, Pope Leo concluded he must act. He ordered letters drafted for the emperor and the patriarch, and designated three trusted advisers, including Cardinal Humbert of Silva Candida, to carry them to Constantinople on his behalf. Leo's choice of Humbert, while understandable given his loyalty and many talents, proved fateful, as the cardinal's zeal for a reforming, unchallenged papacy may have exceeded that of the pope himself. Humbert had earlier been tapped to impose the new papal discipline on various Western prelates and was more than willing to test his blunt methods in the East. Certainly, he was not prepared to treat New Rome's patriarch with anything approaching the respect Cerularius usually commanded.

Since Cerularius was not even notified that a papal legation was on the way, he seems at first to have mistaken Humbert's group for imposters in league with his antagonist General Argyos. It did not seem possible the pope would adopt such a severe and peremptory tone with a fellow patriarch, and he was taken aback to read in Leo's letter that any dissent from Rome amounted to a "confab-

7. Constantine IX Monomachos was actually the third husband of the Empress Zoë, whose husbands and dependants ruled the Byzantine Empire from 1028 to 1054. Zoë's choice of the elderly Constantine was a disaster for the empire, and not only because of the Great Schism. His reign was marked by loss of territory to the Normans and the introduction of ill-advised taxes on his Eastern subjects, which stoked their restiveness at a time when they were sorely needed to assist in defending the empire's frontiers.

ulation of heretics, a conventical of schismatics, and a synagogue of Satan." Understandably, the Roman see's letter to the emperor was far more respectful, and for a while it appeared Humbert's delegation might succeed in prying Byzantium's secular and religious leaders apart. Constantine Monomachos understood full well that his only chance of holding on to lands in southern Italy was through an alliance with the papacy against the Normans. The emperor even agreed to suppress an offending tract by the monk Nicetas Stethatos after Humbert penned a savage rebuttal that included such crude gibes as "You should be called 'drunk' rather than 'monk'!" and "One would not think that you live in the Studite monastery but in a circus or brothel."

True to his aggressive nature, Humbert then proceeded to overplay his hand. On July 16, 1054, he and his fellow legates strode into Hagia Sophia as astonished clergy were preparing to chant the Liturgy and placed on the altar a bull of excommunication against the patriarch, the archbishop of Ochrida and their adherents. Upon leaving the church, the cardinal and his companions stopped, shook the dust from their sandals and exclaimed, "May God behold and judge us!"

But if the legates thought they could treat the patriarch as they might an upstart bishop in the West, they were grossly mistaken. When the populace heard of the curse on their patriarch, they rallied to his support, leaving the emperor no choice but to abandon hope of an anti-Norman alliance. Pressured by growing demonstrations, he bowed to Cerularius's wish to convene a synod, at which Humbert and his associates were condemned and excommunicated. Each side had now pushed the other to the edge of a total rupture. Thanks to Humbert, moreover, the doctrinal issue of the Filioque clause had been resurrected as a major obstacle to reconciliation; Humbert seemed to think the Eastern Church had deleted it at some point from the creed, and leveled this baseless charge in the document the legates left in Hagia Sophia.

Had either side wanted to, there was still opportunity to pull back from the brink. Pope Leo had died before his legates even reached Constantinople, so technically they were in no position to excommunicate in his name. And the patriarch's condemnation was confined for the moment to the legates themselves; it did not extend to the entire Latin Church. But such was Humbert's prestige in Rome that Leo's successors reflexively endorsed the view that he had done little more than discipline a contumacious bishop and that it was up to Cerularius or a successor to seek forgiveness.[8] Easterners were of quite the opposite view: they

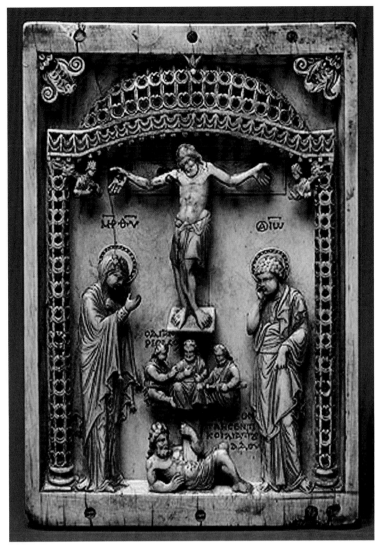

A tenth-century Byzantine ivory plaque depicting the Crucifixion, likely made in Constantinople. It is unique among surviving early Byzantine depictions of the Crucifixion, in that it shows the dying figure of Hades, classical ruler of the underworld, at the base of the cross—signifying Christ's victory over evil.

8. Humbert's version of events, published after his return to Rome, was the only Latin account, and thus was immensely influential for centuries in shaping the Western view of Cerularius. This was especially true regarding the conviction that only the patriarch's scheming forced an otherwise reluctant emperor to side with him. "Mad Michael," Humbert wrote of Cerularius, "stirred up a great rebellion of the common people against the emperor, because the emperor's will had been to cooperate with the legates."

believed the first conciliatory move should come from Rome. Cerularius, in any case, had a more ambitious project in mind. The confrontation had confirmed his belief that the patriarch must wrest independence from the emperor, lest the church be hostage to mere politics, and so, fearless intriguer that he was, Cerularius organized a conspiracy to replace Constantine Monomachos with Isaac Comnenus, after extracting a promise from the latter that he would stay out of ecclesiastical affairs. This pledge, however, turned out to be worth just about what one would expect; Cerularius was deposed one year later by the new emperor, and died shortly thereafter.

The decisive significance of the Schism of 1054 is occasionally disputed by those who note that relations periodically thawed between Rome and Byzantium in the years that followed. But the eleventh-century clash between pope and patriarch deserves its traditional prominence, for it dispelled all lingering doubt on both sides regarding the range of differences that separated them, while sharpening the arguments for each contested practice and belief. The Greek and Latin Churches had been diverging for centuries without fully realizing it; now that their eyes were opened, they were appalled by what they saw, and yet lacked the historical context to grant validity to the other's tradition. Disagreement over the correct form of sacramental bread might seem relatively trivial to a later age, for example, but as Mahlon H. Smith observes, for these disputants, the issue "penetrated practically every area of theology." The Filioque, of course, seemed to raise an even more fundamental doctrinal divide. Meanwhile, overshadowing everything was the question of authority. To Catholics in the West, it was perfectly obvious the pope was the successor to Peter, to whom Christ had left the church, and that Cerularius and his defenders

On a promontory overlooking Lake Ohrid, the Macedonian church of St. Jovan Kaneo, built of brick and stone, is an intriguing blend of Byzantine and Armenian influences. First erected in the ninth century, it was restored in the fourteenth. It was in the see of Archbishop Leo, whose letter of 1053 to the Greek bishop in Trani instigated Western animosity.

were thus in rebellion against a divinely proclaimed order. To Eastern Christians, it was equally apparent that authority was shared by the patriarchs, Rome included, and that while the Roman see might be first among equals, it did not follow that the pope could simply dictate without collegial support.

It is not as if many Christians on both sides, from humble lay folk to theologians and mighty bishops, did not often yearn for a restoration of unity. And attempts were made to achieve it. Even the First Crusade in 1095 was motivated at least in part by a Western desire to defend Eastern Christians from the relentless Muslim pressure. Unfortunately, the crusaders had their own definition of what comprised ecumenical spirit: They drove the Greek patriarch out of Antioch in 1098, and replaced him with a Latin bishop, then compounded this outrage in 1204 with a horrific sack of Constantinople. After that disaster and the humiliating occupation that followed, only military desperation would ever again prompt an emperor to engage in talks aimed at bridging the divide.

The West's response over the centuries has wavered from outright challenges to Orthodoxy, with the establishment of churches under Rome in Orthodox countries, to the Second Vatican Council's positive assessment of the Orthodox faith in the twentieth century and the establishment of a Joint International Commission, which has declared the Catholic and Orthodox "Sister Churches" that are both responsible for maintaining the "one Church of God." However, full rapprochement between East and West still appears distant. None has striven more tirelessly for it than John Paul II, the pope when this chapter was written. Though his efforts met with mixed responses in Athens, Moscow and Sofia, Christians both Orthodox and Catholic pray for and expect reunion as an inevitability. In the words of G. K. Chesterton, they wait for it to happen "like the coming of the comet or the freezing of the star." ■

A historic and long-awaited meeting between Eastern and Western churches occurred in 1964, with the meeting of Pope Paul VI and the patriarch of Constantinople, Athenagoras, in Jerusalem, a meeting re-enacted by Pope John Paul II and Patriarch Bartholomew I in 2004. Although East and West are far from completely reconciled, these important gestures have warmed relations between them.

The barefoot emissaries of Pope Innocent IV, John Carpini and his companion Benedict, pause in their grueling journey across the Asian steppes. Despite advanced age and the dangers of starvation, Mongol attackers and physical deprivations, these zealous Franciscans persevered to reach the court of the great Khan, there to discover Chinese Christianity long established.

CHAPTER 7

An untold story—How all central Asia once teemed with Christians

The first Western missionaries were shocked to find the Mongol capital alive with Christianity, the fruit of fervid evangelism by the Church of the East

For European Christians in the mid-thirteenth century, the immense expanse of Asia was one vast and menacing unknown. Out of Asia, it was true, came beautiful silks, delightful spices and much wealth. But out of Asia also came the ferocious and pitiless hordes of Mongol tribesmen who had so recently pillaged and slaughtered their way through southern Russia and eastern Europe. Nor were the Mongols the first such invaders. Many others had preceded them, so that Asia seemed to Western Christendom a source of unrelenting, murderous barbarism. Into this foreboding peril, in the year 1245, Pope Innocent IV sent an envoy. His mission: to reach and seek the conversion of the fearsome Mongol khan.

His choice for the job must have seemed as unlikely as the timing. John of Plano Carpini was no swordsman or diplomat—merely a pudgy Franciscan friar. But as an early disciple of Francis of Assisi, John had helped to found Francis's new mendicant order; he was no faint-heart. With one equally intrepid companion, Friar Benedict the Pole, he journeyed for nine excruciatingly uncomfortable months across the great Eurasian plain to the lower reaches of the Volga river—where one day they were suddenly and alarmingly snatched up by Mongol horsemen and delivered to the camp of Batu Khan, grandson of the

"We started out most tearfully, not knowing whether we were going to life or death," wrote the weary Friar John of Plano Carpini when the Mongol chieftain Batu told him he must journey onward to the distant court of the Great Khan himself. Already Friar John and his companion had been nine months on the road, and were "so feeble that we could hardly ride; during the whole of that Lent, our only food had been millet with salt and water ... nor had we anything else to drink but snow melted in the kettle."

No doubt a welcome sight to medieval Silk Road travelers journeying through the Kyrgyzstan mountains, this caravanserai, one of the few remaining ones, is located in the Torugart Pass near the Chinese border. Built completely of stone, the tenth century Tash Rabat caravanserai offered a comfortable night's stay, boasting a large central hall, thirty individual rooms, a place for animals to lodge and eating facilities. Local legend suggests that the inn may at one time have been a Nestorian monastery.

storied Genghis, and recently the scourge of Europe at the head of the infamous Golden Horde. Alas, Batu refused to accept their message from Pope Innocent. He insisted they take it to his cousin Kuyuk, the Khakan (Great Khan) of all the Mongols, at his court at Karakorum—five more harrowing months away.[1]

Struggling on, the two Franciscans were finally able to discharge their commission, but not before experiencing a severe shock. Here they were, in deepest Asia, at this supposedly heathen court—and the place was crawling with Christians! The Great Khan's personal secretaries were Christian; so were his advisers and administrators; so were his physicians. In a chapel near the royal tent, regular Christian worship was reverently and very audibly proceeding. And as John would further recount in his *History of the Mongols*, Christian courtiers insisted that Kuyuk himself was about to embrace the faith.

The westerners realized with disdain that these people were Persian heretics, whose disaffected Church of the East—rejecting every plea from Rome and Byzantium—had insisted more than eight centuries earlier upon following the heretical teacher Nestorius. Friar John disapprovingly noted that some of their liturgical practices differed from Western ones, and seemingly some of their beliefs, also. But they were recognizably Christian, and of their mission activities in central Asia, no news whatsoever had hitherto seeped through to Europe.

Indeed, what the two friars saw at the Mongol capital was only a fragment of these activities. Between the fifth and the fifteenth centuries, missionaries from the Persian Empire had traveled the trade routes of Asia to plant the cross from Arabia east to the Pacific Ocean, and from the Indian Subcontinent north to Siberia, converting kings, chieftains and sometimes whole tribes, and establishing thousands of churches. They had conducted, in fact, the most far-ranging evangelistic endeavor in the history of Christianity up to that time.

Not until the twentieth century would Western Christians begin to suspect the true scope of this Church of the East. How could they? After the fifth century, Mesopotamian Christendom was almost completely cut off from the West, for reasons political as well as theological. Within another several hundred years, most of Asia's flourishing Christian

communities would be wiped out, and such evidence as remained of their existence would long be overlooked or misinterpreted. Furthermore, to compound the distress of the few surviving remnants, through the second millennium they would be dismissed by Europeans, despite their vigorous denials, as hopelessly heretical.

The great missionary Church of the East originated in the first century. Among the crowd in Jerusalem that experienced the momentous descent of the Holy Spirit, says the New Testament, were Jews from Persian Parthia, Medea, Elam and Mesopotamia (Acts 2:9). In town to celebrate Passover, most of them would have known about the Crucifixion of Jesus. Some might even have seen him after his Resurrection. Some could have experienced directly the infilling of the Holy Spirit, descending upon the disciples as a mighty wind and tongues of fire. Three thousand reportedly experienced it through Peter's inspired sermon (Acts 2:41).

These people, according to Christian tradition, hastened home to carry the momentous news of the crucified and risen Messiah to fellow Jews throughout Persia. Soon afterward, the apostle Thomas, before going on to preach in India, is believed to have sent a disciple named Thaddeus (Addai in Syriac) to preach in Osrhoene, a small and embattled state perilously squeezed between the Byzantine and Persian Empires. Thence the new faith spread to the kingdom of Adiabene and its capital, Arbela (modern Arbil in Iraq), three hundred miles to the east. (See earlier volume, *A Pinch of Incense*.) Here Jewish Christians became particularly numerous, and soon they reached out to their gentile neighbors.

Tradition credits Addai and two of his converts, Aggai and Mari, with the launching of missionary work throughout Arabia, Persia, Armenia, and east to the Indian border.[2] Historian John Stewart (*Nestorian Missionary Enterprise: The Story of a Church on Fire*) quotes a sixth-century claim that in the time of Bishop Abd Mshikha-Zkha of Arbela, between A.D. 190 and 225, there were some twenty-five episcopal sees between the mountains of Kurdistan and the Persian Gulf (listing by name seventeen of the incumbents). A respected school of theology was established at Edessa, capital of Osrhoene.

Conditions then were propitious for Christianity in Persia and adjacent regions. Zoroastrianism predominated, but the Parthian warrior dynasty that had ruled Persia since about 140 B.C. took little interest in matters religious. Such harassment as occurred was local, instigated by jealous Zoroastrian priests rather than by royal command. Furthermore, despite intermittent warfare between Rome and Persia, Eastern and Western Christians were not yet cut off from each other, allowing regular communication between cities like Edessa (usually Roman-occupied) and Nisibis (some hundred and fifty miles away, in territory usually Persian).

Under the Sassanids who conquered Persia in A.D. 224, its Jewish and Christian minorities could still live in peace, so long as they behaved with discretion.[3] In the early fourth century, however, the situation changed. The Sassanids were Zoroastrians, claiming descent from the ancient Medes and Persians, whose great ambition was to fully restore the worship of Ahura Mazda, god of light, and with it the glorious empire of Cyrus the Great. So they built

2. A fourth-century document called *The Doctrine of Addai* describes how Addai, disciple of the apostle Thomas, healed and converted King Abgar of Edessa, and baptized many of his subjects. Among the first was the royal robe-maker, Aggai, and another future missionary named Mari. Tradition remembers Mari as being, like Thomas, a doubter and pessimist who reported back that the people east of Edessa were worthless heathen and the project hopeless. Urged to keep going, however, he did so—again like Thomas—and reluctantly persevered to final and abundant success.

3. Third-century Sassanid shahs were chiefly concerned with eliminating Manichaeanism, a syncretistic religion then spreading wildly. Its founder, a young aristocrat named Mani, was killed along with many of his followers in vicious persecutions, and Christians too were often included.

new fire temples, and centralized Zoroastrian worship as their state religion. Its priests—called *mobeds* or magi—became exceedingly powerful, and adherence to the national faith became proof of patriotism.

Moreover, about then Christianity became the favored religion of the Roman Empire, automatically rendering Persian Christians suspect of treasonous intentions. In 339, Shah Shapur II started a brutal forty-year campaign against this "religion of Caesar." Memorialized in church annals as "the Great Persecution," it began by double-taxing Christians to finance war against Rome. The Christian *catholicos* (patriarch), Shimun bar Sabbai, refused to help collect it, protesting that his people were too poor—which in that era they likely were. Shimun and a hundred of his priests were therefore arrested, but Shapur reportedly was uneasy about this proceeding. He offered to let them all go free if only Shimun would worship the sun—even just once.[4] No, the catholicos sorrowfully replied, he could not do that because, he said, "The sun went into mourning when its creator died."

So the executions began—with the catholicos last to die. In the midst of the killing, according to legend, a sympathetic palace official named Pusaik discerned that one victim, a friend of his named Hanania, seemed to be faltering in his resolve. "Do not fear, Hanania," he called out. "Shut your eyes that you may open them on the light of Christ!" Guards immediately dragged Pusaik before Shapur, where Pusaik declared that he envied the martyrs their punishment, for he too was a worshiper of Jesus Christ. His work and status at

4. The shah-of-shahs Shapur II ordered the Christian patriarch Shimun to make obeisance to the sun ("even just once") as a test of loyalty to the Persian throne. Zoroastrianism centers upon temples where Ahura Mazda is worshiped as sacred fire, but as god of light and goodness, Ahura Mazda is also associated with the sun, the major source of light. Similarly, rather than bury their dead in the dark earth, Zoroastrians allow sunlight and the birds of the air to deal with their dead. (They still do, as on the Towers of Silence in Bombay.)

court, he said, counted as nothing by comparison. For this wretch, roared the furious Shapur, mere beheading was too mild. "Tear his tongue out by the roots!" he shouted, "so that men may fear me because of him!"

Sixteen thousand believers were recorded by name as dying in the Great Persecution, wrote the Greek ecclesiastical historian Sozomen, along with countless unnamed others, for a total of perhaps two hundred thousand. The royal mandate allowed any minor official to unleash a local massacre, which enabled Zoroastrian priests or vindictive neighbors to vent any grievance. For years, it is said, such outbreaks were endemic throughout the Persian provinces, particularly in Adiabene and among the numerous Christians of outlying territories.

Nuns and monks reportedly were favorite targets, because celibacy offended Zoroastrian belief. Their tormentors frequently offered to spare them without even making them renounce Christ, if only they would agree to marry. Few did. One target was the deaconess Tarbo, sister of Catholicos Shimun, who was accused of using sorcery to inflict vengeful illness upon the Persian empress. Tarbo, with another sister and their servant, was condemned by the chief Mobed to be cut in pieces—a favored method of execution. Then the ailing empress (to complete her cure) was carried on a litter among their bleeding body parts.

Even so, it was claimed, relatively few Christians faltered under torture. Of one group of three hundred, for example, just twenty-five reportedly chose to deny their Lord and save their lives. The reported behavior of some few individuals, however, was deplorable. For example, one degenerate priest, Paul, is said to have abjured his faith to save his wealth, which merely frustrated his persecutor, Narses Namaspur, a notoriously greedy official who coveted precisely that wealth. Narses therefore ordered Paul to behead five consecrated women, thinking he would surely condemn himself by refusing, but the wretched priest did not shrink even

Tenacious survivors for two centuries in Iraq, Christians now comprise three percent of the population and are concentrated in Baghdad and the north near Mosul (the ancient city of Nineveh). This shopkeeper in Arbil (top, facing page), would be a descendant of first-century Christians evangelized by Addai, follower of the apostle Thomas. The Christian village of Al Qosh (bottom, facing page), on the Nineveh plain, looks much as it must have centuries ago. Syriac, an Aramaic language, is still used liturgically in places like St. Matthew monastery (above, left). Sixteen hundred years old and strategically located on Mount Maqloub, it was damaged by bombing during the American invasion of Iraq. Iraq's most famous Christian, Tariq Aziz (above, right), was formerly Deputy Prime Minister to Saddam Hussein. His role as advisor and diplomat echoed the traditional services performed by educated Christians in the Muslim empire.

from this. He killed the horrified women, though in the end it did him no good. Narses put him to the sword regardless, and confiscated his riches.

At times, though, Persian shahs looked kindly upon their Christian subjects, who prudently responded by trying to disassociate themselves from the Roman Empire. In 410, at the Council of Seleucia, they declared their church independent of Rome, and of almost every other patriarchate outside the Persian realm. (The only remaining connection to Western Christendom was a friendly and unofficial one through the patriarchate of Antioch.) In return, Shah Yazdegerd I issued an edict of toleration for his Christian subjects, recognizing them as a *melet*, a distinct people (as the Jews already were) under the monarchy.

The Persian catholicos, now established in the capital city, Seleucia-Ctesiphon on the Tigris River, claimed jurisdiction over most of Asia outside the Roman Empire. And then came the event that would conclusively separate the Eastern Church from all the rest, pinning firmly upon it the enduring and controversial name "Nestorian." The patriarch Nestorius of Constantinople, accused of

The patriarch Nestorius, accused of disputing Christ's divinity, was ousted as a heretic. Western condemnation remained in full force until the past century when doubts arose.

denying complete unity between the fully divine and fully human natures of Christ, was excommunicated as a heretic by the Third Ecumenical Council, which met in Ephesus in 431. Nestorius's books were condemned, and he was banished to Egypt, where he died some twenty years later. (See earlier volume, *Darkness Descends*, chapter 6.)

Persian Christians, increasingly alienated, accused their Western brethren of misrepresentation and theological hairsplitting. They had been represented at the Council of Nicea, and had endorsed the doctrine so meticulously formulated there. But they were not present at Ephesus, and they vehemently refused to acquiesce in its condemnation of Nestorius, whose teaching, they contended, had been distorted. They continued to hold him in high regard, and to revere his mentor, Theodore of Mopsuestia, as their major theologian.

The effect of Nestorianism on the theology of the Church of the East has been debated ever since. His followers certainly dominated it, and were greatly reinforced by refugees from anti-Nestorian heresy-hunters in the Roman Empire[5]. In any case, Western condemnation would remain in full force until the twentieth century, when some scholars would develop serious doubts. "Whether Nestorius himself ever expressed his belief in the crude way he is supposed to have done, and for which he was condemned, is a matter of dispute," concludes historian Laurence E. Browne in *The Eclipse of Christianity in Asia*, "for it is abundantly clear that the Nestorian Church (i.e., the Church of the East) never held the doctrine in that extreme form, and as time went on, its doctrine approximated more and more to what was known as orthodoxy in the West."

5. Nestorian Christians were not the only refugees flooding into Persia in the fifth century. Equally endangered by the failure of the Council of Ephesus, and later of Chalcedon, to solve the conflicts besetting the church were the Monophysites, whose belief about the human-divine union within the nature of Christ was opposite to the alleged heresy of the Nestorians. Organized by the indefatigable bishop Jacob Baradaeus, Monophysites became numerous throughout Egypt and Syria (see earlier volume, *The Sword of Islam*). In the sixth century many fled to Persia, causing bitter power struggles with the Nestorians and resulting in two separate churches.

Meanwhile, although Yazdegerd I largely honored his commitment of 410, dreadful persecutions followed his death ten years later, possibly because so many highborn Zoroastrians were becoming Christian. Bahram V (421–439), his son and successor, conducted a brutal two-year campaign featuring exquisite refinements of cruelty, some of which were detailed in contemporary accounts. Flaying (by stripping the skin from the hands or back, or peeling the face from forehead to chin), was a favorite, along with binding people hand and foot and throwing them into pits to starve to death (or possibly to be slowly devoured by rats).

Imposing evidence of a once thriving Christian population near Maku, Iran, this Armenian church is named for St. Thaddeus, who evangelized and was martyred in this area. Also known as the Black Church (Ghara Kelisa), it now has a service only once a year on the saint's feast day, drawing Armenians from all over Iran. The original church, built early in the Christian era, has been superseded by this seventeenth century structure, incorporating tenth and thirteenth century ruins.

After a three-decade respite, the killings began again under Bahram's son Yazdegerd II (439–457). He is said to have dispatched 153,000 Christians in a single city, Kirkuk in present-day Iraq, by crucifixion, stoning or beheading. This number may be exaggerated, suggests Anglican missionary and historian W. A. Wigram (*Introduction to the History of the Assyrian Church*), but local tradition insists that on the hill of the executions, the gravel was permanently stained red. Also cherished in the East is the story of Tamasgerd, the royal officer in charge of the slaughter, who was so impressed by the courage and faith of the martyrs that at length he insisted upon joining them. Thus Tamasgerd was "baptized in his own blood," and a church bearing his name was later built there.

The accession of Chosroes I (the Great) in 531 inaugurated forty-eight prosperous and relatively peaceful years for Persian Christians. His favorite wife (possibly a Byzantine captive) is said to have been a believer, as was his physician. He employed many more Christians as administrators, and greatly admired their patriarch, Aba. The jealous Zoroastrian magi, however, charged that Aba was an apostate from the state religion, was leading others similarly astray, and was criticizing marriage between close relatives (a Persian custom). All three were capital offenses, and all the charges were true. Aba was indeed a former Zoroastrian, and an evangelical, and determined to cleanse his church of Zoroastrian habits. Chosroes, unable to persuade him to temporize, saved him from death by imprisoning and then exiling him.[6]

Hormizd IV, the otherwise undistinguished son of Chosroes the Great, also eschewed persecution, declaring that his throne stood on four bases: Zoroastrians, Magians (a Zoroastrian variant), Jews and Christians. His son

6. Although conversion from Zoroastrianism to Christianity was a capital offense, it was usually (but not always) commuted to prison or exile. Proselytizing was also illegal, an impossible rule for an evangelical faith. Patriarch Aba in the mid-sixth century had to rule the church from exile, or from prison, for seven years. The monk George of Mount Isla, accused under Chosroes II of apostasy, was first jailed and then executed.

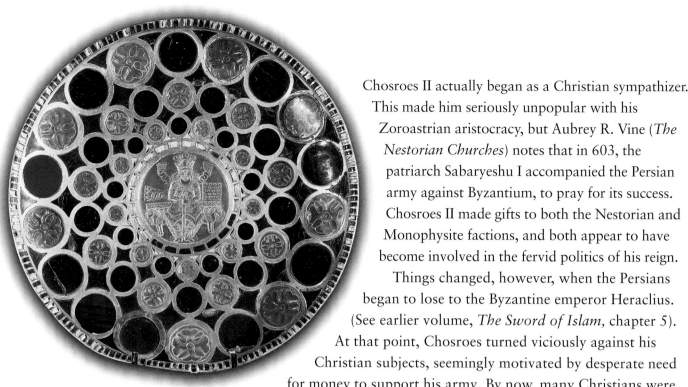

Chosroes the Great sits enthroned on the medallion in the center of this sixth-century cup. The elaborate gold metalwork, embellished with garnets and carved rock crystal, demonstrates the skill and artistry of Sassanian craftsmen, whose designs were copied from Byzantium to China. The cup is housed in the Bibliothèque Nationale de l'Opéra, Paris.

Chosroes II actually began as a Christian sympathizer. This made him seriously unpopular with his Zoroastrian aristocracy, but Aubrey R. Vine (*The Nestorian Churches*) notes that in 603, the patriarch Sabaryeshu I accompanied the Persian army against Byzantium, to pray for its success. Chosroes II made gifts to both the Nestorian and Monophysite factions, and both appear to have become involved in the fervid politics of his reign. Things changed, however, when the Persians began to lose to the Byzantine emperor Heraclius. (See earlier volume, *The Sword of Islam*, chapter 5). At that point, Chosroes turned viciously against his Christian subjects, seemingly motivated by desperate need for money to support his army. By now, many Christians were well-to-do bureaucrats, teachers, lawyers, doctors, merchants and craftsmen. A notable victim this time, for example, was one Yasdin, silversmith to the shah. Yasdin was killed, all his goods confiscated, and his wife brutally tortured, in case she knew of hidden treasure. But the Sassanid epoch was about to end. Chosroes was deposed and killed in 628, and little more than two decades later the weakened realm of Persia would fall to a whirlwind from the deserts of Arabia, Islam.

Helping to preserve some order in this turbulent time was one of the great leaders of the Eastern Church, Patriarch Yeshuyab II, who at one point was able to arrange a peace treaty with Heraclius. More remarkable still, he also convinced this theologically inclined emperor that the Church of the East was indeed orthodox in belief. While Yeshuyab was in Constantinople, Heraclius allowed him to receive communion in the Byzantine Liturgy. This caused a bishop back home to loudly accuse his patriarch of heresy, insisting that he had been bribed to compromise the true faith. "A blow from a friend is worth more than a kiss from an enemy," Yeshuyab gently but firmly responded, and produced a detailed account of all his doings in Constantinople.

Patriarch Yeshuyab also strengthened Nestorian missionary outreach to the Turkish nomads of central Asia, established India as a separate metropolitanate (see sidebar page 188), and is believed to have authorized the first mission to China. Nestorian evangelists had long been busy in Asia and India, and Arabia as well. The faith followed trade routes, and devout traders themselves often acted as missionaries. The major route into southern Arabia, for instance, led from Hira in western Iraq to the city of Najran in the Yemen. By the time of the Muslim invasion, Hira was almost entirely Christian, writes De Lacy O'Leary (*Arabia Before Muhammad*), and according to the Muslim historian Ibn Hisham, the church at Najran was founded by a Syrian trader called Haymiyun. (See *The Sword of Islam*, chapter 1.)

The recurrent persecutions of Christians in Persia meanwhile caused many to flee to the empire's fringes. Far from discouraging them in their beliefs, however, adversity inspired them to greater zeal, and following the traders and settlers came monks from the Persian monasteries and the theological schools of Edessa, Nisibis and Seleucia-Ctesiphon. There were also dramatic happenstances. At the close of the fifth century, for instance, the son of Shah Peroz, Kavad, was passed over in favor of his uncle. Kavad sought refuge with the White Huns, denizens of the central Asian steppes beyond the Oxus River, and in his entourage were two Christian laymen, a bishop and four priests. Kavad later won back his throne (with assistance from Hun warriors), but the Christians remained many years with the tribe—baptizing and teaching them, inventing an alphabet for them, and even persuading them to plant some vegetables and grain.

Mission outreach to far eastern Asia could also travel with these tough nomad raiders, as they fought each other for dominance of the continent. While Rome and Persia repelled or absorbed waves of westward-bound barbarians, the ancient empire of China was similarly harried. Even the famous Great Wall, begun in the third century B.C., was only partially effective. Nomad attackers still managed to infiltrate or smash their way into the fabled Chinese Empire, and sometimes were assimilated and absorbed, in the same way as were barbarian tribes in Rome's frontier provinces.

Persia also had trade connections with China from the fifth century. One important Christian trader, Sergis, is recorded as having settled his household in 578 in Lint'ao, along the Old Silk Road some three hundred miles west of its eastern terminus in central China, Chang'an (later called Sian-fu, and later still Xian). Sinologist and linguist P. Y. Saeki of Waseda University, Tokyo, notes that Chinese books dating from the mid-fifth century cite as places of interest the cities of Merv in Turkmenistan, and Gilan, now in eastern Iran. Both were important Christian centers.

There is also evidence of major mission work within China itself from at least the seventh century, though the most startling would not be discovered until 1623. This was when workmen, digging a foundation at Sian-fu, uncovered the remarkable, and remarkably controversial, Nestorian Monument—a massive black granite slab ten feet high, over three feet wide and about a foot thick. Set up in the courtyard of a nearby Buddhist temple, it was revealed as featuring a cross rising from a lotus blossom. Beneath this, an inscription in Chinese characters declared it to be "A Monument Commemorating the Propagation of the Ta-ch'in Luminous Religion in the Middle Kingdom."

The date on the memorial translates as 781, when Ch'ang-an was the capital of the T'ang emperors. Elegantly chiseled script describes how a missionary named A-lo-pen came there in the year 635, a

Proof of early Chinese Christianity, the Nestorian Monument, ten feet high and mounted on a carved tortoise, now resides in the Forest of Steles Museum, Xian. The T'ang dynasty stele was erected in 781, then buried in 845 at a time of persecution, and finally unearthed in the seventeenth century. The text, in Chinese and Syriac, relates the arrival of Christianity in China and indicates a widespread and well-ordered church.

Four characters from the Nestorian monument describe Christianity as "Ta-ch'in luminous religion," Ta-ch'in being the Chinese expression for the West, or the Roman Empire. Therefore, Christianity is the religion of light that came from the West.

century and a half earlier, from the kingdom of Ta-ch'in (Syria). It recounts the accomplishments of A-lo-pen, his associates and his successors in the following hundred and fifty years. The monument was donated, the inscription notes, by a priest and general named Yazedbouzid, the son of a Nestorian missionary from Balkh, Tahouristan, who is credited with many works of piety, as well as honorable service in the armies of three emperors.[7]

The elaborate inscription contains 1,756 Chinese ideographs and seventy Syriac words. It includes long lists of names (in both languages) of people involved in the mission. But first, it eloquently describes the "Luminous Religion" of its title—the worship of "the unoriginated Lord of the Universe, the mysterious unbegotten Triune Lord," and tells how one Person of this Trinity, the Messiah, came to earth as a man. He brought Life to light mankind and abolished death, and through the Third Person of the Trinity, the Holy Spirit, he opened to mankind the True and Unchanging Way.

"His ministers carry the Cross with them as a Sign," the inscription continues. They travel wherever the sun shines, and try to re-unite those that are lost … proclaiming the Glad Tidings ("joyful sounds") of Love and Charity … Once in seven days they have a bloodless sacrifice ("a sacrifice without the animal"), and thus "cleansing their hearts they regain purity."

This mysterious "Way," it continues, would not have spread so widely without the "Sage," and the Sage would not have been so great without the Way. The Sage almost without doubt is Emperor T'ai-tsung, second ruler of the T'ang dynasty (627–649). "And behold," explains the inscription, "there was a highly virtuous man named A-lo-pen," who decided to bring the Sutras (scriptures) of the True Way to China, through many difficulties and perils. The emperor dispatched a guard of honor to conduct him to the palace, where he worked in the imperial library while translating twelve Sutras, so that the monarch could judge their merits for himself. Finally, "being deeply convinced of the correctness and truth" of the Way, T'ai-tsung issued in 638 an imperial rescript to this effect:

"The Way had not at all times and in all places the selfsame human body. Heaven caused a suitable religion to be instituted for every region and clime so that each one of the races of mankind might be saved. Bishop A-lo-pen of the Kingdom of Ta-ch'in, bringing with him the Sutras and Images, has come from afar...Having carefully examined the scope of his teaching we find it to be mysteriously spiritual and of silent operation...Observing its principal and most essential points, we reached the conclusion that they cover all that is most important in life...This Teaching is helpful to all creatures and beneficial to all men. So let it have free course throughout the Empire."

T'ai-tsung's successors, according to the monument, also observed and supported the Way, sponsoring throughout the land the building of monasteries and temples in which their portraits and the imperial ensigns were prominently featured. At times there was trouble, when the Buddhists raised their voices against the Luminous Religion, or "some inferior Taoist scholars ridiculed and derided it." But the faith was sustained by valiant priests and bishops, who strengthened and reformed it, engaging in the work of conversion ("transforming influence"). This history section concludes with a prayer:

"How vast and extensive is the True Way
Yet how minute and mysterious it is.
Making a great effort to name it,
We declared it to be "Three-in-One."
O Lord, nothing is impossible for thee!
Help thy servants that they may preach!
Hereby we raise this noble monument,
And we praise thee for thy great blessings upon us!"

The author of the inscription identifies himself in Chinese as Ching-Ching (or King-tsing), a Ta-ch'in priest, and in Syriac as "Adam, Priest and Chorepiscopus and Papas of China." A man of this name, incidentally, is also mentioned in both Chinese Buddhist and Christian manuscripts of the era as a prolific translator.

By the time the Nestorian Monument came to light in 1623, a thousand years after the arrival of A-lo-pen in Chang'an, Europe knew more about the Far East. The Venetian traders Nicolo, Maffeo and Marco Polo had traveled extensively there, and Marco's published accounts had been a fourteenth-century sensation. However, though the Jesuit order began work in China during the 1580s, neither these missionaries nor their superiors back home seem to have been aware of the vast Christian presence that previously existed there. Westerners understandably greeted news of the monument with deepest suspicion. An obvious Jesuit forgery, scoffed the European intelligentsia (including the skeptical philosopher Voltaire), and Western scholars would remain similarly dismissive right through the nineteenth century.[8]

By the early twentieth, however, persuasive corroboration was turning up, very disconcerting to the skeptics. Christian manuscripts in both Syriac and Chinese were discovered in Buddhist temples and other caches along the Silk Road, preserved in some instances because the Buddhists had used the back of the manuscripts for their own records. Saeki published his first detailed study of the accumulated data in 1937, then was stymied by what he called "the protracted years of wicked wars," while his own country fought first China and then much of the rest of the world. However, when a friend sent him two newly found manuscripts in 1943—a Syrian hymn in adoration of the Transfiguration of the Lord, dated 720, and a Nestorian Sutra (scripture) on the Origin of Origins, dated 717—he set to work again. The future of Christian missions in the Far East, he declared, "can only be lighted by the lamp of the past."

Without question, these documents sometimes sound a little strange in the ears of modern Christians. Some earlier ones, for example, perhaps translated before the missionaries had a firm grasp of Chinese, occasionally refer to God as "Buddha." They also exhibit a disconcerting tendency to emperor-worship, along with traces of Confucian, Taoist or Buddhist imagery in general. But they are indubitably Christian nonetheless.

Among the oldest is the *Jesus Messiah Sutra*, possibly written by Bishop A-lo-pen himself, which describes how a star "as big as a cartwheel" blazed above the

7. The name of the exemplary priest-cum-army officer who financed the Nestorian Monument, Yazedbouzid, has been translated into Chinese as I-ssu. Linguist P. Y. Saeki also suggests that Bishop A-lo-pen, who headed the original Christian mission in 635, may have actually been named Abraham back home in Persia. China's frontier regions presented an extremely eclectic language mix, harboring as they did a grand diversity of foreigners: Persians, Mongols, Turks, Indians and more.

8. Many European scholars doubted the very existence of the Nestorian Monument, especially after the two-ton slab seemed to vanish in 1907. It turned out that a Danish scholar, Dr. Frits Holm, had offered to buy it for shipment to Europe or America, and indignant Chinese authorities had removed it for greater security to the Pei-lin (Forest of Monuments) in another part of Sian-fu. "I might as well have tried to lift the Rosetta Stone out of the British Museum," Holm commented later, "as to carry away the Ching-Chiao-pei from Sian." But he had meanwhile commissioned local craftsmen to make a replica, which he certified correct in every detail, and which he shipped to the Metropolitan Museum of Art, New York City.

city of *Wu-li-shih-lien* (Jerusalem) when *I-shu Mi-shih-ho* (Jesus Messiah) was born there. After his "immersion for washing" by *Yao-ku-hun* (John), the Messiah healed people, some slowly and some at once, and taught the "Right Way." But at length men who "excelled in wickedness" plotted against I-shu Mi-shih-ho, and forced "the Great King *P'i-lo-tu-ssu*" to condemn him to death. "Thus in charity the Messiah gave up his body … to be sacrificed for all mankind." The document includes moral precepts that parallel familiar biblical texts, but with a difference. Example: "If you happen to see another person laboring very hard, you should assist him by giving him your own power of labor, together with a drink of pure milk."

Those first one hundred and fifty years of Christian mission activity in China were not so trouble-free as the monument's upbeat summary implies.

Christian monks from Persia, reaching Chang'an (now Xian), the Chinese capital, in 635, are welcomed by imperial officials sent to conduct them into the city. The famous Nestorian Monument, discovered in the seventeenth century, describes how the Chinese emperor, probably T'ai-Tsung, set their leader, A-lo-pen, to translating scripture, then sponsored preaching of the faith and establishment of monasteries throughout his realm.

Christianity was competing there with a battery of relatively sophisticated religions: Confucianism and Taoism, both native to China; Buddhism, which probably arrived several hundred years earlier; Zoroastrianism; and the ubiquitous Manichaeanism. Emperor T'ai-Tsung welcomed them all, distributing favors among the major contenders. Having financed Buddhist and Taoist temples in Chang'an, he funded China's first Christian church there in 638. Many more would follow.

The next reign brought more dramatic difficulties in the form of a truly evil empress, the wicked Wu Hou. This woman, reputedly a great beauty, was added to T'ai-Tsung's harem as a child of twelve, and upon his death consigned to a Buddhist monastery. But somehow, Chinese tradition says, she managed to catch the eye of the new emperor, Kao-tsung, when he visited her monastery in 656, and

The hottest, most inhospitable place in China, the Turfan Basin, proved to be the ideal climate to preserve ancient manuscripts and wall paintings, such as this one. The ruined walls of a church near Khocho (or Chotscho) revealed this fresco from the ninth century depicting Palm Sunday. A priest or deacon is holding either an incense box or a chalice while three worshippers hold branches. Head gear identifies the two men as Uighurs, but the woman is clearly Chinese.

9. While Persia's Christian missionaries were first establishing themselves in the Chinese capital in the mid-seventh century, Persia's last Sassanian shah, Yazdegerd III, was fleeing into central Asia before his country's Muslim conquerors. He was killed, but his son found refuge at the T'ang court in Chang'an. The Persian crown prince never regained his country. He died in China, as did his son after him.

to "bewitch" him into making her his concubine. Although such a liaison was universally regarded as deeply sinful, the irresistible Wu Hou completely dominated Kao-Tsung. Determined to supplant his queen, she went so far as to kill her own baby and frame her rival for the murder.

Her ploy worked. The queen was executed (her hands and feet were chopped off and she bled to death), and Hou took her place. After the death of the emperor in 683, this extraordinary woman is said to have deposed her own two sons, started her own dynasty, installed Buddhism as the state religion, and then taken a Buddhist lover. This was, of course, another flagrant moral violation. No matter. The Buddhists declared her to be the Maitreya Buddha ("Buddha of the Future"). By then, Wu-Hou was encouraging anti-Christian mobs to trash churches, which they did with enthusiasm.

Even so, Christians in China managed to hold on. The same was true in their distant homeland, where shortly after their departure, Muslim armies had defeated the Persian shah and captured his capital.[9] Although these new rulers of Persia brutally suppressed Zoroastrianism, they were treating Christians fairly well, probably regarding them as less threatening than the state religion, and as useful administrators.

There is scant reference to the Chinese missions in Persian church records at this time, but the Arabs soon began eyeing Asia, including China. They reportedly sent their first embassy to the T'ang court in 713 via the maritime trade route, and more Christian missionaries went with it. Historian Samuel Hugh Moffett in his magnificent account of the church in the East, *A History of Christianity in Asia*, suggests that experienced Nestorian clergy were used as consultants and interpreters. Thus China is thought to have become a Nestorian metropolitanate in the early eighth century, and Chinese documents note that a Bishop Chi-lieh reached Chang'an with another Arab embassy in 732. (This name also appears on the Nestorian Monument.) Confrontation of two kinds was coming closer, however—a military clash between China and Islam, and a religious clash between Christianity and Islam. The Muslims were destined to win both.

By mid-century, the emperor of China, no longer able to ignore the Arab threat to Tibet and other territories neighboring his own, took action against them. In 751, however, he was decisively defeated at Talas in present-day Kirghistan—a fateful battle that arguably initiated the ultimate Muslim conquest of central Asia. And as the T'ang Empire disintegrated, Christianity seemingly was about to go into total eclipse there.

Many factors doubtless contributed. The largely Christian Uighur confederacy, an important ally of China, which at this stage controlled the Silk Road, decided to make Manichaeanism their official religion, probably because it was a vaguer and more comfortable faith. Islam, first arriving in China with a Muslim army on loan from the caliph at Baghdad, became another strong competitor on its crowded religious scene. Buddhism, the imperial preference, remained strong. The indigenous Confucianists and Taoists continued to harbor deep resentment against all the "foreign" faiths.

Emperor Wu-tsung expelled the foreign missionaries, who had been greatly resented by both the Confucianists and Taoists. Mention of Christianity then faded from the records.

So in 843, foreign missionaries were expelled. The emperor Wu-tsung, a Taoist, ordered the destruction of thousands of Buddhist temples and monasteries. Manichaean books and property were confiscated, and their images burned. Some three thousand Christian, Manichaean and Zoroastrian monks and nuns were commanded to return forthwith to secular life (and specifically ordered to start paying taxes). All non-natives among them were ordered to depart the country forthwith, and thus "cease to confuse Chinese national customs and manners."

The T'ang dynasty and the ninth century ended together. When Guangzhou (Canton) fell to a rebel chief in 878, a reported 120,000 Muslims, Christians and Jews were massacred. After that, Christianity is no longer mentioned in Chinese records. An Arab report dating from the late tenth century is quoted by Bar Hebraeus (1226–1286), Jacobite Primate of the East and an enormously prolific and accomplished scholar. This report, Bar Hebraeus writes, described an encounter in Baghdad with a monk recently returned from China, who said that he and five others had been sent to investigate the situation there, and had found nary a trace of Christian churches or Christian people.

This may not have been entirely true, even at such a low point. It was certainly not the case on the Asian Steppes, where a strong Christian presence up to the thirteenth century is attested by archaeological remains found in Mongolia and Manchuria. In southern Siberia, in the area near Lake Issyk-Kul later inhabited by the Kirghiz people, two graveyards were discovered in the late nineteenth century.[10] Both abounded in thirteenth-century Christian grave-markers for people who include priests, teachers, scholars and even one high official. They bear crosses with inscriptions in Syriac (and sometimes Turkish) indicating many origins: Banus the Uighur, Tatta the Mongol, and Shah Malik, son of George of Tus. A typical epitaph reads: "This is the grave of Pasak—The aim of life is Jesus our Redeemer."

10. Lake Issyk-Kul in southern Siberia is a salt lake, forty miles wide and one hundred twenty miles long, fifty-three hundred feet above sea level, surrounded by mountains. Fed by hot springs, it seldom freezes. In this area were found two extensive thirteenth-century Nestorian cemeteries. "This is the grave of the priest and general Zuma," says an epitaph dated 1272, "a blessed old man.... May our Lord unite his spirit with the spirits of the fathers and saints in eternity."

After all, merchants and monks alike had been zealously preaching the faith throughout Asia from the fourth century onward. Historian Stewart cites evidence of Christians among the Turks in the fifth century, and they not infrequently served as advisers or physicians to the chieftains. The eighth-century Nestorian patriarch Timothy, who sent scores of monks into central Asia to teach, baptize and build churches, wrote to a colleague in 781 about a nomad chief who had led his entire tribe into the faith, and was requesting a bishop to instruct them further.

Another such example is cited by the chronicler Joseph Simonius Assemani, about two hundred years later. A chief of the Keraits, a Turko-Mongol tribe then ranging east and south of Lake Baikal, became hopelessly lost while hunting alone in the mountains. Then he saw a man (or perhaps it was a vision) who identified himself as Mar (Saint) Sergius, and offered to guide him out if he would believe in Jesus Christ. Reaching home safely, the chief inquired of some Christian merchants what he must do. They expounded to him the Christian gospel, which so inspired him that he asked the nearest metropolitan to instruct and baptize him, and two hundred thousand Kerait tribesmen along with him. However true this may have been, Stewart comments, both the Kerait territory, with its capital

A rare Christian monument in China, this seventh century pagoda (right) was examined in 1998 by British scholar Martin Palmer and discovered to have Christian origins. The east-west orientation and the Christian themes represented on the interior bas-relief sculptures positively identify it as Christian. Neglect and earthquakes have damaged the building and its underground passages; restoration work has since been done on the exterior of the building. Palmer suggests that the pagoda was once the library of an adjoining monastery. The stone cross (below), dated 1382 and featuring Chinese and Christian symbols intertwined, is found near Yan Shan at the ruins of the ancient Monastery of the Cross.

Karakorum, and the neighboring Chinese province of Kansu, were reputed to be Christian strongholds before the twelfth century.

About this time, not coincidentally, tales began to filter through to Europe that a fabulously powerful Christian priest-king named Prester (Presbyter) John was ruling a country in deepest Asia. Prester John, who has never ceased to engage Western imaginations, is mentioned by several medieval chroniclers. He was also said to have written to the Byzantine emperor Manuel Comnenus (1143–1180) a letter which began, "John, priest by the power and virtue of God and our Lord Jesus Christ, Lord of Lords, to the sovereign of Constantinople," and went on to inquire "whether you have, like us, the true faith." Prester John informed the emperor that he himself was a zealous and merciful Christian, and overlord to sixty-two lesser kings. His riches were beyond counting, and his domains stretched to "farther India, where reposes the body of St. Thomas the Apostle."

Several Asian chieftains have been proposed as a historical Prester John, with no clear winner. Prince George of the Onguts is a strong candidate, though an equally likely choice would be Toghrul Wang-Khan of the Keraits. In any event, writes Moffett, Toghrul and his people were about to play a significant (if dubious) role in history by lending their support to the young chieftain of a Mongol sub-clan, Temugin by name. With their initial help, Temugin shortly managed to exert control over most of his numerous Mongol neighbors, including the Keraits, and in 1206, he had himself proclaimed Great Khan of the Mongol peoples, under a new name: Genghis.

For the next two decades, Genghis Khan spread death and destruction across two continents. He seized the Silk Road from the Tibetans. He conquered Manchuria, burning Canbaluc (Beijing). With his fourth son, Tolui, he attacked and bloodily defeated two Muslim-held Persian border states. In 1220, the chroniclers credit Toluị with butchering seven hundred thousand people—of both sexes and all ages—in the city of Merv. His Mongols spared no one, the Muslim historian Ibn al-Athir wrote in horror: "They killed women, men and children, they ripped open the bodies of the pregnant and slaughtered the unborn." Genghis's last campaign took him through Afghanistan to the banks of the Indus River.

Genghis maintained his shamanistic religion lifelong,[11] but for political

The Uighurs, Muslims since the tenth century, are native to parts of China as well as Uzbekistan, Kazakhstan and Kyrgyzstan, all countries along the Silk Road. As well as possessing highly developed skills in art, music and medicine, the ancient Uighur people were also widely literate. Their written language and knowledge of printing contributed to the propagation of religious ideas of many faiths: Buddhist, Manichean and Christian.

11. Genghis Khan remained a pagan all his life, but monotheistic influences helped shape his written law. All must believe in one God, Genghis declared, and priests of all kinds were not to be taxed. One of his edicts recommended abstinence from alcohol—or, if that proved impossible, getting drunk no more than three times a month.

The stuff of legends, Prester John squares off against Genghis Khan in this fourteenth century manuscript illustration in From the Travels of Marco Polo *held by the British Library. John was purportedly a priest and ruler of a fabulously wealthy and idyllic Christian state, somewhere in Asia. No doubt intended to enhance his hero status, this illustration depicts him running through Genghis Khan with his sword. A decapitated head lying on the ground adds a grisly detail.*

12. The Christian princess Sorkaktani, wife of Genghis Khan's son Tolui, raised all of her sons to be emperors. The eldest, Mongke, was Great Khan of the Mongols. The second, Kublai, became the celebrated emperor of China. Hulagu, was *ilkhan* (emperor) of Persia. The youngest, Arikbuka, ruled in central Asia.

reasons chose several Christian princesses from important tribes in his confederacy as wives for himself and his sons. The influence of these women, adding to that of Christian courtiers, made itself felt as the Mongol Empire spread across Asia. One princess in particular stands out—Sorkaktani, niece of Genghis's original Kerait benefactor Toghrul Wang-Khan, who was married to Tolui. Widowed young, she devoted herself to the upbringing of her four sons. None of them embraced Christianity, but all were in varying degrees sympathetic to it. This was important, because Sorkaktani managed to see to it that these four grandsons of Genghis took control of his entire empire—despite ferocious competition from myriad other relatives.[12]

In particular, she may deserve credit for a second resurgence of Christianity in China under the rule of her second son, the celebrated Kublai Khan, the magnificence of whose court would so dazzle the Western world. Sorkaktani died in 1252 before Kublai gained full control of his Chinese Empire, but a great-grandson would confer upon her, posthumously, the title of "empress," at ceremonies that included Nestorian liturgies. Both Muslim and Christian historians heap praise upon Sorkaktani; Bar Hebraeus effusively calling her a sincere and true Christian, comparable to the saintly Helena, mother of Constantine.

Meanwhile, the turbulent and violent Mongol conglomerate imposed order, of a sort, upon Asia. For some hundred and fifty years, roughly 1220 to 1370, it kept open a road to the West—an admittedly tenuous and hazardous one, but a road nevertheless. For the first time, European traders and Christian missionaries from Rome could journey to inner Asia, with John of Plano Carpini and Benedict the Pole (as described above) pioneering one route in 1245.

In their footsteps seven years later came William of Rubruck, another papal envoy, who reached the court of the Great Khan Mongke. William was even more appalled than John at the Mongol Christians. Being Nestorian, they were to him heretics by definition, but he also criticized them for absence of episcopal supervision, deplorable theology, and terrible morals. Among other sins, he charged, the priests were drunks and usurers, dressed like Buddhists, used shamanist divination and charms, and sometimes married several wives.

In his account of Mongke's court, William described a debate in which, at the request of the khakan himself, he spoke for Western Christianity against the Manichaeans, Muslims, Nestorian Christians and Buddhists who thronged the place. His arguments reduced the Buddhist spokesman to silence, he claimed, so he felt that he won that debate. But he won no souls, he adds with touching candor: "No one said 'I believe.'" A private discussion with Mongke ended on a similar note, which William attributes to the dissolute life of the local Christian priests. "God gave you the scriptures," the skeptical khan told him, "and you do not keep them. He gave us shamans; we do what they tell us and we live in peace."

Be that as it may, the Nestorian church—the Church of the East—had long since established metropolitanates at Ray, near present-day Teheran; Rewardashir on the way to India; Sarbaziyeh farther southeast; Merv on the road to China; in Tibet; and five more along the Old Silk Road—at Herat, Samarkand, Kashgar, Almalik and Navekath, in Uighur territory north of Kashgar. Furthermore, as the first Europeans to travel to China would soon discover, the Nestorian Church was still there, too—having either gone underground after the fall of the T'ang dynasty, or returned later with the Mongol invaders.

Nicolo and Maffeo Polo reached "far Cathay" in 1266, and Nicolo's son Marco subsequently spent many years there. Marco's published reports mention Nestorian Christian communities throughout the empire, and churches in many Chinese cities.[13] In Kanchou, capital of Kansu province, he writes, there were three large Nestorian churches, one of which may have been the monastery

13. The Polos found at the Pacific port city of Foochow a group they call "secret Christians," who had a sacred book that Maffeo and Marco identified as a psalter. These people said that the faith had been delivered to them seven hundred years ago "by three apostles of the seventy who had gone preaching throughout the world." Could these three apostles have been the original evangelists to Persia—Addai, Aggai and Mari—and could these "secret" Christians in Foochow have been the descendents of seventh-century A-lo-pen converts? It is altogether possible.

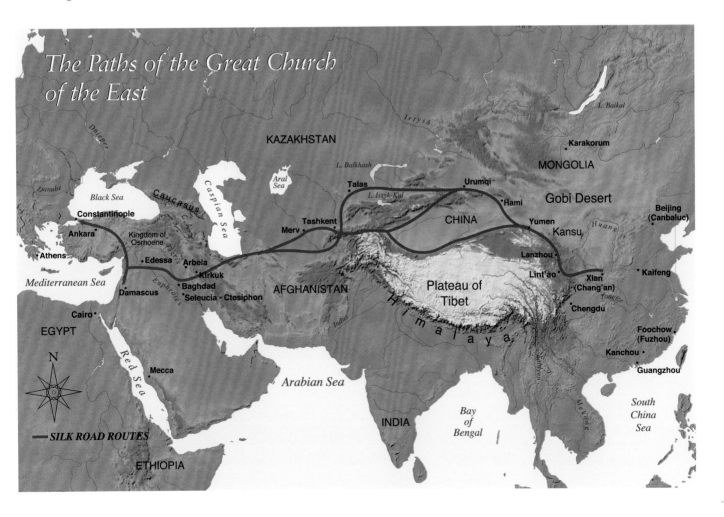

The Paths of the Great Church of the East

SILK ROAD ROUTES

where Queen Sorkaktani was buried, and in the southeastern provinces of Chekiang and Fukien there were many more Christians.

Kublai Khan developed a preference for Buddhism, the religion of his wife, and humbly studied it under a renowned teacher, but he maintained careful balance among his empire's religions: Buddhists and Taoists, who were jealous of each other; Confucianists, who included most of the native Chinese bureaucracy (which he deeply distrusted, but had to endure); Nestorian Christians, now greatly increasing in numbers; and Muslims, the latest arrivals. It was also essential, for his

In the steps of 'Doubting' Thomas

Evidence mounts that early Christians planted a lasting church in India possibly explaining the quick success of later missions from the West

In the seventh century, when missionaries from Persia were just beginning to translate scripture for the Chinese emperor T'ai-Tsung, tradition holds that Christianity had long since been established in India, where the apostle Thomas first preached it nearly six hundred years earlier (see previous volume, *The Veil is Torn*). Landing at Cranganore in South India, St. Thomas is believed to have ranged north almost to Afghanistan, an itinerary even more extensive than St. Paul's. But strong tradition is not the only evidence that "doubting Thomas"—and many courageous disciples after him—had effectively spread the faith throughout the Indian Subcontinent. There are artifacts as well, such as stone crosses with Pahlavi inscriptions that date from the Sassanid era.

After the fall of the Persian Empire to Islam in the seventh century, Christians in India were almost entirely cut off, and information about them is sparse. Enough remains, however, to show that they carried on regardless. The records of the Nestorian patriarchate at Baghdad, known as the Church of the East, reveal a tenuous but continuing Indian connection. For example, in the late ninth century, the Punjab city of Gandispur (later Shahabad) in northern India is listed as the seat of a metropolitanate. This presupposes the existence there of between six and twelve episcopal sees.

Nonecclesiastical sources include the geographer Cosmas Indicopleustes (Cosmas the Indian navigator), who in 525 reported substantial Christian communities in the Ganges Valley, Ceylon, Burma, Siam, Cochin China, and Tonkin. In the thirteenth century, Marco Polo described six great kingdoms in central India. Three were Muslim, he said, and three were Christian monarchies that claimed St. Thomas as patron.[1]

On the southeast coast, Mylapur (now part of the city of Chenai) is the traditional site of the apostle's martyrdom in A.D. 72. Here, too, his efforts and those of his successors apparently bore fruit. Historian John Stewart (*Nestorian Missionary Enterprise: The Story of a Church on Fire*) quotes a fifteenth-century traveler, Nicolo Conti, who calculated that there were then a thousand Christians in Mylapur alone, and many thousands more "scattered all over India, as the Jews are scattered among us." (They were the only people in India, Conti added, who "confine themselves to one solitary mate.")

There are even intriguing indications that Nestorian missionaries traveled into Burma and Thailand, and onward to such Malaysian islands as Java, Sumatra and Borneo. In 1503, for instance, Patriarch Elijah V of the Church of the East appointed a metropolitan for Java. A traveler who accompanied Syrian merchants to Burma in 1506 reported that one local prince there had a thousand Christians in his service.

Despite all this, although Western historians do acknowledge a Christian presence in India at least by the fourth century, they have never credited St. Thomas, or subsequent Persian evangelists, as having real impact upon its overwhelmingly Hindu population. In Western eyes, serious evangelization began there only in the sixteenth century, when European missionaries first arrived in force—and immediately reported gratifying numbers of conversions.

Quite aside from any other evidence, of course, this instant harvest might reasonably be considered significant in itself—an indication, that is, that seeds of faith had already been planted and nurtured there. Indian Christians believe that although their ancestors had been martyred over the years by disapproving Hindu rulers, and hammered hard by Muslim invaders, too, many Christian communities

Mongol warriors, that Kublai take part in such festivals as the summer ceremony of the White Mare's Milk, to honor the spirits of the earth and the air.

A Nestorian metropolitanate was established at Canbaluc, Kublai's capital, and Christian courtiers were extremely influential. A physician and scientist named Ai-hsueh was put in charge of a government department specifically created to deal with Christian affairs, and later headed the Han-lin Academy, an important scholastic center. In due course, Ai-hsueh's five sons—Elijah, Denha, Issa, George and Luke—also held important administrative positions. Another

Young girls in a Kerala church reflect generations of Christianity in India, many families proudly claiming descent from converts of the Apostle Thomas. Christian missionaries are credited with the high level of literacy in Kerala state.

nevertheless still survived in the sixteenth century. Some were forcibly "Latinized" by Portuguese colonizers and Jesuit missionaries, and others later became "Eastern Rite Uniate" churches in communion with Rome. Still others managed to retain or restore their connection to Nestorian and Jacobite Syrian patriarchates, and to maintain their liturgies and scriptures in Syriac or Aramaic.

In the next five hundred years, things would become ever more complex, as other European powers displaced the Portuguese, as Protestant missionaries were added to the religious mix, and as Indian Christians struggled hard for ecclesiastical self-determination.[2] Today, at least seven distinct groups—two of them Catholic and one Protestant—consider themselves "St. Thomas Christians," under such names as Malankara, Malabar, Assyrian, Mar Thoma and Syrian Orthodox. Disparate though they are, however, they emphasize their common heritage. The saint's reputed tomb in the Roman Catholic Church at Mylapur, for example, is a pilgrim site for Indian Christians of every stripe.

Furthermore, they appear to share a continued dedication to evangelism. Although few in number by comparison with Hindus and Muslims, Christians are India's third largest religious group. The *Encyclopedia Britannica Yearbook (2004)* lists them as 6.03 percent of the total population of 1.065 billion. Be it noted,

however, that this amounts to some sixty-three million people (more than the population of Great Britain and twice that of Canada), and the state of Kerala on the southwest coast is twenty-two percent Christian.[3]

St. Thomas, that renowned pessimist, would surely be pleased—and characteristically surprised that things didn't turn out worse. ■

1. Indian historians believe that the Nestorian Church in India was reinforced by a number of major immigrations of Persian traders, settlers and refugees. One likely was caused by the drastic persecutions of Shapur II in the fourth century, and coincidentally led by another Thomas—Thomas of Cana. A second may have occurred in the eighth century. Still another, early in the ninth, apparently founded the city of Quilon in the southwestern district of Kerala, with royal approval. Inscribed copper plates, some of which still exist, record the arrangements made with local officials.

2. In the late nineteenth century, Pope Leo XIII established in India three archdioceses and eight dioceses, most of them in the southwest. Since the Second Vatican Council in the 1960s, Latin has given way to local languages, and a dozen more dioceses have been added.

3. In another interesting statistic, the Indian government in 1990 proclaimed Kerala to be one hundred percent literate. This circumstance was considered so remarkable as to be included in the *Guinness Book of World Records.*

notable court figure was the Ongut chieftain, Prince George, a staunch ally in Kublai's fight for power. Marco Polo thought George might be sixth in direct descent from the legendary Prester John, which seems unlikely. But he was a distinguished monarch, scholar and general, a devout Christian, and he was married to the daughter of Timur, the next emperor of China.

A vivid example of Kublai's policy of sectarian balance occurred after a bitter internal conflict in 1287. A young prince called Nayan, a baptized Nestorian Christian, in alliance with disgruntled Mongol relatives, led an army against the aging emperor under the banner of the cross. Nayan was defeated, captured and killed. But later, according to Polo, when some of Kublai's courtiers taunted the Christians, saying that Nayan's defeat showed that their God was powerless, the emperor decisively silenced them. Nayan was a traitor and his cause unjust, he declared, and therefore the cross of the Christian God did well not to help him. And that Easter, Kublai made a point of having the Gospel book ceremoniously presented to him so he could devoutly kiss it.

Marco Polo, who for a time advised Kublai on Western affairs, and even served three years as a district governor, was likely not so sympathetic. He held the Nestorians in utter contempt. They were the "worst heretics," he wrote, and since their patriarch appointed all sorts of prelates to preach everywhere, it was spreading fast: "Heretics make heretics." Kublai himself would embrace Christianity, Polo believed, if only it were better presented to him, by real Christians.

Other westerners who encountered Nestorian Christians were more favorably impressed, however. Interestingly, while the Polos were investigating Cathay, a pair of Mongol Christian monks, Mark and Sauma, embarked upon an equally momentous journey westward, leaving Peking about 1275, on a pilgrimage to Jerusalem. Mark was an Ongut, about thirty years old. Sauma, a Uighur, may have been the son of an archdeacon who is listed as an early adviser to Kublai. These two struggled through war-torn central Asia to Persia, where they marveled at the holy sites—and where the Nestorian patriarch, Denha, unexpectedly consecrated Mark as metropolitan bishop of Cathay and the Onguts.

Patriarch Denha urged Mark to return forthwith to his homeland, which he tried for years to do, but Asia presented an impassable chaos of warring Turk and Mongol factions. Then Patriarch Denha died, and to Mark's stunned astonishment, the Persian bishops insisted on electing him—a man who could not even speak Syriac. But perhaps the bishops thought (no doubt correctly) that just now the Mongol language might be more useful anyhow. So Mark became patriarch of all Asia as Yaballaha III, a post he filled with distinction from 1281 to 1317. He never saw China again, however, and perhaps not Jerusalem either. But his companion Sauma, who also stayed in Persia and became a prominent bishop there, got to travel right through Europe.

For in 1287, Sauma was chosen by the Mongol *ilkhan* (emperor) of Persia to head an embassy to the pope and to two Western monarchs. His mission failed in that it produced no military support for Mongol Persia, but theologically it seems to have been a success. At Rome, Bishop Sauma found that the pope had just died, but friendly and interested cardinals intently quizzed him as to why a Mongol ruler had sent a Christian ecclesiastic as ambassador. Did they perhaps politely refrain from adding "a *heretical* Christian ecclesiastic?" Possibly Sauma felt this was implied, for he took pains to explain how his country had been evangelized by St. Thomas, St. Addai and St. Mari.

Moreover, he told the Latins, "many of our fathers have gone to the lands of the Mongols, the Turks and the Chinese, and have taught them. Today many Mongols are Christians. There are princes and queens who have been baptized and confess Christ.... No one has been sent to us Orientals from the Pope. The holy Apostles aforesaid taught us, and we still hold today what they handed down to us." Then he added, with dignity, "I am come from distant lands not to discuss or teach my belief, but to pay my respects to my lord the Pope and to the relics of the Saints, and to deliver the messages of the King and of the Catholicos. If you please, let us have done with discussion."

Bishop Sauma spoke with brave confidence and serene faith, yet at that point less than one hundred years of flourishing life remained to the great Church of the East. In the coming century, it would suffer almost total annihilation, in large part at the hands of once-Christian Mongols, in that tragic and heroic welter of Christian self-assurance and false assumption known to history as the Crusades—whose story will be told in the next volume. ■

Alphonse Marie Mucha, born in Moravia, the future Czech Republic, in 1860, soared to wide acclaim in Paris as one of the founders of the Art Nouveau movement soon after the turn of the twentieth century. While his illustrations for theater posters and magazines became the talk of the art world, he never did lose his love for his homeland and the Slav peoples. His commission to paint a series of murals for the Lord Mayor's Hall in Prague led him also to create what he called The Slav Epic, a series of magnificent paintings chronicling major events in the history of the Slav nations. Three are reproduced in this chapter. The above is entitled, The Slavs in Their Original Homeland. The others are reproduced on pages 209 and 210. But Mucha's renown was short-lived. He died in relative obscurity in 1939.

CHAPTER 8

The amazing Slavs subdue their masters by ably serving them

Hundreds of thousands pour in from the East, absorb the nomads who enslaved them, embrace Christ, and bring all Eastern Europe into the faith

I n the year 591, the Byzantine emperor Maurice took advantage of a lull in the wars with Persia to visit the empire's barbarian-infested eastern frontiers. Somewhere in Asia Minor, his scouts seized a party of three armed men whose "arms," as it turned out, were some sort of musical instruments. The emperor curtly interrogated them. Who were they? What were they doing? What were these instruments for? They were Slavs, the three explained through interpreters, from the Western Sea (by which they probably meant the Baltic). The khagan of the ferocious Avars had demanded that their tribe send warriors to help in his wars, and these three had been dispatched as envoys with the tribe's reply, to this effect: "We are a peaceful people who play zithers, not war trumpets. We have no iron. We have no weapons. We are of no use to you as soldiers. But we will gladly entertain you."

This message was not well received, said the musical trio. So enraged was the khagan that he forbade them to return home. But they had escaped, and now after fifteen months on the road, they begged the Byzantine emperor for sanctuary. They could have been spies, of course, but the emperor believed them. The Avars, as he well knew, were the latest wave of nomadic plunderers to come out of central Asia. Besides, Maurice was a pious man, fascinated by the unprecedented notion of an

AIIICITEV TENTVIITANO

One of a series of frescoes in the richly decorated Church of the Nativity, Arbanasi, Bulgaria, this group of musicians reflects the Slavs' love of music and storytelling. The emperor Maurice provided sanctuary for three musicians such as these, who had escaped from the fearsome Avars.

entirely pacifist people, trying to live without war in a world drenched in blood. He granted them safe passage to the nearest Byzantine city.

This story, one of the early mentions in Byzantine annals of the Slavic people, accurately portrays them as the least warlike of all the tribes competing for territory in central Europe during the Dark Ages. Throughout the sixth and seventh centuries, as the Germanic and other groups fought their way into Roman territory, Slavs poured by hundreds of thousands into the vacated regions behind them. But rarely were they left in peace. Slavs were the "soft anvil" upon which successive warrior cultures pounded their "hard hammers," writes Austrian historian Theodore Peisker in the *Cambridge Medieval History*. So thoroughly entrenched grew their reputation for docility that the name Slav came to designate a human being in complete servitude.[1] Yet by culturally absorbing their overlords and tormentors, the enduring Slavs would ultimately inherit most of the territory.

This magnificent resilience can be most easily explained by farming and birth rate. The original cradle of the proto-Slav people, known as Polesie, apparently lay somewhere within the fertile region west of the Dnieper River, east of the Carpathian Mountains, north of the nomad-dominated steppes and south of modern Warsaw. Predominantly fair-haired and blue-eyed, this Indo-European folk seem to have concentrated entirely on agriculture. The Romans noted that Slavs characteristically lived in primitive villages and largely lacked class

1. To the Slavs themselves, their name likely signified everyone who shared the Slavonic language (literally "those who can understand each other"). But others, observing the chronic subjugation of the Slavic peoples by wave after wave of oppressors, began to use the term "slave" to mean those subjected to domination by others.

distinctions. Cultivation apparently enabled them to support large families, but as subsistence farmers, they did not readily organize themselves for war. Although Slavs sometimes fought vigorously among themselves, when menaced by a more militaristic power they would typically yield.

Slavic family life was rigidly patriarchal and resolutely monogamous. Wives were chattels, bought or abducted by the men. (Memory of the latter practice would survive into the twentieth century in premarital mock abductions, boisterous but good-humored.) Emperor Maurice described them as "hardened to heat, frost, wet, nakedness and hunger," and "well-disposed to strangers." The sixth-century Greek historian Procopius admired their gentle temperament. Later

The Slavs were like a soft anvil pounded by the hard hammers of fiercer tribes, but these peaceful folk were able to absorb and outlast their successive tormentors and overlords.

commentators remarked on their exceptional hospitality and love of music.

Historian Peisker praises the same traits, while voicing some common nineteenth-century generalizations about other alleged Slavic ways: "Void of all enterprise, the Slav leaves others to trade with the fruits of his labor—and they drain him to the last farthing. Drunkenness is his only hateful quality: otherwise he has very attractive traits. He is thrifty almost to avarice … and shows an endurance that harmonizes little with his slender physique. He is in no way aggressive but rather dreamy, confiding, not at all malicious, good tempered, not without dignity, very hospitable, and a lover of amusement."

Massive migrations began in the third century. As more warlike barbarians conquered new territories, Slav peasants followed and settled in areas north to the Baltic Sea, east to the Oka River (south of Moscow), southeast as far as Kiev and southwest to the Carpathians. Slavery greatly accelerated this diaspora, Nordic traders and Asian nomads hunting Slavs like game and transporting their hardworking, cooperative captives to Europe, Asia and even Africa.[2]

In the late sixth century, the warlike Avar tribes were menacing the Byzantine Empire all along its northern frontier. Under Maurice, the imperial army won five decisive battles early in the seventh, and repelled a combined Avar-Slav attack on Constantinople in 617.[3] For the better part of two centuries, however, much of the land formally designated as Avar territory was in fact occupied by resettled Slavs who produced food and other goods for their nomadic masters. They also served—reluctantly—as infantry in support of the formidable Avar cavalry. Poorly armed and trained, they were only motivated to fight because mounted Avars would kill anyone who tried to retreat.

In one form or another, Slavic blood came to dominate most of eastern Europe. Because the Avars were spread too thinly to effectively dominate all of their subjects, independent Slavic territories began to appear. One such, under a leader named Walluc, occupied the Carinthian region of southern Austria. To the

2. Being easy prey for slavers, the pacifist Slavs developed certain subterfuges. According to several early histories, they used one particularly interesting strategy in the soggy Pinsk marshlands that bordered their ancestral territory. Totally immersing themselves in the bog pools, they would breathe through hollow reeds until the marauders had passed by.

3. The Avars were not without admirers within the Byzantine Empire, even in Constantinople itself. British author Tim Newark describes, in *The Barbarians: Wars and Warriors of the Dark Ages*, how a coterie of "wild young men" in the Byzantine capital took to emulating the hairstyles and clothing of the Eurasian marauders while "robbing people at night [and] rioting during the day." Little was done to stop them.

north reigned a Slavicized Frankish prince named Samo, whose domain possibly ran as far west as what is now Bavaria. Smaller independent Slav jurisdictions sprouted in the Alps and along the valley of the Elbe River in eastern Germany.

Slavs resisted Christianity, not necessarily because they rejected its principles, but because supposed Christians were often their most vicious tormentors. For example, when an envoy from the Frankish king Dagobert threatened to invade Samo's region, Samo politely assured him that Dagobert was welcome to his kingdom so long as he "maintained friendship" with its people. The envoy contemptuously replied that Christian Franks could never be friends with pagan dogs. "Then if you are the servants of God, and we are God's dogs," Samo countered, "we are permitted to bite you when you ceaselessly act against his will."[4]

Centuries of subjugation instilled in the Slavic soul a powerful desire for justice, Peisker contends. "The appeal to law and not to the sword is the basis of Old Slavonic thought and aspiration," and Slavic blood fertilized the soil of Europe in their pursuit of "social and religious dreams of an evangelical way of life.... This movement was democratic, not communistic—a wonderful theoretic union of human perfection with spiritual purity in the midst of a society saturated with selfishness." The power of the essentially pacific Slavic

The Byzantine emperor suffered a disastrous defeat at the hands of the Bulgars. They chased his legions across the Danube and slaughtered any who failed to make their escape.

culture was such that it first transformed the predatory Avars, he maintains, and after them the Bulgars, the next wave of pagan nomads.

Small predatory bands of Bulgars, yet another population from the mysterious lands east of the Black Sea, appeared in the Balkans during the late 400s, and occasionally served Byzantium as mercenaries. A century and a half later, they were well established in their first kingdom east of the Sea of Azov, and what historians call the Old Bulgarian Empire reached its zenith in the 600s, under a powerful khagan named Kubrat, who ruled for six decades. (The term "khan" and its variants derive from the Mongolian language.) Then it was extinguished by new invaders, the Khazars (see sidebar, page 200), while four of Kubrat's five sons migrated farther west.

The most successful was the third son, Asperuch, who resettled his large following around the Danube Delta, where Emperor Constantine IV, mindful of previous depredations by Huns and Avars, led a major assault on them—and suffered a disastrous defeat. The triumphant Bulgars chased his legions across the Danube, slaughtering all stragglers. Then they pressed south and west into the lands that would become their European home, much of which was already occupied by Slavic tribes.

The Slavs capitulated, although the two cultures diverged dramatically. The Bulgars practiced polygamy, for instance, and their women wore the veil, while the men wore turbans. Nonetheless, the obliging Slavs helped the Bulgars expand, muscling Byzantium to the south and the weakening Avars to north and west. The heavily fortified Bulgarian capital was Pliska, 190 miles northwest of Constantinople. The Byzantines periodically tried to regain the lost territory, and frequently had to contend with further Bulgar assaults. One emperor actually invited them to attack Constantinople itself.[5]

In the early ninth century, a cunning warrior named Krum, possibly descended from Khagan Kubrat's fourth son, vanquished the Avars in the onetime Roman province of Pannonia (a portion of modern Hungary and Austria). As sublime khan, Krum united Bulgar tribes until his realm stretched from the Black Sea far into the rugged Balkans, and the empress Irene had to pay him protection money. But Nicephorus I, who succeeded Irene in 802, was determined to confront him. During a lull in Byzantium's constant fight against the Islamic Empire on his southeastern border, Nicephorus attacked—and failed. Worse still, the failure inspired Krum to march on Macedonia the following year. There he managed to trick the defenders of the frontier fortress of Sardica into opening their gates, and slaughtered the entire garrison of six thousand men.

Nicephorus responded briskly by seizing Pliska, that city being nearly undefended at the time. (He wrote home to Constantinople, with satisfaction, that he spent a pleasant Easter enjoying the comforts of Krum's palace.) The

[5]. Byzantine-Bulgar relations were chronically tangled. Emperor Justinian II, for example, was deposed in 695, six years after suffering a major defeat by the Bulgars. His nose and tongue were slit by his triumphant rival and he was exiled. Nothing daunted, the disfigured ex-emperor made an alliance with the Bulgar khagan, Tervel, to help him assault Constantinople in 705 and regain his throne—then Justinian turned and attacked Tervel. (See earlier volume, *The Sword of Islam*, chapter 10.)

Nicolas Roerich painted The Slavs on the Dnieper *in 1905, a folk art rendition of a settlement of ancient Slavs. Sturdy Viking-style boats, strong people and vibrant primary colors suggest prosperity and strength in early Slav society. The painting is in the State Museum, St. Petersburg, Russia.*

combatants then retired to their respective capitals until the spring of 811, when Nicephorus decided to eliminate Krum. With a mighty army that included battle-hardened legions from the Muslim front, he bore down on Pliska. Krum tried to parley. Nicephorus refused, routed the khan from his stronghold, torched it, and put all its inhabitants—irrespective of age or sex—to the sword.

Again the khan tried to parley. Again the emperor refused. Instead, he chased the fleeing Bulgar warriors into a narrow mountain pass—and there met disaster, for they were able to take cover and ambush their pursuers. Nicephorus, realizing his mistake too late, exclaimed, "Even were we birds, we could not hope to escape." On that night of July 26, the Bulgarians fell upon his troops and butchered most of them, including the emperor. His son and successor, Stauracius, escaped but died later of his wounds. The severed head of Nicephorus was gleefully displayed on a pike, then prepared for a new use. The skull, lined with silver, became a drinking goblet used by Krum to celebrate his victory with a Slavonic toast: *Zdravitsa*—that is, "To your good health!"[6]

Krum's use of a Slavonic word is a small but significant indication of his attitude toward the Slavs, who by then enjoyed more or less equal social status.

Pursuing the khan's warriors, Nicephorus was caught in an ambush. 'Even if we were birds, we could not hope to escape,' he cried. He was slain and his skull turned into a drinking cup.

The Bulgar ambassador to Constantinople, for example, was a Slav. Krum realized that the relatively sedentary, productive, law-abiding Slavs could supply the social and economic savvy his people needed, and among other innovations he promulgated a code of laws. (One of these, incidentally, banned cultivation of grapes, perhaps an attempt to curb the bibulous Slavs.) Krum saw no value in Christianity, however, although it was spreading among his subjects. He reputedly would use Byzantine captives as craftsmen and bureaucrats only if they would renounce their faith (the other option being death).

Further Bulgar gains in Thrace and Macedonia in 812 culminated in the defeat at Versinicia of a far larger Byzantine force. Just six days later, Krum was before the walls of Constantinople, conducting a grotesque exhibition of barbarism. While he paraded about with his concubines, his troops sacrificed both humans and animals on pagan altars. Then, with Emperor Leo V still refusing to surrender, the Bulgars embarked on a bloody rampage through the suburbs outside the walls.

Krum offered to raise the siege if the Byzantines would pay him a vast indemnity, and would display for his selection all their most beautiful women. He wanted to choose a few for his already extensive harem. The emperor craftily suggested that he and Krum and a few aides meet unarmed on the shore outside the walls, to discuss these matters. This they did—and at a prearranged signal three assassins, secreted in a nearby hut, burst out to attack the Bulgars. But the trick

6. Some eleven hundred years later, the Russian composer Sergey Prokofiev would use Krum's toast, "Zdravitsa!" as the title of a cantata he wrote (under duress) to celebrate the birthday of Soviet dictator Josef Stalin—a far more accomplished mass murderer than Supreme Khagan Krum, Emperor Nicephorus or any other tyrant of antiquity. Tyrants change little over the centuries, except to become more efficient in their killing.

failed. Krum leaped on his horse and galloped off, barely nicked by one arrow.

The orgy of death and destruction he now unleashed was beyond anything Constantinople had yet seen. Thousands were massacred. Captives, women and children included, were herded like cattle to the barbarian lands north of the Danube. Scores of churches, palaces, bridges and forts became smoking ruins. A successful counterattack by Leo near the Bulgarian coastal city of Mesembria (now Nesebûr) only quickened Krum's thirst for revenge. But in April 814, while he was recruiting more Slavs and Avars and amassing armaments for another monumental assault on Constantinople, a blood vessel burst in his brain. The sublime Khan was no more, and one of Christianity's major bastions was thereby spared what might well have been final destruction.

Mercifully for both sides, Krum's son and successor, Omurtag, negotiated a durable peace with Byzantium, although the accompanying ceremonies scandalized church and state authorities alike. Leo had to express his sincerity by performing pagan rites that included swearing on a sword and sacrificing a dog, while Omurtag swore an oath in the name of God. Though some saw subsequent

The Scylitzes Chronicle *portrays Bulgars besieging the city of Constantinople. In this illustration above, the Bulgar leader Deleanos receives a fellow commander in his tent; the tents of the Bulgar army are on the right. Below, the Byzantines burst out of the city in an attempt to rout the Bulgars.*

The Khazar compromise

A strange nomadic people resolves the Muslim-Christian issue by opting for Judaism;
for two centuries they prevail between the Black and Caspian, then vanish from history

Among the Turkic and Mongol peoples who roared at unpredictable intervals and with hurricane force from the Asian steppes, the most intriguing are the Khazars, dominant between the Caspian and Black seas from the eighth through the tenth centuries.[1] Speaking a Turkic tongue, yet frequently fair-skinned and even red-haired, they consistently blocked Islam's advance toward eastern Europe. They never became Muslim—but did not accept Christ either. Instead, they adopted Judaism *en masse*, a relatively rare circumstance. Moreover, despite the conversion of these ferocious warriors to the Jewish faith, and despite the fact that they also seem to have been industrious traders and craftsmen, the Khazars disappeared from history without leaving a single written record of their passing.

They apparently originated in the Caucasus, then spread north and westward. At their fullest strength in the late eighth century, they were exacting tribute from the Alans, Goths, Greeks, Magyars and Bulgars. Their capital was at Itil, where the Volga River flows into the Caspian Sea. There, during the winter months, lived their *khagan*, a secluded and seemingly ritualized monarch on whom depended the welfare of the state. Only he of all Khazar males could let his hair grow long and free, loosely bound with a red band; all other men wore braids. According to Muslim sources, a khagan was ritually strangled when his reign had lasted forty years. An actively governing official, known as the *bec*, seems to have gradually usurped the royal power.

Under their unremitting military discipline, the Khazars frequently executed their own troops after a defeat. Yet their peacetime crafts were impressive, ranging from the making of leather clothing to silver jewelry and bronze mirrors. Some historians credit them with the manufacture of Europe's first paper and glass.

Khazar traders roamed as far northwest as Sweden, buying and selling furs and slaves, while silk, coral, pearls and other luxuries traveled from China to Itil and thence to Europe. They established extensive farms and orchards (some irrigated), and made wine production a major business. They lived in felt tents and clay houses, reserving brick for palaces and other public buildings.

Khazars likely followed a shamanistic religion that deified natural forces, and Judaism may initially have reached them through traders. However, Greek-speaking Jewish artisans had long been resident in Roman colonies along the Black Sea and in the Crimea, Jewish communities already existed in the Balkans, and Jewish refugees eventually entered Khazaria from Muslim lands as well. Although details of their conversion are scarce, author Kevin Alan Brook in *The Jews of Khazaria* strongly theorizes that a crucial debate between Christian, Muslim and Jewish teachers took place before the khagan and the bec in the summer of 861.

Backing his thesis are certain documented facts. For one, in 860 the Byzantine emperor Michael III sent to the Khazars, at their own request, the missionary Cyril. According to a life of Cyril written by his brother Methodius, the khagan insisted in an ensuing debate that his people were intended by God to be illiterate (Cyril and Methodius being widely known as the originators of the Slavonic alphabet). Methodius also writes that the Khazar ruler already had some knowledge of Jewish beliefs.

According to Muslim sources, the bec asked the Muslim envoys whether they preferred Judaism or Christianity. Judaism, they replied. Then the bec put the same question to the Christians, and they acknowledged that they preferred Judaism over Islam. Therefore, the bec reasoned, since Judaism was older, and respected by both the others, it was obviously the best option. Judaism may also, of course, have offered a shield against both Christian and Muslim neighbors. Jewish sources claim that the victories and personal influence of a certain great warrior of mixed Khazar and Jewish parentage was another factor.

No scholarly authority seriously disputes the Khazar conversion, which is well attested by medieval Jewish scholarship from Spain and Egypt. The form adopted was orthodox. It included circumcision, Sabbath observance, ritual washing, avoiding the flesh of scripturally forbidden animals, and other practices laid down in the Torah. How far Judaism penetrated the population beyond the Khazar nobility has been debated, but Brook concludes that most Khazars became Jewish.

Nemesis for the Khazars came from the North, where the Viking Rus established themselves midway down the Volga River before 840. Their fleets progressed downstream toward Itil, which lacked a navy, and Viking pirates infested the region. After a few initial victories, the Khazars were eliminated by a Rus-Byzantium alliance early in the eleventh century. Fleeing survivors probably mingled with earlier Jewish communities in eastern Europe. Migration statistics of any kind are unavailable, and the absence of records means that time has left only a tantalizing trace of this unique people. ∎

1. A roll call of just the better-known nomad peoples that attacked Europe between the fourth and fourteenth centuries would include the Alans, Huns, Avars, Magyars, Scythians, Bulgars, Cimmerians, Seljuk Turks, Mongols and Tatars.

plagues and earthquakes as divine retribution for such sacrilege, it brought a thirty-year peace—almost unprecedented for the times.

Omurtag continued his father's policies regarding the Slavs, and Slavonic became the *de facto* official language. Only the military establishment remained purely Bulgar. From the Byzantine Greeks he imported architecture, art and a written alphabet, but one Greek import he vigorously and brutally resisted: Christianity. To expose secret Christians in his realms, he insisted that everyone eat meat during Lent. Any man who refused to renounce his faith was killed, and his wife and children enslaved.

Peace with Byzantium allowed Omurtag to challenge the Franks in the Slav-inhabited regions north and west of his fortress at Belgrade. His youngest son, Malamir, who succeeded him in 831, added Macedonia and the northern Greek Peninsula to the Bulgar realm. But Malamir first had to deal with his older brother, Enravotas, who had been persuaded by his Greek slave to believe in Jesus Christ. British historian Steven Runciman, in *A History of the First Bulgarian Empire*, suggests this was a Byzantine plot, to unsettle the enemy.

Hating Christianity, Omurtag insisted all must eat meat at Lent. Any man who refused to renounce his faith was to be killed, and his wife and children sent into slavery.

However that may be, Enravotas held firm in his faith. When his brother Malamir had him killed, he became Bulgaria's first recognized martyr.

This may have impressed the youthful mind of the next Bulgarian khan, Boris, a great-grandson of Krum, who equaled his ancestor in statecraft. Boris brought his people into the Christian faith despite many obstacles, one of which was his uneasy relationship with neighboring Moravia. A coalition of Slavic tribes, the Moravians occupied an area that would one day encompass the Czech and Slovak republics, along with parts of Hungary, Austria and Poland. They were ruled by a prince named Rostislav, and he and Boris appear to have concluded, quite independently, that formal conversion of their countries to Christianity was necessary and probably inevitable.

The steps that Rostislav and Boris took to accomplish this would significantly exacerbate the uneasy relationship of Rome and Constantinople. Each Slav ruler was justifiably suspicious of the other, and of the Christian nations on their respective doorsteps, so each sought alliance with a more distant Christian power. In 862, Rostislav reached out to Patriarch Photius of Constantinople. Boris signed a treaty with the Frankish king, Louis the Pious, which also linked him to Pope Nicholas. But Boris's alliance with Rome prompted Constantinople to attack Bulgaria's thinly defended eastern flank. He had to capitulate, formally recognizing the temporal authority of the emperor and the spiritual authority of the patriarch in Constantinople. He was baptized in September 865, with the Byzantine emperor as godfather.

Many of his pagan chieftains consequently rose in a violent insurrection that nearly cost him his life, but Boris prevailed. He then secured his future by executing some fifty ringleaders (along with their children, to eliminate any revenge-seekers). Still, the Bulgars regarded the Greek priests, now flooding their land, as emissaries of their longtime enemy. Furthermore, they complained, these supposed missionaries treated them contemptuously, and seemed none too competent, either. When one Greek priest was revealed as a complete fraud, they cut off his nose and ears and deported him. Besides, Patriarch Photius insulted Boris with a letter the Bulgar monarch deemed patronizing—describing Boris as "the fruit of my labors" and lecturing him on the finer points of Byzantine theology.[7]

In exasperation, or confusion (or possibly both), Boris again approached Pope Nicholas I, requesting missionaries from Rome and asking many questions about Christianity, which the pope answered in truly exemplary fashion (See sidebar, page 204). Nicholas also promised to assign Bulgaria its own bishops immediately, and an archbishop as soon as the number of Christians warranted. Boris, anxious to keep the Bulgarian Church as free as possible from both Constantinople and Rome, was delighted. He expelled all the Greek priests and welcomed the Romans.

Familiarity of language and geographical proximity might sooner or later have returned Bulgaria to the Eastern Church in any case, but the process was now hastened by a seemingly fortuitous series of events. Emperor Michael III, "the Drunkard," who had been proclaimed emperor at age two, had spent his entire reign in the shadow of his mother, Theodora, and had developed into a thorough wastrel. In 867, at the age of twenty-seven, he was murdered by the man who would succeed him, Basil I "the Macedonian." (See page 137.) Emperor Basil removed Photius from the patriarchy and restored the previously ousted Ignatius. That same year, Pope Nicholas died, and his successor, Adrian II, persistently ignored Bulgarian requests for their archbishop.

Since Boris's central concern was still autonomy for the Bulgarian Church, he again turned eastward, and he got results. A major ecclesiastical council, held in Constantinople and attended by all concerned, agreed that this was where Bulgaria belonged. Patriarch Ignatius immediately assigned for it an archbishop and several bishops. Boris at last was satisfied. In Byzantium, he had perceived, the church tended to be subordinate to the state.

But the clinching argument for Boris, who aspired to unite his people by both

Emperor Michael III in a defining moment of Slav history. He receives envoys of the Moravian prince Rotislav, who, recognizing the benefits of Christianity, has requested missionaries who speak the Slavic languages. From the Radziwill Chronicle, an early history of Russia.

7. Two apocryphal stories of the conversion of the Bulgar khan Boris reflect the importance of women and art in spreading the faith. The first asserts that Boris's embrace of Christianity was inspired by his sister, who had become a Christian while a prisoner in Constantinople. The second relates that a painting of *The Last Judgment*, rich in terrifying detail, convinced the pagan khan that he must quit his heathen ways.

religion and language, may have been that the Eastern Church was ready to permit worship in the vernacular, while Rome insisted on Latin for all. In fact, a Slavic alphabet had recently been developed by two Greek missionaries in Moravia, Cyril and Methodius, who were even then translating into Slavonic the Christian Gospels and the Eastern liturgy. This monumental accomplishment would lead to the conversion of Europe's entire Slavic population, most of it to the Eastern Church. It would also earn sainthood for both translators.

Uniquely suited to the job, the two were brothers, born in the Aegean city of Thessalonica. Their father, a government official, served a regional population largely comprised of Macedonian Slavs, and the brothers grew up among them. Besides, Cyril in particular was said to possess a particular gift for language, a prodigious thirst for knowledge, rigorous self-discipline and intense devotion to God. At fifteen,

Translation of the Gospels and Orthodox liturgies into Slavonic led to the conversion of Europe's entire Slavic population, and would earn sainthood for Cyril and Methodius.

he was sent to the imperial school in Constantinople, where the future patriarch Photius was a teacher, and where he became acquainted with the boy-emperor Michael III, then only six. Later on, both these relationships would matter.

At twenty-four, Cyril was attached to a diplomatic mission to the new Arab capital of Samara, north of Baghdad, where he is said to have made a memorable impression on the Abbasid courtiers.[8] Elder brother Methodius governed a Slavic region outside Thessalonica for ten years. In 855, after palace intrigues broke their links to the court of Emperor Michael III, both men retreated to a monastery on Mount Olympus. Later, their status restored, they were members of an imperial delegation attempting to improve relations with the Khazars.

In 862, however, Cyril's old mentor Photius asked them to handle a request from Prince Rostislav of Moravia. "Christian teachers have been among us already, from Italy, Greece and Germany, teaching us contradictory doctrines," Rostislav had told the patriarch, "but we are simple Slavs and we want someone to teach us the whole truth." Further, he wanted it done in their own language. Irish missionaries had preached in the region since the late 700s, and Rome had considerable influence there, but in ecclesiastical matters, Rostislav was of one mind with Boris of Bulgaria; he wanted an autonomous church for Moravia.

Cyril and Methodius were providentially at hand, and already preparing for such a job. Historian A. P. Vlasto writes in *The Entry of the Slavs into Christendom* that Cyril had begun working on a Slavonic alphabet at least seven years earlier, and he now completed the thirty-eight-letter system that would evolve into the Cyrillic alphabet. The letters were symbols such as circles, triangles and crosses (these three respectively inspired by eternity, the Trinity and the Crucifixion), designed to express the unique phonetics of Slavonic. A biography written shortly after his death claims that the first words Cyril translated were

8. The Muslims of Samara ostracized local Christians by painting devils on the exteriors of their homes. When Cyril was asked the meaning of these images, he cleverly replied that these devils must be fleeing the homes of faithful Christians, because they found them inhospitable. He presumed there were no devils on the outside of Muslim homes, he added, because "they dwell inside with the inhabitants."

"Iskoni b_ Slovo, i Slovo b_ u Boga, i Bog b_ Slovo"—the magnificent opening lines of St. John's Gospel ("In the beginning was the Word, and the Word was with God, and the Word was God").

Within the year, the brothers were in Moravia, establishing a school to teach the new alphabet and train priests. They were bitterly resented by the Latin priests already there, mainly Bavarians, who considered their linguistic

A few questions troubled Khan Boris

Was sex on Sundays allowed, or chariot racing? Was underwear in church mandatory? Pope Nicholas's exhaustive answers shed light on ninth-century Christian lifestyles

May Christian spouses have sex on Sundays? How about during Lent? Must Christians wear undergarments in church? Should they participate in chariot races? And what about working on weekends? To the newly converted ruler of a kingdom still largely and obstinately pagan, such everyday questions loomed large. Just what sort of behavior did this religion called Christianity expect, anyhow?

The ruler concerned was the Bulgarian khan, Boris, baptized just a year earlier in 865. The authority to whom he directed his queries was none other than Pope Nicholas I. When he asked Patriarch Photius of Constantinople for instruction, the khan complained, Photius had confused him with complex theological pronouncements, and talk of creeds and ecumenical councils. Boris, a practical man, needed practical answers. When, for example, could he execute criminals? How could he justifiably wage war against other Christian nations? How should he treat his remaining pagan subjects? And by the way, could he still use his pagan healing stone?

Khan Boris's one hundred and six questions provide a unique window on the life and thought of a man ruling a chaotic land during a very tumultuous ninth century, and Pope Nicholas's response is a remarkable dissertation that answers them clearly, completely, and also diplomatically. The pope explains basic church rules governing fasting, work and marriage, emphatically stating that bigamy is a worse crime than murder. Sex on Sundays was prohibited, he writes, for "if one should cease from all worldly labor on Sunday ... how much more should one beware of carnal pleasure and every sort of bodily pollution?" But in Lent, by contrast, "it would be completely licit for a man to sleep with his wife without contamination." Undergarments, says Nicholas, are unimportant; the Bulgars may wear them or not, according to preference—but women must cover their heads, and men must be hatless in church.

He bans participation in chariot races—unwelcome news for Boris, a great race enthusiast—but offers some consolation: "Because we cannot yet persuade you to abstain from the games at all times, since you, weak as you are, cannot yet ascend to the mountain to receive the highest commandments of God ... at least spend more time intent upon prayer, abstinence and every kind of penance during Lent and at times of fasting."

Pope Nicholas dismisses the contention that no work should be done on Saturday; people who insist on this are "men of a perverse spirit" and "preachers of the Antichrist." On Sunday, however, a Christian must indeed "cease from earthly labor and devote himself to prayers in every way," for it is "the Redeemer himself, our Lord Jesus Christ, who is the true Sabbath."

As for backsliders among his converted subjects, Boris should first allow the church to persuade them to return to Christ "like a mother, like a teacher." If this fails, however, they can be "rightly oppressed" for "God often arouses the powers against the deniers of Christ and the deserters of baptism."

Right of sanctuary must be rigidly respected. If the pagans of Old Rome "sought indemnity by fleeing to the asylum of the Temple of Romulus, how much more should those who flee to the Temple of Christ receive remission?" But the pope takes issue with standard Bulgarian treatment of suspects. He suggests reliance on credible witnesses, rather than "beating the criminal's head with lashes and pricking his sides with iron goads until he came up with the truth."

He urges clemency for military deserters, escaped slaves, and border guards who unwittingly allow either category to flee the country. If judgment or execution becomes unavoidable, however, Boris should try not to administer them on holy days: "For although both can perhaps be exercised without fault, nevertheless it is fitting that ... a person who comes to divine service should not be implicated in secular business."

endeavors downright heretical. But Cyril and Methodius, unlike most church and state authorities on both sides of the East–West divide, really seem to have been more interested in evangelizing than ecclesiastical politicking. Recognizing the deep Western roots of the Moravian Church, they tried to collaborate with both Rome and Constantinople. Cyril eventually translated both the Western and the Eastern liturgies into Slavonic, and taught both.

In wartime, the khan should act "with greater mildness concerning any parents who are captured," and "spare their lives for the love of the God who delivered them into his [Boris's] hands." Wars must neither be declared nor fought on "the most celebrated days venerated by all Christians," and the decision to fight must be accompanied by "attending church, prayer, forgiving sinners, confession, receiving communion, opening the jails, loosing the fetters and granting liberty to servants, to those broken and weak, and captives, and distributing alms to the needy."

What if a Christian nation breaks a treaty, the khan asks, and declares war on Bulgaria? Pope Nicholas seems reluctant to offer a general rule. The local bishop, he suggests, will better understand "the circumstances of the affair, the nature of the moment, the characters of the people, and the justice of the parties," and thus can better "intimate what should be done."

Boris should reason with subjects who insist on remaining pagan, and if they refuse to listen, should "remove them from your service and friendship." But "violence should by no means be inflicted upon them to make them believers. For everything which is not voluntary cannot be good."

The khan had specifically inquired about the status of many Bulgarians baptized by "a certain lying Greek [who] claimed that he was a priest although he was not." Pope Nicholas gently rebukes him for punishing this pretend priest, since his "simulation nevertheless conferred salvation on a great many." Even Judas, he observes, "baptized many in [Christ's] name." As for priests who continue to give communion despite scandalous behavior, Nicholas states firmly that "no one, no matter how much he has been polluted, can pollute the divine sacraments which are the purging remedies of all contagions, nor can a ray of the sun, even though it passes through sewers and latrines, attract any contamination from there."

The letters exchanged by these two men illuminate two very distinct lifestyles. One is a great warrior grappling for a semblance of civilization and an understanding of morality, despite the barbarism of his country and his own nature. The other is one of the greatest of the medieval popes, drawn into the secular world through his determination to spread the gospel of Jesus Christ. Together they vividly personify the spirit that weaves through the Middle Ages. ■

Ever patient, Pope Nicholas I responded to a barrage of questions from the newly baptized Bulgarian khan, Boris. Boris requested practical guidance on behalf of his people, pagan and struggling to adopt Christian practices, which Nicholas provided with insight and compassion. A detail from a painting by Raphael in the National Gallery, London.

The brothers' success nevertheless made Rome nervous, and in 867 Pope Nicholas summoned them to Rome. On the way, they detoured into the adjacent Slavic realm of Pannonia. Its ruler, Prince Kocel, was also interested in an autonomous Slavic Church. He accepted copies of the Slavonic gospels and liturgies, and offered Cyril and Methodius fifty disciples to train for the priesthood.

Their reception was quite different in Venice, where the Italian clergy, ardent "trilingualists," assailed them with furious argumentation. Only Hebrew, Greek and Latin should be used for liturgical worship, they insisted, because these were the languages of the inscription on Christ's cross. Cyril's response, as recorded by his Slavonic biographer, was a rhetorical masterpiece: "Does not God send the rain equally upon all? Does He not permit the sun to shine upon all? Do we not all equally breathe the air? Are you not ashamed to recognize only three tongues, as though all other nations and races were blind and deaf? Tell me, do you make God a powerless God, Who cannot bestow equal powers on all nations; or do you make Him an envious God Who refuses to do so?"

They reached Rome shortly after the death of Pope Nicholas. His successor, Adrian II, now realizing that Rome could lose the Slavs altogether on the language issue, approved the use of the Slavonic for preaching and teaching in Moravia. He also allowed several of their protégés to be ordained as priests, and proposed that Cyril himself become bishop of Moravia. But at this crowning moment, Cyril fell mortally ill. Recognizing that death was imminent, on Christmas Day he had himself tonsured a monk, and fifty days later, on February 14, 869, he died at age forty-two. On Adrian's orders, he was given a funeral fit for a pope, attended by Greeks and Romans alike.[9]

Methodius carried on their work. He returned to their adopted land, with the pope's blessing, as archbishop of Sirmium, responsible for the Slavs of Moravia, Slovakia and Pannonia. This honor was both blessing and curse. Western clergy formerly responsible to the Bavarian bishops of Salzburg and Passau were horrified to find a Greek in charge—and a Greek who in their eyes was corrupting the church with his Slavonic liturgies. Moreover, Prince Rostislav's nephew, Svatopluk, governor of Nitra, was currently conspiring with the Germans to depose his uncle. Svatopluk found it expedient to charge Methodius with violating Christian doctrine and trespassing on another bishop's jurisdiction.

The aging missionary was tortured, horsewhipped by a Bavarian bishop, and confined to a monastery, while Rostislav fared far worse—he was blinded, and imprisoned until his death. Two and a half years later, Methodius was freed at the request of a new pope, John VIII, and resumed his mission, although under dramatically changed circumstances. Pope John rejected the Slavonic liturgy and Svatopluk ruled at the pleasure of the Germans. In Pannonia, Prince Kocel died while putting down a Croatian insurrection, which halted development of the Slavonic Church there. Svatopluk was an effective military leader, however, who expanded the Moravian Empire into adjacent Slavic regions. Methodius and his missionaries, following the troops, made many converts in the new regions, and their popularity among the Slavs of central Europe afforded some protection

9. Cyril's history after his death proved almost as varied as his life. He asked Methodius to bury him at the Mount Olympus monastery where they had spent time together, but his remains became a pawn in the struggle between Rome and Constantinople. Pope Adrian II ordered him interred in St. Peter's Basilica in Rome. Methodius arranged a compromise: interment in Rome, but at the Basilica of St. Clement, the first-century pope and martyr whose remains Cyril reputedly found during his mission to the Khazars. But when the Normans destroyed St. Clement's in 1084, Cyril had to be relocated, then moved back when it was rebuilt, then moved again in the late eighteenth century, when the French attacked Rome. After that, says Jesuit historian Michael Lacko, a private Roman family safeguarded Cyril's relics until 1963, when they were returned to St. Clement's.

from Svatopluk and hostile Latin clergy. Even so, they were relentlessly harassed, particularly by a priest named Wiching.

Wiching was probably responsible for another formal rebuke from Rome in 879. Methodius was accused this time of outright heresy, of using Slavonic liturgically, and of failing to add the *filioque*—the phrase "and from the Son"— to the assertion in the Nicene Creed that the Holy Spirit "proceeds from the Father." (The last allegation was a curious one; Rome itself would not officially adopt this change for another thirty-five years.) Once again, Methodius had to troop off to Rome, where he easily defended himself, and won another papal endorsement for the Slavonic liturgy.

Pope John also told him to carry on as archbishop of Greater Moravia, though he terminated his jurisdiction over Pannonia. But Methodius's nemesis, Wiching, was made bishop of Nitra. As such, he was nominally answerable to Methodius, but since he had the ear of Svatopluk, his real power was considerable. So was his cunning. When the beleaguered missionary returned to Moravia in 880, he encountered a widespread and very solid misapprehension that the pope had in fact found him guilty, and replaced him with Wiching. The author of these lies? The mendacious bishop himself, no doubt.

Now well into his sixties, Methodius must have been growing weary of plots. In 881-882, he traveled to Constantinople one last time and visited his old friend Photius. The meeting by all accounts was cordial; Photius did not complain that

Cyril and Methodius evangelizing the Moravians in an early twentieth-century illustration. Cyril had already begun creating a Slavonic alphabet when summoned by Rotislav, enabling him to translate both the Catholic and Orthodox liturgies into the language of the people.

Cyril and Methodius are canonized and honored as "Apostles to the Slavs" in the Orthodox church. Although the Slavonic church did not take hold in Moravia, the founding work of the two brothers established the Slavonic language in churches of other Balkan countries. This icon is from the Trojan Monastery in Bulgaria.

the brothers had fallen in with the pope. Indeed, after his own long, tempestuous relationship with Rome, Photius had recently negotiated an accord with the pope that acknowledged him as patriarch of Constantinople. Returning to Moravia, Methodius resumed the translation of religious texts, including the Old Testament, into Slavonic. And he excommunicated Wiching and some of his confederates—a vain attempt to safeguard his own followers and successors.

That was one of the last earthly acts of Archbishop Methodius. He died at Easter 885, and his disciples, in an exquisitely fitting farewell, made a point of conducting his funeral rites in Latin, Greek—and Slavonic. But his death marked the beginning of the end for that language in Moravia. Wiching persuaded the next pope, Stephen V, to make him archbishop, to totally ban the Slavonic liturgy, and to approve the purging of followers of Cyril and Methodius. Many were arrested. Some fled. Some were sold as slaves.

The future of the Slavonic Church would be determined elsewhere, with Bulgaria playing the pivotal role. Methodius had reportedly left copies of all the Slavonic texts in Constantinople on his last visit there along with a group of disciples (one of whom was the khagan Boris's youngest son, Simeon), who were to found a training school for missionaries to Bulgaria. Meanwhile, many Moravian clergy sought haven in Bulgaria. Boris welcomed them all, envisioning them as founders of a fully Slavicized and Christian Bulgaria. Confident that his nation was firmly set on this path, Boris then turned over the throne to his eldest son, Vladimir, and retired to a monastery.

Vladimir proved to be a lax Christian, however, and a pawn of the stubbornly pagan Bulgar aristocracy. Four years later, Boris therefore replaced him with Simeon, who was made of much sterner stuff. Simeon the Great, as he came to be known, reigned from 893 to 927, presiding over a florescence of art, culture, commerce and—not least—faith. Written Slavonic evolved from Cyril's original notation into the more Greek-influenced Cyrillic, while still retaining the name of the saintly linguist.[10] Translation of religious texts became a large-scale enterprise. Simeon also discarded the titles "khan" and "khagan" in favor of the Slavonic "czar" (from the Latin caesar).

10. Though the word "cyrillic" derives, of course, from Cyril, it was actually only when dying that the saintly Cyril decided to be tonsured a monk and took that name. Throughout his career he was known by his baptismal name, Constantine.

Simeon was a fighter, too. When a trade dispute again triggered war with Byzantium, the Greeks sought lethal assistance from the Magyars, the latest nomads out of the Ural Mountains. The Bulgars beat them back, and a decade later, twice stormed the gates of Constantinople. Simeon also battled the Serbs and Croats, extending his reach from the Black Sea to the Adriatic. Seemingly his greatest desire, however, was to become emperor of Byzantium, and after persistent failure he persuaded the pope to declare him "Emperor of Rome and the Balkans" instead. As such, he appointed a patriarch for Bulgaria, a presumptuous move steadfastly ignored by Constantinople.

With Simeon's death in 927 his war-stressed empire collapsed into secession (by the western provinces) and invasion (by Serbs and Magyars). It even endured a short-lived Kievan occupation in the 960s, but the Byzantines delivered the deathblow. Emperor Basil II "the Bulgar-slayer," invaded three times between 981 and 1014, and crowned his final victory with an act of brutality so stupendously cruel as to stupefy even that callous age. When his army took prisoner fifteen thousand Bulgar soldiers, Basil had ninety-nine men out of every hundred blinded. The hundredth man he left with just one eye, so that he could guide his sightless comrades home. Then he turned them all loose.

Samuel, fourth czar since Simeon, was reportedly so horrified by the sight of his stumbling army that he collapsed and died, and within a few years, the last vestiges of the Bulgar Empire were absorbed into Byzantium, where they would lie dormant for some two centuries. But the work of Cyril and Methodius, and

Mucha's visionary painting, The Introduction of the Slavonic Liturgy, *blends pagan and Christian images in its celebration of the first Liturgy served in the language of the people.*

their royal sponsors, had sown the seeds of Christianity wide and deep in Bulgar territory—so deep that it would survive both pitiless cruelty from fellow Christians, and the coming assaults of Islamic and Turkish invaders. Through it all, the Bulgars would remain loyal to the Eastern Church.

In some other regions, the ecclesiastical orientation of the Slavs was yet unresolved, but Latin jurisdiction naturally tended to prevail in the more westerly areas. So it was with Bohemia, precursor of the twentieth-century Czech Republic. Settled by Slavs in the six and seventh centuries, Bohemia remained pagan until the late 800s, when it fell under Christian influence. A Czech legend relates how Borivoj, a Slav chieftain from Prague, led his country into the faith after a humiliating incident at the Moravian court. As a heathen, so the story goes, he was expected to sit on the floor to eat, while Christian dignitaries dined in style at tables.

Some sources suggest that Borivoj was baptized by Methodius himself, and it is altogether likely that priests trained by Methodius catechized his subjects. But the disintegration of Moravia forced Bohemia to look westward for security, and its introduction to faith in Jesus Christ proceeded under direction from Rome.

Czar Simeon of Bulgaria, an enthusiastic patron of arts and letters, spawned a golden age of Bulgarian culture. Mucha's portrayal shows Simeon in his court surrounded by the intellectuals of his day, writers, philosophers and scribes.

One particular Bohemian, incidentally, would become well known in England in the nineteenth century, by way of a popular Christmas carol—Borivoj's grandson, Wenceslas.[11] Reputedly a gentle, pious soul, whose brief life emphasized charity for the poor, this young ruler had absorbed his religious convictions from his grandmother, an early Bohemian convert who was assassinated by her pagan daughter-in-law, Wenceslas's mother. He himself was murdered in 929, at the age of twenty-two, by his power-hungry brother, thereby qualifying as a Christian martyr and a hero of the Czech people.

Wenceslas, a gentle soul who emphasized charity to the poor, was murdered at the age of 22 by his power-hungry brother. His name lives on in a popular English Christmas carol.

The next Slavic flock to enter the Christian fold was Poland. In the mid-tenth century, the disparate tribes east of Germany and north of Bohemia were led by a dominant chief named Mieszko (or Mieczyslaw). Mieszko may have been an illiterate barbarian, observes historian Vlasto, but he was no fool. Recognizing a formidable power in the mighty German Empire just across the Oder River, he followed the advice Methodius had given another Slavic prince many years earlier: "Better to embrace Christianity voluntarily and retain your independence than to be forcibly baptized in foreign captivity."

So Prince Mieszko invited in missionaries from his nonthreatening southern neighbor, Bohemia. He also wed the daughter of its king, Boleslaw, and their marriage became one of the many instances in the conversion of Europe where, as St. Paul put it, "the unbelieving husband is saved through the believing wife." (I Cor. 7:14) The bride traveled north in 964 accompanied by priests, liturgies and scripture translations. Two years later Mieszko was baptized, subsequently persuaded the pope to create a Polish diocese under direct papal supervision, and in the next two decades extended his territory from the mouth of the Oder to the borders of Baltic Prussia and the Kievan state. Finally, trying to ensure strong Christian support on his western border, he arranged his renowned "Donation of Poland" to the pope, just before his death in 992.[12]

Under Mieszko's son Boleslaw, "the Brave," Poland experienced a blossoming of Christianity, commerce and conquest, its influence spreading from the Baltic beyond the Carpathians, and east of the Vistula River. Emperor Otto III formally recognized Boleslaw and his kingdom, and the pope appointed an archbishop for Poland. The Latin language and the Latin rite dominated from the beginning. Mieszko and Boleslaw both sanctioned conversion by force, and anyone who broke a religious fast, for instance, risked having his teeth knocked out. After Boleslaw died in 1025, parts of Poland rapidly reverted to paganism. Mobs of peasants roamed the country murdering clergymen, nobles and government officials, and ransacking churches, convents and castles.

But there is also some evidence that the unrest, especially in the South, was

11. The Christmas carol *Good King Wenceslas*, written in 1853 by the noted English translator and hymnographer John Mason Neale, remained popular right through the twentieth century, to the dismay of some modernists and post-modernists. In the 1960s, one student of carols, Elizabeth Poston, condemned it as "ponderous moral doggerel," and attacked Neale for "debasing" a thirteenth-century spring carol from which he borrowed the melody. Though Wenceslas is certainly remembered for his charitable acts, his mission to relieve a poor man on a snowy night is a fable invented by Neale.

12. Needing Christian allies, but wary of the imperial Germans, around 990, Prince Mieszko of Poland dispatched an embassy to Rome that purported to bestow control of his kingdom upon Pope John XV. This so-called "Donation of Poland" is recorded in a document, the *Dagome index*, which is regarded as genuine. The close relationship then initiated would culminate ten centuries later in elevation of the first Polish pope, John Paul II.

due to conflict between Latin loyalists and Moravian supporters of Slavonic traditions. Not until 1039, with the reign of Kazimierz, great-grandson of Mieszko I, was order restored in Poland. Kazimierz insisted on Latin rule and usage, although the country's written language, as in Bohemia, was influenced by the Slavonic alphabet of Cyril and Methodius. Thus the work of the two Greek brothers, who accomplished one of the great missionary achievements of the Eastern Church, is inextricably interwoven with the political and religious history of virtually all Slavdom.

Ironically, however, in Byzantium's home territory in the eighth century, these supposedly "peaceful Slavs" had begun rolling back the frontier of the empire itself, supplanting the Greeks as far south as Thessalonica and infiltrating most of the Balkan Peninsula's interior as well. The Greeks clung to a few seaports, but even some of their islands, including Crete, were subject to Slav incursions. In the North, Slavonic-speakers occupied Macedonia, effectively blocking the *Via Egnatia,* the old imperial highway linking east and west—a physical separation that added to the estrangement of Rome and Constantinople.

Arriving Slavs took up farming and settled in small villages, while the Greek cities and towns fell to ruin. The newcomers shunned them utterly, calling them "walled tombs," but this resistance to urbanization, and to organization, proved their undoing in Greece. By the mid-ninth century, the Byzantine reconquest was almost complete, and the Slavic population was converting to Christianity. Moreover, in Greece they would ultimately lose not only their language, but all cultural distinction as well—a rare instance of a large Slavic population succumbing to assimilation.

Such was by no means the case in the rest of the Balkan area, however. In the seventh century, their northernmost territories, eventually to be known as Croatia and Slovenia, were heavily populated by pagan Slavs along the northern part of the Dalmatian coast and east to the Drava River. The Dalmatian Croats became especially turbulent, looting churches, extorting protection payments and practicing piracy on the Adriatic, even occasionally raiding Italian ports.

As always, pope and patriarch both sought Croat and Slovene souls. The patriarch had an initial advantage, as the Slavonic alphabet and liturgy migrated south from Moravia and Pannonia, but in the early tenth century, Croatia opted irrevocably for Rome. Mild measures against the use of Slavonic became compulsory measures. Eastern Slavic

Gold, pearls, and precious gems adorn the fourteenth-century crown of the kings of Bohemia, one of the Bohemian treasures stored in St. Vitus Cathedral in Prague, and exhibited only on special national holidays. Some of the stones in this crown are among the largest of their kind in the world.

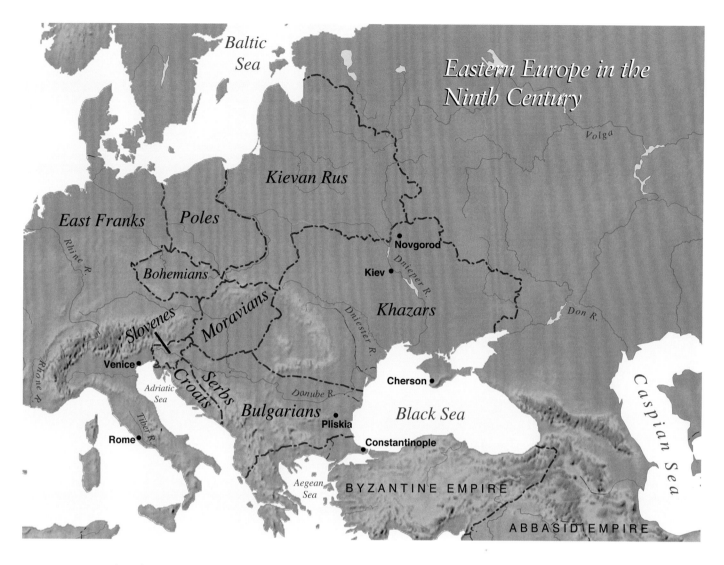

priests were ordered to cut their hair and beards; men who could not speak Latin were refused ordination; Methodius was branded a heretic; and Cyril's alphabet suffered guilt by association. The Eastern Church lingered on only in rural parishes and monasteries along the Dalmatian coast. Croatians and Slovenians would consequently maintain their Slavic language and culture, but their alphabet would be Latin and their church Roman.

Meanwhile, a few hundred miles to the southeast, in the valleys of the Drina and Ibar rivers, a different destiny awaited another group of Slavs. Little is known of the Serbs before the ninth century, when they began to impinge upon Byzantium, and missionaries from Moravia and Bohemia began spreading literacy and Christianity. By the eleventh, the locus of Serbian power shifted west to latter-day Montenegro and the southern Dalmatian coast. In the twelfth, it gained cohesion and still more territory under its first significant leader, Symeon Nemanja (not to be confused with Simeon of Bulgaria).

Eastern Serbia was inevitably influenced by the Eastern Church, and the Dalmatian side by the Western, a circumstance sharply illustrated by the Nemanja dynasty. Vukan Nemanja, who governed Montenegro, married a relative of the pope and embraced the West. His brother Stephen, governor of the interior, married a Byzantine princess and remained with the East. The inevitable conflict was mediated by a third brother, Rastko—though not under that name. In 1191, Rastko secretly became a monk on the famous monastic peninsula of Mount Athos, taking the name Sava. Seventeen years later he returned, to play a key role in establishing the independent Serbian Orthodox Church, and to become its first archbishop—and before very long, its patron saint.[13]

Both Serbia and Bulgaria harbored the Bogomil heresy, an uncompromising belief that the material world is hopelessly evil, and Satan's exclusive domain. The country most infected with Bogomilism, however, was the last Slavic Balkan realm, Bosnia-Herzegovina, which never did fully resolve its Christian orientation. Straddling the very edge of the religious chasm between East and West, Bosnia-Herzegovina evolved into a patchwork of Western and Eastern communities, and eventually—after the Turkish invasion of the late fifteenth century—Muslim as well. Nevertheless, it was still culturally Slavic, like most of central Europe.[14]

At the very center of the Slavic world was one glaring cultural anomaly. Hungary was not slavicized, and never would be. The chosen home of the fearsome Magyars, it became a permanent wedge between the Slavs of the North and South. Magyar durability apparently owed much to Magyar temperament. Reportedly more ruthless even than the Huns, they exterminated whole populations, sparing only young women for use as sexual slaves. At their horrifying arrival in the late ninth century, terrorized Christian populations associated them with Gog and Magog, Satan's dreadful harbingers of the Apocalypse as described in Revelation 20:8.

Temporarily blocked by the Bulgars, the Magyars crossed the Danube in the tenth century, seizing the territories once ruled by the Slavic princes Svatopluk and Kocel. They repeatedly attacked Germany, France and Italy (and Constantinople at least once), until the Germans stopped them at Merseberg in Saxony in 933, and at Lechfield in Bavaria in 955. (See chapter 3.) Thoroughly chastened, the Magyars settled down on the Hungarian plain.

Christian influence from surrounding areas also seems to have been a factor in Magyar cultural independence. A powerful prince named Geza apparently decided that his people could not survive as a pagan enclave. He married a Polish Christian named Adelaide, who in 985 arranged the baptism of her husband and their ten-year-old heir, Stephen. Coming to his throne in 997, Stephen was known as a devout Christian who liberated his slaves, and built churches and monasteries. By then, too, the papacy was allowing national churches some autonomy (although not on language). For the Magyars, Pope Sylvester II authorized a church free of German supervision in 1001. This ensured for the second millennium Hungary's allegiance to the West.

The greatest Slavic colossus of all would arise from another union, this time with Nordic barbarians first known to eastern Europeans as Varangians, and later as the Rus. Elsewhere, of course, the close relatives of those gentry were called Vikings, or Northmen. (See chapter 4.) Indefatigable pirate-merchants, they came in the eighth century from Scandinavia, via the Gulf of Finland and

13. Five years after the Serbian prince Rastko secretly became a monk, taking the monastic name Sava, his father King Symeon abdicated and did likewise. Father and son founded the monastery of Hilandar on Mount Athos, the center of medieval Serbian culture, and Sava later returned to Serbia to help establish the Orthodox Church there. He would be named his country's patron saint. Together, writes A. P. Vlasto (*The Entry of the Slavs into Christendom*), Sava and Symeon represent "dynasty and church, the twin pillars of the Serbian state, and the source of its remarkable strength."

14. One Balkan area that did not fall to the Slavs was the southern part of the ancient Roman province of Illyricum, across the Adriatic Sea from Italy. It became Albania, named for its dominant tribe, the Albanoi, who spoke an old Illyrian language. Ruled by Byzantium for a thousand years, Christian Albania would resist the invading Ottoman Turks until 1506—half a century after Constantinople fell. Then they repeatedly rebelled, until the Ottomans initiated a particularly brutal campaign to Islamize them. Some two thirds eventually became Muslim. Curiously, Albania would also supply two-dozen grand viziers (prime ministers) of Turkey.

Hungary became the permanent home of the migratory Magyars, fierce raiders and the terror of Europe. Arpad, here taking possession of the land, became their first ruler, uniting seven Magyar tribes and settling on the Hungarian plain around the Danube.

the network of navigable waterways that traverses the great plains between the Baltic, Black and Caspian seas. The eastern Slavs, who earlier used some of these rivers to move north from their prehistoric Polesie homeland, watched with interest as the Varangians built a fortified settlement at Novgorod.

And then, according to the primary source of early Russian history, *The Chronicle of Bygone Years*, written around 1100, the Slavs approached the Varangians. "Our land is vast and rich but there is no order in it," they told the new arrivals. "Come and rule over us." The Scandinavians needed no second asking. With a few modest portages in the Valdai Hills, they had discovered, the Volga, Don and Dnieper river systems could handily carry them to the fabled lands of the Khazars, Byzantines and Arabs. By expelling its Khazar overlords, they next took the Slavic city of Kiev on the Dnieper where northern forest met southern grassland. From Kiev in 860, two hundred boatloads of Varangian warriors launched their first attack on Constantinople.[15]

Patriarch Photius of Constantinople initially persuaded the Rus to accept some Christian evangelists, an arrangement that lasted only until a ruthless Viking chief named Oleg, a Thor-worshiping polygamist, seized central power

15. Patriarch Photius wrote of the Rus attack on Constantinople that a "hailstorm of barbarians burst forth" like a "wild boar," and "devoured the inhabitants … sparing nothing from man to beast, not respecting female weakness, not pitying tender infants, not reverencing the hoary hairs of old men … but boldly thrusting their sword through persons of every age and sex." The bloodbath was avenged when a storm swamped the departing Rus in their booty-laden longships—after Photius prayed over the robe of the Holy Virgin.

16. Legend has it that the Rus leader, Oleg, was warned by a soothsayer that his favorite horse would cause his death. He therefore ceased riding the animal and retired him to pasture. When he heard some years later that the horse had died, however, he decided to pay his respects. Resting his foot on the animal's skull, he was delivering a eulogy to his beloved steed when a snake emerged from inside the skull, and bit him.

and threw them out. Oleg also built Kiev into what he proclaimed to be "the mother of Rus cities," before he died, according to legend, from a snakebite in 913.[16] His successor was Igor, a scion of the Rurikid family that had established Novgorod, thus launching the dynasty that would preside over the Rus emergence as a Slavic and Christian power. Integral to this process was Igor's wife, Olga, who became regent in 945, after her husband was captured and hideously executed.

His captors, says *The Chronicle*, were a recalcitrant Slav group who tied Igor between two bent-over sapling trees, then released them to tear him apart. Olga, tall, handsome and formidable, is described by Vladimir Volkoff in his 1984 biography, *Vladimir the Russian Viking*, as a "petticoated Machiavelli with a touch of sadism." She amply punished her husband's killers, burying some alive and burning down their chief town. But a decade later, Olga suddenly mellowed, became an ardent Christian, and traveled to Constantinople to discuss the conversion of her people. Then, dissatisfied with what she considered cavalier treatment by the Byzantines, she did what other monarchs had done. She contacted Rome.

By then the Varangians had acquired, likely from Bulgaria, the Cyrillic alphabet and some knowledge of Christianity, although most of them remained stubbornly heathen. Volkoff imagines Olga's son, Sviatoslav, for example, as dearly loving his mother, but vehemently rejecting her religion. "Mother," he might have said, "my retinue will laugh at me if I become a do-gooder. Yours is not a faith for soldiers and princes." Sviatoslav became king in 962, gave his pious mother a Christian funeral when the time came, and reigned a proper pagan, barring Roman missionaries, although he did not deliberately persecute Christians. Fearless in battle, he headed victorious campaigns against the Khazars, Bulgars, Greeks and more.

As an ardent polygamist, Sviatoslav had the customary complement of children, but three were predominant: Yaropolk and Oleg, sons of his primary wife; and Vladimir, born of a tryst with Olga's Slavic servant. Vladimir, although

More ruthless than Huns, the Magyars slew entire populations, only sparing young women to serve as their sexual slaves. Terrorized Christians saw them as forerunners of Satan.

ridiculed by his half brothers as the "son of a slave," was raised within the royal family, and was in fact Olga's particular favorite. He trained eagerly in martial arts, writes Volkoff, quickly maturing into a formidable warrior. Fonder of conquest than governing, Sviatoslav divided his kingdom's administration among these three sons, while he concentrated on conquering Bulgaria. Yaropolk got Kiev and environs, Oleg the southern lands, and Vladimir the original Viking settlement at Novgorod.

Whether any other dispensation would have worked is unlikely; certainly this one did not. When the king died on his way home from a defeat by Byzantine forces, Yaropolk of Kiev immediately attacked and killed Oleg. Vladimir, not yet twenty, escaped a similar fate by fleeing to Sweden. There he recruited such a sizable army of Varangian mercenaries that two years later Yaropolk surrendered Kiev without a fight. Vladimir thereupon killed his half brother, amply avenging those childhood taunts.

The year was 978. Christianity was the dominant faith in most of Europe, and spreading. Vladimir's cherished (and later sainted) grandmother had explained her faith to him, and he now took as his third wife Yaropolk's widow, a Greek and a former nun. Furthermore, his closest friend, Olaf, son of a murdered king of Norway, was a Christian. (Rescued from slavery in Estonia, Olaf had been adopted into Sviatoslav's household.) Nevertheless, one of Vladimir's first projects as king was a pagan revival that installed images of Slavic gods, headed by a huge wooden idol of Perun, god of thunder and lightning, the Slavic Thor. In Kiev before the image of Perun, with its silver head and golden mustache, regular bloody sacrifices were performed.

An efficient administrator and ambitious imperialist, Vladimir was even more renowned for drinking, feasting and fornicating. He reputedly had four wives, and more than a thousand concubines. But suddenly, while still in his twenties, he mysteriously changed character, and even began to seriously consider the religion he once rejected. Was he influenced by Olga and Olaf? Was he sated with hedonistic pleasures? Was it divine inspiration? All of these, and more? Whatever the explanation, he proceeded with notable deliberation.

First Vladimir carefully examined all options, says *The Chronicle*, inviting Western and Eastern Christians, Jewish and Muslim spokesmen to make their case. Then he sent agents to observe these religions in their homelands. Islam he summarily rejected for banning pork and alcohol. "For the Rus," he said, "drinking is their only joy. We cannot be without it." The Judaism of the Khazars he dismissed, when told that Jews seemingly had so offended their God that he gave their homeland to others. Latin liturgies were austere, his envoys reported, and Latin priests obsessed with fasting. But in Constantinople, according to *The Chronicles*, his agents were absolutely dazzled. "The Greeks led us to edifices where they worship their God," they told Vladimir, "and we knew not whether we were in heaven or on earth. For on earth there is no such splendor, or such beauty.... We know only that God dwells there among men."

As fate would have it, Emperor Basil II needed help just then against both an internal rival and the Bulgars, and Vladimir still had some thousands of Viking mercenaries on his hands, hungry for war and pillage. He was happy to donate these now expendable warriors to the emperor's service, but in return he wanted recognition of his impending conversion to Eastern Christianity, and something even more substantial: Basil's sister Anna in marriage. The desperate emperor reluctantly agreed. Anna, however, did not agree at all.

The royal groom and bride were to meet in the spring of 988 near Cherson, the strategic Byzantine port city near the mouth of the Dnieper. In accord with the agreement, Vladimir dispatched six thousand Viking mercenaries to Constantinople, where they would earn fame as the elite "Varangian Guard" (see sidebar page 142). Then he waited for his bride. Instead, apologetic envoys arrived with the news that Anna didn't want him for a husband, and was refusing to leave Constantinople. Always decisive, Vladimir laid siege to Cherson. It surrendered after eight months, and the

Viking traders haggle with Mongol and Persian caravaners on the Volga River, bartering fur pelts and an even more valuable commodity, captive slave girls, for such Asian luxury goods as silk, metalwork and coins. The latter, being carefully weighed at left, have been discovered in many Viking treasure hordes. The mustached totem in the background represents a Norse god, and the skull of a sacrificial ox hangs at top right.

Oleg, the legendary Varangian warrior considered to be the founder of the Kievan Rus state, captured Kiev from the Khazars in 880. In this lithograph by V. Vaznetzov, now in the Bibliothèque des Arts Décoratifs, Paris, Oleg meets the soothsayer who prophesies about his death.

17. By 1250, Prince Vladimir the Great, the Christian convert ruler who brought the Rus into the faith, was declared by the Russian Orthodox Church a saint "Equal to the Apostles," in recognition of this great work of evangelization. Among other things, he is also credited with inspiring a major victory against the Swedish army on July 15, 1240, won by Russian forces along the Neva River, after they invoked the intercession of the great prince who had died on that day in 1015.

terrified people awaited the usual Viking pillage and slaughter. But Vladimir, now committed to Christianity, said he was not interested in pillage and slaughter. All he wanted was his wife.

Since the empire now faced the loss of its crucial base on the Black Sea, Anna had no choice. Thus in the summer of 989 the twenty-five-year-old princess finally walked ashore, beautiful and imperial in white satin and gold filigree, accompanied by essential ecclesiastical personages also in full regalia. Vladimir was now baptized, says *The Chronicle*, along with "many of his companions." Legend has it that in the meantime he had been stricken blind, and that the baptismal waters miraculously restored his sight. And now the marriage too could take place—the marriage that not only transformed Vladimir into a monogamous Christian, but also wedded the eastern Slavs to the Eastern Church from that moment onward.

As a bride-gift, he restored Cherson to his brother-in-law Basil. Back in Kiev, he ordered the destruction of every pagan idol. Perun, savagely mutilated, was sent down the Dnieper, to be destroyed in its wild cataracts. And now, Vladimir summoned his people for baptism. With the selfsame liturgical formula that the Orthodox Church would still use in the twenty-first century, Anna's Greek priests performed the traditional exorcism of evil: "The Lord puts you under ban, O devil...." Then they hallowed the waters of the Dnieper in the age-old baptismal blessing, making the whole river holy.

Kievans responded in their hundreds, according to *The Chronicle*, plunging eagerly into the water. "O God, who hast created heaven, earth, sea and all that is in them, look down upon these thy new men," Vladimir prayed over his shivering people, "and cause them to know Thee who art the true God, even as other Christian nations do...." Thus began the official conversion of Russia.[17]

It proceeded so speedily as to suggest that Christianity had already spread widely among the Rus, but the postscript to Vladimir's proclamation may also have been persuasive: "Any man who fails to respond, let him consider himself my foe." Nor was the process entirely peaceful. Novgorod's pagans rebelled, for example. They were violently subdued and forcibly baptized, but paganism lingered in the North into the thirteenth century. Still, Vladimir seemingly tried to proceed peacefully. He built some four hundred churches, among them the immense oaken St. Sophia in Kiev, with its thirteen domes. Probably dedicated to the Blessed Virgin, it was called the Church of the Tithe because Vladimir dedicated one tenth of his revenue to its clergy and charities.

He also established schools, insisted that young people attend them, organized mass baptisms, liberated slaves, and presented his previous wives and concubines to deserving friends. He and his sons personally distributed food and drink to the poor, and organized regular Sunday feasts to replace the pagan bacchanals of old. He reputedly tried to restrict military operations to defense alone, usually against the Pechenegs, a group of ferocious eastern tribes who constantly harried the Rus. It is said he even tried to reduce the use of capital punishment in domestic law.

Bulgarian missionary priests doubtless helped to entrench the Slavonic language, and in the remaining quarter-century of his reign, Vladimir established the pattern of church-state governance that would prevail on one form or another in Russia until the Communist revolution of the twentieth century. He also created a legal system that made the church the arbiter of family matters, and cast the monarch as the "earthly representative of Christ," equally responsible for the material and spiritual welfare of his people.

Like so many medieval monarchs, Vladimir was blessed with a superfluity of offspring, including ten legitimate sons by previous wives, and two by Anna. He appointed them all as princes and grand dukes to administer specific regions, with Yaroslav, the eldest, in Novgorod. Included on equal terms was his nephew, Sviatopolk, son of the brother he had killed (and whose widow he had married). Vladimir made him prince of Turov, near the Polish border. Even when Sviatopolk conspired against him, the grand prince merely imprisoned him briefly, and subsequently kept him near Kiev.

Yaroslav was likely his choice until he defied his father in 1014, when Vladimir's thoughts seemingly shifted towards

The Radizwill Chronicle *records the conversion of Vladimir after his envoys witness an Orthodox service in Constantinople and "knew not whether they were in heaven or in earth." The top illustration in its upper half portrays the envoys at the service in Hagia Sophia cathedral. In the lower half they report back to Vladimir. The bottom illustration shows the conversion of Vladimir's grandmother, Olga. Her influence on her grandson did not become evident until twenty-eight years after her death when he adopted Christianity and led the way for all Russia to do the same.*

Bitter memories live on

A 'little Slavonic island in a German sea' became a footnote of history as the Wends were brutally subjugated by their German rulers

Just before Christmas 1854, the sailing vessel *Ben Nevis* completed a tumultuous, seven-week transatlantic journey from Liverpool, England, docking at last at Galveston, Texas. The five hundred passengers, who had survived rough seas and rampant cholera, undoubtedly said a prayer of thanks before moving on to Houston, the city that many of them eventually called home. To the locals, they probably seemed just another batch of poor German immigrants seeking prosperity. Not so. The newcomers were Wends, an ancient but minute people of Slavic origin, seeking a privilege that had eluded them for more than a thousand years: the right to speak their own language and live without persecution. (Though they are known best as the "Wends," the people themselves prefer to be called "Sorbs," a term less used because it becomes confused with Serbian Slavs.)

The Wends appear in the earliest historic references to the Slavic peoples, says historian George R. Nielson (*In Search of a Home*), but have been little noticed because they were so few in number, and had never formed an independent state. In the sixth century, they followed westward-moving Germanic tribes into a broad area known as Lusatia, between the Oder and Elbe rivers, stretching from fifty miles southeast of Berlin to the border of the later Czech Republic, and including parts of Poland. While some Wends continued west into Saxony, most developed their own culture in Lusatia's woodlands and meadows.

But before long the German Franks, anxious to secure the eastern border of their Christian Empire, found themselves confronted there by an entrenched thicket of pagan Saxons and Slavs. As A. P. Vlasto notes in *The Entry of the Slavs into Christendom*, the Germans openly coveted the best Slav lands, and the busy, prosperous Slav ports that offered access to the northern Baltic trade route. Initially the Germans merely conducted raids, selling their many Slavic captives as slaves, usually to the Muslims.

The actual subjugation of the Lusatian Wends began in the early tenth century. It would take nearly three hundred years to completely subdue, Germanize and Christianize them, a process whose events were engraved in Wend memory. Early in the twentieth century, Jacob Barth, their preeminent poet and a student of theology, wrote:

> Oh, how appalling was the carnage,
> Oh, how hellish the slaughter!
> The gallows resounded with screams and curses
> As the hounds tore into the masses.
> The priests, all the while, chanted psalms
> And litanies and sang hymns.
> Horrified by the sight of it all,
> The sun itself took flight.
> Hrabanus entered into his chronicle
> (while praying on his knees):
> "Charlemagne brought the Gospel to the Wends
> To the greater glory of God."

Wends (or Sorbs) still comprise a minority in Lusatia, Germany, where their language has been kept alive. These traditionally dressed Wends prepare for Easter with the decorating of eggs. The twentieth century has seen the emigration of numbers of these people to Australia and the United States.

Ironically, the kings who subjugated the Wends of Lusatia, beginning with Henry the Fowler (912-936) and his son Otto the Great (936-973), were of Saxon blood. The Saxons, Vlasto writes, were seemingly determined to subject the pagan Slavs to the same treatment they themselves received from Charlemagne: "The recent converts became, as often, more rabid and extreme in their turn." And while "Henry's policy did not yet amount to a systematic 'baptism or death,' this soon became a commonplace Saxon attitude."

Individual free choice in religion may have been scarcely comprehensible to people bound by tradition and clan loyalties, whether Saxon or Wendish, but cultural resistance could run deep. In 983, pagan Wends rebelled, razing Hamburg and clearing out the Germans from virtually all territory beyond the Elbe. Although the Germans regained Lusatia in a bloody fifteen-year campaign, for almost two centuries there was continuous strife.

In 1168, the Wends bitterly conceded defeat and began a sorrowful period of decline as an impoverished underclass, dispossessed of their property, banned from skilled jobs, required to speak only German. Lusatia and the Wends, described by author Gerald Stone in *The Smallest Slavonic Nation* as a "little Slavonic island in a German sea," became a mere footnote of history.

By the early twenty-first century there were fewer than seventy thousand Wends in the entire world, the majority Lutheran and a substantial minority Roman Catholic. While the Wends still consider the town of Bautzen in eastern Germany their capital, only one thousand of its forty-four thousand inhabitants are Wendish, and assimilation is every bit as potent in Texas as Germany. So a Slavic people that has survived epochal persecution now faces a more graceful dissolution through assimilation. ∎

Aerial view of Chersonesos, the ancient Cherson, with the newly renovated St. Volodymyr's Church, taken in 2001. The entrance to Sevastopol Harbor is in the distance. The ancient Black Sea port is the alleged site of Vladimir's baptism in 988.

Boris, Anna's elder son, and after that, the stalwart but pious prince of Rostov, who was deservedly popular with the people. But the grand prince appointed no definite successor. Four serious problems confronted him in 1015: Yaroslav's defiance; Sviatopolk's continued scheming; Pecheneg attacks on the East; and personal illness. In fact, he was fatally ill. No sooner had he commissioned Boris to march against the Pechenegs than Vladimir, Grand Prince of Kiev and all the Rus, died at his summer palace. He was in his late fifties.

Hardly had he been interred beside Anna and Olga in the Church of the Tithe when conflict erupted. Sviatopolk, who must have spent the last three decades nursing hatred of his uncle and cousins, swiftly dispatched assassins to murder Boris (on his way back from battle), as well as Boris's devoted younger brother, Gleb.[18] He then seized the throne, with some help from Poland, but did not hold it long. From Novgorod, Yaroslav managed to duplicate his father's initial strategy, and finished off cousin Sviatopolk.

Yaroslav reigned long and well enough to be accounted "the Wise." He expanded Kievan territory to include the last Slavic tribes in a realm that would be ruled by the Rurikid dynasty for another five centuries. In the next two, the Russian Orthodox Church would grow to encompass the entire realm, and would subsequently survive a millennium of persecution by Muslims, Mongols, Turks and Communists. In fact, during the period of Mongol domination, the patriarchy of Moscow would succeed Constantinople as chief bastion and defender of Eastern Christendom, and by the twenty-first century it would have missionary dioceses throughout Europe, the Americas, Africa, Australia and the Middle East. ■

18. The two sons of Grand Prince Vladimir and Princess Anna are revered as saints by the Russian Orthodox Church. Boris and Gleb, called "the Passion-Bearers," were assassinated on the orders of their cousin, Sviatopolk, later known as "the Accursed," who wished to seize the throne. Boris, warned of Sviatopolk's intent, refused either to flee or to defend himself against one he considered his brother. Dismissing his army, he awaited the assassins, praying: "Lord Jesus, thou didst accept thy Passion on account of our sins. Grant me also the strength to accept my passion." The younger Gleb, when told that Boris was dead, did likewise.

O epic-famed, god-haunted Central Sea,
Heave careless of the deep wrong done to thee.

— Thomas Hardy, Genoa and the Mediterranean

The rugged coast of rocky Crete looks out upon the
Mediterranean. The Muslims captured the island in 826,
enslaved the Christian inhabitants and held it for 135 years.
From Crete, they waged a century-long reign of terror
against the Christian inhabitants of the whole Aegean area.
The great sea, tranquil by summer, raging in winter, as
Hardy observes, has seen many "deep wrongs." But its
beauty has long left man awestruck. "The grand object of
traveling," wrote the British essayist Samuel Johnson, "is to
see the shores of the Mediterranean."

CHAPTER 9

The Norman intruders foil Islam's campaign to kill off Christianity

Muslim raiders occupy Sicily, take over Provence, block the Alpine passes, and repeatedly hit Rome until the now-Christian Vikings drive them off

For more than eight hundred years, the Mediterranean Sea had teemed every spring, summer and fall with mercantile traffic. Only the daring or desperate ventured out on its treacherous waters in the gale-ridden months from November to March, but in the sailing season, hundreds of ships crisscrossed its four-hundred-mile width, hauling grain from the Nile Delta and North Africa, exotic commodities from the Far East, and passengers in every direction. Out of this trade the great ports of Barcelona, Marseilles, Ostia, Bari, Corinth, Naples, Thessalonica, Tyre, Alexandria and Carthage had been born and prospered, uniting in a single civilization southern Europe, western Asia, and North Africa.

In the fifty years that followed the close of the seventh century, however, all this abruptly changed. The whirlwind Muslim conquest of Syria, Palestine, Egypt, North Africa and the Iberian Peninsula gave Islam total control of the east, west and south coasts of the great sea, leaving only its north shores in Christian hands, and transforming the Mediterranean's three-thousand-mile length of virtually tideless salt water into a war zone, almost bereft of mercantile traffic.

For the next three hundred and fifty years, from the mid-700s to the late 1000s, Muslim forces strove to conquer that remaining north coast, and along with it what little was left of the Christian religion. How perilously close they came to success few Christians, then or now, would ever realize. For most of those years, Christian ports along that north coast were under repeated Muslim attack. Three times, Muslim armies would assail Rome itself. One Rome-bound assault force would be beaten back at sea by an elderly and ailing warrior-pope with no naval experience, who personally assembled a grab-bag fleet, captained it to victory, and saved the city.

By the year 1100, the Muslims would be stopped, and all their conquests along the north coast east of Spain recovered. But the chief factor in their defeat would be a new player in the Mediterranean theater, the people known as the Normans, descendants of the Vikings who had settled in northern France, abandoned their tribal past, and with skill and zeal adopted the feudal system. Devout Christians though they now claimed to be, and in many respects doubtless were, they would move into Italy as brigands and mercenaries in search of booty, land, and slaves. The Muslims would quickly learn to hate and fear this new enemy, but no more than the Mediterranean Christians, much of whose land the Normans would unceremoniously usurp for themselves. For the Muslims, however, this dismaying reversal in the eleventh century would come after three centuries of almost unremitting victory, when the Christian lands on the north coast had seemed theirs for the taking.

Go back those three hundred years to the middle of the 700s, and one views Islam on the verge of a grand and final triumph that appeared inevitable. Its only decision was what to attack first. Christian Sicily looked attractive, the ten-thousand-square-mile island whose bulk divided the eastern Mediterranean from the western, its south coast only two days' good sailing from the African shore, its northernmost point a mere two miles from the toe of the Italian Peninsula. But then, too, there was Christian Crete, lying south of Greece. Its land was mountainous, its coasts hazardous and its ports few, but it was closer than Sicily to the big Muslim base at Alexandria, and once taken, it would offer easy access to all the Christian islands of the Aegean. Churches could be quickly pillaged there, wealthy towns looted, babies and the aged slaughtered, and the able-bodied brought back to slave markets in Alexandria and Damascus, the comely women trans-shipped east to well-paying Turks and Mongols.

Finally, there was the great sea's western basin. From Barcelona, the big port on the Spanish coast now in Muslim hands, corsairs could hit the whole southern littoral of Christian Provence, perhaps even take the port of Marseilles. Then the Christian islands of Corsica and Sardinia would be easy prey. Furthermore, a relatively small land force could hold the passes of the Alps, cutting off Italy from the Frankish and German Christians to the North, when the great day came for the knockout blow on Christian Rome.

Yet there were problems. By 750, Islam was already ceasing to be a single political entity as the Muslim Empire fragmented. Spain, which the Muslims called al-Andalus or Andalusia, had always shown tendencies to independence, and in 765 declared a separate caliphate. The Berbers of North Africa, now based at Tunis, soon did the same. Even Muslim Egypt was beginning to make its own plans. And it was in 750 that the Umayyad caliphs at Damascus were overthrown. Their mortal enemies, the triumphant Abbasids, lost no time transplanting the Arab capital to Baghdad, moving themselves and their priorities away from the Mediterranean.

From the viewpoint of Mediterranean Muslims, that was unfortunate. Conquering Christendom in the West meant first gaining undisputed control of the Mediterranean. It was superbly navigable. Other than in the winter, it was one of the world's most benevolent bodies of water. Its tides, measured in fractions of an inch, produced none of the terrifying coastal currents created by the big ocean tides.[1] The Mediterranean skies are so sunny that more water evaporates out of it than flows into it from its three major rivers—the Nile, the Po and the Rhone. The loss is replenished, however, from the Black Sea whose four "Big D" rivers—the Don, the Dniester, the Dnieper and the Danube—cause an outflow into the Aegean and Mediterranean. At its western extremity, the Mediterranean swaps water with the Atlantic through the Strait of Gibraltar, its own heavier, more saline flow running outbound along the bottom, while the waters of the Atlantic run inbound along the surface at up to nine miles an hour. This phenomenon, incidentally, made it notoriously difficult for medieval vessels to transit the strait outbound.[2]

The Mediterranean's winter gales come out of the northeast, turning its waters into a churning cauldron that can send even heavy modern vessels running for port. Its four terrible winds have names. The *mistral* sweeps over the Gulf of Genoa. The *bora* rips across the Adriatic, then crosses the Italian peninsula to become the *tramontana* over Sicily and Malta. The subsidiary sea, the Aegean, suffers the terrors of the *vardarac*. The winds move into the northwest in spring and become gentle breezes, making for an easy passage from north to south or west to east. Northbound or westbound traffic must fight head winds, the westbound working along the north coast between the islands to take advantage

1. Medieval sailors recognized at least one notable exception to the Mediterranean's tidal tranquility, in the two-mile-wide Strait of Messina between Italy and Sicily. According to the twelfth-century Muslim traveler Ibn Jubayr, "the sea in this strait pours through like the bursting of a dam." Homer's legendary king Odysseus had to pass through a narrow channel guarded by two monsters: on one side Charybdis, which sucked ships into a great whirlpool; on the other side Scylla, a vicious reef. Tradition places these in the Messina Strait. Today the whirlpool is a gentle circular current, and no reef exists opposite it. Sea conditions may have changed—or maybe there never was such a place.

2. In the magnificent German movie, *Das Boot* ("The Boat"), a U-boat passes the Gibraltar Strait undetected by simply cutting its engines and drifting silently along the bottom on the outbound current.

A mosque perched on the Gibraltar shore is evidence of one of the many peoples who have staked a claim to the "Rock." The name Gibraltar derives from the Arabic Gebel Tariq, *or Tariq's Mountain.* Tariq ibn Zihad captured the Iberian Peninsula for Islam in 711.

For centuries an important commercial link in the Mediterranean world, Byzantine Rhodes was repeatedly attacked by Muslim raiders. The fifteenth century Fortress of St. Nicholas was crucial to Rhodes' defense, protecting the entrance to Mandraki harbor near the site of the ancient Colossus.

of the onshore and offshore breezes of morning and evening. As long as the Christians held the north shore ports, this gave them a powerful advantage.

The warship of the age was the *dromon*—small and fast, with two banks of oars, a square sail on a main mast, and a small mast forward that carried a triangular "lateen" sail. Earlier models included a bow ram, below the waterline, to charge and sink enemy vessels. This was later replaced by a high, beak-like structure used as a bridge, so that boarding parties could capture rather than sink the enemy. Constantinople-based dromons carried siphons at the bow to project Greek fire, an early medieval variant of napalm, so decisive in turning back the Muslim assault on Constantinople in 717. (See earlier volume, *The Sword of Islam*, chapter 10.) Little is known of Muslim ships during the period, except that they were probably patterned on the Byzantine dromon. As the years passed, ships grew larger; one twelfth-century Egyptian vessel is recorded as carrying one hundred and forty oarsmen plus marines, sailors and officers.

Being in part oar-powered, the dromon had certain advantages over sailing vessels. It could cruise at nearly four miles an hour on a dead-calm sea. In battle, it could achieve seven to ten miles per hour for short bursts (i.e., up to twenty minutes), until the oarsmen were exhausted. But it had two major disadvantages. Each oarsman required a half-gallon of fresh water per day, so that a vessel must carry about one hundred eighteen-gallon barrels of water for a twenty-day cruise. That left little room for anything else.

More critical still, oars must be mounted close to the water to gain the maximum sweep, which gave oared ships a short freeboard (the distance from gunwale to waterline). This meant they could not take heavy seas, and must remain close to land. If they ventured out too far, the consequences could be quick and devastating. An oared dromon could be swamped by a single wave, with the loss of all aboard, and fleets of several hundred vessels could go down in one storm.

As the big Muslim offensive opened at the close of the eighth century, such a catastrophe happened to the mighty fleet sent in September 808 by the warrior sultan Harun against the Mediterranean island of Rhodes. The Muslims failed to take Rhodes, and the fleet commander later tried to pillage the tomb of St. Nicholas at the port of Myra, and robbed the wrong grave. Then, as his fleet headed home in October, a storm arose and sank most of it. Muslim or no, the awestruck commander fell on his knees and begged St. Nicholas to forgive him. He personally survived the disaster.

For the rest of the ninth century and well into the tenth, however, the Muslims suffered few defeats. Their strategy had not varied from the days of Muhammad. First came *razzias*, or raids, followed by temporary occupation, and finally conquest. Malta fell in 800, followed in 809 and 810 by Corsica and Sardinia. In

After he had botched an attempt to rob the tomb of St. Nicholas and a storm had sunk most of his ships, the Muslim leader fell to his knees and begged the saint to forgive him.

813, the Muslims raided Nice on the French coast. On the west coast of Italy, they hit Civitavecchia so hard that this supply port for nearby Rome was abandoned and left a ghost town. (It has lately revived as a port of call for cruise ships visiting Rome.) True to form, they kept up the momentum, invading Crete in 826, Sicily in 827, Italy in 836, and the south coast of France in 838.

The invasion of Crete came about curiously. In a crackdown on religious non-conformity, the Umayyad governor of Spain deported ten thousand Muslim dissidents. The deportees sought refuge in Egypt, where they found another rebellion brewing. So they left their families in Egypt and joined a successful raid against Crete, whose inhabitants they enslaved. But as they prepared to return to Egypt, they found that their own leader had burned their boats. They would get no welcome back in Egypt, he contended; they had better stay in Crete. But what about their families? That was simple, their leader countered—marry the women they'd just enslaved and start new ones!

For the next century and a half, the Muslims based on Crete wreaked havoc on the Christian islands of the Aegean, reducing some to wilderness. Twenty-nine Aegean towns were taken and the inhabitants enslaved. Even the burgeoning monasteries of Mount Athos had to be evacuated. Three times, Byzantine armies tried to recapture Crete. Two were destroyed trying to land. One actually got ashore and defeated the Muslim defenders—then postponed mop-up operations

In their campaign to conquer the north coast of the Mediterranean, the Muslims first attacked Sicily in 827. It took years to drive out the Byzantines; this illustration from the Scylitzes Chronicle shows the siege of Messina in 843.

until the next day, made camp and got drunk. There was no next day for them. Surviving Muslims slaughtered them in a night attack, and then pursued their escaping commander to the isle of Cos, where he was captured and crucified.

The Muslim invasion of Sicily began with one of history's veritable soap operas. Euphemios, the Byzantine naval commander, either seduced or coerced a nun into marrying him. Her two brothers protested to the emperor, who ordered the admiral's arrest. If found guilty, he would lose his nose. Euphemios took action. He and his sailors defeated and executed the Byzantine governor. Then Euphemios, declaring himself emperor, sought the support of the North African Muslims against the inevitable imperial reprisal. Amiably agreeing, they arrived with ten thousand foot soldiers and seven hundred cavalry, carried in some seventy ships, and informed Euphemios that Sicily would now be Muslim. In the ensuing struggle, Euphemios was stabbed to death by his wife's brothers.

Over the next two generations the Muslims took one Sicilian town after another. Palermo fell in 831, Messina in 843. Syracuse held on heroically until 878, when the Muslims finally claimed it. Sicily, stepping-stone to Italy, had indeed become a Muslim state. During the Sicilian campaign, however, there had been one prescient event, when a small fleet sailed down the Adriatic to help the defenders. It was easily beaten off, but in hindsight, a new Christian power had arrived on the scene. The ships had come from Venice, whose fleets in the future would not be so easily repelled.

Strife among Christians also allowed the Muslims to gain control of the south coast of France, and Liutprand of Cremona, a tenth-century historian and bishop, leaves a record of how this calamity began. About twenty Spanish Muslims, he writes, were forced ashore one night by a storm. They found themselves near the little town of Fraxinetum (now Garde Freinet in Provence). Breaking into a small manor house, they murdered the inhabitants, then discovered an oddity about the place. A particularly dangerous species of cactus grew thick all around it, a plant whose thorns were like small swords that could fatally impale a man. They also found a hidden trail through the cactus, leading up a hill that overlooked the town. What a superb site for a fort, they thought, but how could twenty men keep control of it once the people of the area discovered their presence?

They need not have worried, Liutprand continues. When the neighboring Christians found them, they recruited the Muslims' help in fighting another Christian group. Soon the Muslims made themselves indispensable and Liutprand laments the outcome. The Muslims, he says, "who in themselves were of insignificant strength, after crushing one faction with the help of another, increased their own numbers by continual reinforcements from Spain, and soon were attacking everywhere those whom at first they seemed to defend. In the fury of their onslaughts, they exterminated the whole people and left no survivors, so that all the district began to tremble." The fort at Fraxinetum became an unassailable Muslim base that terrorized southern France for the next two hundred years.

The invaders suffered a brief setback when Charlemagne broke through into Spain and took Barcelona in 797, but without a fleet, he could not use it as a base. Throughout the 800s, nearly all initiative remained with the Muslims.

The town of Gortyna on the island of Crete, so ancient that it was mentioned by Homer, was destroyed in the Muslim invasion of 825, and now lies completely in ruins. This church was dedicated to St. Titus, correspondent of St. Paul and the first bishop of the island.

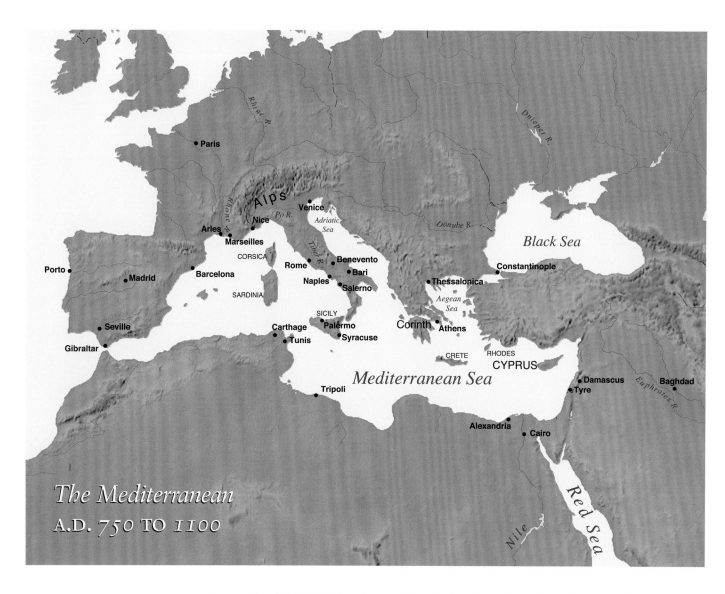

The Mediterranean
A.D. 750 TO 1100

Marseilles fell in 838, but it was already desolate since all trade across the Mediterranean had been stopped.[3] Striking inland, the Muslims hit Arles in 842, and worked their way up the populous Rhone Valley. In 852 they took back Barcelona. Meanwhile, they set up camps in the Alpine passes and looted the traffic between Italy and Germany.

"Muslim corsairs succeeded in establishing what amounted to a Muslim province in southern France," writes historian John H. Pryor (*Geography, Technology, and War: Studies in the Maritime History of the Mediterranean*). Henri Pirenne (*Mohammed and Charlemagne*) is even more doleful. "From the Gulf of Lyons and the Riviera to the mouth of the Tiber," he writes, "the coast was ravaged by war and pirates whom the Christians, having no fleet, were powerless to resist. The ports and the cities were deserted. The link with the Orient was severed, and there was no communication with the Saracen (Muslim) coasts. There was nothing but death."

The Muslims meanwhile crossed from Sicily and invaded southern Italy. Again taking advantage of Christian feuds, a small force hired itself out to the governor of Bari to fight the Lombards. Instead, the Muslim mercenaries stole through the night, murdered the governor, called in reinforcements, defeated the

3. The disappearance of trans-Mediterranean trade in the eighth century finally ended the use of papyrus, the ancient forerunner of paper, in nearly all government and scholarly documents, says the historian Henri Pirenne (*Mohammed and Charlemagne*). Papyrus was made from the plant of that name native to the Nile Delta. However, the use of papyrus had been declining in northern Europe in favor of parchment or vellum, made from the untanned skin of sheep, calves and goats, and better suited to books with separate leaves. Papyrus documents were usually rolled.

Lombards, and captured the city that commands the approaches to the Adriatic. The Muslim commander proclaimed himself "sultan of Bari," and they advanced up the Adriatic coast to imperil Venice.

As he and his compatriots discovered, Italy was another easy target, because the Christians were chronically at war with one another. Three powers jostled for supremacy. The Frankish–German Empire, now run by descendants of Charlemagne, held sway in the North. The papal state, known as the Republic of St. Peter, controlled the center within the Frankish Empire, along with the Lombards whose king was Frankish. The Byzantine Empire uncertainly clung to the South. Naples and the two nearby ports of Amalfi and Gaeta, though nominally Byzantine, were in effect independent. Like the other Italian factions, Naples was so wholly absorbed in the threat posed by its immediate neighbors that it failed to recognize the Muslim enemy advancing upon it from his new bases in Sicily and at Bari. In 836, Naples actually called in the Muslims as allies against the Lombards. The Muslims obliged, beat back the Lombards, then helped themselves to Taranto, the big port on Italy's south coast.

Not all Christians were quite so myopic, however. As so frequently happens in the Christian story, one man read the situation correctly. Louis II, Frankish king and grandson of Charlemagne, dedicated his life to ousting the Muslims, and a chaotic life it was, fraught with danger not only from the Muslims but from his fellow Christians—from his father's two brothers, who constantly sought to disinherit him; from the Lombard nobility, who persistently challenged his authority; from bishops, who resented his insistence on sustaining his grandfather's control of the church; from the Byzantine Empire,

Charlemagne, pensively surveying the Mediterranean from his fortress at Narbonne, realizes that without an effective navy, the Christian lands of the sea's northern shore must be overrun by Vikings and Muslim raiders from Spain and North Africa.

which he distrusted and despised; and from factions within his own court. In two respects, however, he was greatly blessed. He was a deeply committed Christian, and this commitment was to stop the Muslims. Second, he had Engelberga, his devoted, highly competent and very beautiful wife, who ran his kingdom from their capital at Pavia when he was at war. And at war Louis remained for nearly all of his thirty-three-year reign.

His first serious collision with the Muslims proved a failure. It came in the fateful year 846, when an invading force landed at the mouth of the Tiber, captured the two harbor towns of Porto and Ostia, then rapidly advanced up the

Louis died, embittered by the greed and hate surrounding him, and his empire came within an ace of falling apart. Then, in John VIII, the right man appeared at the right time.

4. Churches could be "profaned" (desecrated) in many ways. In one dubious account, cited by the classic historian Edward Gibbon, a Muslim raider is accused of having "profaned" a convent at Salerno in 873 by spreading his bedding on the chapel altar and each night deflowering there a Christian nun. One nun put up such a fight, however, that a roof beam was dislodged, fell on the man and killed him.

5. The Christian recovery of Bari presents a historical puzzle. To secure Byzantine help, Louis II promised his daughter in marriage to the Byzantine emperor, Basil I. When Louis canceled the marriage, however, the Byzantine fleet sailed away. Louis then lifted the siege of Bari, leaving behind a token force. As he marched away, the Muslim defenders left the walls and attacked his rearguard—whereupon Louis returned and took the city. The unanswered question is: why did he cancel the wedding? Some historians blame the schism between Rome and Constantinople, then at one of its crisis points. Others see it as a ruse to draw the defenders from the walls.

left bank, assembled before the walls of Rome and laid siege to the city. The churches of Saints Peter and Paul, which lay outside the walls, were ransacked and "profaned."[4] Called in to save the city, Louis's force was not adequate to dislodge the invaders. But a subsequent attack by the margrave of Spoleto beat them off. When the retreating Muslim fleet was lost in a storm, Christians credited its destruction to the hand of God. The chronicle known as *The Annals of St. Bertin* records some of the aftermath: "The sea tossed up some of the corpses on the shore, still clutching treasures to their breasts. When these were found, they were taken back to the tomb of the apostle Peter."

But Louis stopped the Muslim offensive in central Italy the following year with a decisive victory near Benevento. He crushed their army in southern Italy in 852, then began the task of recovering Bari. This took more than fifteen years, and required of him a humiliating compromise. He had to summon the help of the Byzantine fleet, which defeated the Muslims at sea, so that reinforcements from Egypt and Sicily were cut off, and Louis personally led his triumphant troops into the city. Although this victory was achieved through the unusual spectacle of the Byzantine East and Frankish West working together, it did not bring about an East–West accord. It had the reverse effect, the Byzantines loudly claiming credit for the city's fall, Louis issuing a jeering response that the Byzantines had been too late with too little and that his troops had in fact done the job.[5] Even so, writes Pirenne, the recovery of Bari probably saved Venice, doomed Muslim efforts in the Adriatic, and made their eventual expulsion from Italy a virtual certainty.

Fortune turned against Louis the following year, however, when he was captured while putting down a rebellion in Benevento. His two envious uncles (brothers of his father, who had inherited the other segments of Charlemagne's empire) assumed him dead, and moved in to seize his Italian possessions. His wife successfully fought them off. Louis died three years later in 874, at the age of fifty, embattled to the end, with the Muslims before him and the conniving Christian nobility behind. "He was sick of a world which no longer seemed to contain anything save hate, sordid greed and treachery," writes the historian Henri Daniel-Rops (*The Church in the Dark Ages*). With his death, the Byzantines occupied Bari.

"The forces of disintegration which had been attacking the empire ever since Charlemagne's death," Daniel-Rops comments, "were very near to triumph." But they did not triumph. Once again, the right man turned up in the right place at the right time. Three years before Louis died, the papacy fell to the aged and ailing John VIII. Once again the Muslims were assembling for an attack on Rome, and a massive Muslim assault force was expected any day off the Italian coast. The pressing Christian need was for a top-notch admiral to meet them at sea, a skilled general to halt them if they landed, and a shrewd diplomat to pull the feuding Christians together. Pope John was no sailor, no soldier, had never been a diplomat, and was a frail seventy-year-old.

The details of what followed are sketchy at best, but the outcome is not. Unable to secure a concerted Christian effort, the old pope hurled himself into the military role. He built a wall around the churches of Peter and Paul, some remnants of which survive to this day, organized construction of a fleet of small, fast dromons, recruited crews, and personally took command. "The pope himself assumed the duties both of a general and an admiral," writes the *Catholic Encyclopedia*. "To guard the 'city of the old dotard Peter,' as the Muslims contemptuously called Rome, John himself patrolled the coast. He overtook the pirate fleet off the promontory of Circe, and was completely victorious over them." A contemporary account says, "The insolent invaders were drowned in a bath of blood."

The enemy had been beaten off, but no one knew better than Pope John that he would certainly be back. Unless Christians could somehow be unified, and another Louis II found to give the Muslim threat top priority, then sooner or later Rome would fall, and Western Christianity along with it. But where was such a leader to be found? Pope John desperately searched for the right man.

The imperial crown was first conferred on Louis's uncle, known as Charles the Bald, who talked confidently, but did nothing except stir up further feuding among the Christian monarchs. When Charles died, the crown was passed to Louis's cousin, a feeble-minded epileptic known to history as Charles the Fat. When he likewise proved useless, and Naples again allied itself with the Muslims

Although now ruined and overtaken by vegetation, the San Giovanni degli Eremiti, a landmark in Palermo, Sicily, is a beautiful example of twelfth-century Muslim-Norman architecture. The five red cupolas are definitively Muslim, a style of architecture much admired by King Roger II, the Norman builder of the church. The bell tower and cloister are typically Norman.

The fighting ships of a war-torn sea

The dromon was versatile, fast in battle, yet easily swamped in heavy weather, but nothing equaled the lithe-hulled Viking vessels at withstanding crashing waves

When Rome controlled the Mediterranean at the dawn of the Christian era, the great inland sea was a vast commercial highway, where ships hauling grain cargoes from African ports to the opposite coast grew ever larger. After the Muslim conquest of Syria, Palestine, Egypt, North Africa and Spain, however, the Mediterranean became a war zone for the next four centuries. Designed for fighting, not for commerce, ships grew smaller and faster and more maneuverable.

Chief among them was the dromon, portrayed in the sketch below and in the three at the top of the page opposite. Usually powered by both oars and sails, the dromon could make a steady four knots (roughly 4.5 miles per hour) under oars, in the frequent dead calms of summer. In battle it could make six to nine knots—for up to twenty minutes, before the oarsmen dropped exhausted. These were significant advantages. Its disadvantage lay in its short freeboard (i.e., the distance from gunwale to the waterline), which meant that it could easily be swamped in storms, and must therefore stay close to shore.

Below is the double-mast Byzantine dromon used in the centuries-long conflict. The single-mast vessel (top right, opposite) is a Muslim craft, unusual in depending on sail alone. The bas-relief (top left, opposite) from the Leaning Tower at Pisa, Italy, dated between 1000 and 1150, is believed to be a Christian representation of two dromons delivering souls to the port of heaven. Beneath it is a bas-relief from the historic fortress town of Aigues-Mortes in France, fifty miles west of Marseilles. Note the bow deck for boarding enemy vessels.

Other occasional visitors to the Mediterranean included the lithe vessels of the Vikings (see chapter 4), although their true sphere of operation was the open Atlantic, where their relatively high freeboard enabled them to withstand ocean storms, and their flexible hulls could bend before the crashing of the waves. ■

TOM LOVELL
NATIONAL GEOGRAPHIC

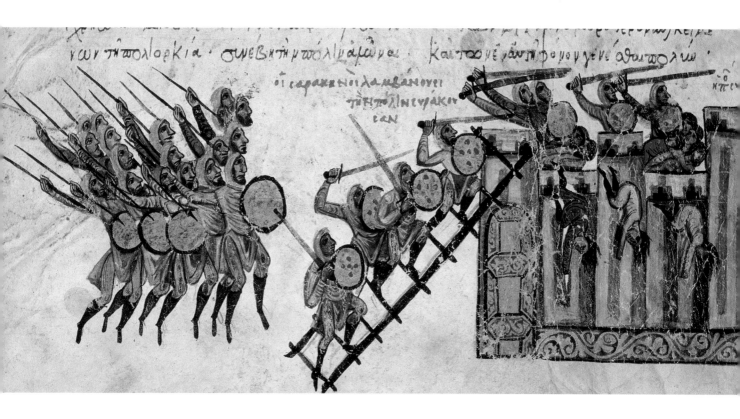

οι σαρακηνοι λαμβανουσι την πολιν ευρακον σαν

Briefly the capital of the Byzantine Empire in the seventh century, Syracuse changed hands many times. It fell to the Arabs in 878, then to the Normans two hundred years later. Byzantines defending the city are illustrated here, from the Scylitzes Chronicle.

to ward off the Lombards, Pope John tried one last expedient. He issued an appeal on behalf of an entity that had never before been invoked. He called it "Christendom," and by it, he meant all the states that called on Jesus Christ as savior. This, of course, included Byzantium, now marking its "golden era" under the direction of the brilliant Macedonian emperors.

The Macedonians heard the call, and the tide gradually began to turn, but it was too late for the ailing John VIII. In his machinations to save his church, he had made many enemies. In December 882, those enemies prevailed, first poisoning him, and when he failed to succumb, beating him to death with a hammer. History accords him a mixed assessment. "He was totally absorbed in aims of temporal dominion," writes the nineteenth-century historian Ferdinand Gregorovius. He was "ambiguous, intriguing, sophistic, unscrupulous." And yet, "he put kings to shame and covered his memory with military renown.... His name shines with royal splendor in the temporal history of the papacy."

The Muslims continued their raids against the north coast while the area around the toe of Italy became a wilderness. In 890, they set up a base at Saracinesco near Rome, and another in the Sabine Hills, though no serious attack against the city itself was mounted. The tenth century began as woefully as the ninth, with raids and devastation on all Christian coastal territories. Then in 931 came what Pirenne calls "an extraordinary incident." A Muslim squadron was defeated off the French coast. The oddity lay in the fact that its nemesis was a Byzantine fleet, a long way from home, and it proved an omen for the next three decades. In 961, the emperor Nicephorus Phocas recovered Crete and attacks on the Aegean islands ceased. Four years later, the Byzantines recaptured Cyprus, and that same year they sank an entire Egyptian fleet off Tarsus.

Then at Salerno, thirty-five miles southeast of Naples on Italy's west coast, there was another unusual occurrence. A party of forty foreign pilgrims[6] was spending the night there, when Muslim raiders struck. The visitors, appalled and humiliated at the feeble resistance offered by the locals, borrowed weapons and horses from the prince of Salerno, caught up with the raiders, slaughtered some of them, and sent the rest fleeing for their lives. That was in 999, the last year of the first Christian millennium. The visitors were Normans. The decisive player had finally entered the game.

"The career of the Normans in South Italy and Sicily," writes the historian John Julius Norwich in *A History of Venice*, "is one of the great epics of European history." It is less an epic of the Normans, however, than of a single Norman family.[7] The family's patriarch, Tancred of Hauteville, was a minor noble in the service of the Duke of Normandy. Little else is known of him—not

Norman visitors, humiliated by the feeble local resistance to Muslim raiders, pursued and drove off the invaders. The key player had finally arrived on the scene.

even which of Normandy's three Hautevilles was his original home. One fact is certain, however. He had twelve sons—five by his first wife Muriel and seven by his second, Fressenda—and at least three daughters.

Big families like this had little to leave their many children, so these Norman sons customarily sought their fortunes elsewhere, chiefly in Italy. But this Norman movement was not, like the Norman invasion of England some sixty years later, an official state endeavor. They came to Italy in small groups. It was "free enterprise," writes one history, and the enterprise began with pillage, rape, murder and destruction. "The contempt for them of the [Italian] princes was mixed with fear," writes Edward Gibbon in his *Decline and Fall of the Roman Empire*, "and the fear of the natives was mingled with hatred and resentment." The twelfth-century historian, Amatus of Montecassino, portrays them as "riding cheerfully through the meadows and gardens—happy and joyful, cavorting hither and thither," on their mission of death. All this notwithstanding, the sons of Tancred of Hauteville and their descendants personally created much of the history of southern Italy and Sicily for the next one hundred and sixty-five years.

In Italy's ceaseless internecine feuds, demand for fighters was always brisk, and the Hautevilles, all twelve reared to be knights, were superb fighters. They hired themselves out to all parties, but always made sure that no feudal potentate became so powerful over the others that he didn't need them any more. So indispensable did the Normans make themselves to the Duke of Naples that he assigned to some of the Hautevilles, and other Norman leaders, the fortress and district of Aversa, just outside the city.

From this base, they joined one of the recurring Byzantine attempts to regain Sicily. William Hauteville, oldest of the twelve, took part in the attack along with

6. Throughout the 900s, pilgrimages became an increasingly common Christian devotion. The principal destinations were Rome, St. James of Compostela in northwest Spain, and Jerusalem—where Christian pilgrims were generally tolerated. At sea, however, pilgrims took their chances with Muslim raiders, whose sympathies were far from assured.

7. The story of how the Vikings who settled in northern France became the Normans is told in chapter 3.

his next two brothers. William struck down and killed the emir of Syracuse, earning the sobriquet "Iron Arm," but the Byzantine invasion failed, and the Byzantines likewise failed to pay off the Normans. In reprisal, the Hautevilles invaded Apulia, the Byzantine province along the heel of the Italian "boot," taking one town after another. Here they became so hated that the second brother, Drogo Hauteville, was assassinated, and Pope Leo IX organized a polyglot army from Italy and Germany to drive them out.

The pope failed. In June 1053, the Normans defeated the papal army at Civitate on the Fortore River, northwest of modern Foggia. They captured the pope, too, and then as devout Christians, knelt before him, kissed his feet and asked his forgiveness. Leo accepted their pleas before retiring to Benevento,

Normans captured Pope Leo, and then, being devout Christians, knelt before him, kissed his feet and begged forgiveness. The pope granted their plea, but died soon afterwards.

where, conscience-stricken over the men slain at Civitate, he died brokenhearted. Another horrendous problem, namely the collapsing relations with the Greek church, doubtless also weighed upon his tortured soul. (See chapter 6.) Seven years (and four more popes) after Leo's death, however, the formidable Hildebrand, who became pope as Gregory VII, saw the Normans as a solution, not a problem. They were proclaiming themselves champions of the papacy. They strongly backed Gregory's reform of the papal election process, which denied the German emperors a role, and is still in use to this day. In return, Gregory made them dukes of Apulia and Calabria, and any other territories they might be able to wrest from Byzantine control.

The leadership of the Hautevilles had by this time been taken over by Robert, eldest of the seven sons of Tancred's second wife, and known as Guiscard, "the Crafty." (The name was well earned. His followers gleefully relate how Robert posed as a corpse, and was borne for burial by his men into a wealthy monastery. Then the "deceased" suddenly arose from its coffin, terrorized the monks, and looted the place.) Men feared Robert's booming voice, but rejoiced to serve under him. How women reacted to him is disclosed by the snooty, but plainly captivated Byzantine princess Anna Comnena: "Though of insignificant origin, he is in temper tyrannical, in mind most cunning, brave in action … stature so lofty he surpasses even the tallest, complexion ruddy, hair flaxen, shoulders broad, eyes that emit sparks of fire, frame well-built where nature required breadth, from tip to toe well proportioned.… Powerful characters are ever like this, people say, even though they be of somewhat obscure descent."

Under Robert's direction, the Normans first cleared the Byzantines out of Apulia, and then out of their remaining province of Calabria. They retook Bari in 1071, ending altogether the Greek political presence in Italy. Five years later, the Lombard city of Salerno fell to them, complete with its renowned school of

medicine. Thus, the once fearsome Lombards, terror of Gregory the Great more than four centuries earlier, existed no longer in southern Italy. But the Normans' most lasting accomplishment in the Mediterranean remained to be achieved: the reconquest for Christianity of Sicily, something Byzantium had been futilely attempting for years.

In this endeavor, the man many consider the greatest of the Hauteville brothers plays the

The Palatine Chapel in the city of Palermo (chapel to the Norman kings' palace) is stunning in its decoration, incorporating elements of the Romanesque, Muslim and Byzantine cultures resident in Sicily in the twelfth century. The dome (above) has the traditional Pantocrator icon, with iconographic mosaics covering the walls and ceiling (below).

major role. Roger was the twelfth son of Tancred Hauteville, and the last to arrive in Italy. His biographer, the Norman monk Geoffrey of Malaterra, paints a striking portrait of him: "tall, well proportioned, eloquent, clever, prudent in counsel, intrepid in arms, agreeable and courteous in all things"—in short, much as Anna Comnena had depicted his older brother. All this wasn't enough, however, to win him the beautiful Judith of Evreux back in Normandy. How could a kinswoman of the future William the Conqueror marry a man of such inferior rank?

Roger II, Norman king of Sicily, is crowned in this twelfth-century Byzantine mosaic (right) from Palermo, Italy. A detail (left) from King Roger's coronation mantle with the tree of life and a lion killing a camel (emblematic of the Norman struggle against Islam). The mantle is now housed in the Kunsthistorisches Museum, Vienna.

So the spurned Roger left Normandy, joined Robert in the Calabrian campaign, and soon made himself Robert's indispensable second in command. In 1060, the brothers tackled Sicily, when one Muslim emir provided an opportunity by seeking their aid against another. Roger launched an advance attack by night, and landed on the coast five miles south of Messina. Next day, he caught the defenders unaware, and took the city before brother Robert had even embarked with the main body of his troops and their Muslim allies. Two more Sicilian towns surrendered without resistance, but by then, Roger had departed for the mainland. There had been an opportune turn of events back in Normandy.

Duke William, it seems, had seriously quarreled with his half brother, the abbot of St. Evreux, a monastery renowned for the magnificence of its music. The abbot and his monks fled for Italy, taking with him three children for whom the abbot was godfather. One of them was Judith, about seventeen years old. Duke Robert made them all welcome in Italy. The abbot established a new monastery there, and in one of its first services he married Judith of Evreux to Roger Hauteville. The wedding music, people said, was magnificent.

Roger by now was a powerful Norman magnate. Or was he? He had conquered towns and castles in his brother's cause—but Robert "Guiscard" had made him lord of none of them. Up to then, Roger had not much cared. Now he did, if only because he needed an adequate title for his wellborn wife. A terrible row ensued,[8] resolved by an agreement that each brother would get half of the estates. In the end,

8. The quarrel between Roger and Robert Hauteville has elements of both tragedy and comedy. The parsimonious Robert, exasperated with his brother's whining for compensation, imprisoned him. Roger escaped to the town of Gerace, whose people closed their gates against the pursuing Robert. Robert gained entry in disguise, was sheltered by two friends, but was discovered. Both friends were killed and Robert made prisoner. Suddenly, Roger burst on the scene, demanding to confront his brother. But when Robert was produced, the brothers burst into tears, embraced each other, and all was forgiven. Henceforth, they vowed, everything would be split fifty-fifty. However, they continued to wrangle over details for the rest of their lives.

Roger became Grand Duke of Sicily, Robert Duke of southern Italy. Roger's son, as King Roger II of Sicily, would in due course unite the two domains.

But at the time of the marriage, the conquest of Sicily had barely begun, and in 1062, Judith found herself right in the middle of it. The Normans had taken the town of Troina, sixty miles southwest of Messina, and twenty west of famous Mount Etna.[9] Leaving Judith with the garrison there, Roger moved on to the next Norman target. The Muslims, seeing his wife as the ideal hostage to recover the whole island, attacked the town in force, assisted by Greek Christians, who by now hated the Normans as much as the Muslims did.

Roger raced back to Troina, made his way past the Muslim positions, then closeted the garrison in a local fort that stood atop a four-thousand foot mountain, and got set for a siege. Short of food, fuel and manpower, his men were hopelessly unprepared for winter, which came early. Roger and Judith took turns wearing their one woolen cloak by day; both slept under it by night. Then fortune favored the Normans. Aware that their quarry would soon have to surrender, the besiegers grew overconfident, and one night most of them got drunk on the local wine. Silently over the snows stole Roger and his men, slaughtered the enemy, and finished the wine.

The following year the Muslims, genuinely alarmed, sent thousands of troops in from Africa, landed them on Sicily's east coast—probably at Syracuse—and prepared to wipe out the small, upstart Norman force. The showdown came at Cerami, fifteen miles northwest of Troina. There the Norman force of seven hundred knights (plus attendants and infantry) so startled the huge Muslim army of fifteen thousand, says contemporary historian Geoffrey Malaterra, that the Muslims panicked and fled. The Normans looted their camp, hunted down fugitives, killed hundreds of them and sold the rest into slavery. Thanking God for their victory, they sent a special gift to Hildebrand—four prize camels. Hildebrand's reaction is not recorded.

Palermo next fell in 1072, to a two-pronged Norman attack—Roger by land, Robert by sea.[10] Palermo was no mean prize, either. Over the years, Muslims had moved to it from all over the Mediterranean, giving it at one point three hundred mosques, beautiful parks, and gardens with fountains. Some called it the "paradise of the Mediterranean." Roger's rule proved as tolerant as that of the early Umayyads in Spain. Muslims were allowed freedom of worship, Greeks permitted to retain the Eastern form of Christianity.[11] It took the Normans another eighteen years to free the rest of the island from Muslim power, and the Normans held it until 1194. (Then, after a civil war, the Holy Roman Emperor became king of Sicily and Germans succeeded the Normans in southern Italy.)

The final offensive of the Normans in the Mediterranean proved as disastrous as their Sicilian enterprise had been successful. Their fleets crossed the Adriatic and began a costly and ultimately unsuccessful attempt to take over the Byzantine Empire. Some of the consequences were both lasting and devastating. The ecclesiastical schism between East and West was affirmed as a

9. Mount Etna, one of the world's most active volcanoes, has been erupting for about a half million years.

10. During one Norman assault on Palermo, Robert's army suddenly was attacked by tarantula spiders, whose bites caused great pain, swelling, and chronic flatulence. The experience so shook the Normans that they retreated. Curiously, the "true" tarantula spider, named for Taranto, Italy, does not bite, is not poisonous, and flees for cover if disturbed. However, the name came to apply to other spiders that are very poisonous indeed. Historians conclude that Robert's troops must have disturbed the habitat of some other, less friendly spider than the amiable Italian tarantula.

11. Some of the grandeur of the Norman court at Palermo can still be seen. The ceiling of the palace chapel is covered with Byzantine mosaics. The king's private chamber still displays gold mosaics of swans, peacocks and lions. In the Church of the Martorama, there are mosaic portraits of Roger II, and a Byzantine hymn to the Virgin, inscribed in Arabic around the base of the dome, evidences the plurality of religious observance there in the era of the Norman kings.

military and political schism as well, with the Greek church as unsuccessful in Italy and Sicily as the Latin church was to prove in Greece and most of the Balkans. Further, the Normans held their lands on papal authority, giving the See of Peter a powerful legal hold on the churches and government of southern Italy.

Beyond all this, however, a new method had been approved for Christian outreach. It could now be military. The Normans fought in Italy (as in the

Cefalu is a picturesque city on the island of Sicily, boasting centuries of architectural achievement. The twin towers of the twelfth-century Norman Cathedral are visible from the sea (left, bottom). A style known as Sicilian Romanesque, the cathedral (left, top) was built under the patronage of King Roger II in 1131. The interior is famous for its mosaics, including the Pantocrator in the dome (above, right).

invasion of England) under a papal banner with automatic indulgence promised to all who fell in battle. "Be not afraid," cried Robert Guiscard to his little army before the Battle of Cerami. "We have Jesus Christ with us who says, 'If you have faith as a grain of mustard seed you shall tell the mountains to move and they shall move (Matt. 17:20), and nothing shall be impossible to you.'" Upon this they charged, and an astonishing victory followed. It was a powerful message. In the two centuries immediately ahead, it would be heard often. ∎

Muslim Spain: model of tolerance

For one hundred years Christians fared well—until one criticized Muhammad,
setting off the 'era of the martyrs,' a purge some blame on the Christians themselves

I
t was midwinter in the year 750, and two frightened brothers, aged about twenty and thirteen, were hiding on the eastern bank of the Euphrates. Of all the Umayyad dynasty that had ruled the Arab Empire for nearly a century, only they remained alive. The victorious Abbasid faction had slaughtered the rest of their kin, and now the straining ears of the fugitives caught the muffled tread of approaching soldiers. Desperately they plunged into the wide river, but the younger lad rapidly weakened in the current. Glancing over his shoulder, the older youth saw his brother turn back—then saw the Abbasid warriors seize him on the bank and lop off his head.

The survivor, Abd al-Rahman ibn Mu'awiya, reached the far bank, says the contemporary chronicle *Akbar Majmu'a*. He fled across the Arabian desert towards North Africa, the homeland of his Berber mother. He found no welcome among Muslim leaders in Egypt, Libya or the Maghreb.[1] Across the Strait of Gibraltar, however, where the Iberian Peninsula had fallen to Arab and Berber invaders a generation earlier, Umayyad loyalties were still strong. Furthermore, the conquerors were vastly outnumbered by its eight million subjugated Visigoths and Romans.

They were also divided among themselves—Arabs against Berbers—a conflict that had begun in North Africa when Arab governors demanded tribute from Berber tribes, newly converted to Islam, and seized their lovelier daughters as concubines. The Berbers consequently embraced Islam's puritanical Kharijite strain, based on simple virtues and equality of all believers, and rose in rebellion both in Morocco and across the strait. In fact, Iberia's Arab masters had lately been saved only by the fortuitous arrival of seven thousand Umayyad troops, who like Abd al-Rahman had fled the Abbasid takeover.

So in 755, the Umayyad prince made his bid for control of al-Andalus, the Arabic name for the peninsula's broad southern expanse. (Al-Andalus would later evolve into "Andalusia.") He handily defeated the Abbasid governor outside his capital, Cordoba, because troops deserted in large numbers to join the new Umayyad champion. Even so, Abd al-Rahman is said to have narrowly escaped death at the hands of his own men, when he forbade them to ravage the palace and harem. But the last of the Umayyads survived this as well, and the grateful Cordobans acknowledged the tall young man as their emir.

When Abbasid sympathizers launched a counterattack, Abd al-Rahman successfully defeated them, too—and then sent an altogether instructive message back to Baghdad,

1. The Maghreb is the region of northwestern Africa that now includes Tunisia, Algeria and Morocco. The Arabic term means "Island of the West," a graphic description of the fertile strip between the sea of sand (the Sahara) and the Mediterranean. The federal research division of the U.S. Library of Congress notes that a literal translation of Maghreb would be "the time or place of the sunset" (similar to "Occident" in Latin and English), differentiating the westernmost conquests from the Mashriq, Islam's eastern homeland.

the new Abbasid capital. He had the Abbasid leaders in Spain decapitated, and their pickled heads wrapped in the black Abbasid flag and packed in a bag. "Praise be to God," the horrified Abbasid caliph reportedly cried, "for placing the sea between me and such a demon!" As for the tiny remnant of Christian Spain, driven by the original Muslim conquerors into the mountainous northwest, it posed no immediate threat.

Abd al-Rahman reigned thirty-two years, founding in al-Andalus an independent Umayyad caliphate that would dazzle the world with its material abundance, graceful architecture and impressive scholarship. It would also inadvertently aid in the defense of Christendom, since the Baghdad caliphs—although their empire still stretched from the Indian Ocean to the Atlantic—could no longer easily dispatch armies into western Europe through Spain. The Andalusian Umayyads themselves would make constant forays into the promising lands beyond the Pyrenees, but the Franks were able to block the limited forces of Iberian Islam.

Organized into twenty administrative provinces, al-Andalus enjoyed a revival of production and trade, which had languished under the Visigoths. Disused Roman mines were reactivated to produce gold, silver, copper, cinnabar (mercury sulfide), lead and iron. Roman irrigation systems were reclaimed and upgraded to allow the introduction of such semitropical crops as oranges, sugar cane, coconuts, dates, pomegranates and bananas. The Moorish waterwheel, its deep metal

scoops gleaming like pearl as they revolved, fascinated Andalusian poets. "She sobs and weeps her streams of sparkling water. She weeps and the garden smiles with many a petal … " wrote Mahbub the Grammarian in the eleventh century. Among the Umayyad sympathizers who thronged in from Syria were skilled craftsmen, artists and scholars. Around Cordoba's Great Mosque and royal palace, with its schools and government offices, an immense bazaar of thousands of shops sprouted in a warren of noisy, narrow streets. The citizenry learned about fashion, wearing brilliant silk robes in

One of the many schools that sprang up around Cordoba's Great Mosque. Craftsmen, artists and scholars from Syria, North Africa and even Europe flocked to the Umayyad capital of al-Andalus. A nineteenth-century engraving from The Illustrated History of the World, *published by Ward and Lock.*

spring, white in high summer and furred or quilted winter garments.

Neither Abd al-Rahman nor his immediate successors severely persecuted Christians and Jews. Assigned a second-class status, these "infidels" could discreetly practice their religions, so long as they paid the heavy taxes prescribed by the Qur'an for non-Muslims. They prospered along with the Muslims of al-Andalus, some achieved high office, and a hundred years later the Cordoba district would still have seven churches and four monasteries. But Christianity itself did not in fact thrive. To the contrary, the preferential taxes provided a strong incentive to embrace Islam, and many Visigoth landowners did so to keep their estates and titles. Before long, too, intermarriage blurred both religious and racial distinctions.

The Berber–Arab racial blend was known as Moro, after Mauritania in northwestern Africa (whose people are still called Moors). Over time, as most of the Andalusian population became Muslim in religion, such Christians as maintained their faith were called "Mozarabs," because even they were heavily influenced by Islam. In the mid-ninth century, the *Indiculus Luminosus* (cited by T. W. Arnold in *The Preaching of Islam*) complained: "Our Christian young men, with their elegant airs and fluent speech, are showy in their dress and carriage, and are famed for the learning of the Gentiles; intoxicated with Arab eloquence, they greedily handle,

eagerly devour and zealously discuss the books of the Chaldeans" (i.e., Muslims). Not one Mozarab in a hundred, the chronicler added, could write a simple letter in Latin, but "a countless rabble of all kinds of them" could compose Arabic poetry.

Even so, the Umayyad regime was never completely secure. Toledo, the former Visigoth capital, was especially suspected of revolutionary conspiracy, and in 797 the caliph al-Hakam took action against it. He summoned Toledo's leading men to a feast. Accompanied by his very young son, the future Abd al-Rahman II, al-Hakam led his guests into one of the city's deep defensive trenches. Once trapped there, say the early chronicles, seven hundred Toledans were butchered and buried on the spot. (The little prince, it was said, was consequently afflicted with a lifelong habit of nervous eye-blinking.) In 805, the relentless al-Hakam crucified seventy-two leading citizens of Cordoba for allegedly plotting against him. Later still, when harsh taxes sparked massive rebellion, he employed his Christian-led palace guard to crucify three hundred dissidents.

Tricked and trapped in a narrow trench, conspiracy suspects were killed outright.

Al-Hakam's son Abd al-Rahman II (832–852), while siring forty-five sons and forty-two daughters, found time and energy to consolidate his realm. When a Viking fleet attacked Lisbon and then Seville, his troops thoroughly thrashed the marauders, killing a thousand and enslaving four hundred. He also built a fleet to protect his coasts, and one Muslim historian reports that royal revenue rose more than fifty percent. During his reign, however, there occurred the "epoch of the martyrs." It began about 850, when a group of Muslims asked a priest named Perfectus to share his views on Christ and Muhammad. Perfectus, fully aware that "showing disrespect for the Prophet" was a capital offense, declined. But when the Muslims persisted, promising to protect him, he told them that Muhammad was one of the false prophets foretold by Jesus, and a man whose marital activity had rendered him a moral reprobate. His questioners, deeply offended, reported him after all, and Perfectus, holding to his statements, was beheaded.

Much more worrisome to Muslim authorities was the case of Isaac, an educated Mozarab aristocrat of high government rank, who became a monk. In June 851, Isaac declared before a senior Islamic judge that Muhammad was languishing in hell for misleading the Arabs. That official, after anxious consultation with the caliph, condemned Isaac to death; his headless corpse was soon dangling upside down in public view. Sanctius, a young soldier, committed the same willful defiance two days later, and suffered the same fate. He was followed within forty-eight hours by six men with monastic connections. One chronicler records their words as: "We profess Christ to be truly God, and your prophet to be a precursor of antichrist and an author of profane doctrine." When three more such individuals appeared a month later, Abd al-Rahman II ordered the arrest of all Christian priests in Cordoba, hoping to contain what must have seemed to him a suicidal contagion.

But more deaths

Le Mezquita (below), Cordoba's cathedral built around the former Great Mosque, towers above a sixteen-arch Roman bridge, rebuilt by the ancient city's Moorish conquerors. The arched interior of Le Mezquita (bottom) clearly shows its Islamic origins. Long a favored destination for Christian pilgrims, the cathedral now also attracts Muslims visiting their ancient holy sites of al-Andalus.

The Ark and rising flood, illustrated in the Beatus in Apocalypsin, *an eighth-century manuscript composed by the abbot of St. Martin de Leibana monastery, Spain. Christianity continued to coexist with Islam in al-Andalus—but uneasily, and sometimes violently.*

followed. One martyr was Flora, whose Muslim father had died when she was a child. She was subsequently raised a Christian, but under Islamic law was considered Muslim, and therefore apostate. This too was a capital offense. Reported to the authorities by her influential Muslim brother, Flora was severely whipped and then, when she refused to abjure Christ, was executed. Details of nine more female martyrs and many men were recorded up to 859, when the scholar and historian Eulogius was himself beheaded.

The epoch of martyrs was controversial both then and later. This self-destructive defiance was unnecessary, some Mozarab leaders contended, and indeed wrong, since Islam did not forbid anyone to believe that Jesus Christ was God. Sympathetic Muslims also begged Christians to desist. One friendly courtier told Eulogius, "If stupid and idiotic individuals have been carried away to such lamentable ruin, what is it that compels you, who are outstanding in wisdom and illustrious in manner of life, to commit yourself to this deadly ruin,

suppressing the natural love of life?" But the martyrs believed they were truly called to proclaim the divinity of Jesus Christ. "The order of preaching is enjoined upon us," Eulogius wrote, "and it befits our faith that we extend its light...."

The erudite nineteenth-century orientalist Reinhardt Dozy severely disapproves the Spanish martyrdoms. In his *Histoire des musulmans d'Espagne* he dismisses them as religious presumption and cultural resentment: "Feeling sanctified in their pride, exasperated at the outrages they received, and pushed by a feverish need to act, priests, monks, and a small number of like-minded laymen would not resign themselves to suffer in silence...." But later Christian commentators agree with Eulogius. A complacent Mozarab population, they reason, was drifting into massive apostasy, and needed just such beacons of self-sacrifice.

The glory of Islamic Cordoba arguably climaxed under Abd al-Rahman III (921–961), the first Spanish Umayyad to officially declare himself caliph in al-Andalus. This red-haired ruler spoke the local language and reputedly ruled with exemplary tolerance—and lavish style. The chronicles describe his court as involving some fourteen thousand people. They were housed in four hundred buildings, which incorporated some forty-three hundred marble columns. The fish in his ornamental ponds were said to require twelve hundred loaves of bread daily. Another pool, filled with constantly moving quicksilver, reflected sunlight with dazzling purity.

For the reception of one Frankish

embassy, Abd al-Rahman III had the very streets covered in costly carpets. Mail-clad warriors formed an archway with their upheld swords along the route. Entering the palace, the story goes, the Christians bowed to a silk-clothed dignitary on a brocade-draped throne, thinking him Abd al-Rahman. "Raise your heads," their guide advised. "This is but a slave of his slaves." They encountered several more equally august figures, only to hear the same message. Finally the Franks beheld a solitary man, simply dressed and seated on a bed of sand. Before him lay a small fire, a sword and a copy of the Qur'an. "Behold the ruler!" their guide announced.

Nevertheless, the Cordoban caliphate lasted only so long as it could keep its varied population in line. During the reign of the child-caliph Hisham II, a former royal tutor seized power. Best known as al-Mansur, "the Victorious," he did so by bringing masses of fanatically loyal Berber troops from North Africa, supported by extremist Islamic clerics, which destroyed the fragile balance of al-Andalus. After the death of the ironfisted al-Mansur, the realm fragmented into small principalities known as "taifas," whose leaders frequently blended cruel crudity with refined sensuality. For example, al-Mu'tatid, who ruled in Seville from 1042 to 1069, was capable of using his enemies' skulls as flowerpots—and also of composing fine verse. One day, it was said, while watching a breeze on the Guadalquivir River, al-Mu'tatid improvised aloud: *The wind scuffs the river and makes it chain mail....* A female serf, working nearby, replied

with a couplet of her own: *Chain mail for fighting, could water avail."* Al-Mu'tatid and the beautiful slave became lovers, and then loyal and lifelong mates.

The Christian Visigoth remnants in the northwest had meanwhile been merging with the native Basques and Cantabrian mountaineers of Asturias, people never subdued even by the Roman Empire. The result was a notably tough fighting breed. Since their first victory against the Muslim forces at Covadonga in 722, they had been expanding their domain with raid and counterraid, punctuated by larger-scale battles. The names of their new kingdoms—Castile, Leon, Navarre and Aragon—rang like battle cries across Western Christendom, awakening aspirations for "reconquest." Northward, too, trickled streams of Mozarabs not content to live within the polity of al-Andalus. These

The annual pageant of Christians and Moors in Alcoi, eastern Spain. The colorful celebration commemorates the Christian reconquest of the town in 1276, after centuries of warfare. Tradition holds that the Christian forces were eventually victorious thanks to the miraculous aid of St. George.

refugees planted self-reliant settlements over the broad, high tableland of central Spain, fighting alongside the emerging Spanish feudal aristocracy. Slowly but inexorably the Muslim frontier was driven south.

Deeply inspiring to this resurgent North was devotion to St. James the Apostle. Popular belief held that he had preached in Roman Iberia, and that after his death, his body was returned there. Its reputed resting place at Compostela in Galicia became western Europe's most popular pilgrimage destination, drawing tens of thousands. Furthermore, St. James (*San Diego* in Spanish) metamorphosed into a warrior. The chronicles maintain that his apparition participated in at least thirty-eight battles. Most notably, a blindingly bright figure, mounted on a pale horse and bearing a white banner, inspired the Christian forces at Simancas in 939, when King Ramiro II of Leon massively defeated the Cordoban army and Abd al-Rahman III himself barely escaped alive.[2]

Yet these northern kingdoms could not unite politically. Bound to the Visigoth custom of dividing a kingdom between sons, they continually split, and often fought each other. From this chaos in the eleventh century emerged one Rodrigo Diaz de Vivar, known as El Cid (Arabic for "the lord"), who would become the most famous of Spanish Christian champions. At twenty-two, he led the troops of Castile, and he married a niece of the king. When a disputed royal succession divided Castile, however, El Cid embroiled himself in the civil war that followed, and his unauthorized raid against the Muslim kingdom of Toledo prompted Alfonso VI of Castile–Leon to exile him. Although still devoted to his angry king, El Cid took service with the Muslim ruler of Saragossa.

He subsequently defeated both Muslim and Christian armies, all the while protesting his unswerving loyalty to the implacable Alfonso.

Toledo fell to King Alfonso himself in 1085, after which he subdued some of the Muslim-ruled taifas, and demanded heavy tribute from them. This caused the rulers of these principalities to seek aid from a Muslim sect that had taken power in North Africa, the Almoravids, although they actually had little in common with that puritanical sect, formed among desert nomads who despised high taxes, vast harems and civilization in general. The Almoravids crossed the Strait of Gibraltar in 1086, and their well-ordered infantry, supported by imported Turkish archers, quickly took over most of Muslim Spain.

El Cid, now master of Valencia in eastern Spain, achieved some remarkable victories against the newcomers. Ever the chivalrous knight, this Christian Spaniard reputedly never suffered defeat in battle, and insisted to the end on his fealty to his liege lord Alfonso VI. After El Cid's death, when reinvigorated Muslim armies pressed Alfonso hard, he retreated back to the far North. The king's only son—offspring, incidentally, of a Moorish mother—died in battle, and the Christian cause went into eclipse.

In centuries to come, the escalating clash with Spanish Christians would harden the originally generous spirit of al-Andalus. The Almoravids, and their equally puritanical North African successors, the Almohads, had no use for religious tolerance—an attitude, it must be said, shared by their Christian enemies. The stage was set for the long and bitter battle for the Iberian Peninsula. ■

2. The sole previous claim to warrior status of St. James the Great, powerful patron of Spanish battles, was that the Lord Jesus playfully nicknamed him, and his brother John, "Boanerges" (Sons of Thunder) on account of their vehemence. Beheaded by Herod Agrippa in A.D. 44, (Acts 12:2) James, the brother of John, was the first apostle martyred. Historians consider it unlikely that St. James ever visited Iberia.

*In this painting by Julius Köckert from the
Maximilianeum Collection, Munich, the Abbasid caliph
Haroun al-Rashid at the age of twenty receives envoys
from Charlemagne, bearing the correspondence, tributes
and gifts customarily exchanged by kings and emperors.
Haroun was a patron of the arts, a highly capable
administrator, and one of Islam's greatest generals.*

The Abbasid take-over begins a disintegration of pan-Islamic unity

The new capital Baghdad sees a cultural flowering until the caliphs lose control and renegade sects slay tens of thousands in the Muslim heartland

I t was a party to remember, and six Muslim historians have recorded it for posterity. The host was Abdullah ibn Ali, military commander for (and uncle of) the first Abbasid caliph. Victorious at last over the rival Umayyad dynasty, which had ruled Islam from Damascus for ninety years, the Abbasids were now bent on exterminating every last Umayyad supporter. The Umayyads were hiding, so it was said, in the very "bowels of the earth." But eighty of them had been caught, and on this night of June 25, 750, at the little town of Abu Futrus, near Jaffa on the Mediterranean coast, they were paraded into a grand Abbasid victory banquet. At a signal from Abdullah they were hacked to pieces, and then covered with carpets. The party proceeded amid the dying groans of any still alive.

Hatred can run deep in Islam, as it would among Christians in the years ahead, but this hatred had a history even older than Islam. It was rooted in the Arabian past: the northern herdsman hating the southern farmer, the roving Bedouin hating the townsman, family feuds enduring for generations. There were also other powerful causes for hatred between Abbasid and Umayyad. Religious authority was involved, each faction believing itself divinely commissioned to rule the Muslim world.

The Abbasids were led by descendants of Muhammad's stalwart Uncle Abbas, and

One of the oldest cities in the world, Damascus was the seat of the Umayyad caliphate for just under a century, creating a vibrant center for artists and artisans. This painting, from the city's Azm Palace Museum, illustrates Damascus in the seventeenth century. The eighth-century Great Mosque, on the right, is still a landmark.

supporting them—for the moment—were the followers of Ali, foster son and unswerving supporter of the Prophet. They represented, in short, the Prophet's actual kinsmen. The Umayyads' claim, by contrast, was based solely on precedent. Their ancestors were the traditional leaders of Mecca, who had fiercely opposed the Prophet until his military success became irreversible, when they belatedly joined him.

Muhammad himself had not appointed his successors, but later a process to do so had been established. However, said the Abbasids, the Umayyads had used that process to cheat Abbas and Ali, and Ali's son Hussein, of the rightful succession. According to their opponents, the Umayyads had established at Damascus a false, cynical, opportunistic and unholy distortion of the true faith. No wonder their government was riddled with corruption! Everyone knew, for example, that a provincial governor under Caliph Hisam (724–743) had appropriated some fifty-two million *dirham*, and given up only some of it under torture. Clearly there were many more like him. Just look at the staggering opulence of the caliphs' court! Look at the thousands of slaves who supported their grandiloquent lifestyle, their gambling, their horseracing, their hunting! Consider the hounds of Caliph Yazid I (680–683), with their gold anklets and personal slaves! Consider also that Yazid himself actually composed and encouraged instrumental music, though the Prophet had condemned it as "the devil's muezzin!"

Worse still was the drinking. The Prophet had banned alcohol, but one Umayyad caliph trained a monkey as his drinking companion, and another actually swam in a pool of wine, gulping it by the mouthful. Dissipation had spread even to holy Medina and Mecca, where palatial whorehouses were staffed by Persian and Byzantine slave girls who beguiled Muslims with incense, soft music and wine. Singers and dancers performed at the Sacred Pilgrimage itself. At Ta'if, near Mecca, the beauteous A'isha bint Talha, great-granddaughter of Muhammad's closest friend Abu Bakr, and namesake of the Prophet's beloved wife, had been married three times—and refused to veil her face. Allah had bestowed her beauty upon her, she said, so it was her clear duty to display it.

The Abbasids promised a very different Islamic government. Besides providing legitimate rule and moral reform, they vowed to restore true Muslim equality. When the Arabs conquered Persia in the name of Allah, many of its

The opulence and immorality of the Umayyad court was notorious. One caliph trained his pet monkey as his drinking companion; another's hounds had gold anklets and personal slaves.

people embraced Islam, but the Umayyads consigned them to second-class status. Heartily resentful, these converts rallied to the black Abbasid banner, the Prophet's own flag. And so in April 750, the rebel chieftain Abu al-Abbas, namesake and great-great-grandson of the Prophet's uncle, was able to crush the Umayyads, banishing their white banner from Damascus.

The new regime, the third to rule the Muslim Empire, would prove to be its longest-lasting.[1] The Abbasid dynasty would endure for five centuries, although its caliphs would actually rule for only one. Thereafter they would be merely the puppets of foreign intruders and invaders, while the vast empire that stretched from the Atlantic Ocean to India fragmented into separate states. One surviving Umayyad would found his own durable dynasty in Spain. Egypt and North Africa would break away, and even parts of Arabia and Persia.

The Abbasids began piously enough. Caliph Abu al-Abbas wore the actual cloak of the Prophet when leading the Friday prayers, while ruthlessly securing his regime. The last Umayyad caliph was discovered hiding in an Egyptian church, and his head was dispatched to Damascus. Al-Abbas adopted the honorific *al-Safah*, "the Blood-shedder" and made good on the title. The executioner's carpet beside the throne became a permanent fixture, as did the office of executioner, and torture chambers in the palace basements. Even dead Umayyad caliphs were not spared. Their bones were dug up and their graves desecrated.[2]

Like the Umayyads, al-Abbas had to rely on Persian bureaucrats, making his administration, also like theirs, more Persian than Arab. The caliph held absolute power, but customarily acted through his vizier (prime minister), emirs (generals) and qadis (judges). Most of these were Persian, and many were Christian. The chief judge, however, had to be a stalwart Muslim with theological training, since the Abbasids did try, as promised, to base their legal system on the *Shari'a*. That is, they tried to apply the Qur'anic legal system—derived from rules

1. The first Arab caliphate ruled at Mecca and Medina from 632 to 661. Second came the Umayyad caliphate, which reigned from Damascus from 661 to 750. The third, the Abbasid, ruled mostly from Baghdad from 750 to 1258— a total of 508 years.

2. So great was the desecration of Umayyad graves after the Abbasid takeover that the second Abbasid caliph, al-Mansur, issued strict orders about his own burial. When al-Mansur died in 770, wrote the chronicler Ibn al-Athir, one hundred graves were dug—and his body secretly buried somewhere else.

established by Muhammad for a tribal community in the desert—to the political, economic, social and judicial requirements of an intercontinental empire.

They did not succeed, but neither has any Muslim ruler since. Generations of Muslim jurists, observes Middle East expert Daniel Pipes (*In the Path of God: Islam and Political Power*), have failed to make the Shari'a practicable without changing its traditional formulas—and the slightest change is considered questionable if not unthinkable. As a simple example, the Prophet set taxes for his Muslim followers very low, since in his time plunder and non-Muslim taxpayers amply provided for state requirements. Such was no longer the case in Persia, and to move beyond the limitations of the Shari'a an entire parallel system of tariffs and tolls had to be set up.[3]

The same was true in almost every area. As one instance, the commander of

Al-Mansur spared no expense in building a magnificent capital. Baghdad was famed for its huge walls and wondrous gardens, and the Palace of the Golden Gate soared high over all.

3. Islam early imposed onerous taxes upon *dhimmis* (i.e., non-Muslims such as Christians and Jews), not only to provide state revenue, since Muslims themselves were lightly taxed, but also to encourage conversion to Islam. In Persia, the incentive seems to have worked so well, however, that state revenues were seriously eroded, and state authorities became noticeably uninterested in further conversions to Islam. They could not afford them.

4. The job of the Abbasid postal service, writes historian J. B. Bury (*A History of the Eastern Roman Empire*), was not just to deliver the imperial mail, but to monitor the far-flung imperial administration. It was a giant espionage system, strongly reminding Bury of the Czarist secret police circa 1900. Local postmasters sent to the caliph all sorts of useful information—such as whether a governor was dallying too long with his latest slave girl. The spy net also reputedly used merchants, travelers of all sorts, and hundreds of nosey old women.

the caliph's bodyguard oversaw a police force and courts that handled trade regulations, debt repayment, and such moral transgressions as gambling and the sale of alcohol. He was even expected to prevent such infractions as elderly men dyeing their gray beards black to falsely beguile young women. Meanwhile, the Shari'a became restricted over time mostly to family and ecclesiastical law.

Some public institutions inherited from the Persians and Umayyads worked well, however. The Abbasids extended the Khorasan Road right to the border of China, and they expanded the vitally important postal service. Its hundreds of miles of horse, mule and camel relays connected the empire and delivered the imperial mail, but was at least equally valued as the caliph's primary spy network. Each local agent passed on to the postmaster general all news of interest, including in particular bureaucratic misdeeds.[4]

When al-Abbas died of smallpox four years into his reign, his brother became caliph by eliminating two other contenders. Tall, slender, dark and stern, he assumed the title *al-Mansur*, "Victorious Through God," and consolidated his position with even less scruple than his brother. Al-Mansur had Uncle Abdullah, his rival for the caliphate, imaginatively murdered by imprisoning him in a house with salt foundations. When flooded, reports the historian al-Tabari, it collapsed upon its inhabitant. The new caliph's most powerful lieutenant (and therefore potential rival) was neatly eliminated by inviting him to a banquet where he was assassinated. Dissident Alyite factions, soon thoroughly disillusioned with their allies, had to be similarly dealt with.

Meanwhile, al-Mansur completed in a brisk four years the project for which he is best remembered: his new capital, constructed by one hundred thousand workmen on the west bank of the Tigris River. The city of Baghdad (Gift of God) was destined to rival even Constantinople and to be the scene of Islam's first great cultural flowering. Not that this was the caliph's particular intention, notes J. B. Bury in his *History of the Later Roman Empire*, for he reputedly was an abstemious man, almost niggardly. Absorbed by natural science, history, grammar and law, al-Mansur shunned splendid clothes, rich pageantry and the arts of all kinds, particularly music. One day, encountering a slave playing a tambourine, he had the instrument smashed over the man's head.

But for Baghdad, no magnificence was spared. Designed as a circle four miles in circumference (and thus known as the Round City), it featured three massive concentric walls of sun-dried brick, with four great gateways on north, south, east and west. The one-hundred-and-thirty-foot dome of the caliph's Palace of the Golden Gate soared high within the inner wall. Outside the walls, al-Mansur had a second residence, the Palace of Eternity, surrounded by wondrous gardens, and farther north another palace for the heir apparent. Also outside the walls was the commercial city, intersected by canals, with an assigned quarter for each business and trade.

Three bridges gave access to suburbs on the opposite bank of the Tigris. The Christian Quarter, known as *Dar al-Rum* ("Abode of the Romans"), with its churches and monasteries, was in one of these. Throughout the city were public baths—sumptuous, steam-heated marble bathhouses with mosaic floors and refreshment rooms. As the empire prospered, the produce of the fertile Tigris–Euphrates Valley flowed into the capital, while Arab merchants extended their trade routes to deal in Chinese silk and porcelain, Indian spices, Asian jewels and minerals, Scandinavian furs, African ivory, and slaves both black and white.

With the move of the Abbasid caliphate to Baghdad, that city blossomed into a large and wealthy center of culture, medicine, science and learning. The gilded domes and minarets of the Kadhimain Mosque are typical of the lavishly decorated religious buildings with their intricate tile work, marble floors and mirror mosaics.

This was the city that would inspire stories of the fictional Aladdin, Ali Baba and the forty thieves, and Sinbad the sailor. Their adventures, based on Persian stories with many Arab additions, would entertain generations to come in the *Arabian Nights*. Baghdad would "witness the most momentous intellectual awakening in the history of Islam," writes Philip K. Hitti in his monumental *History of the Arabs*. Amid its luxury and intrigue, the Christian physician-scholar Hunayn ibn Ishaq al-Ibadi translated the works of major Greek thinkers, and paid for each book with its equivalent weight in gold. But Hunayn was no toady. When the caliph ordered him to produce a poison for one of his enemies, Hunayn refused and was jailed for a year. Why such defiance, demanded the caliph, upon his physician's release. Two reasons, replied Hunayn. His religion required him to love his enemies, not poison them, and his profession forbade him to do harm.

Almost all the caliphs employed Christian physicians, and the impressive medical lore amassed by the Muslim Empire came largely from Greek, Persian and sometimes Indian sources. It would in due course be transmitted into Europe by way of Muslim Spain and Sicily. Muslim physicians added to this store of medical knowledge, of course, the most illustrious being the ninth-century diagnostician, surgeon and chemist al-Razi (known in the West as Rhazes), a prolific writer who also built and administered Baghdad's hospital. Equally famous is the physician, philosopher and poet Ibn Sina (Latinized as Avicenna), who codified Greco–Muslim medical knowledge in one comprehensive and remarkably accurate volume. Translated into Latin, it became one of Europe's chief medical resources until the seventeenth century.

The Abbasids displayed an insatiable appetite for every sort of knowledge—astronomy, mathematics, astrology, alchemy, optics, geography, music theory, psychology, politics, philosophy and metaphysics—that they could import from India and Byzantium. The words for arithmetic, geometry,

The Abbasids displayed an insatiable appetite for knowledge. Scholarship and literature flourished at their courts, and Arabic became the language of learning.

geography and music in both Latin and Arabic originate from Greek. There ensued a veritable orgy of translation, as Nestorian Christian scholars commissioned by the caliphs rendered into Syriac and Arabic all the great Hellenists: Galen, Hypocrites, Euclid, Ptolemy, Plato, Aristotle.

Muslim scholars responded by building upon this "new" learning in practically every field, and soon Arabic became the recognized language of learning throughout the Islamic world. Among the scholars were historian–theologians like al-Tabari and the historian–geographer al-Masudi. And finally, there were purely literary works, including love stories from the lively courts of the caliphs, which became immensely popular in western lands, as did the haunting love poetry of the *Rubaiyat* of the Persian Umar al-Khayyam. Al-Khayyam, quite typically, was a scientist as well: an accomplished astronomer who reformed the Islamic calendar.[5]

These intellectual developments quickly took institutional form, beginning with the "House of Wisdom," a combined translation center, academy, library and observatory. Observatories and hospitals served as teaching centers, as did mosques, and Baghdad's first university-style institute, the *Nizamiyah*; would survive for centuries. Libraries both private and public opened in major cities, while literary, poetry and debating salons were favored entertainment in wealthy homes. The result, although something the Prophet had never predicted, was a brilliant society centered on the glittering city of Baghdad.

But the Muslim Empire was becoming ever less Arab. Although Baghdad remained firmly Muslim in faith, and Arabic the legal language, Persian influence prevailed in dress, food, songs, stories and popular culture generally, as well as government. Abroad, although the caliph was everywhere unfailingly mentioned in the formal Friday sermon, the empire was fracturing both theologically and politically.

Both presented intractable problems, and they worked in tandem. Theologically, the Abbasids held to the position espoused by their Umayyad predecessors, based on literal interpretation of the Qur'an and assiduous

5. While massive scholarly translation was proceeding under Abbasid auspices, the materials used changed significantly, from parchment (or papyrus) to paper. The Persians had learned from the Chinese how to manufacture it. By 794, Baghdad's first paper mill was operating, and Ja'far, Haroun al-Rashid's powerful vizier, ordered parchment replaced by paper for all government use.

collection and assessment by their scholars of the *Hadith* (traditions). Adhering to this *Sunna* ("middle path" or "orthodox way"), they came to be called "Sunnis." But their Alyite allies were developing increasingly contrary views. They revered Hussein as a veritable saint and Ali as the last legitimate caliph, with a seemingly boundless devotion. They even amended the Islamic declaration of faith to read: "There is no God but God and Muhammad is his Prophet, and Ali is his vice-regent (*wali*)."

The Alyites preferred to call their leader *imam*, which simply means "leader," rather than caliph. They believed, however, that as Ali's direct descendant, their imam inherited all Muhammad's power—spiritual as well as temporal—and was therefore incapable of error or sin. The Abbasids contemptuously dismissed them and their beliefs as a mere *Shi'a*, a sect, and the name stuck. The Alyites would henceforth be known as Shi'ite, i.e., "sectarians."

The early Abbasid caliphs actively persecuted them, even desecrating and destroying the tombs of Ali and Hussein. The Shi'ites, who were strong in Persia, caused the Abbasids endless grief in return, but the toll on Shi'ite leadership was high. In little more than a century, eleven Shi'a imams died by poison, execution or in battle. Their historians hold that the twelfth, a descendant of Hussein, disappeared without trace in the cave below the Great Mosque at Samara. He thus

Many brilliant scholars flourished during the Abbasid caliphate in Persia. Umar al-Khayyam, known to Westerners for his Rubaiyat, was famous during his lifetime as a mathematician and astronomer. H. M. Burton portrays him (above), working out a reform of the Persian calendar. Ibn Sina (left), sits in the august company of Galen and Hippocrates, an indication of the esteem in which this tenth-century Persian physician was held. The woodcut is from a sixteenth-century European medical book.

6. The Shi'ite tendency to fragment into myriad factions seems to have been predicted by the Prophet. According to a tradition reported by the revered *Hadith* master Ibn al-Jawzi, Muhammad once said, "The Israelites have been divided into seventy-one or seventy-two sects, but my community shall be divided into seventy-three." It probably has, and most have been Shi'ite.

became the "hidden" or "expected" imam, and his devotees await his return as the *Mahdi*, the "divinely appointed one," who will finally restore true Islam and conquer the world in its name. All this was, and would remain, the belief of the main Shi'a body, still known as Twelvers.

However, the Shi'ite had a chronic tendency to split.[6] For example, their sixth imam, before his death, named as his successor his elder son Isma'il. But then, supposedly discovering that Isma'il was intemperate as to wine, he appointed his younger son Musa instead. Though most of his followers accepted this decision, some argued that an imam, being infallible, was incapable of such an offense. For the Ismai'lis, therefore, Isma'il became the seventh imam, who would very soon return as the Mahdi. Meanwhile, they developed on the basis of the number seven a mathematical cosmogony, which purported to explain the universe and all history. They held that the Qur'an must be interpreted as allegory to reveal its inner meanings, and espoused such beliefs as transmigration of souls.

Under the leadership of a Persian named Abdullah, Ismai'li missionaries spread across the Islamic world, secretly

View of Cairo by Jean-Leon Gerome, a nineteenth-century view of the city chosen as the capital of the Fatimid caliphate. The spread of the Fatimids in North Africa effectively cut off Christians there from their fellows in Europe.

initiating converts both Persian and Arab into these esoteric doctrines.

The Ismai'lis in time continued to split into further sects. Among the most striking were the egalitarian Qarmatians (or Carmathians), founded late in the ninth century by a pupil of Abdullah, Hamdan Qarmat, who believed that all things must be held in common (including wives, some sources say). Their intensely communal beliefs, says Hitti, have caused some modern historians to call them "the Bolsheviks of Islam." They also resembled the early Bolsheviks in their readiness to shed blood, including that of fellow Muslims. At the end of the ninth century, they founded a Qarmatian state on the Persian Gulf, from which they wreaked havoc into the eleventh.

Also of considerable duration—some two and a half centuries—were the Fatimids, another Ismai'li offshoot whose leader, Sa'id ibn Hussein, claimed descent from Fatima, daughter of the Prophet and wife of Ali. After much clandestine advance work in North Africa to announce his advent as the Mahdi, Sa'id arrived there in the guise of a merchant. He was jailed nonetheless by the suspicious Abbasid-appointed governor, a Sunni already operating as a virtually independent ruler, but was rescued by supporters. Successfully eliminating the ruling regime, he was proclaimed Imam Ubaydullah al-Mahdi in 909.

Imam Ubaydullah ruled North Africa for twenty-five years, energetically expanding his territory from Morocco to Egypt, and his progeny proved equally industrious. His son raided the coasts of France and Italy, and his grandson the Spanish coast. In 958, the Fatimids advanced west to the Atlantic. In 969, they

A mad caliph and an obstinate light

He destroys Helena's Church of the Holy Sepulchre and proclaims himself divine, and to this day controversy swirls around Jerusalem's inexplicable lighting of lamps

Christian pilgrims in the eleventh century revered the Church of the Holy Sepulchre in Jerusalem as the veritable center of the universe. What place could be more sacred than this magnificent structure, erected seven hundred years earlier by Emperor Constantine I and his mother, St. Helena, on Mount Golgotha, on the very site of the Crucifixion and entombment of Jesus Christ?

Furthermore, it was here, every year at Eastertide—with the great church darkening and packed tight with devout pilgrims—that the miraculous Paschal Fire would appear out of nothing and inexplicably light the lamps on the sacred tomb of the Lord. So when word got round in the year 1009 that Christendom's holiest church had been razed to the ground by order of the Egyptian caliph al-Hakim, Christians everywhere reacted in shock and horror.

Indignation at Caliph al-Hakim ibn Amr Allah, some say, may actually have contributed to the launching of the Crusades. It most certainly enhanced his reputation as "the Mad Fatimid Caliph"—not that this reputation needed enhancing. During his twenty-five-year reign, al-Hakim conducted the era's worst persecutions of Christians and Jews. He later capped even this by declaring himself to be divine, and cruelly harassing his Muslim subjects instead. Indeed, his destruction of the Church of the Holy Sepulchre may have seemed to Muslims one of al-Hakim's saner acts.[1]

Christian celebrations there, so close to the revered al-Aqsa Mosque, were regarded by Muslim authorities as particularly repugnant and none more than the loud and jubilant worship on Holy Saturday. "Under the very eyes of Muslims," complained one observer, there occurred "a number of hateful things which are not right to hear or look upon." Muslims had two reactions to this. Some were upset because they believed the "Miracle of the Holy Fire" to be a fake, produced through some ecclesiastical hocus-pocus. Others were even more upset because they feared it might actually be real.

In 1008, a traveling Ismai'li missionary assured al-Hakim that the Holy Fire was obviously Christian trickery designed to fool gullible pilgrims, so the indignant caliph had the church demolished stone by stone. The very rock of the Lord's sepulchre was attacked with pickaxes, horrified Christians learned. In the next four years, at al-Hakim's further command, churches and monasteries throughout Palestine, Syria and Egypt were pillaged and destroyed, bishops arrested and tortured, graveyards desecrated, and the Christian and Jewish faiths driven underground. Thousands of Christians, say the chroniclers, lost heart and became Muslim. (A good many are thought to have recanted later, however.)

All this, uncharacteristic of Muslim rule generally, was entirely in character for al-Hakim. The blue-eyed son of a Russian Christian mother, he became the sixth Fatimid caliph in 996, at age eleven, on the death of his accomplished and notably tolerant father, al-Aziz. By age eighteen, he took to randomly torturing and killing his high court officials, both Christian and Muslim. As a fervent Shi'ite, he pronounced curses against the early caliphs and Companions of the Prophet, and had these denunciations inscribed on mosques, then later ordered them removed. Women must not leave their houses, he decreed, and therefore banned manufacture of women's shoes. A certain vegetable dish was forbidden because it was a favorite of the eighth-century caliph Mu'awiya, enemy of Ali, the revered Shi'ite protagonist.

But al-Hakim seemingly crossed into true insanity after an influential Shi'ite prophet, al-Darazi, began proclaiming him divine. Urged on as well by his vizier (prime minister), a Persian mystic, the Mad Caliph tried to suppress such central Islamic practices as the Ramadan fast and the Hijaz pilgrimage. The Islamic "great proclamation"—*In the name of Allah, the merciful, the compassionate*—became *In the name of al-Hakim, the merciful, the compassionate*. This sparked riots in Cairo. Historian Laurence E. Browne, in *The Eclipse of Christianity in Asia*, says that al-Darazi prudently retired to Lebanon, "where he founded the sect of the Druze, who to this day worship al-Hakim as god." Then, in February 1021, the Mad Caliph simply disappeared, possibly murdered on orders from his sister, whom he had accused of being unchaste.

In due course, things settled down. Al-Hakim's son made a treaty with the Byzantine Empire, which helped local Christians rebuild the Church of the Holy Sepulchre by 1048. Furthermore, the Holy Fire resumed its annual appearance and, say the faithful, has continued to do so right to the present day.

So has impassioned argument about it. Is it miracle, or is it fake? The eleventh-century Muslim scholar al-Biruni took no stand either way: "A story is told in connection with the Saturday of the Resurrection that astonishes the investigator, and whose basis is impossible to discover." In 1834 an English traveler, Robert Curzon, reacted with typical nineteenth-century scepticism: "It seems wonderful that so barefaced a trick should continue to be practiced every year in these enlightened times." (The fact that several hundred participants died of asphyxiation that year in the packed church, a fate narrowly escaped by Curzon himself, may not have enhanced his objectivity. Actually, such incidents have been surprisingly few, though nowadays fire extinguishers are noticeably at hand.)

But accounts are on record from many believers. In 1106, for instance, the Russian abbot Daniel ecstatically described how, at about the ninth hour "the Holy Light suddenly illumined the Holy Sepulchre, stunningly bright and splendid." Abbot Daniel was referring to the elaborate stone *edicule* (literally "little house"), in effect a chapel built around the actual tomb. The presiding bishop had entered with a candle taken from Prince Baldwin, the Crusader ruler of Jerusalem, Daniel continued, and "it was from the prince's candle that we lit ours.... Someone who has not shared in the excitement of that day cannot possibly believe that all I saw is true."

The account nearly nine centuries later of another pilgrim, Niels Christian Hvidt, provides a more detailed description of the manifestation on April 18, 1998. This was Holy Saturday calculated (as always) according to the Julian calendar, and the ceremony was conducted (as always) under Orthodox auspices. Would-be worshipers were camped all round the church, Hvidt

The famous miracle of the Holy Fire resumed once the Church of the Holy Sepulchre was rebuilt in 1048. This painting, The Sacred Fire of Jerusalem, *by Eugene Alexis Girardet, captures something of the awe and excitement of the holy event.*

writes, hoping to squeeze into it. That morning, Arab Christians began dancing "ferociously" inside it, chanting loudly to the beat of drummers seated upon the shoulders of the dancers.

At about 1:00 p.m., however, silence fell upon the crowd. A little later, Israeli officials elbowed their way through. Their role, one fulfilled by Turk and Arab authorities before them, was to eliminate the possibility of trickery. They entered the edicule to search for any lighting device, and then sealed its doors with wax. The worshipers, chanting *Kyrie Eleison* (Lord have mercy), continued to wait in the dark. At last came the Greek Orthodox patriarch of Jerusalem, Diodorus I, heading a procession that thrice circled the edicule. Then the patriarch, stripped of his liturgical vestments and wearing only a simple white gown, broke the seals and carried two unlit candles into the tomb.

Pilgrim Hvidt had interviewed Patriarch Diodorus beforehand, asking him what happens next. "I find my way through the darkness towards the inner chamber," the patriarch told him, "and fall on my knees. I say certain prayers which have been handed down through the centuries, and having said them, I wait." Then, after varying intervals, "from the core of the very stone on which Jesus lay, an indefinable light pours forth.... Sometimes it covers just the stone, while other times it gives light to the whole sepulchre, so that people who stand outside and look into it see it filled with light. The light does not burn—I have never had my beard burned in all the sixteen years I have been patriarch in Jerusalem and have received the Holy Fire."

Eventually, Diodorus continued, the light forms a column "in which the fire is of a different nature," from which candles can be lit. These he takes out to the Armenian and Coptic patriarchs, whence the light is passed to all the jostling, ecstatically chanting people. Participants frequently have insisted, however, that their own candles were lit directly by strange bluish flames that danced about the chapel.

"I believe it to be no coincidence that the Holy Fire comes exactly on this spot," Patriarch Diodorus told Hvidt. "In Matt. 28:3, it says that when Christ rose from the dead, an angel came, dressed all in a fearful light ... I believe that is the same light that appears miraculously every Easter Saturday. Christ wants to remind us that his resurrection is a reality, and not just a myth."

Whatever the explanation, one fact seems inescapable. The Mad Caliph failed to extinguish either the church or the light of Christ's Resurrection. As John's Gospel says (1:5): "The light shines in the darkness and the darkness cannot put it out." ■

1. Known in the West as the Church of the Holy Sepulchre, this hallowed basilica has always been known to the Orthodox East as the Church of the Resurrection. This name, incidentally, provided Arabic-speaking Muslims with a contemptuous pun. It translates into Arabic as *Kanisat al-Qiyama*, and historian F. E. Peters notes in *Jerusalem* that contemporary Muslims delighted in derisively referring to it instead as the *Kanisat al-Qumama* "Church of the Dung Heap."

conquered Egypt, and by 991 controlled most of Syria as well, where they had to contend with the Qarmatians. They also provided Egypt, for a time, with wealth and good government. Under the fifth imam, Nizar al-Aziz (975–996), the Shi'ite Egyptian caliphate was more powerful by far than the Sunni Abbasids of Baghdad.

Al-Aziz built a new capital, Cairo, described by a visitor in the next century as a beautiful and singularly law-abiding city of brick houses five and six stories high, with many shops, lighted streets, eight great mosques, canals, magnificent bridges and gates, and of course, palaces. Al-Aziz's own palace, with which he hoped one day to dazzle the defeated Abbasid caliph of Baghdad, was especially impressive. Under the tolerant rule of al-Aziz, other faiths, Christians included, fared well. He had a Christian vizier, and his Russian wife, mother of his heir, was also Christian. Indeed, she was the sister of two patriarchs. Tolerance would

Christians and Jews were tolerated as 'people of the Book,' and only sporadically were they offered the stark choice of either converting to Islam or execution.

vanish from Cairo, however, in the reign of al-Hakim (996–1021), the strange, troubled, blue-eyed son of al-Aziz. (See sidebar, page 264.)

Al-Hakim was not typical of Muslim treatment of subject peoples in this era, however. It varied greatly throughout the Muslim world, but only sporadically were Christians and Jews faced with the stark choice of "Islam or the sword." The Prophet had classified them as "people of the Book," to be tolerated as an inferior class, so in Persia they were organized as separate groups (*melets*), under their own leaders. These *dhimmis* were not fully recognized in law, and had to pay heavy taxes. In addition, onerous and frequently humiliating restrictions were often prescribed, though not always applied. Laurence E. Browne, in *The Eclipse of Christianity in Asia*, quotes the eleventh-century Muslim lawyer Mawardi to explain that two categories of law applied to Christians. The first category was absolute and always obligatory, the second not necessarily so.

The first category included the following: Dhimmis must never denigrate the holy Qur'an, or the Prophet, or the Muslim faith; they must not attempt to amorously approach or marry a Muslim woman; they must not "turn a Muslim from the faith or harm him in person or possessions," nor aid his enemies. First category rules were invariably and fiercely enforced. The restrictions of the second category, which were much more sporadic, required Christians to wear an identifying garment, and possess no building higher than Muslim ones. They must not offend Muslim ears by their summonses to prayer or by making claims about their Messiah. They must refrain from "drinking wine publicly and displaying their crosses and swine." They were forbidden to ride any animal more grandiose than a mule, or to own slaves.

Similar restrictions applied to Jews, and the Umayyad caliphs extended melet status to a people Muhammad probably never imagined, the Zoroastrians. The Jews,

The tenth century Tokali Kilise Church in Goreme, Cappadocia, Turkey, is richly decorated with frescoes, such as the one here of Jesus and St. Paul baptizing the first Christians. The oldest known rock church in the area, it was built into a cave.

relatively few in number, were not seen as a threat and were very useful, handling most of Baghdad's financial and business affairs. They supported rabbinical schools and synagogues, and far from being suppressed, seem to have been highly esteemed. A twelfth-century account tells how their chief, called the *exilarch* or "prince of captivity," arrived at an audience with the caliph, robed and turbaned in silk and preceded by a servant crying "Make way for our lord, the son of David."

Christians specialized in government, education, finance and medicine, bringing influence and wealth to themselves and their churches. An example is the physician Jurgis (George) ibn Bakhtishu, called in to cure Caliph al-Mansur of persistent stomach trouble. Ibn Bakhtishu subsequently ran the court medical practice, and so did his descendants for six illustrious generations. As Arabic professor T. W. Arnold observes in *The Cambridge Medieval History*, Christian prosperity is amply indicated by the size of the bribes the Nestorian churches could produce when necessary. Another indication is the size and number of magnificent church buildings erected throughout the caliphate between 760 and 1180—although building new churches was theoretically not allowed.

Muslims naturally resented this preferment, especially since Christians seem not always to have been as deferential as they should. They further suspected that many Christian converts to Islam did so insincerely, for worldly advancement, and they frequently complained that the unconverted were not obeying the dhimmi rules. Christians were not wearing the distinctive garments as required, or were hiding them under other clothing, they said. Their noisy summonses to church services were attracting crowds who "ogled" them, and wealthy Christians were not all paying the proper tax. And some of these infidels, protested one irate Muslim, were actually presuming to use Muslim names like "Hassan and Hussein and Fadl and Ali … and there is nothing left but that they should be called Muhammad...."

Such complaints sometimes got results. In 758, al-Mansur confiscated church treasures. A later caliph briefly enforced all the rules, and had new and borderland churches demolished. Another deposed and imprisoned the Nestorian patriarch, destroyed some churches, expropriated several monasteries, and required Christians to put devil images on their gates, sew yellow patches on their clothing, and reduce grave monuments to ground level. Anti-Christian mobs attacked churches on occasion, sometimes despite official protection. In one instance, the caliph ordered a damaged church rebuilt, but during the process, the mob burned it down again. Few attacks on life and limb are recorded, however, either from official policy or mob action, and these occurred mostly during frontier fighting between Muslims and their Byzantine adversaries.

Within the empire, much Muslim–Christian intercourse was amiable enough. On a formal level, both produced apologetics for their own beliefs, and held debates. The Muslims, Browne remarks, were little impressed by Christian arguments, but he detects "a wistful looking towards Jesus to supply something that was not to be found in Islam." This may have resulted from daily contact of the common people of both faiths. Moreover, as more and more Christians became Muslims, there appears in Islam a noticeable infiltration of Christian ideas and outright borrowings. Miracles began to be attributed to the Prophet, for example, prophecies about him were discovered in the Old Testament, and Hadiths appeared that attributed to him sayings remarkably like those of Jesus. "If any man suffers, or a brother of his suffers," says a prayer of that era, "let him say, 'Our Lord God who art in heaven, hallowed be thy name, thy power is in heaven and on earth; as thy mercy is in heaven, so practice thy mercy upon earth; forgive us our fault and our sins, thou art the Lord of the good men; send down mercy from thy mercy, and healing from thy healing, on this pain, that it may be healed again.'"

There is also evidence that adherents of both faiths sometimes honored the memory and tomb of the same saints, and by the eleventh century they habitually shared in each other's festivals. On occasion, it is thought, Muslims

Lost until 1881, the Nemrut Dag statues are now a UNESCO World Heritage Site. A burial monument to the first-century B.C. ruler Antiochus I, the mountainside mausoleum is located north of Edessa, near Samosata, Turkey, an area soaked in blood from historic Christian-Muslim battles.

even attended Christian liturgies. Finally, Islam produced the Sufis, Islamic holy men clearly influenced by the ubiquitous Christian monks of the East, with a possible touch of Buddhism as well. The Sufis firmly established themselves despite the deep repugnance of both Sunnis and Shi'ites for the basic monkish principles of asceticism and (even more) of celibacy.[7]

Yet very few Muslims became Christian, while increasing numbers of Christians went the other way. This was quite the opposite to the outcome in Europe, where Roman missionaries brought wave after wave of barbarian conquerors into the faith. Historians offer various explanations. Browne suggests that the churches of the East must have lost faith and zeal since the early days, when they so valiantly embraced martyrdom under the Persian shahs. British historian Aubrey R. Vine (*The Nestorian Churches*) agrees that an increasingly material outlook caused Persian Christians to lose their grip on "the essentials of their faith." Henri Pirenne in *Muhammad and Charlemagne* writes that the fact a Christian's faith was mostly ignored was "the most effective means of detaching him from it." And as Pipes emphasizes, apostasy from Islam (where the Qur'anic penalty was, and is, death) has been a relative rarity at any time.

Meanwhile, whatever else might engage the attention of the Arab caliphs, they never long ignored one obligation: jihad (holy war) against Byzantium. In 718, the emperor Leo III had foiled an all-out Umayyad effort to conquer Constantinople. Their massive fleet had withdrawn in defeat and disgrace from the Sea of Marmara (see previous volume, *The Sword of Islam*, chapter 10). But since then Muslim armies had repeatedly crossed the Taurus Mountains and descended upon the Christian communities of Asia Minor, pillaging, marching the inhabitants away into slavery, and occupying the territory until Christian forces expelled them.

In 727, ten years after the great siege of Constantinople, they were back attacking Nicea, only sixty miles from the capital. In 730 they took the city of Caesarea in Cappadocia. In the last year of Leo's life, 739, he confronted a Muslim army of ninety thousand at Acroïnum, on the western edge of the Anatolian plateau (now in Turkey) and routed them, having been warned of their approach by an ingenious defense system of mountain-to-mountain signal lights that the Byzantines had devised.[8]

The Abbasid takeover eleven years later caused a lull in border hostilities, but in 782 the third caliph, al-Mahdi, resolved to demonstrate the prowess of the new regime by driving right through to the Asiatic shore of the Bosporus opposite Constantinople. His second son, Haroun, eighteen years old and in command of the army, routed the Byzantines, then deeply divided by the iconoclast controversy (see chapter 5). He obliged the empress Irene, regent for her twelve-year-old son, Constantine VI, to plead for a humiliating and expensive peace. Haroun's jubilant father bestowed upon him the title *al-Rashid*, the "Well-Guided," and designated him second heir to the throne.

Four years later, in August 785, al-Mahdi died at age forty-three. By then he had decided to make Haroun his heir, and not his elder son, Musa al-Hadi. Nevertheless, Musa, with Haroun's acquiescence, did reign for one year—a year

7. Sufi mystics, men seeking direct experience of God, appeared in the ninth century, and by the twelfth, when organized Sufi fraternities formed, had won the acquiescence of most orthodox Muslims. The name comes from the *suf* (wool) robes they adopted from Christian monks, along with asceticism, celibacy, meditation, vigils and litanies.

8. The timely warning that enabled Emperor Leo III to repel the Muslim army at Acroïnum was sent by signal fire from the fortress of Lulon, which guarded the northern end of the pass through the Taurus Mountains known as the Cilician Gates—often the frontier between the Muslim and Byzantine Empires. From Lulon the news was relayed by seven other hilltop stations until it could be read from the lighthouse in the Great Palace at Constantinople.

of mutual suspicion and recrimination, before he too died on September 15, 786.[9] Next day Haroun al-Rashid, at twenty-two, saw to the burial of his brother and accepted oaths of allegiance from Baghdad notables. Wearing Abbasid black, he rode upon a white horse to al-Mansur's mosque in the Round City to lead midday prayers, while his subjects shouted their joy from rooftops and windows. Young, intelligent and energetic, Haroun took over when the empire was headed for its zenith of power, culture and wealth, and became in the popular mind its most admired and best-loved caliph. His political style, observes the British soldier–historian John Bagot Glubb in *Haroon al Rasheed and the Great Abbasids*, was relatively conciliatory—internally anyhow. The only blood shed at his accession was that of one especially defiant subject, and he released from prison numerous Alyites.

Abbasid qualms about luxury had by now been wholly suppressed, and the caliphs were rivalling in self-indulgence the once-despised Umayyads. Haroun's father, al-Mahdi, had made the pilgrimage to Mecca, for instance, with camel-loads of mountain ice wrapped in sacking to cool his drinks. (His ancestors,

Quick-tempered but compassionate, Haroun al-Rashid would often mix incognito with his people in Baghdad's night streets. He was widely esteemed and immensely popular.

snorts Glubb, "had crossed these deserts with a handful of dates…. and a goatskin of muddy water.") In lavish spending and carousing, however, Haroun's court would eclipse all others. Being particularly fond of music, he held one festival involving two thousand singers. His favorite "cup companion" was the celebrated libertine poet Abu Nuwas, who enlivened their revels with paeans to wine and women. Haroun's brother, Ibrahim, was himself a celebrated singer and lute-player, and his heir, al-Amin, spent several fortunes building animal-shaped barges for all-night parties on the Tigris. Fashionable Muslims simply ignored the Prophet's strictures against alcohol. Others contended that Muhammad knew only about fermented dates; the splendid wines now readily available from Christian monasteries and Jewish merchants were quite another matter.

Haroun built polo grounds and a boat harbor on the Tigris, and for his beloved empress, his cousin Zubaida, laid out another palace and more gardens. Tableware, Zubaida decreed, must always be of silver or gold, studded with jewels, and their food of the finest. Yet Haroun also had a social conscience. Discovering that one exotic dish consisted of one hundred and fifty fish tongues and cost a thousand dirhams, he immediately sent two servants to give the fish tongues to the first beggar he encountered, and also to distribute a thousand dirhams to the poor. Tall and well built, with thick, curly, black hair and a short beard, Haroun is said to have been emotional, impulsive, quick-tempered and compassionate—a volatile combination. At night, it was said, he often mixed incognito with his people in Baghdad's streets. That may help account for his legendary popularity.

9. Historians disagree about how and why the caliph al-Mahdi died at forty-three. He may have been killed in a hunting accident, or more likely, have been poisoned by one of his concubines. As to "why," John Bagot Glubb (*Haroon al Rasheed and the Great Abbasids*) lists three theories. One, the concubine gave him the poison in mistake for an aphrodisiac. Two, she intended it for a rival concubine, not al-Mahdi, and fatally bungled the delivery. Three, she was bribed by his eldest son, Musa, who knew his father had decided to make his brother the next caliph.

But he was a serious man, taking pains with the education of his two eldest sons: al-Ma'mun, child of a favorite concubine; and al-Amin, slightly younger, Zubaida's only child.[10] He was reputedly pious, and certainly a warrior, turning Tarsus in Cilicia into a fortress, and launching yearly assaults on the Byzantine frontier. Sometimes the Byzantines fought back; sometimes they bought him off. After the emperor Nicephorus I took over from Irene in 802, however, the mood in Constantinople changed. Nicephorus repudiated the tribute that Irene had paid ("female weakness" he called it), and demanded the money back. Haroun, in apoplectic rage, seized a pen and scrawled upon the back of the emperor's defiant missive: "From Haroun, Prince of the Faithful, to Nicephorus, the Roman dog. I have read your letter, you son of a heathen mother. You will see my reply before you hear it."

His army, 135,000 strong, set out almost immediately for the Byzantine frontier. Nicephorus, his bluff called, had to hastily agree to continue the tribute, and the Muslim army headed home. But then the emperor reneged on his agreement, reasoning that Haroun's army could not return through the high Taurus passes in dead of winter. He was wrong again. Back they came, burning and looting and gathering captives. This time, Nicephorus even promised to pay in specially minted coins stamped with the likenesses of Haroun and his designated heirs—but again he did not deliver. So in 806 the caliph himself, wearing a peaked cap emblazoned "Raider and Pilgrim," led a summer attack that captured Heraclea. Another force struck the island of Cyprus, reportedly taking seventeen thousand prisoners, including its Orthodox bishop. Only then did Nicephorus pay all the tribute arrears.

But ill fortune now switched to the Muslim side. Sensing that he would not live to see old age, Haroun conducted his two oldest sons to the sacred Ka'ba at Mecca, split the empire between them, and made each swear to and sign a concordat to respect this arrangement. The document was then pinned to the wall, but promptly fell off, a bad omen—and an accurate one. Haroun died seven years later in March 809, of an abdominal affliction, at forty-six. Within four years, the brothers were at war, with Zubaida's son, al-Amin, besieged in the city of Baghdad by his half brother, al-Ma'mun. So fierce did the fighting become that the beautiful Round City was wrecked before al-Amin tried to escape by night across the Tigris, was caught, and was summarily beheaded.

Baghdad's devout Muslims might well have concluded that the wrong man won, for al-Ma'mun was theologically very suspect. He backed the Mu'tazilites, a

The tales of the Arabian Nights *are based on the court of Haroun al-Rashid, here shown as a young man in an Indian miniature from the Bibliothèque Nationale, Paris. Scheherazade spun her nightly tales, weaving legends with real people such as al-Rashid, creating stories that are still beloved in the West as well as the East.*

10. "The Prince of the Faithful is entrusting to you the being dearest to his heart," wrote Haroun al-Rashid to the tutor of his eldest son. "He gives you full authority over his son, and will warn him that it is his duty to obey you.... Teach him to read the Qur'an and instruct him in the traditions of the Prophet. Beautify his mind with poetry and teach him how to behave.... Do not be so severe as to kill the natural activity of his mind, or so indulgent that he becomes accustomed to idleness. Try as far as you can to lead him by kindness, but if he rejects it, then use severity and assert your authority."

freethinking movement within Islam dating from Umayyad times and derived from Greek, Persian and Indian thought. The Mu'tazilites believed in free will. Worse still, they utterly rejected the orthodox Sunni belief that the Qur'an in its Arabic form is, as Hitti puts it, "the identical reproduction of a celestial original," but rather that it was "created." If the Qur'an was in effect "eternal," they contended, it must be a rival to God himself. In 833, al-Ma'mun proclaimed that all his Muslim subjects must affirm this view, and set up an inquisition to enforce his edict, provoking sturdy opposition and periods of severe suffering for unwilling Muslims.

Although Bury notes that al-Ma'mun spent more money trying to rebuild Haroun's court than he did on the defense of the Syrian frontier, his twenty-year reign was one of almost constant warfare against recusant movements in his empire. He died on such a campaign in 833. A third Haroun son, al-Mu'tasim, succeeded him, and it was he who had to contend with Byzantium. A new Byzantine emperor, Theophilus, attacked the Muslim fortress of Zapetra, al-Mu'tasim's birthplace, on the Melitene Plain along the Euphrates. Al-Mu'tasim's response was to wipe out the Christian city of Amorion, which fell after a two-week siege—betrayed, it was said, from within. The Muslims destroyed the walls, burned a church in which many citizens had taken refuge, and slaughtered, by one estimate, thirty thousand people. More than a thousand nuns were "delivered to the outrages of the Turkish and Moorish slaves," writes Bury, quoting al-Tabari. Many prisoners perished on the arduous march back to

Still a place of pilgrimage for Shi'ite Muslims, the Great Mosque was built in the ninth century as part of the Abbasid city at Samara, Iraq. The largest mosque in the world, its minaret is the most striking feature, rising to a height of over 150 feet.

Mesopotamia, or were killed on the way when supplies and water ran short.

There was one more consequence. Probably only the highest-ranking captives survived, writes Judith Herrin in *Women in Purple, Rulers of Medieval Byzantium*, and efforts to ransom them were only partially successful. Forty-two of these officers, after seven years in Muslim captivity, were confronted with the final choice: Islam or the sword. Refusing to abjure their faith, they were beheaded on the banks of the Tigris; their bodies, thrown in the river, miraculously did not sink.[11] But al-Mu'tasim's projected next blow against Byzantium proved a costly disaster. He built four hundred ships in Syria to attack Constantinople. The fleet sailed in 842, and all but seven vessels were wrecked in a storm off the southwest coast of Asia Minor. Al-Mu'tasim, who had died that year, was spared this news, as well as the much worse news that followed. With his reign, the glorious century of Baghdad's Abbasid caliphate came to an end, and two centuries of hideous chaos ensued. Amorion would be their last external military victory, and internally they were about to lose control of their empire and even of their court.

The immediate cause was a serious error of judgment by al-Mu'tasim himself. Son of a Turkish slave girl, he apparently felt secure in creating a separate royal bodyguard of four thousand Turks to safeguard his interests against hostile elements in the regular army. However, these Turk mercenaries became so unruly as to make life in the capital intolerable. The wrathful citizenry threatened insurrection, and in 836 al-Mu'tasim had to move them

and his government sixty miles north to Samara. Succeeding caliphs became the prisoners and puppets of these Turkish officers, who appointed and disposed of them at will.[12]

The return of the court to Baghdad fifty-six years later made no difference. The Turkish soldiers were still very much in evidence, conniving with influential slaves, eunuchs and the women of the teeming harems, and life was chancy. In the relatively long reign of the puppet caliph al-Muqtadir (908–932) twenty-three viziers were either fired or murdered. The actual ruler by now was a eunuch who took the title "commander of commanders" and had his name added to the Friday state prayers. He was likely complicit in the assassination of Caliph al-Muqtadir by Berber soldiers, and in having two more caliphs deposed, blinded, and thrown out to beg on the streets.

Seeming rescuers appeared in 945. A people known as the Buwaihids, after their leader, Buwai, who claimed descent from Persia's Sassanid kings, appeared with troops before Baghdad and ordered the Turks out. A Turkish people themselves, they

11. The faithful Byzantine officers seized at this final Abbasid victory are memorialized by the Eastern Church as the Forty-two Martyrs of Amorion.

12. During the fifty-six years that Samara functioned as the Abbasid capital, only one unhappy caliph managed to escape. As al-Tabari recorded this saga, the slave mother of the unfortunate Al-Mustain (862–866) connived to depose him so she could share supreme power with two Turkish generals. Al-Mustain managed to escape the palace in 865, reach Baghdad, and barricade himself in the suburb of Rusafah, but the Turkish Guard was in hot pursuit. The ensuing siege, Bury remarks, was as fatal to the city's old eastern quarters as the four-year fight between al-Amin and al-Ma'mun had been to the central city.

had migrated into the empire by way of Shiraz in southwestern Iran, where they had embraced Shi'ite Islam. Baghdad's resident Turkish soldiery fled, and the caliph, al-Mustakfi, formally greeted the Buwaihid leader, appointing him "commander of commanders." He had no choice, of course, but he quickly found that his rescuers were worse than the Turkish guard. In 946, they blinded and deposed him, and sent him to join his two predecessors in poverty. For the next hundred and ten years, the Buwaihids ruled in the name of the powerless caliphs.

Meanwhile, the Abbasid Empire was disintegrating. In the tenth century, both North Africa and Spain officially broke away under rival caliphs, which produced the spectacle of three caliphs reigning at once. From the late ninth century, rebellions devastated Iraq, Syria and Asia Minor. One of the nastiest, led by a wily Arab who claimed to be the Alyite messiah, rallied to rebellion the desperate black

The vicious Qarmatian revolt inflicted nearly a century of murder and looting. In 930, they pillaged Mecca, slaughtered 30,000, and carted off the Black Stone.

slaves of the Euphrates saltpeter mines. Over fourteen bloody years, they slaughtered the populace of Basra and three other cities, fighting off all comers.[13] The equally vicious Qarmatian Revolt, named for its Ismai'li leader, inflicted nearly a hundred years of murder and looting on Syria and Mesopotamia. In 930, Qarmatians pillaged Mecca, slaughtered thirty thousand fellow Muslims there, and carted off the Black Stone from the Ka'ba. For a decade, they ignored frantic pleas for its return and large ransom offers, writes the historian Juwayni, then threw it one Friday into the mosque at Kufa. Attached was a note: "By command we took it, and by command we have brought it back."

As the tenth century conferred chaos and misery on the Muslim Empire, it conferred a military triumph on Byzantium, accomplished by a brilliant general named Nicephorus Phocas, (not to be confused with the emperor Nicephorus I, who had fared so badly at the hands of Haroun). This Nicephorus was a general who regained Crete from Muslim pirates, and also Calabria in southern Italy, as reported in the last chapter. He now turned his attention eastward, and in 962 took Aleppo in Syria, where he destroyed the palace and reportedly killed ten thousand defenders. At the death of Emperor Romanus II, Phocas was proclaimed Nicephorus II by his devoted troops. To strengthen his claim to the throne, he married Romanus's widow, Theophano, and then went right on fighting in Cilicia and Syria for the next four years, taking and retaking Tarsus, and seizing numerous other towns. Meanwhile, a Byzantine admiral defeated an Egyptian fleet and recovered Cyprus, regaining control of the whole eastern Mediterranean. At last, in 969, Phocas's army took possession of his main objective: Antioch, capital of Syria and illustrious city of Christian patriarchs and councils, which would remain in Christian hands for the next century.

But by then Nicephorus Phocas was dead, assassinated that same year by a

13. When the black slaves who worked the saltpeter mines of the Euphrates Delta rose in rebellion, their bloody, fourteen-year rampage chiefly spread mayhem across Mesopotamia and even threatened Baghdad. Like their former Arab masters, they preferred beheading as a method of execution, and amassed severed heads by the thousands. Finding themselves burdened with altogether too many after a bloody attack on Basra, it is said, they floated them down the canal to the city to be identified by their relatives.

fellow general, John Tzimisces, who was his wife's lover. Tzimisces married Theophano, becoming her third imperial husband, and continued Phocas's Syrian crusade. His troops first fought off an attack on Antioch by the Egyptian Fatimids, and then began an invasion of northern Mesopotamia. By 973, the frantic Baghdad populace was demanding jihad against Byzantium, writes A. A. Vaile in the *Cambridge Medieval History*, and threatening revolution.

This brought Tzimisces himself to the eastern front, where he produced a series of stunning victories. In 975, after concluding an alliance with Armenia, he led the imperial army out of Antioch on what became a triumphal march. Damascus voluntarily surrendered. Tiberias, Nazareth and Caesarea did likewise when he turned south into Palestine. Reaching Nazareth and Mount Tabor, writes historian Henri Daniel-Rops (*The Church in the Dark Ages*), his jubilant soldiers "mingled their prayers with shouts of victory." Why Tzimisces did not go on to Jerusalem itself, which had actually sent a message pleading not to be sacked, is unclear. Turning to the coast instead, he captured Beirut, Sidon and Byblos—but was defeated at Tripolis and retired to Antioch. That winter he fell ill, probably of typhus, and died in 976.

Any dream Tzimisces may have had of freeing Jerusalem died with him. His successor, Basil II, who ruled Byzantium for the next half-century, concentrated on extending Christendom north by converting more of the Slav peoples. But one

Nicephorus Phocas makes his triumphal entry into Constantinople in this medieval illumination. Having waged many successful conquests in Syria, Italy and Crete, he was proclaimed emperor by his army and marched to Constantinople to claim the throne.

Cylindrical Seljuk tombs near Ab-e-Garm, Iran, were lavishly decorated with designs and Qur'anic verses, reflecting the importance of the individual buried within. The brief period of the Seljuk dynasty in Iran was relatively stable, allowing vigorous trade and a flourishing culture in education and the arts, particularly architecture.

14. A certain Ahmad ibn Fadlan, who prior to their conversion to Islam visited the Oghuz Turks from whom the Seljuks descend, recorded his disgust with them. They do not wash themselves after defecation or urination, he complains, and never bathe. Visitors caught washing have to pay fines. During a visit to one family, the mother casually uncovered her privates and scratched them, causing Ahmad to cover his face in acute embarrassment. Her husband, who thought this hilariously funny, jocularly informed him that he might admire but not touch. The Oghuz were scrupulously chaste; adulterers, if caught, were torn in two.

major reason he could do this was that Phocas and Tzimisces had moved the Muslim–Byzantine frontier nearly two hundred miles farther away from Constantinople. Another was that Islam lay enfeebled in spirit and rent by violent sectarianism.

Nevertheless, events in the great grasslands of central Asia would soon enormously strengthen the Islamic cause in general, and the Abbasid caliphate in particular. Late in the tenth century, a chieftain of the Turkish Oghuz tribe, Seljuk by name, led his clan into Muslim territory. In two generations, while at some stage becoming fervent Sunni Muslims, they carved themselves a domain in and around Khorasan. In December 1055, a grandson of Seljuk, Tughril Beg, descended with his wild horsemen upon Baghdad, and the Shi'ite Buwaihids fled.

The hapless caliph welcomed them as deliverers, and deliverers they proved to be, restoring the long mistreated Sunni caliphs to full dignity, while Tughril contented himself with running his government under the title *sultan* ("he with authority"). To Baghdad's Muslims, gentrified by three centuries of leisurely living, the Seljuks appeared uncouth barbarians, foreign in tongue and personally unclean. On the plus side, however, they quickly regained much of the empire.[14] After Tughril died childless in 1063, his nephew Alp Arslan proved equally effective, first reclaiming Mecca and Medina from the Fatimids, then confronting the Byzantines.

Constantinople had been anxiously monitoring the Seljuks. Emperor Basil II persuaded Christian Armenia and Georgia to place themselves under Byzantine protection—a decided error, writes historian Tamara Talbot Rice (*The Seljuks in Asia Minor*). More than eight decades of military neglect had elapsed since the days of Tzimisces, and the now-decrepit Byzantine army would prove incapable of defending even its own territory. The showdown occurred in 1071 at Manzikert, near the Armenian–Byzantine border (now Malazgirt in Turkey). Alp Arslan's adversary was Romanus IV, emperor since 1067, and a man destined for a truly tragic end.

His predecessor, Constantine X, had on his deathbed required his wife, the empress Eudoxia, to swear she would not remarry, so that their seventeen-year-old son could accede unchallenged as Michael VII. Eudoxia decided, with reason, to repudiate this oath. Asia Minor, Byzantium's breadbasket and source of its best soldiers, was again living in dread—now of recurring and ferocious Seljuk raids. In the Armenian capital, Ani, a city for which Arab historians claimed an improbable population of seven hundred thousand, the Seljuks blocked the streets with corpses. In Sebastea, the new invaders reportedly left no one alive, while stripping the place of every moveable asset. They annually hit Edessa and Antioch. At Ardzen, says one account, Christians were incinerated in their churches. "Lift your eyes," it continues, "and look. Your sons are taken into slavery, your infants smashed without pity, your youths given to the flames, your venerable ancients thrown down in public places, your virgins—raised gently and in comfort—dishonored and marched off on foot into slavery."

This was no time for a boy emperor, Eudoxia reasoned, so oath or no oath, she chose as her husband Romanus Diogenes, a stalwart officer with a fine battle record.[15] But uncontrolled bureaucracy in Constantinople had reduced the army to penury. Soldiers often went unpaid, dependable local militia had been supplanted by undependable mercenaries, experienced generals were replaced by court sycophants. Meanwhile, Monophysite Armenia, prime source of fine soldiers, had been utterly

Uncontrolled bureaucracy had reduced the army to penury. Soldiers went unpaid, dependable militia were supplanted, experienced generals were replaced by court sycophants.

alienated by recurring attempts to force the Armenians into Greek Christianity.

So it was a ragtag army that Romanus led out in 1069, to find and destroy Alp Arslan somewhere in Mesopotamia or Armenia, and all the omens were foreboding. A dove, for example, landed on the emperor's hand. Did that mean he should seek peace, not war? A pole snapped in the imperial tent, and then fire destroyed it. What might this mean? For two seasons Romanus tracked Alp Arslan, while the Turks cannily avoided confronting the heavily armored Byzantine cavalry. At length, in the summer of 1071, with his army numbering sixty to one hundred thousand men, and with a thousand carts hauling siege machinery, Romanus headed directly into Armenia at Manzikert. This threatened the Persian heartland beyond it, and Alp Arslan was two hundred and fifty miles away, besieging the Fatimids at Edessa. The sultan swiftly recognized the danger, however, and moved more quickly on Manzikert than Romanus thought possible. One of the pivotal battles of history was now at hand.[16]

The emperor's characteristic confidence seemed diminished, making him moody, irritable, and incautious. He sent his best troops to forage for supplies thirty miles away, and continued into Armenia. Then, curiously, his scouts encountered a small Seljuk force. Romanus sent a cavalry unit to investigate. It did not return, and at evening he discovered why. Alp Arslan's entire army was directly in front of him. The Byzantine troops nonetheless bivouacked for the night. In the darkness, Seljuk warriors thundered through their encampment, loosing lethal volleys of arrows. With morning there came a further surprise: a truce offer, not from Alp Arslan but from the caliph himself in Baghdad. Romanus rejected it. To stop the raids, he knew, he must break the Seljuk army once and for all. But where were the troops he had sent to forage? He could not have guessed the grim truth.

15. An amusing although dubious story spread through Constantinople after the death of Constantine X. The proposed remarriage of the empress Eudoxia, contrary to her promise, met vigorous opposition from the patriarch of Constantinople. An oath, he declared, was an oath. But the man she wants to marry is your brother, he was told. That put a different light on the matter, said the patriarch, and approved the marriage. He discovered too late that her intended was in fact someone else.

16. The best modern history of the Battle of Manzikert, almost the only history in English of the pivotal encounter, was written by Alfred Friendly, a distinguished Washington D.C. journalist and popular historian. It is entitled *The Dreadful Day* and from it this summary account is largely drawn.

Encountering part of the Seljuk force, they had run for home—a mass desertion. Unable to delay longer, the emperor ordered attack formation.

In two columns, his men moved steadily against an enemy that seemed to evaporate before them. But then from the heights on either flank came the Seljuk horsemen—light, fast, and deadly—shooting into the packed Byzantine ranks, splitting one column from the other, spreading disarray. Halting his advance, Romanus about-faced, in order to retrace his steps and relieve the men behind. This move was misinterpreted as a sign that the emperor had surrendered, or possibly fallen. Panicking, the Byzantines fled the field. The emperor, fighting ferociously in the garb of a simple soldier, was recognized, overcome and captured.

The defeat was decisive. The sultan first forced his imperial prisoner to kiss the ground before him, after which he treated him with great dignity. Moreover, since he was then more concerned with the Fatimids in Egypt than the Christians in Constantinople, he offered terms. For a heavy and immediate cash payment, plus an annual levy, Alp Arslan promised he would restore all Byzantine lands and allies to their previous status. The two empires would live at peace. Romanus agreed and was released. But meanwhile, as he soon learned, his stepson Michael had been proclaimed in his stead and had repudiated the treaty. The wrathful Alp Arslan swore a mighty oath:

> The Romans (i.e., Byzantines) are atheists. From today on, the peace with them is broken and the oath which linked them with the Persians no longer exists. From now on, the worshipers of the cross will be immolated by the sword and all Christian countries will be delivered into slavery.

Alp Arslan himself died less than a year later, stabbed to death by a prisoner he was personally executing. He had failed to dislodge the Fatimids from Syria

and Palestine, but his son, Malik Shah, finished that job. After that, the fearsome Seljuk dynasty disintegrated into endless wrangling over the succession. Romanus's fate was worse by far. History would hold him accountable for the military disaster that began Byzantium's four-century-long downfall, and his efforts to regain the throne also ended in hideous personal disaster. Twice he formed armies and fought the supporters of Michael VII. Twice he was defeated, and when finally captured was severely beaten and blinded. The Byzantine historian John Scylitzes describes his terrible fate, and his noble acceptance of it:

> Carried forth on a cheap beast of burden like a decaying corpse, his eyes gouged out and his face and head swollen and full of worms and stench, he lived on a few days in pain and smelling foully, and finally died, settling his ashes in the island of Prote [in the Sea of Marmara], where he had built a new monastery. He was richly buried by his wife, the queen Eudoxia, leaving behind himself the memory of trials and misfortunes which surpass hearing. But in such great misfortunes, he uttered no blasphemy or curse, but continued to give thanks to God, bearing cheerfully what befell him.

This ended Romanus's misfortunes, but not Byzantium's. Court feuds and internecine intrigues continued for a further nine years, with Christian contenders frequently hiring or allying with Muslim forces against Christian rivals, until Alexius I, first of the Comnenian dynasty and a diplomatic genius, brought the turmoil to an end. He also sent a desperate call to Rome for Western help against the continuing encroachment of Islam. The appeal was rejected, or so he probably thought. Then one day in the spring of 1097, a small army of knights from across Western Europe arrived in Constantinople. Their goal: the reconquest of Christian Anatolia, Syria, Palestine, Egypt and North Africa. After nearly half a millennium, the great Christian counterattack against Islam, known to history as the Crusades, was about to begin. ■

Erzurum, north of Manzikert, was one of the important cities occupied by the Seljuks after their decisive victory over the Byzantines at Manzikert in 1071, which gave them access to most of central and eastern Anatolia. This view is typical of the bleak landscape near Erzurum.

PREVIOUS VOLUMES IN THIS SERIES

VOLUME ONE:

The Veil is Torn
A.D. 30 to A.D. 70
Pentecost to the
Destruction of Jerusalem

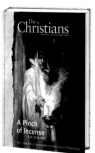

VOLUME TWO:

A Pinch of Incense
A.D. 70 to 250
From the Fall of Jerusalem
to the Decian Persecution

VOLUME THREE:

By This Sign
A.D. 250 to 350
From the Decian Persecution
to the Constantine Era

VOLUME FOUR:

Darkness Descends
A.D. 350 to 565
The Fall of the
Western Roman Empire

VOLUME FIVE:

The Sword of Islam
A.D. 565 to 740
The Muslim Onslaught all
but Destroys Christendom

For additional copies of this book, or others in this series:

Write: Box 530 • Pembina, ND 58271 USA   or
10333 - 178 St • Edmonton, AB T5S 1R5 Canada
Call toll-free in North America: **1-800-853-5402**
On line: **www.christianhistoryproject.com**

NEW CONTRIBUTORS TO THIS VOLUME

PAUL BUNNER, former executive editor of *Alberta Report* newsmagazine and a freelance writer in Edmonton, wrote the chapter on the conversion of the Slavs on page 192.

VINCENT CARROLL, a Denver, Colorado, journalist and author, is not a new contributor, though in this volume he gives us Chapter 6, his first full chapter, describing the East-West schism in Christianity. Editorial page editor of the *Rocky Mountain News*, he is also co-author of *Christianity on Trial: Arguments Against Anti-Religious Bigotry*.

K. MACDONALD CORBETT of Falkland, B.C., who has been a reporter, columnist and editor for more than forty years in the U.S., Canada and Israel, wrote the sidebar on the Christian use of relics on page 30.

MATTHEW FRANCIS, who holds a Master of Arts degree in theology from the University of Manchester and is a former instructor in religion at Nazarene College, Calgary, wrote the subchapter on the Golden Age of Byzantium on page 137.

LOUISE HENEIN, who holds a Master's of Library Science, is the volume's picture editor. She also wrote the subchapter on nuns on page 34 and the sidebar on Hildegard of Bingen, page 40.

LESLIE TAILLEFER, of Edmonton, Alberta, did the sketches of Hildegard of Bingen and the painting of the Nestorian missionaries at the court of the Chinese emperor on pages 180 and 181.

BIBLIOGRAPHY

Abelard, Peter and Heloise. *The Letters of Abelard and Heloise.* Harmondsworth: Penguin, 1974.

Addison, James Thayer. *The Medieval Missionary: A Study of the Conversion of Northern Europe, A.D. 500-1300.* New York: International Missionary Council, 1936.

Allott, Stephen. *Alcuin of York, c. A.D. 735 to 804: his life and letters.* York: William Sessions, 1974.

Andrae, Tor. *Les Origines de l'Islam et le Christianisme.* Paris: Adrien-Maisonneuve, 1955.

Anglo-Saxon Chronicle. http://sunsite.berkeley.edu/OMACL/Anglo/.

The Annals of St-Bertin. New York: Manchester University, 1991.

Aprem, Mar. *Council of Ephesus of 431.* Trichur, India: Mar Narsai Press, 1978.

———. *The Nestorian Fathers.* Trichur, India: Mar Narsai Press, 1976.

———. *Nestorian Missions.* Trichur, India: Mar Narsai Press, 1976.

Arvites, James Anthony. *Irene: Woman Emperor of Constantinople, Her Life and Times.* Ph.D. diss.: University of Mississippi, 1979.

Atiya, Aziz S. *History of eastern Christianity.* London: Methuen, 1968.

Baggley, John. *Doors of Perception: Icons and Their Spiritual Significance.* Oxford: Mowbray, 1987.

Barmby, James. *Gregory the Great.* New York: Pott, Young, 1879.

Barnes, Harry Elmer. *The History of Western Civilization.* New York: Harcourt, Brace and Company, 1935.

Bell, Richard. "The Origin of Islam in its Christian Environment." In *Gunning Lecture, Edinburgh University, 1925.* London: Frank Cass, 1968.

Bishai, Wilson B. *Islamic History of the Middle East: Backgrounds, Development, and Fall of the Arab Empire.* Boston: Allyn and Bacon, 1968.

Boissonnade, Prosper. *Life and Work in Medieval Europe: Fifth to Fifteenth Centuries.* London: Routledge and Kegan Paul, 1949.

Boniface, Saint. *The Letters of Saint Boniface.* New York: Norton, 1976.

Brown, R. Allen. *The Normans.* Woodbridge: Boydell & Brewer, 1984.

Browne, Laurence E. *The Eclipse of Christianity in Asia: From the Time of Muhammad till the Fourteenth Century.* New York: H. Fertig, 1967.

Browning, Robert. *Justinian and Theodora.* London: Thames and Hudson, 1987.

Bury, J. B. *A History of the Eastern Roman empire from the fall of Irene to the accession of Basil I. (802-867).* London: Macmillan, 1912.

———. *A History of the Later Roman empire. From Arcadius to Irene.(395 A.D. to 800 A.D.)* Amsterdam: Hakkert, 1966.

Cahen, Claude. *Pre-Ottoman Turkey: A General Survey of the Material and Spiritual Culture and History, c. 1071-1330.* New York: Taplinger, 1968.

Cahill, Thomas. *How the Irish Saved Civilization: The Untold Story of Ireland's Heroic Role from the Fall of Rome to the Rise of Medieval Europe.* New York: Nan A. Talese, Doubleday, ca. 1995.

The Cambridge Medieval History. New York: Macmillan, 1911-36.

Carabine, Deirdre. *John Scottus Eriugena.* New York: Oxford University Press, 2000.

The Catholic Encyclopedia. www.newadvent.org.

Cavarnos, Constantine. *Orthodox Iconography: Four Essays.* Belmont, MA: Institute for Byzantine and Modern Greek Studies, 1977.

Chamberlin, Russell. *Charlemagne: Emperor of the Western World.* London: Grafton, 1986.

Congar, Yves. *After Nine Hundred Years: The Background of the Schism Between the Eastern and Western Churches.* Westport, CT: Greenwood Press, 1978.

Coulton, G. G. *Five Centuries of Religion.* Cambridge: Cambridge University Press, 1923-1950.

———. *Life in the Middle Ages.* Cambridge: Cambridge University Press, 1928-30.

———. *Medieval Panorama: the English Scene from Conquest to Reformation.* London: Cambridge University Press, 1938.

Daniel-Rops, Henri. *The Church in the Dark Ages.* London: Dent, 1963.

Davis, R. H. C. *The Normans and their myth.* London: Thames and Hudson, 1976.

Décarreaux, Jean. *Monks and Civilization: From the Barbarian Invasions to the Reign of Charlemagne.* London: Allen & Unwin, 1964.

Downey, Glanville. *A History of Antioch in Syria: from Seleucus to the Arab Conquest.* Princeton, NJ: Princeton University Press, 1961.

Duckett, Eleanor. *Alcuin, Friend of Charlemagne: His World and his Work.* New York: Macmillan, 1951.

———. *Alfred the Great and His England.* Chicago: University of Chicago Press, 1956.

———. *The Wandering Saints of the Early Middle Ages.* New York: Norton, 1959.

Dvornik, Francis. *Byzantine missions among the Slavs: SS. Constantine-Cyril and Methodius.* New Brunswick, NJ: Rutgers University Press, 1970.

———. *The Photian Schism, History and Legend.* Cambridge [Eng.]: Cambridge University Press, 1948.

Einhard and the Monk of St Gall. *Early Lives of Charlemagne.* New York: Cooper Square, 1966.

Evans, Joan. *Monastic Life at Cluny, 910-1157.* Hamden, CT: Archon Books, 1968.

Every, George. *The Byzantine Patriarchate, 451-1204.* London: S. P. C. K., 1962.

Fisher, D. J. V. *The Anglo-Saxon Age, c.400-1042.* London: Longman, 1973.

Frend, W. H. C. *The Rise of Christianity.* Philadelphia, PA: Fortress, 1984.

Friendly, Alfred. *The Dreadful Day: the Battle of Manzikert, 1071.* London: Hutchinson, 1981.

Fuller, J. F. C. *The Decisive Battles of the Western World.* London: Granada, 1970.

Gardner, Alice. *Theodore of Studium, His Life and Times.* London: E. Arnold, 1905.

Gibb, H. A. R. *Mohammedanism: An Historical Survey.* New York: Oxford University Press, 1961.

Gibbon, Edward. *Decline and Fall of the Roman Empire.* www.ccel.org.

Glick, Thomas F. *Islamic and Christian Spain in the Early Middle Ages.* Princeton, NJ: Princeton University Press, 1979.

Glubb, John Bagot. *Haroon al Rasheed and the Great Abbasids.* London, Hodder and Stoughton, 1976.

———. *The Great Arab Conquests.* London: Hodder and Stoughton, 1963.

Goubert, Paul. "Les Rapports de Khosrau II Roi des Rois Sassanide avec L'Empereur Maurice." In *Actes du VIIe Congrès des Études Byzantines, Bruxelles 1948.* Nendeln: Kraus, 1966-1979.

Gregoire, Henri. "An Armenian Dynasty On The Byzantine Throne." In *Armenian Quarterly 1* (1946).

Haight, Anne Lyon. *Hroswitha of Gandersheim: Her Life, Times, and Works, and a Comprehensive Bibliography.* New York: Hroswitha Club, 1965.

Hamadeh, Muhammad Maher. *Muhammad the Prophet: A Selected Bibliography.* Thesis. Ann Arbor, MI: 1965.

Hammer-Purgstall, Joseph. *The History of the Assassins, Derived from Oriental Sources.* New York: B. Franklin, 1968.

Haugh, Richard S. *Photius and the Carolingians: The Trinitarian Controversy.* Belmont, MA: Nordland, 1975.

Havighurst, Alfred F., ed. *The Pirenne Thesis: Analysis, Criticism, and Revision.* Lexington, MA: Heath, 1976.

Heath, R. G. "The Western Schism of the Franks and the Filioque." In *Journal of Ecclesiastical History 23* (1972), 97-113.

Helmoldus, Presbyter Bosoviensis. *The Chronicle of the Slavs.* New York: Columbia University Press, 1935.

Herrin, Judith. *Women in purple: Rulers of Medieval Byzantium.* Princeton, NJ: Princeton University Press, 2001.

Hitti, Philip K. *History of the Arabs.* London: Macmillan, 1946.

Holt, P. M., Ann K. S. Lambton and Bernard Lewis, eds. *The Cambridge History of Islam.* Cambridge: Cambridge University Press, 1970.

Hunt, Noreen. *Cluniac monasticism in the Central Middle Ages.* London: Macmillan, 1971.

———. *Cluny under Saint Hugh, 1049-1109.* London: E. Arnold, 1967.

Jackson, Gabriel. *The Making of Medieval Spain.* London: Thames and Hudson, 1972.

Johnson, Paul. *A History of Christianity.* New York: Penguin, 1976.

Jones, Gwyn. *A History of the Vikings.* New York: Oxford University Press, 1984.

Joseph, John. *The Nestorians and their Muslim Neighbors: A Study of Western Influence on their Relations.* Princeton: Princeton University Press, 1961.

Kendrick, T. D. *A History of the Vikings.* London: Methuen, 1930.

Kidd, B. J. *History of the church to A.D. 461.* Oxford: Clarendon Press, 1922.

Kirkby, Michael Hasloch. *The Vikings.* New York: Dutton, 1977.

Knowles, David. *Christian Monasticism.* New York: McGraw-Hill, 1969.

Kraemer, Joel L. *Humanism in the Renaissance of Islam: the Cultural Revival During the Buyid Age.* Leiden, The Netherlands: E. J. Brill, 1986.

Kritzeck, James. *Peter the Venerable and Islam.* Princeton, NJ: Princeton University Press, 1964.

Lacko, Michael. *Saints Cyril and Methodius.* Rome: Slovak Editions, 1963.

Lane-Poole, Stanley. *The Moors in Spain.* London: T. Fisher Unwin, 1888.

Lang, David Marsh. *Armenia, Cradle of Civilization.* Boston: Allen & Unwin, 1978.

Latouche, Robert. *The Birth of Western Economy: Economic Aspects of the Dark Ages.* New York: Barnes & Noble, 1961.

Latourette, Kenneth Scott. *A History of Christianity.* New York: Harper & Row, 1953.

———. *A History of the Expansion of Christianity, v. 2 The Thousand Years of Uncertainty.* New York: Harper & Brothers, 1937-45.

———. *The History of Christianity.* Berkley: Blackie & Sons, Glasgow, 1929.

Leclercq, Jean. *The Love of Learning and the Desire for God: A Study of Monastic Culture.* New York: Fordham University Press, 1961.

Lindsay, Jack. *The Normans and Their World.* London: Hart-Davis, MacGibbon, 1973.

Little, Lester K. *Religious Poverty and the Profit Economy in Medieval Europe.* Ithaca, NY: Cornell University Press, 1978.

Liudprand, bishop of Cremona. *The Works of Liudprand of Cremona.* London: Routledge, 1930.

Livermore, H. V. *The Origins of Spain and Portugal.* London: George Allen & Unwin, 1971.

Lyon, Bryce Dale. *The Origins of the Middle Ages: Pirenne's Challenge to Gibbon.* New York: Norton, 1972.

MacKay, Angus. *Spain in the Middle Ages: From Frontier to Empire, 1000-1500.* London: Macmillan, 1977.

Maddocks, Fiona. *Hildegard of Bingen: the Woman of her Age.* New York: Doubleday, 2001.

Markus, R. A. *Gregory the Great and His World.* New York: Cambridge University Press, 1997.

Martin, Edward James. *A History of the Iconoclastic Controversy.* New York: AMS Press, 1978.

Menander, Protector. *The History of Menander the Guardsman.* Liverpool: Cairns, 1985.

Milis, Ludovicus. *Angelic Monks and Earthly Men: Monasticism and its Meaning to Medieval Society.* Rochester, NY: Boydell Press, 1992.

Montalembert, Charles Forbes. *The Monks of the West: from St. Benedict to St. Bernard.* New York: AMS Press, 1966.

Morris, Rosemary. *Monks and Laymen in Byzantium, 843-1118.* New York: Cambridge University Press, 1995.

Muir, William. *Annals of the Early Caliphate: From the Death of Mahomet to the Omeyyad and Abbaside Dynasties A.H. XI-LXI (A.D. 632-680) from original sources.* Amsterdam: Oriental Press, 1968.

Muntaner, Ramón. *The Chronicle of Muntaner.* London: The Hakluyt Society, 1920-21.

Neill, Stephen. *A History of Christianity in India, 1707-1858.* New York: Cambridge University Press, 1985.

Newark, Timothy. *The Barbarians: Warriors & Wars of the Dark Ages.* Poole, Dorset: Blandford, 1985.

Newman, Barbara, ed. *Voice of the Living Light: Hildegard of Bingen and Her World.* Berkeley: University of California Press, 1998.

Newman, John Henry. *Certain Difficulties Felt by Anglicans in Catholic Teaching, v. 1.* www.newmanreader.org.

Nicephorus, Saint. *An Eyewitness to History: The Short History of Nikephoros our Holy Father the Patriarch of Constantinople.* Brookline, MA: Hellenic College [1989?].

Nicholas I, Pope. *The Responses of Pope Nicholas I to the Questions of the Bulgars A.D. 866.* www.fordham.edu.

Norwich, John Julius. *A History of Venice.* New York: Knopf, 1982.

O'Leary, De Lacy. *Arabia before Muhammad.* London: K. Paul, Trench, Trubner, 1927.

Olrik, Axel. *Viking Civilization.* New York: W. W. Norton, 1930.

Paul, the Deacon. *History of the Lombards.* Philadelphia: University of Pennsylvania Press, 1974.

Peddie, John. *Alfred: Warrior King.* Thrupp, Stroud, Gloucestershire: Sutton, 1999.

Pipes, Daniel. *In the path of God: Islam and Political Power.* New York: Basic Books, 1983.

Pirenne, Henri. *History of Europe from the invasions to the XVI century.* London: Allen & Unwin, 1939.

———. *Mohammed and Charlemagne.* Cleveland, OH: World Pub., 1957.

Power, Eileen. *Medieval English Nunneries, c. 1275 to 1535.* Cheshire, CT: Biblo & Tannen, 1988.

Pryor, John H. *Geography, Technology, and War: Studies in the Maritime History of the Mediterranean, 649-1571.* New York: Cambridge University Press, 1988.

Putnam, Emily James. *The Lady: Studies of Certain Significant Phases of Her History.* Chicago: University of Chicago Press, 1970.

Read, Jan. *The Moors in Spain and Portugal.* Totowa, NJ: Rowman and Littlefield, 1975.

Rice, Tamara Talbot. *The Seljuks in Asia Minor.* London: Thames and Hudson, 1961.

Roberts, Paul Craig. "The Pirenne Thesis, Economies or Civilizations: Towards Reformulation." In *Classica et mediaevalia 25* (1964): 297-315.

Robertson, Elizabeth. "*An Anchorhold of her own.*" *In* Equally in God's Image: Women in the Middle Ages. *New York: P. Lang, 1990.*

Rodinson, Maxime. *Mohammed. New York: Pantheon Books, 1971.*

Rohan, Michael Scott and Allan J. Scott. *The Hammer and the Cross.* Oxford, England: Alder, 1980.

Ruether, Rosemary Radford. *Visionary Women: Three Medieval Mystics.* Minneapolis, MN: Fortress Press, 2002.

Runciman, Steven. *A History of the First Bulgarian Empire.* London: G. Bell & Sons, 1930.

———. *The Eastern Schism.* Oxford: Clarendon Press, 1963.

Saeki, Yoshiro. *The Nestorian Documents and Relics in China.* Tokyo: Toho Bunkwa Gakuin: Academy of Oriental Culture, Tokyo Institute, 1951.

Saunders, J. J. *A History of Medieval Islam.* New York: Barnes & Noble, 1965.

Shaban, M. A. *Islamic History: A New Interpretation.* Cambridge [Eng.]: Cambridge University Press, 1971.

Shaw, Stanford J. *History of the Ottoman Empire and Modern Turkey.* New York: Cambridge University Press, 1976.

Simocatta, Theophylact. *The History of Theophylact Simocatta.* New York: Oxford University Press, 1986.

Sladden, John Cyril. *Boniface of Devon: Apostle of Germany.* Exeter [Eng.]: Paternoster Press, 1980.

Smalley, Beryl. *Historians in the Middle Ages.* London: Thames & Hudson, 1974.

Smith, Mahlon H. *And Taking Bread: Cerularius and the Azyme Controversy of 1054.* Paris: Beauchesne, 1978.

Socrates, Scholasticus. *Ecclesiastical History.* www.ccel.org.

Stewart, John. *Nestorian Missionary Enterprise.* Edinburgh: T. & T. Clark, 1928.

Stone, Gerald. *The Smallest Slavonic Nation: the Sorbs of Lusatia.* London: Athlene Press, 1972.

Stoyanov, Yuri. *Hidden tradition in Europe.* New York: Arkana, 1994.

Stratos, Andreas N. *Byzantium in the Seventh Century.* Amsterdam: Adolf M. Hakkert, 1968.

Sturlason, Snorre. *Heimskringla: or, The Lives of the Norse kings.* Cambridge: W. Heffer & Sons, 1932.

Taylor, Henry Osborn. *The Mediaeval Mind: A History of the Development of Thought and Emotion in the Middle Ages.* Cambridge, MA: Harvard University Press, 1949.

Thompson, James Westfall. *A History of Historical Writing.* Glouchester, MA: P. Smith, 1967.

Thorpe, Lewis G. M., trans. *Two lives of Charlemagne.* Baltimore: Penguin Books, 1969.

Tout, T. F. *The Empire and the Papacy, 918-1273.* London: Rivingtons, 1941.

Trimingham, J. Spencer. *Christianity Among the Arabs in Pre-Islamic Times.* New York: Longman, 1979.

Turtledove, Harry. *The Immediate Successors of Justinian.* Ph.D. diss., University of California, Los Angeles, 1977.

———, trans. *The Chronicle of Theophanes.* Philadelphia, PA: University of Pennsylvania Press, 1982.

Vasiliev, A. A. *History of the Byzantine Empire, 324-1453.* Madison: University of Wisconsin Press, 1958.

Venarde, Bruce L. *Women's Monasticism and Medieval Society: Nunneries in France and England, 890-1215.* Cornell University Press, 1999.

Vine, Aubrey R. *The Nestorian Churches: A Concise History of Nestorian Christianity in Asia from the Persian Schism to the Modern Assyrians.* London: Independent Press Ltd., 1937.

Vlasto, A. P. *The Entry of the Slavs into Christendom: An Introduction to the Medieval History of the Slavs.* Cambridge: University Press, 1970.

Volkoff, Vladimir. *Vladimir the Russian Viking.* London: Honeyglen, 1984.

Waissenberger, Robert, ed. *Die Turken vor Wien. Europa und die Entwicklung an der Donau 1683.* Salzburg: Residenz Verlag, 1982.

Wallace-Hadrill, J. M. *The Barbarian West, 400-1000.* Malden, MA: Blackwell, 1996.

Whitby, Michael. *Emperor Maurice and his historian: Theophylact Simocatta on Persian and Balkan warfare.* New York: Oxford University Press, 1988.

White, Lynn Townsend. *Medieval technology and social change.* New York: Oxford University Press, 1964.

Widukind, von Korvei. *The Three Books of the Deeds of the Saxons.* Translated with introduction, notes, and bibliography, by Raymund F. Wood. Diss., 1949.

Williams, Stephen and Gerard Friell. *Theodosius: The Empire at Bay.* New Haven, CT: Yale University Press, 1995.

Zarnecki, George. *The monastic achievement.* New York: McGraw-Hill, 1972.

PHOTOGRAPHIC CREDITS

INDEX

Subsequent volumes bring the Christian story to the end of the twentieth century